D1715825

Attitudes In and Around Organizations

FOUNDATIONS FOR ORGANIZATIONAL SCIENCE
A Sage Publications Series

Series Editor

David Whetten, *Brigham Young University*

Editors

Peter J. Frost, *University of British Columbia*
Anne S. Huff, *University of Colorado* and *Cranfield University* (UK)
Benjamin Schneider, *University of Maryland*
M. Susan Taylor, *University of Maryland*
Andrew Van de Ven, *University of Minnesota*

The FOUNDATIONS FOR ORGANIZATIONAL SCIENCE series supports the development of students, faculty, and prospective organizational science professionals through the publication of texts authored by leading organizational scientists. Each volume provides a highly personal, hands-on introduction to a core topic or theory and challenges the reader to explore promising avenues for future theory development and empirical application.

Books in This Series

PUBLISHING IN THE ORGANIZATIONAL SCIENCES, 2nd Edition
Edited by L. L. Cummings and Peter J. Frost

SENSEMAKING IN ORGANIZATIONS
Karl E. Weick

INSTITUTIONS AND ORGANIZATIONS
W. Richard Scott

RHYTHMS OF ACADEMIC LIFE
Peter J. Frost and M. Susan Taylor

RESEARCHERS HOOKED ON TEACHING:
Noted Scholars Discuss the Synergies of Teaching and Research
Rae André and Peter J. Frost

THE PSYCHOLOGY OF DECISION MAKING: People in Organizations
Lee Roy Beach

ORGANIZATIONAL JUSTICE AND HUMAN RESOURCE MANAGEMENT
Robert Folger and Russell Cropanzano

RECRUITING EMPLOYEES: Individual and Organizational Perspectives
Alison E. Barber

ATTITUDES IN AND AROUND ORGANIZATIONS
Arthur P. Brief

IDENTITY IN ORGANIZATIONS: Building Theory Through Conversations
Edited by David Whetten and Paul Godfrey

PERSONNEL SELECTION: A Theoretical Approach
Neal Schmitt and David Chan

Arthur P. Brief

Attitudes In and Around Organizations

Foundations for
Organizational
Science
A Sage Publications Series

SAGE Publications
International Educational and Professional Publisher
Thousand Oaks   London   New Delhi

For information:

SAGE Publications, Inc.
2455 Teller Road
Thousand Oaks, California 91320
E-mail: order@sagepub.com

SAGE Publications Ltd.
6 Bonhill Street
London EC2A 4PU
United Kingdom

SAGE Publications India Pvt. Ltd.
M-32 Market
Greater Kailash I
New Delhi 110 048 India

Printed in the United States of America

Library of Congress Cataloging-in-Publication Data

Brief, Arthur P., 1946-
    Attitudes in and around organizations / by Arthur P. Brief.
       p. cm. — (Foundations for organizational science)
    Includes bibliographical references and index.
    ISBN 0-7619-0096-9 (acid-free paper)
    ISBN 0-7619-0097-7 (pbk.: acid-free paper)
    1. Job satisfaction. 2. Industrial sociology. 3. Employee
attitudes I. Title. II. Series.
    HF5549.5.J63 B734 1998
    158.7—ddc21   98-19719

This book is printed on acid-free paper.

98 99 00 01 02 03 10 9 8 7 6 5 4 3 2 1

Acquiring Editor:	Marquita Flemming
Editorial Assistant:	Frances Borghi
Production Editor:	Wendy Westgate
Production Assistant:	Nevair Kabakian
Designer/Typesetter:	Janelle LeMaster
Cover Designer:	Candice Harman
Indexer:	Jean Casalegno

Many people have helped shape who I am.
This book is dedicated to two of them.
One was with me in the beginning with
unconditional love and still is there.
The other joined my life during my graduate
student years and now is gone. His "love,"
if you can call it that, was never unconditional.
It was of the tough variety, the type I believe that
shapes wayward students into reasonably
confident and competent professionals.

To Mom
and LLC

Contents

Introduction to the Series

The title of this series, **Foundations for Organizational Science** (FOS), denotes a distinctive focus. FOS books are educational aids for mastering the core theories, essential tools, and emerging perspectives that constitute the field of organizational science (broadly defined to include organizational behavior, organizational theory, human resource management, and business strategy). The primary objective of this series is to support ongoing professional development among established scholars.

The series was born out of many long conversations among several colleagues, including Peter Frost, Anne Huff, Rick Mowday, Ben Schneider, Susan Taylor, and Andy Van de Ven, over a number of years. From those discussions, we concluded that there has been a major gap in our professional literature, as characterized by the following comment: "If I, or one of my students, want to learn about population ecology, diversification strategies, group dynamics, or personnel selection, we are pretty much limited to academic journal articles or books that are written either for content experts or practitioners. Wouldn't it be wonderful to have access to the teaching notes from a course taught by a master teacher of this topic?"

The plans for compiling a set of learning materials focusing on professional development emerged from our extended discussions of common experiences and observations, including the following:

1. While serving as editors of journals, program organizers for professional association meetings, and mentors for new faculty members, we have observed wide variance in theoretical knowledge and tool proficiency in our field. To the extent that this outcome reflects available learning opportunities, we hope that this series will help "level the playing field."

2. We have all "taught" in doctoral and junior faculty consortia prior to our professional meetings and have been struck by how often the participants comment, "I wish that the rest of the meetings [paper sessions and symposia] were as informative." Such observations got us thinking—Are our doctoral courses more like paper sessions or doctoral consortia? What type of course would constitute a learning experience analogous to attending a doctoral consortium? What materials would we need to teach such a course? We hope that the books in this series have the "touch and feel" of a doctoral consortium workshop.

3. We all have had some exposure to the emerging "virtual university" in which faculty and students in major doctoral programs share their distinctive competencies, either through periodic jointly sponsored seminars or through distance learning technology, and we would like to see these opportunities diffused more broadly. We hope that reading our authors' accounts will be the next best thing to observing them in action.

4. We see some of the master scholars in our field reaching the later stages of their careers, and we would like to "bottle" their experience and insight for future generations. Therefore, this series is an attempt to disseminate "best practices" across space and time.

To address these objectives, we ask authors in this series to pass along their "craft knowledge" to students and faculty beyond the boundaries of their local institutions by writing from the perspective of seasoned teachers and mentors. Specifically, we encourage them to invite readers into their classrooms (to gain an understanding of the past, present, and future of scholarship in particular areas from the perspective of their firsthand experience), as well as into their offices and hallway conversations (to gain insights into the subtleties and nuances of exemplary professional practice).

By explicitly focusing on an introductory doctoral seminar setting, we encourage our authors to address the interests and needs of nonexpert students and colleagues who are looking for answers to questions such as the following: Why is this topic important? How did it originate and how has it evolved? How is it different from related topics? What do we actually know about this topic? How does one effectively communicate this information to students and practitioners? What are the methodological pitfalls and conceptual dead ends that should be avoided? What are the most/least promising opportunities for theory development and empirical study in this area? What questions/situations/phenomena are not well suited for this theory or tool? What is the most interesting work in progress? What are the most critical gaps in our current understanding that need to be addressed during the next 5 years?

We are pleased to share our dream with you, and we encourage your suggestions for how these books can better satisfy your learning needs—as a newcomer to the field preparing for prelims or developing a research proposal, or as an established scholar seeking to broaden your knowledge and proficiency.

DAVID A. WHETTEN
SERIES EDITOR

Preface

This book would not be without Ben Schneider. He conceived of the idea of a book on job attitudes and (after agreeing to broaden the scope to attitudes in and around organizations) persuaded me to write it. I still do not know whether I should thank him for the latter. I do know, however, that he has earned my respect and affection for always being there for me as a supportive colleague, providing both task and socioemotional support through the years. Often, folks express appreciation to their families for supporting their writing endeavors. Candidly, my wife and daughter were pretty insulated from this project and simply continued, during its writing, to punctuate my life with joy. Cora Scott, my administrative assistant at Tulane (who feels like family), is the one who bore the burden of me while this book was being produced. I will not go into the gory details, but she deserves sainthood. Several colleagues provided comments on what is in the pages ahead. To them, I am not only appreciative but also apologetic because I too often ignored their sage advice. These terrific colleagues include Sue Ashford, Joerg Dietz, Rob Folger, Jennifer George, Erika Hayes, Doug Pugh, Janet Ruscher, and Howie Weiss.

A preface sometimes supplies a statement of purpose or scope. This one does not. The "lay of the land" is described in Chapter 1. I do want to note here, however, the style in which the book is written. I was advised to write it as if I were having a conversation with one of my doctoral students. I thought this was great advice; often, I heeded it. So, in places, my language may seem to some a bit too casual. Please do not let it get in the way of the content. I do have a serious message to deliver; I hope that it's presented in ways that help rather than hinder.

Have a good read!

ARTHUR P. BRIEF

1 Attitudes

MUCH ADO ABOUT SOMETHING

Few, if any, organizational scientists disagree that attitudes play a central role in the discipline. Mere mention of the "attitude" concept evokes in the minds of most the study of job satisfaction. Often accompanying this cognitive representation of research on attitudes in the organizational sciences is a yawn or some other behavioral manifestation of boredom. This less-than-enthusiastic reaction is understandable. Attitude research is old hat; what is new or faddish tends to attract more interest than the enduring (Dunnette, 1966). By old hat, I mean that by the 1930s, Allport (1935) had declared attitudes to be social psychology's "most distinctive and indispensable concept" (p. 798), and Thurstone (e.g., 1931) had developed quantitatively sophisticated methods for their measurement (cf. Greenwald & Banaji, 1995). By the 1970s, Locke (1976) had counted more than 3,300 studies on *the* primary attitude investigated by organizational scientists—job satisfaction. It is easy to appreciate, therefore, why—after more than a half century of intensive study—the topic of attitudes may not now inflame the intellectual passions of the organizational scholar. Obviously, by now, so much scholarly attention must have resulted in logically and empirically defensible answers to all important research questions.

Wrong. This book is far from strictly a historical account. For example, although the literature on job satisfaction will be reviewed (albeit relatively briefly), I will emphasize what we as organizational scholars might want to learn about job satisfaction regarding research questions that have not been adequately attended to or have not even been posed previously. More important, as the title, *Attitudes In and Around Organizations,* suggests, the book does not address just job satisfaction. It also is concerned, for instance, with how the attitudes people bring with them to the workplace (e.g., their racial attitudes) affect thoughts, feelings, and actions in organizations and how the attitudes of those around (i.e., outside) an organization are affected by the organization.

By broadly construing the set of attitudes that are and should be attended to in the organizational sciences and by focusing on what new might be learned about the origins and functions of these attitudes, this book is intended to generate some heat. That is, my grandest goal for the book is that the passions of its readers, be they new initiates to the organizational sciences or seasoned veterans, are ignited to pursue the study of attitudes in and around organizations. Where there is heat, enlightenment is sure to follow.

The rest of this introductory chapter provides a taste of what's to come in two ways. First, brief examples will be supplied to demonstrate how research on attitudes in the organizational sciences has paid off and how it will continue to do so. Second, short descriptions of the remaining chapters will be presented. Neither the examples nor descriptions to follow will adequately suggest what the book is not. In particular, it is not an exhaustive catalog of research findings on job satisfaction. As indicated above, the book is balanced more toward looking ahead, rather than back. Readers more exclusively interested in what is known about job satisfaction should see, for example, the now classic chapter by Locke (1976) and Cranny, Smith, and Stone's (1992) recently edited volume.

The Payoffs

It seems to many organizational scientists that the usefulness of studying attitudes lies in their observed relationships to behaviors deemed to be important. Many of these relationships will be noted in the chapters to come. To preview what's ahead, I'll share something of what we have learned about the

relationship between job satisfaction and job performance, perhaps the behavior of interest to most organizational scientists.

Much evidence indicates that individual job satisfaction generally is *not*
significantly related to individual *task* performance (e.g., Brayfield & Crockett,
1955; Iaffaldano & Muchinsky, 1985; Vroom, 1964). Likely because this finding, evident in the literature for more than 40 years, flies in the face of
conventional wisdom (e.g., happy workers are more productive), researchers
have continued to pursue the search for a satisfaction-performance relationship. Largely because of the efforts of Organ and his colleagues (e.g., Bateman
& Organ, 1983; Organ, 1988a, 1990; Smith, Organ, & Near, 1983), that search
has paid off.

Organ's work focuses on organizational citizenship behaviors (OCBs)
rather than task performance. *Task performance* can be thought of as the
proficiency with which people perform activities that are formally recognized
as part of their jobs (Borman & Motowidlo, 1993). These role-prescribed
(Katz & Kahn, 1978) activities often are those identified by the job analysis
techniques of the industrial psychologist. Alternatively, OCBs less frequently
are thought of as in-role and, therefore, are more discretionary in nature. They
include, for example, volunteering to help out a coworker and to take on other
duties beyond regularly assigned ones.[1] Generally speaking, OCBs can be
thought of as forms of contextual performance (e.g., Motowidlo & Van
Scotter, 1994); indicators of it and task performance compose overall assessments of how well people do their jobs (Mackenzie, Podsakoff, & Fetter, 1991;
Orr, Sackett, & Mercer, 1989). Somewhat more precisely, *contextual performance* refers to the contributions people make to an environment supportive
of task performance.

As suggested above, research does show that although a consistent job
satisfaction-task performance relationship remains elusive, job satisfaction
often has been found to be related to contextual performance in the form of
OCBs (Organ & Ryan, 1995). Theoretically, the relative discretionary nature
of contextual performance helps explain this difference in findings. That is,
because contextual performance entails more volition than task performance
(Borman & Motowidlo, 1993), it should be more sensitive to factors such as
how satisfied people are with their jobs. It is reasonable to believe, for example,
that people who are more satisfied with how their employers treat them are
more likely to volunteer to take on duties beyond those regularly assigned to
them (e.g., Organ, 1988a).

The full story of the job satisfaction-job performance relationship remains
to be told in the chapters ahead. What has been told, however, does dem-

onstrate that a research focus on attitudes is perceptive. More than a decade ago, the correlation between satisfaction and performance was labeled an illusory one, a perceived relationship between two variables that we logically or intuitively think should interrelate but that do not (Iaffaldano & Muchinsky, 1985). Today, because of the persistence of several tenacious organizational scholars (e.g., Organ, 1988a), we know logic and intuition sometimes can surmount what is taken as an empirical fact. Other "facts" in the organizational literature remain to be scrutinized adequately. As the following example shows, such careful and critical examination of the taken for granted might also yield unforeseen insights.

To demonstrate what the future may hold by continuing to look at the old in a new light, I will again focus on the job satisfaction construct. In the organizational literature, job satisfaction is commonly thought of as an affective reaction (i.e., how people feel about their jobs). Locke (1976), for example, defines job satisfaction "as a pleasurable or positive emotional state resulting from an appraisal of one's job or job experiences" (p. 1300). This view of job satisfaction can be traced to early studies in which workers' feelings were of explicit concern (e.g., Hersey, 1932) and to the idea, long evident in social psychology, that feelings are a component of attitudes (e.g., Allport, 1935). Regarding the social psychology literature, a two-component model of attitudes—one affective, the other cognitive—is well established (e.g., Bagozzi & Burnkrant, 1979; Crites, Fabrigar, & Petty, 1994; Petty & Cacioppo, 1986a; Zajonc & Markus, 1982). Despite this recognition of the two-component model, it rarely has been addressed in the organizational literature.[2] Only one study has assessed the affective and cognitive content of often used measures of job satisfaction (Brief & Roberson, 1989), with disturbing findings. In part, we observed that scores on two commonly used measures of job satisfaction, that is, the Job Descriptive Index (Smith, Kendall, & Hulin, 1969) and the Minnesota Satisfaction Questionnaire (Weiss, Dawis, England, & Lofquist, 1967) reflect relatively little affective content of the attitude construct. More simply stated, measures of job satisfaction may not adequately capture how people *feel* about their jobs.

A mismatch between conceptualization and measurement, in and of itself, clearly is troublesome. It is only symptomatic, however, of a larger problem noted earlier—the failure of the organizational community to adequately attend to the distinctiveness of the affective and cognitive components of the attitude construct. This failure is reflected in that none of the following possibilities have been empirically addressed in the organizational literature: (a) An individual may hold an attitude as measured by an index of one component and yet hold a different attitude in his or her standing on the other component (e.g., Rosenberg & Hovland, 1960); (b) each component has separate antecedents (e.g., Greenwald, 1968); (c) the different components differently predict the same criterion variable (e.g., Millar & Tesser, 1986); and (d) predictions are more precise to the extent that the components are consistent with one another (e.g., Rosenberg, 1968b). Given these possibilities, what might we learn by looking, for example, at job satisfaction in a new light that recognizes its components? For instance, it may be the case that job satisfaction does predict task performance when the thoughts and feelings workers have about their jobs are in alignment. But again, no one now knows how affective-cognitive consistency affects the job satisfaction-task performance relationship. I hope that this book will help stimulate others to generate such knowledge.

Thus far, I have demonstrated the payoffs attached to studying attitudes in the organizational sciences by sharing a little bit of what we already have learned and of what we might learn through approaching the familiar in innovative ways. I will close this discussion of payoffs by speculating what a focus on the *un*familiar might bring.

Universally, it seems, attitudes in the organizational sciences are viewed as operating in a conscious mode. This universality, for example, is evident in the almost exclusive practice of using self-reports to measure attitudes (i.e., of directly asking people their attitudes). Alternatively, might it be the case that people in and around organizations hold attitudes of which they are unconscious (i.e., unaware)? Evidence outside the organizational sciences indicates the answer is yes (e.g., Greenwald & Banaji, 1995). Thus, it is quite possible, for instance, that prospective employees, coworkers, and customers belonging to the same demographic group (e.g., Blacks) might be discriminated against by organizational members who *un*knowingly harbor negative attitudes toward that demographic group. Various works, for example, by Dovidio and Gaertner (e.g., 1991), support such a possibility. The argument evident in these works goes something like this: Some people, because they embrace egalitarian values, are at least cognitively neutral toward Blacks yet have negative feelings toward them. To avoid this conflict between the cognitive and affective components of their attitudes toward Blacks, they exclude from consciousness their negative feelings. Moreover, they act on their unconscious negative feelings only when they think they have a plausible, seemingly nonprejudicial reason for doing so. For instance, a manager may not hire a Black person for a sales position because the manager thinks the White customer base would be more receptive to people of the customers' own race, yet the manager's unconscious negative feelings toward Blacks contributed to or drove the decision (Brief, Buttram, Elliott, Reizenstein, & McCline, 1995). This sort of possibility awaits detailed examination in the organizational sciences; again, we have assumed attitudes are conscious. Although the study of unconscious attitudes in and around organizations likely will be methodologically challenging, we probably will unmask, by moving away from an exclusive reliance on direct assessments of attitudes, a host of interesting attitude-behavior relationships not previously recognized.

In sum, the above examples were intended to demonstrate that we in the organizational sciences (a) have accumulated a substantial body of knowledge about attitudes and (b) have the opportunity to learn considerably more by pursuing answers to familiar questions in innovative ways and by addressing questions not yet posed. As stated earlier and detailed a bit more below, this book will summarize what we know about attitudes in the organizational sciences and, more important, suggest what we might discover by adopting novel means, both conceptually and methodologically, for exploring attitudes in and around organizations. I use the phrase "might discover," rather than "will discover," because I have been socialized to write like the typical scientist who feels compelled to hedge all assertions. Putting 20 plus years of hedging aside, I am convinced of what the future will hold in the organizational sciences, and it is exciting. Attitudes commonly will be conceived of at all organizational levels of analysis as well as on both sides of an organization's boundary; theoretically driven interventions for changing attitudes will be frequent objects of study; and a variety of attitudes, not now investigated, will be considered indicators of how well organizations function economically, politically, and socially. The task before me is not only to get readers to envision this future but also to enlist readers in enacting it.

A Road Map

The six chapters to come begin by covering familiar territory and progressively move into more and more uncharted areas. The next chapter, for example, provides an overview of the job satisfaction literature. In it, definitions, dimensions, and measures of job satisfaction will be discussed; theories and empirical findings regarding both the origins and functions of the construct will be surveyed; and conceptual and methodological recommendations will be offered regarding future research needs. These recommendations largely will be limited to linear extensions of the extant job satisfaction literature; more radical departures will be recommended in later chapters.

The forthcoming suggestions to deviate from the traditional concerns of those who study attitudes in organizations can be traced to ideas that are not originally mine. Rather, I often found them in the social psychological literature, which initially was and largely remains the home of attitude research. The purpose of Chapter 3, therefore, is to provide some foundation in how social psychologists study attitudes. Given the breadth and depth of these approaches to the study of attitudes, the chapter offers only a selective view of the social psychology literature. The topics to be surveyed include what an attitude is and how its components can be conceptualized, ways of measuring attitudes, the impact of attitudes on behaviors, attitude formation and change, and the resistance of attitudes to change efforts. The ideas contained in these surveys will do more than inform the study of job satisfaction; they frequently will help frame a host of other issues to be raised in the chapters that follow.

Chapter 4 explicitly returns to the topic of job satisfaction, to demonstrate that an exciting, fresh approach to studying the construct is afoot. Consistent with that aim, the chapter opens with a redefinition of job satisfaction. Next, antecedents of the "new" job satisfaction are explored, followed by a detailed consideration of its likely organizational consequences. The chapter closes with an outline of what the next wave of job satisfaction might look like. The chapter is sprinkled liberally with speculations, particularly about job satisfaction construed at higher levels of analysis.

Much of Chapter 5 has to do with racial attitudes. Although these attitudes obviously are important in and of themselves, they were selected to represent the larger set of attitudes people bring with them to the workplace. Following a brief introduction to the idea of "attitudinal baggage," the chapter discusses the historical and contemporary nature of racial attitudes in the United States. The implications of this discussion for the workplace then will be presented, along with a host of pressing research questions sensitive to a variety of targets of discrimination in the United States and beyond. The chapter ends by returning to the more general theme of the attitudes people bring to work and how those attitudes might be modified by organizations.

The chapters described above all deal with the attitudes of organizational insiders. The focus shifts in Chapter 6 to a concern for the attitudes of those beyond the boundaries of an organization. Groups of people not conventionally thought of as organizational insiders but whose attitudes are organizationally relevant include, for example, stockholders, government officials (legislators and regulators), suppliers, potential employees, and the public at large. The chapter focuses on one particularly important group of outsiders—customers—to demonstrate how organizations affect the attitudes of people beyond their boundaries. After an introduction to the general topic of outsider attitudes (particularly that of goodwill), the nature of customer satisfaction, especially how it is described in the marketing literature, will be discussed. The chapter then reviews the effects of organizations on customer satisfaction and offers ways of enhancing our understanding of observed relationships. Finally, a broader view of the effects of organizations on outsider attitudes will be adopted to pose a set of research questions about how organizations may seek to influence salient attitudes in their environments.

The last chapter of the book presents an argument that the study of attitudes in and around organizations can be thought of as contemporary history and, therefore, that the theories derived from this study are temporally bound. This argument is advanced by demonstrating how the nature of work in America changed during the 1980s and 1990s and how those changes affected the study of job attitudes. This chapter, like the preceding ones, is intended more to raise questions than to answer them. My aspirations go beyond stimulating readers to seek answers to the questions I have posed. My grandest aim is to arouse readers to create their own puzzles about attitudes in and around organizations that they themselves want to solve. Such imaginative acts finally will bury attitude research as an endeavor forever plodding along in a mechanical fashion. A glimpse at what I hope will rise in its place lies in the pages ahead.

Notes

1. For more on OCBs and like constructs, see, for instance, Brief and Motowidlo (1986), George and Brief (1992), Van Dyne, Graham, and Dienesch (1994), and Van Dyne, Cummings, and Parks, (1995).

2. For exceptions, see, for example, Organ and Near (1985) and Weiss and Cropanzano (1996).

2 Job Satisfaction Reconsidered

The above title is borrowed from Walter Nord (1977). I do so not only because it informs what this chapter is about—a reconsideration of the job satisfaction literature. The title also reflects that the chapter captures some of the distinctly critical tone of Nord's journal article, in which he stated, "Some of the most interesting characteristics of the existing research are revealed not by the results of what we have studied, but by an examination of the topics that have gone unanalyzed" (p. 1026). Thus, what is to come is intended to provide an appreciation of what we know *and* of what we might want to learn.

The chapter unfolds as follows. First, a working definition of the *job satisfaction* construct is taken from the literature, and I discuss how its facets have been construed. In this discussion, conventional measures of these construals are noted. Next, I survey a variety of theoretical approaches that have been used to explain where a person's job satisfaction comes from. This survey is punctuated by exemplary research findings. Third, a number of investigated consequences of job satisfaction and theories addressing them are reviewed. I close the chapter by discussing why some issues were not raised in it.

As I emphasized in the introductory chapter, what follows in no way will constitute a comprehensive review, critique, and integration of the job satisfaction literature. One simple reason for this is that the literature is too vast. Although Locke (1976) estimated that by 1972, more than 3,300 studies had been published on job satisfaction, the number had grown to more than 12,400 by 1991 (Spector, 1996)! What is to come, therefore, necessarily reflects my judgment as to what we know and do not know about job satisfaction, on the basis of how it has been investigated. In Chapter 4, I will return to the study of job satisfaction to explore what we might learn by departing from history.

A Working Definition

I reviewed numerous definitions of job satisfaction and could not identify one that was totally pleasing. Because job satisfaction is an attitude toward one's job, I viewed the alternative definitions by how the concept of attitude typically is construed. As will become more apparent in the next chapter in which the attitude concept is tackled, definitions of job satisfaction do not seem to be derived from what is thought to constitute an attitude. Simply for now, an attitude has two components, one affective and the other cognitive (e.g., Crites, Fabrigar, & Petty, 1994), yet job satisfaction tends to be defined conceptually only in affective terms. One recent departure from this tendency is the definition implied by Motowidlo (1996), who suggests that job satisfaction is a judgment about the favorability of one's work environment. If he had gone on to recognize more explicitly that such an evaluative judgment can be reflected in thoughts *and* feelings, I would have been pleased.

Regardless of the problems with how job satisfaction is defined, one still needs some idea of what the construct means to review the literature addressing it. Thus, I take as a working definition Locke's (1976). He defined job satisfaction as "a pleasurable or positive emotional state resulting from the appraisal of one's job or job experiences" (p. 1300). I chose Locke's definition because it appears to be widely used. Also, it is consistent with other definitions evident in the literature. For instance, Cranny, Smith, and Stone (1992) defined job satisfaction as "an affective (that is, emotional) reaction to a job, that results from the incumbent's comparison of actual outcomes with those that are desired (expected, deserved, and so on)" (p. 1). Weiss and Cropanzano (1996) observed that it is curious that this definition, like others (e.g., Lofquist & Dawis, 1969; Porter, Lawler, & Hackman, 1975), includes the presumed causes of the construct (i.e., outcome-standard comparisons). I will have more to say on this difficulty later in the chapter.

The Dimensions

Often, investigators have been interested in how satisfied people are with different elements of their jobs. Such interest in the dimensions or facets of job satisfaction is easily understood because the elements of jobs (e.g., tasks, relationships, and rewards) readily come to mind, and satisfaction with virtually any of them, depending on the goals of the researcher, can be argued to be important. I am unaware, however, of any theory that leads to the systematic identification of these elements and/or to understanding when satisfaction with a particular element is more important than some other element. For example, assume that I wanted to examine the relationship between job satisfaction and employee turnover. It would be helpful to know what facets of job satisfaction I should investigate and which of those facets is most likely to be predictive of turnover. Not only does theory fail to speak to these questions in regard to turnover, but again there is a void of theory that explicitly entails reasoning about which facets of job satisfaction ought to be considered and their relative importance for understanding any given criterion variable (other than overall job satisfaction itself). The meaning of work literature (e.g., Brief & Nord, 1990a) does suggest the elements of jobs that such a facet-focused theory about job satisfaction might include. Vroom (1964), for instance, identified five properties of jobs in seeking to answer the question, "Why do people work?" Those properties are financial renumeration, expenditure of energy, production of goods and services, social interaction, and social status. One could assert, on the basis of Vroom's discussion of these properties, that satisfaction with each of them is salient to understanding a person's decision to work, to become psychologically involved in a job, or to leave a job. Beyond this point, regrettably, Vroom's discussion of the properties is not particularly helpful. He states that there is "no basis for judging the relative influence of these different properties" (p. 43). Moreover, I have not found that need theories (e.g., Maslow, 1943) directly translate into propositions about the relative importance of satisfaction with specific job elements. Partially, this is because any particular job element (e.g., pay) too easily could be argued to be involved with satisfying two or more needs (e.g., physiological, safety, and esteem). More helpful to me has been to consider what might be the essential purpose or function of a job in people's lives.

In a series of articles (e.g., Brief & Aldag, 1989, 1994; Brief & Atieh, 1987; Brief, Konovsky, George, Goodwin, & Link, 1995; Doran, Stone, Brief, & George, 1991; George & Brief, 1990), I have asserted that the economic elements of a job are dominant, given life circumstances characterized by challenging financial demands (e.g., being a primary breadwinner with several mouths to feed). This none-too-surprising observation suggests facet importance is a product of nonjob factors (e.g., a person's family configuration). Thus, for example, as long as a worker faces challenging financial demands, her satisfaction with pay will contribute more to her experienced quality of life than her satisfaction with the tasks she performs or with her interpersonal relationships at work. This assertion becomes more significant if one accepts the position, as I do, that many, if not most, workers, even in a rich country such as the United States, confront significant financial demands during virtually all their working lives. In 1993, the median family income in America was less than $37,000; in 1992, almost 8,000,000 families lived in poverty. The potential importance of the economic elements of jobs is not really visible in the literature. As Nord (1977) noted, researchers have not adequately emphasized the study of so-called extrinsic sources (e.g., pay) of job satisfaction, as much as can be justified. He attributed this deficiency to investigators' assumption that because workers generally have their financial needs met, they primarily are concerned with fulfilling higher-order needs. (This assumption might be attributable to the relatively secure financial position occupied by university faculty.) Almost 20 years after Nord's observation, it appears that the economic elements of jobs remain inadequately emphasized (Brief & Aldag, 1994), although there appears to be an increased interest in satisfaction with pay. This interest, however, is expressed narrowly as measuring the construct and understanding its antecedents. Questions concerning the consequences of satisfaction with pay or with any other economic job element rarely have been raised. Later in the chapter, I will return to research on satisfaction with pay.

Of course, the above discussion of when this or that facet of job satisfaction might be more or less important to a worker does not constitute a theory. Once again, such a theory, likely rooted in the literature on the meaning of work, awaits to be developed. Nevertheless, facets of job satisfactions are studied and, therefore, measured. Indeed, it seems that the facets considered are those gauged by two popular measures: the Job Descriptive Index (JDI; Smith, Kendall, & Hulin, 1969) and the Minnesota Satisfaction Questionnaire (MSQ; Weiss, Dawis, Lofquist, & England, 1966). The JDI taps satisfaction with coworkers, pay, promotion opportunities, supervision, and the work itself. Each of these is measured by a scale composed of 9 to 18 adjectives to which a person responds "yes," "uncertain," or "no" in regard to how descriptive the adjective is of his or her job. For instance, examples of the adjectives used to measure satisfaction with coworkers include *boring* (reverse scored), *responsible,* and *intelligent.* Presumably, therefore, a person who describes coworkers as *intelligent* is more satisfied with them. Smith et al. (1969) detailed the methodological care taken in developing the JDI, and Cook, Hepworth, Wall, and Warr (1981) provided a generally favorable assessment of its known psychometric properties. But as the sample coworker scale items provided show, the JDI is not an obvious indicator of how workers *feel* about their jobs; as previously suggested, its structure (i.e., the facets addressed) is not dictated explicitly by a strong theoretical rationale.

The MSQ was constructed to operationalize the satisfaction part of Dawis, Lofquist, and Weiss's (1968) theory of work adjustment. The MSQ is composed of 100 items intended to assess satisfaction with 20 aspects of the work environment (called work reinforcers) that pertain to 20 psychological needs. These specific needs were not explicated in the theory of work adjustment. So the MSQ's facets of job satisfaction, like those of the JDI, were not theoretically identified. The breadth of a 20-facet measure, nevertheless, is impressive. Those facets are ability utilization, achievement, activity, advancement, authority, company policies and practices, compensation, coworkers, creativity, independence, moral values, recognition, responsibility, security, social service, social status, supervision-human relation, supervision-technical, variety, and working conditions. I, for one, could not have intuited a set this large. Persons respond to each of the five items, tapping each of these facets by indicating on a five-point scale how satisfied they are with the aspect of their jobs specified by the item. The following items from the satisfaction with coworkers scale exemplify the content of the MSQ: "the chance to develop close friendships with my coworkers," "the friendliness of my coworkers," and "the way my coworkers are easy to make friends with." Clearly, the JDI and MSQ appear to offer quite different ways of tapping presumably the same variable, satisfaction with coworkers. This also is the case for the other facets the measures have in common. Thus, researchers face a real choice in deciding between the two. I prefer the MSQ simply because it directly asks how satisfied people are and because it taps a much longer set of facets. But as Chapter 4 will show, I am not really pleased with either of the popular options. See Cook et al. (1981) for several other options.

Recently, there has not been much work on multifaceted measures of job satisfaction. Conceptually, Schneider, Gunnarson, and Wheeler (1992) have proposed that "the addition of present and future opportunities to the measurement of job facet satisfaction will improve the relationship between the sum of facet satisfaction and index of overall job satisfaction" (p. 55). Their proposition is derived from the idea that opportunities are in themselves satisfying (e.g., Miller & Monge, 1986). For empirical results consistent with Schneider et al.'s proposition, see Ospina (1996); in the next section, I will have more to say about the facet-overall job satisfaction relationship.

Although satisfaction with pay, as has been noted, generally has not been emphasized adequately in the literature, its measurement recently has been addressed. Heneman and Schwab (1985) developed the Pay Satisfaction Questionnaire, which purportedly gauges satisfaction with pay level, pay raises, structure/administration, and benefits. The results of studies assessing the factor structure of this questionnaire, however, lead one to question whether these distinct dimensions are tapped (cf. Miceli & Lane, 1991). Beyond concern with measurement, Miceli and Lane, building on the work of Heneman (1985), have advanced multiple models of the determinants of pay satisfaction. Their models are influenced strongly by the literature on justice in the workplace (e.g., Greenberg, 1987) and do not fully reflect the possibility that the reactions of employees to their pay are conditioned by such nonjob factors as financial demands. For instance, I suspect that with all else equal in the workplace, Worker A, unattached with no dependents, would be more satisfied earning Pay Level Z than would Worker B, with an unemployed spouse and three dependent children.

To summarize, organizational scientists have some theoretical work to do in regard to better understanding the dimensions of job satisfaction and the relative importance of those dimensions for explaining any given phenomenon. Moreover, in studying the facets of job satisfaction, we need to be careful in selecting among alternative measures (recognizing that those alternatives may not be conceptually equivalent) and in avoiding the availability of a *seemingly* acceptable alternative driving our research agendas (as suggested by Kaplan's, 1964, "law of the instrument"). Finally, although not explicitly concerned with the relative importance of satisfaction with pay, researchers have begun to more seriously focus on the measurement of pay satisfaction and its determinants. These models likely could be improved by a fuller consideration of the economic functions of work in people's lives. In the section below on overall job satisfaction, some of the issues raised in discussing the dimensions will reappear.

Overall Job Satisfaction

Given what was said above about how dimensions of job satisfaction have been identified, it should not come as a surprise that summing across facet scores (e.g., adding together a respondent's scores on the JDI's coworkers pay, promotion opportunities, etc. scales) is not equivalent to measuring overall (i.e., general or global) job satisfaction. Scarpello and Campbell (1983) provide an informative demonstration of this nonequivalence. In part, the researchers examined the relationship between the sum of MSQ facets and a single-item measure of global job satisfaction: "How satisfied are you with your job in general?" Such single-item measures often have been included in large-scale surveys such as the General Social Survey (e.g., Davis, 1982). Scarpello and Campbell concluded that their results "argue against the common practice of using sum of facet satisfaction as the measure of overall job satisfaction" (p. 595). The correlation between the sum of the MSQ facets and the general measure was only .32. Moreover, they asserted that their one-item, five-point global rating of overall job satisfaction is reliable and inclusive and that the whole, represented by this global measure, is more complex than the sum of the presently measured parts.[1] Thus, until we have a theory-driven multifaceted measure of job satisfaction, an attractive way of gauging the overall construct also is quite simple, a single item such as the one used by Scarpello and Campbell. Taking simplicity and, as will be discussed in Chapter 4, psychometric rigor, one step further is Kunin's (1955) single-item measure of overall job satisfaction, the faces scale (see Figure 2.1). Respondents to the item place a check under a face that indicates how they feel about their job in general.[2]

The various measures that have been described all are direct, paper-and-pencil, self-reported ratings of job satisfaction.[3] This form of measurement is by far the most popular in the literature, but interesting options exist that are underused.

Back in 1976, Locke stated, "It is unfortunate that interviews have been used relatively infrequently to assess job satisfaction" (p. 1336). He went on to say that this was because of the following potential advantages to interviews:

> The meaning of the responses can be determined, contradictions can be explained and corrected, individuals with poor self-insight can be assessed more accurately; misinterpretations of items can be corrected, etc. Furthermore, interviews can probe more in-depth and can use an approach to question-asking which is best

Circle the face that best describes how you feel about your job *in general*.

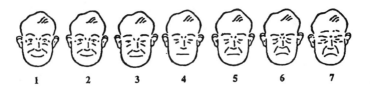

Figure 2.1. Faces Scale: Sample Items
SOURCE: Adapted from "Construction of a New Type of Attitude Measure," by T. Kunin, 1955, *Personnel Psychology, 8,* pp. 65-78. Used with permission.

suited for each individual based on his knowledge, degree of education, and perspective. (p. 1336)

Today, I fully concur but also want to go further. Before I do so, let me urge the reader to take a look at the interview schedule used in the classic study by Hoppock (1935, pp. 57-59). It provides a good example to be replicated.

Now, to move ahead or, as will be shown, perhaps backward. To methodologically respond to the theoretical needs previously noted (e.g., a better understanding of the dimensions of job satisfaction and their relative importance), the field likely would benefit tremendously from a *grounded theory* approach (Glaser & Strauss, 1967). According to Strauss and Corbin (1990), this strategy "is a qualitative research *method* that uses a *systematic* set of *procedures* to develop an inductively derived . . . *theory* about a *phenomenon*" (p. 24). Although a few examples of the use of qualitative techniques in the recent job satisfaction literature can be identified (e.g., Taber, 1991), I am unaware of any attempts to develop a grounded theory. Developing such a theory would signal how little we may know and how much we might learn from observing and listening to workers. A terrific starting point for thinking about how to proceed with doing the sort of research required is Hersey (1932), although the terms *grounded theory* or *job satisfaction* appear nowhere in the text. According to Hersey, the purpose of his study was "to discover and formulate through intensive analysis of a group of representative men, general prerequisites for successful adjustment which would in turn apply in principle to all groups of male workers" (p. 5). He used a variety of research techniques, including observing his small group of participants while they worked, recording their conversation, repeatedly interviewing them at work about their daily activities and feelings, and visiting with them in their homes during the evening. On the basis of the data collected by these and other means, Hersey formulated numerous proposals about the "ideal plant environment" that entailed describing *a congenial job; sound working conditions; security; satisfactory renumeration; justice, equality, and independence;* and *understanding and efficient supervision.* Although these terms likely seem familiar, Hersey's interpretation of them is not necessarily commonplace. For example, he discussed security not only in reference to unemployment and arbitrary dismissal but also in regard to accidents, illness, and old age. Later in the book, I will draw a bit from this wealth of ideas. For now, I move on to more conventional approaches to understanding the antecedents of job satisfaction.

Antecedents

Why do some people report that they are highly satisfied with their jobs and others report considerably lower levels of job satisfaction? In initially responding to this question, I will go over much of the territory covered by Locke (1976). That is, I will review some of the answers he provided, updating them when appropriate. Then, I will move into territory discovered (or at least the meaningfully enlarged) since Locke's review of the job satisfaction literature.

Person-environment (P-E) fit models, either implicitly or explicitly, have dominated how organizational psychologists have thought about the causes of job satisfaction. Dawis (1992) provides an informative history of this way of thinking. According to him, it began with Schaffer (1953), who built on the work of Murray (1938). Schaffer found that average need satisfaction correlated with overall job satisfaction and that need satisfaction for the highest-strength needs correlated most strongly with overall job satisfaction. These findings indicate that work environments that fulfill a person's important needs are satisfying (i.e., there is a fit between what the environment has to offer and what the person needs). Porter (1961) operationalized P-E fit by calculating need satisfaction from responses to two questions: "How much is there now?" (environment), and "How much should there be?" (person). French and his colleagues at the University of Michigan (e.g., French & Kahn,

1962) defined fit objectively and subjectively as (a) person demands (e.g., needs) to be met by environmental supplies and (b) environmental demands (i.e., role requirements) to be met by the person's supplies (i.e., abilities).

Research based on P-E fit defined in these ways has yielded expected fit-satisfaction relationships (e.g., Harrison, 1978). In Holland's (e.g., 1985) theory of vocational choice, vocational satisfaction depends on the fit between an individual's personality (essentially reflecting a person's needs) and the environment in which he or she works. Considerable evidence indicates that fit thought of in this way also is related to job satisfaction (e.g., Assouline & Meir, 1987; Gottfredson & Holland, 1990; Mount & Muchinsky, 1978). Katzell (1964) emphasized fit in regard to personal values and job characteristics. Locke (1976), too, emphasized values, rather than needs, as was done, for instance, by Schaffer and Porter. Although Locke employed Rand's (1964) conception of a *value* as what one acts to gain or keep, I find Rokeach's (e.g., 1968, 1973) approach more attractive because of the distinction he draws and its concreteness. He distinguished between two types of values: *terminal values,* or desired end states of existence worth striving for, and *instrumental values,* or desirable modes of behavior instrumental to the attainment of terminal values. In addition, Rokeach provides what he argues are complete lists of both types of values. See Table 2.1 for the lists and Braithwaite and Law (1985) for more on Rokeach's research.

Thus, one can think about a satisfying job in both the degree to which it facilitates the attainment of those *terminal* values most important to a person and the degree to which it allows or encourages behaviors consistent with those *instrumental* values most important to the person. Therefore, a job may be unsatisfying although it facilitates attaining an important end state (e.g., comfortable life) because it also requires the person to behave inconsistently with an important mode of conduct (e.g., being honest). To date, Rokeach's approach to values or more contemporary extensions of it (e.g., Schwartz, 1990) have yet to be applied to understanding job satisfaction. Such applications, nevertheless, are promising as a way of addressing the fit-satisfaction relationship from a values perspective. An additional and methodologically intriguing approach to the relationship is provided by Chatman and her colleagues (e.g., Chatman, 1991; O'Reilly, Chatman, & Caldwell, 1991) that entails a means of assessing an organization's values and the fit between those values and individuals.

The Work Adjustment Project at the University of Minnesota (which yielded the MSQ) perhaps is the most sustained effort to assess relationships

Table 2.1   Rokeach's List of Terminal and Instrumental Values

Terminal Values

A comfortable life	Inner harmony
(A prosperous life)	(Freedom from inner conflict)
An exciting life	Mature love
(A stimulating, active life)	(Sexual and spiritual love)
A sense of accomplishment	National security
(Lasting contribution)	(Protection from attack)
A world at peace	Pleasure
(Free of war and conflict)	(An enjoyable, leisurely life)
A world of beauty	Salvation
(Beauty of nature and the arts)	(Saved, eternal life)
Equality	Self-respect
(Brotherhood, equal opportunity for all)	(Self-esteem)
Family security	Social recognition
(Taking care of loved ones)	(Respect, admiration)
Freedom	True friendship
(Independence, free choice)	(Close companionship)
Happiness	Wisdom
(Contentedness)	(A mature understanding of life)

Instrumental Values

Ambitious	Imaginative
(Hard-working, aspiring)	(Daring, creative)
Broadminded	Independent
(Open-minded)	(Self-reliant, self-sufficient)
Capable	Intellectual
(Competent, effective)	(Intelligent, reflective)
Cheerful	Logical
(Lighthearted, joyful)	(Consistent, rational)
Clean	Loving
(Neat, tidy)	(Affectionate, tender)
Courageous	Obedient
(Standing up for your beliefs)	(Dutiful, respectful)
Forgiving	Polite
(Willing to pardon others)	(Courteous, well-mannered)
Helpful	Responsible
(Working for the welfare of others)	(Dependable, reliable)
Honest	Self-controlled
(Sincere, truthful)	(Restrained, self-disciplined)

SOURCE: Adapted from *Understanding Human Values* (pp. 133-134), by M. Rokeach, 1979, New York: Free Press. Reprinted with the permission of The Free Press, a Division of Simon & Schuster, from *Understanding Human Values* by Milton Rokeach. Copyright © 1979 by The Free Press.

between P-E fit and job satisfaction (Weiss et al., 1967). In this program of research, fit was operationalized by two sorts of questions: "How important to you in your ideal job is X?" (to assess a person's needs), and "How well is this job described by X?" (to assess the environment), with X being the 20 dimensions gauged in the MSQ (e.g., ability utilization, compensation, and security). Researchers often have found fit approached in this way to be related to job satisfaction (cf. Dawis, 1992).

In the above discussion, the person side of the P-E fit equation was characterized as either values or needs. As implied in that discussion, those who have adopted a value characterization were not guided by a specific framework, such as Rokeach's (e.g., 1968), in selecting the particular values of interest. Alternatively, however, a number of investigators who have adopted a need characterization were guided by specific, need content theories. Below, I turn to these theories and leave behind the general notion of P-E fit. Those readers wanting to know more about P-E fit and job satisfaction should see Edwards (1991) and Kristof (1996).

Need Theories

Three theories specifying the needs to be fulfilled if workers are to be satisfied with their jobs have captured the interests of organizational scientists: Maslow's (e.g., 1943, 1968) need hierarchy theory; Herzberg's (e.g., 1968; Herzberg, Mausner, & Snyderman, 1959) motivator-hygiene theory; and Alderfer's (1969, 1972) existence, relatedness, and growth (ERG) theory. Maslow identified five categories of innate and prepotent human needs (physiological, safety, belongingness, esteem, and self-actualization). These needs, according to him, are arranged in a hierarchy such that as a lower-order need (e.g., belongingness) becomes satisfied, the next higher-order need (e.g., esteem) becomes manifest. Moreover, because this process occurs gradually and not in a rigid step function, two or more needs are salient at any given time (assuming one's physiological needs are at least partially satisfied). Although Maslow's theory is relatively simple to understand, appears consistent with lay understandings of the concept of needs, and may seem to some to characterize a bastardized version of the "American dream," its scientific merit largely is a closed issue. For the reasons noted, the theory may have some heuristic value, but ample empirical evidence questions Maslow's categorization of human needs and proposed hierarchical structure (e.g., Hall & Nougaim, 1968; Rauschenberger, Schmitt, & Hunter, 1980; Wahba & Bridwell, 1976).[4]

Alderfer's (e.g., 1969) ERG theory stands as an alternative to Maslow's. He posited existence (e.g., the needs for food, water, clothing, shelter, and a secure and safe environment), relatedness (e.g., the needs to share thoughts and feelings and to have open two-way communications), and growth (e.g., the needs for self-development and for creative and productive work) as three primary need categories also arranged in a hierarchy but less strictly so than the one proposed by Maslow. Distinguishing Alderfer's theory the most from Maslow's, however, is the frustration-regression hypothesis that states that the failure to satisfy a higher-order need (e.g., relatedness) results in the next lower-order need (e.g., existence) becoming more important. Research other than Alderfer's on ERG theory is sparse; therefore, given the similarities between Alderfer's and Maslow's theories, I tend to *assume* the failures to support the latter generalize to the former. Nevertheless, I find Alderfer's frustration-regression hypothesis intriguing, and I like the way he tries to link specific organizational outcomes to the satisfaction of specific needs (e.g., pay to existence needs). I just wish we had more data.

The scientific merit of the third theory of interest, Herzberg's (e.g., Herzberg et al., 1959) *motivator-hygiene* (or two-factor) theory, also is a closed issue but perhaps should not be. Essentially, he posited that the factors (e.g., achievement, recognition, and responsibility—called motivators or satisfiers) that cause job satisfaction are different from the ones (e.g., company policy and administration, supervision, and coworkers—called hygiene or maintenance factors or dissatisfiers) that cause job *dis*satisfaction. This proposition implies that job dissatisfaction is not the opposite of job satisfaction, as commonly accepted in the organizational sciences. Herzberg's theoretical position and how he empirically went about identifying satisfiers and dissatisfiers have been criticized soundly, with due cause (e.g., House & Wigdor, 1967; King, 1970; Whitsett & Winslow, 1967). Indeed, by the 1970s, Korman (1971) concluded that research findings contradicting Herzberg's had "effectively laid the Herzberg theory to rest" (p. 179). I concur with Pinder (1984), however, who stated that "one is left, more than twenty years later not really knowing whether to take the theory seriously" (p. 28). My concurrence with him does not stem from any significant disagreements with the critiques of Herzberg's research methods; rather, it is tied to how job satisfaction has been operationalized in tests of the theory. In the chapters ahead, I will reconsider job satisfaction as affect and introduce evidence suggesting that positive and negative affect likely are independent of one another. Thus, of the ideas advanced by Herzberg, I remain somewhat attached to the possibility that job dissatisfaction is not necessarily the opposite of job satisfaction.[5]

In sum, I am not particularly impressed with cumulative empirical evidence in support of available need theories. This conclusion is consistent with Salancik and Pfeffer's (1977) critique of need theories. I note this although some of the arguments in their influential article have been questioned successfully (e.g., Stone, 1992). With all the evidence in place, we still do not have (a) a consistently verified taxonomy of human needs (b) that is justifiably linked to specific job elements, goals, or outcomes and (c) that can be used to help explain how the relative importance of a need changes across contexts (e.g., work or family) or through time. All three of these characterizations seem essential if a need theory is to help us better understand the causes of job satisfaction.[6]

I am afraid that where we ought to go from here is not back to refine the theories I have reviewed; rather, we must bite the bullet by attempting to construct a need theory from the ground up or abandon such theories as conceptual tools for addressing the causes of job satisfaction. Theory construction also was my answer to the confusion about the dimensions of job satisfaction. As I noted in my discussion of that confusion, the lack of a viable need theory was a source of the difficulty. If we had the right sort of need theory, we then would be better able to identify the facets of job satisfaction and to posit when a given facet of satisfaction is salient for understanding a given phenomenon. I hope someone picks up the challenge of constructing a more viable need theory; until then, we must look elsewhere, as I do below, for insights to job satisfaction.

Other Theoretical Approaches:
The Earlier Models

By "earlier models," I mean those that appeared in the literature more than a quarter of a century ago and, for one reason or another, remain worthy of note. I hope that these reasons will become apparent. I begin with March and Simon's (1958) work. They posited three causes of job satisfaction: (a) the greater the conformity of job characteristics (reality) to the self-characterization (ego-ideal) held by the individual, the higher the level of satisfaction; (b) the greater the predictability of instrumental relationships on the job, the higher the level of satisfaction; and (c) the greater the compatibility of work requirements with the requirements of other roles, the higher the level of satisfaction. The first proposition is an intriguing form of the person-environment fit idea; it is consistent with self-discrepancy theory (Higgins,

1987), which has received considerable empirical support in the social psychology literature (e.g., Higgins, Bond, Klien, & Strauman, 1986; Scott & O'Hara, 1993; Strauman, 1992). Essentially, the theory asserts that *self-esteem* is defined as a match between how a person sees him- or herself and how a person wants to see him- or herself. Moreover, Higgins, Simon, and Wells (1988) have speculated how actual-ideal self-discrepancies might inform the study of job satisfaction. I am unaware, however, of either March and Simon's proposition or Higgins et al.'s speculations having been pursued in the organizational literature.

March and Simon's (1958) second proposition also remains to be pursued. The notion that predictability has value is consistent with a variety of empirical evidence in the organizational sciences, for example, the findings pertaining to the effects of realistic job previews (Wanous, Poland, Premack, & Davis, 1992). The influence of the predictability of instrumental relationships on job satisfaction, however, has yet to be precisely assessed, at least to my knowledge. Of course, to do so would require identifying these instrumental work relationships. March and Simon's discussion of them is vague at best. For instance, rather than defining what they mean by an *instrumental relationship,* March and Simon provide examples of them such as the following: For a factory manager, the relationship between costs and volume of production is instrumental.

The literature on work-family conflicts (e.g., Greenhaus & Beutell, 1985) is supportive of March and Simon's (1958) third proposition regarding the compatibility of nonwork and work roles. But we have yet to systematically examine how the fit between other nonwork roles (e.g., church member or political party affiliate) and work roles might affect job satisfaction. An observant Jew who is expected to work on Saturdays and a liberal Democrat surrounded by conservative Republican coworkers may not report being highly satisfied with their jobs. In total, it seems worthwhile to attend to March and Simon's three propositions, yet they in no way represent a complete theory of job satisfaction. Thus, although the knowledge that might be gained by pursuing them could help flesh out our appreciation of particular causes of job satisfaction, I am doubtful such research would lead to a more holistic understanding of the job attitude.

More theoretically rich approaches to job satisfaction can be found in various treatments of the *organizational justice* concept. Jacques (1956) was one of the first to investigate the justice concept of equity in the workplace. He reasoned that a state of disequilibrium is created within a person when his or her actual level of pay deviates from the equitable level, regardless of the direction of the disparity. Jacques observed that if actual pay does fall below the equitable level, then workers experience dissatisfaction. Homans (1961), Patchen (1961), and Adams (1963) developed more detailed conceptions of equity based on rewards and deprivation, with Adam's (e.g., 1965) ideas capturing the most attention in the organizational sciences.[7] It now is clear that inequity, defined as a person's perceived ratio of inputs to outcomes standing psychologically unequal to that person's perception of some other's input-output ratio, is associated with dissatisfaction. Equity theory and the research flowing from it, however, have been critiqued, for example, for the ambiguities attached to identifying inputs and outcomes and the comparison other. For a current assessment of the theory, see Mowday (1996).

Equity theory can be thought of as concerned with *distributive justice,* referring to the distribution of outcomes (e.g., rewards). Following the publication of Folger and Greenberg (1985), organizational scientists broadened their interests in justice to include procedural as well as distributive concerns. Procedural justice shifts attention from *what* was decided to *how* decisions were made to distribute rewards (Cropanzano & Folger, 1996). That is, it is concerned with the perceived fairness of organizational processes. Research indicates that procedures affect job attitudes most when distributive outcomes are negative (Brockner & Wiesenfeld, 1996).[8] In other words, when workers receive outcomes they judge to be unfair, perceptions of procedural fairness protect them against the levels of dissatisfaction they might have otherwise experienced.

The preceeding two paragraphs in no way adequately portray the prominent position that justice concerns have come to occupy in the organizational literature. I urge the interested reader to see excellent articles by Greenberg (1987, 1990a) that frame theoretical and empirical work in the area as well as a number of pieces that may significantly extend the literature (e.g., Bies, 1987; Folger, 1993; Folger, Konovsky, & Cropanzano, 1992; Greenberg, 1990b; Greenberg & Scott, 1996; Kulik & Ambrose, 1992). The organizational literature on distributive and procedural justice is impressive; nevertheless, two aspects of it I find somewhat troublesome. First, with few exceptions (e.g., Greenberg, 1993), the research on organizational justice is too psychological, that is, it fails to get outside the heads of the workers studied. For example, in a typical study, perceptions of the fairness of a performance appraisal system might be measured within one organization, and scores on that measure might be correlated with scores on a measure of job satisfaction. Then, on the basis of observed significant correlations between the two, the investigator concludes fair appraisal procedures are important. My problem is that in this typical study, conducted in one organization, actual procedures likely were held constant (or at best, variance in procedures was constrained). I would like to see more justice research across contexts in which procedures are known to actually vary in significant ways. In this way, variations in context could be linked to perceptions of fairness, and we could be more certain that one is not just studying individual differences in perceptions of fairness. Simply, I want to know context-perception-attitude linkages. Such knowledge would enable us to identify better how to alter organizational processes to promote satisfaction.

My other problem with the justice literature concerns the distribution of *what* and procedures for *what*. The message in the literature seems to be that fairness always matters. Personally, I care considerably about how my dean makes pay decisions and the amount allocated to me; alternatively, I am really not very concerned with where my office mail box is located or how the decision was made to locate it. We need theory and research addressing what outcomes and procedures are important to workers. Certainly, the answer is not all outcomes and all procedures. In sum, theory and data (as well as my personal values) indicate that just organizations are likely to have more satisfied members than are unjust ones. We must learn more, however, about what constitutes a just organization.

Some of my concerns with the organizational justice literature are analogous to difficulties I see with the research on Hackman and Oldham's (1975) *job characteristics model,* another approach to understanding the causes of job satisfaction. This model, essentially a variant of earlier works by Turner and Lawrence (1965) and Hackman and Lawler (1971), posits that workers' perceptions of a set of task attributes (i.e., skill variety, autonomy, task identity, task significance, and feedback) are associated positively with satisfaction. Thus, for example, a worker who sees her job as entailing the use of a variety of valued skills, a reasonable degree of discretion over how and when work is done, the production of a whole or significant part of a product or service, activities whose consequences are significant to the lives of others, and the generation of information about how well she is performing will report being satisfied with what she is doing on her job.

The Hackman and Oldham (1975) model and the empirical examinations of it have been criticized soundly (Aldag, Barr, & Brief, 1981; Roberts & Glick, 1981); many of these criticisms, however, addressed the relationships between the perceived task characteristics and job performance, not job satisfaction. Cumulatively, the data do indicate a positive perceived task characteristic-job attitude association (e.g., Fried & Ferris, 1987; Loher, Noe, Moeller, & Fitzgerald, 1985). It also appears that the relationship is reciprocal. James and his associates (e.g., James & Jones, 1980; James & Tetrick, 1986) have argued, on the basis of notions about higher-order cognitive information processing, that task perceptions contribute positively to job satisfaction *and* vice versa; moreover, their arguments have been supported empirically (e.g., Mathieu, Hofmann, & Farr, 1993). Therefore, workers who are satisfied with their jobs see more variety, autonomy, task identity, and so forth in their jobs. Thus, a simple zero order correlation between task perceptions and job attitudes should not be interpreted only as the latter causing the former.[9]

Now to my concerns with the job characteristics literature: In their report of a field experiment, Lawler, Hackman, and Kaufman (1973) described their failure to alter fully the task perceptions they had intended to by manipulating actual task attributes. This failure points to the lack of understanding of the relationships between actual task attributes and perceptions of them. This gap in our knowledge is compounded because in many field studies employing a survey research design, task perception-job attitude relationships have been investigated in a sample of workers occupying essentially the same job; often, individual differences in task perceptions, not differences in actual task attributes, have been studied. For example, I studied the relationships in a sample of general duty staff nurses (Brief & Aldag, 1978). To make matters worse, in that same study, I committed another not uncommon error. I used Hackman and Oldman's (1975) Job Diagnostic Survey (JDS) to measure task perceptions and Smith et al.'s (1969) Job Descriptive Index (JDI) to measure satisfaction with the work itself. Both measures contain items asking workers how much variety they see in their jobs; thus, it is none too surprising that scores on the measures are correlated significantly. Those were errors made out of ignorance; I now know better. Nevertheless, my study exemplifies, along with Lawler et al.'s, why we need to attend to the linkages among actual task attributes-task perceptions-job attitudes, with the latter gauged in ways nonredundant with task perceptions measures (e.g., do *not* use the JDS and JDI together).[10]

But the problems do not stop there. Outside the laboratory, task attributes and perceptions of them covary with a bunch of other stuff, for example, pay and, more than likely, status, organizational level, and maybe even employment security (e.g., Campion & Berger, 1990; Dunham, 1977). The potential import of these covariations is suggested in two studies. In a field study, Locke,

Sirota, and Wolfson's (1976) participants did not respond as predicted when their jobs were enriched; they told the investigators this was because they expected that when their jobs required them to use more skills and to perform more significant tasks, for example, they would earn more money—which they did not. The host organization apparently anticipated the benefits of job enrichment without increased labor costs. In their study of voluntary job transfers, Simond and Orife (1975) observed that workers invariably chose higher-paying jobs over enriched ones when given the option. Thus, it can be seen that the covariants of tasks, at least money, matter to workers. I would not be surprised to learn that the relationship between task perceptions and job satisfaction, statistically controlling for these covariants, is quite modest. I await such investigations in the literature. In the meantime, I am somewhat optimistic about the future of the job characteristic model, given Campion and McClelland's (e.g., 1993) expansion of it. In their work, a distinction is made between *task enlargement* (i.e., adding requirements to the job for doing other tasks on the same product) and *knowledge enlargement* (adding requirements to the job for understanding procedures or rules relating to different products), with the former shown to *reduce* satisfaction and the latter to *increase* it.[11]

In closing this section, I will briefly note three other earlier models that probably should have received more research attention than they have. The *Cornell model* (Smith et al., 1969), as described by Hulin (1991), conceptualizes job satisfaction as a function of what people receive from their jobs in relation to what they expected to get, judged by their frames of reference for evaluating the outcomes in questions. The more unique part of this conceptualization is the frames-of-reference notion, which is a product of a person's work experiences or what he or she sees others experiencing in regard to work outcomes received. In tests of the Cornell model, frames of reference have been operationalized as the economic conditions in workers' communities (e.g., Hulin, 1966). I would like to see the effects of frames of reference on job satisfaction pursued further by more precisely indexing the extra-workplace variables that are thought to serve as standards for comparison. For example, frames of reference might be conceived of at the *occupational* level and gauged by unemployment rate, proportion of full-time workers, wage levels, and the like.

The second model is Porter and Lawler's (1968). This model posits that job satisfaction is a function of job performance that is equitably rewarded (i.e., performance leads to rewards, which in turn lead to satisfaction, with the reward-satisfaction relationship moderated by equity perceptions). Although some data speak to the proposition (e.g., Wanous, 1974), I do not remember any direct test of it. If such a test were undertaken, the research likely would benefit from being framed to recognize distinctions between distributive and procedural justice as well as between task and contextual performance. (The latter distinction was discussed in Chapter 1.) Porter and Lawler's original proposition, given the state of knowledge when it was posed, referred only to task performance and distributive justice. It seems plausible, for example, that job satisfaction also may be a function of contextual performance (e.g., helping and cooperating with others) that is rewarded on the basis of the use of fair procedures.

Finally, I want to take note of Hage's (1965) *axiomatic theory of organizations*. This approach is different from all the above because it treats job satisfaction as an organizational-level construct. Hage posits the higher the stratification, centralization, efficiency, and formalization of an organization, the lower the job satisfaction; the higher its complexity, the higher the satisfaction. I find some of these predictions both quite logical *and* troublesome. For instance, is a price of reducing cost per unit of output per year (i.e., of increasing efficiency) really reduced satisfaction? Available data provide no clear answer; nevertheless, I suspect the relationship too often holds. Hage's theory, along with structural-functional theories in general, regrettably, is out of vogue. But in the organizational sciences, fortunately, we are beginning to see job satisfaction treated at levels of analysis above the individual. Articles by George (1990) and Ostroff (1992) are terrific examples of what can be learned by construing job satisfaction at levels above the individual.[12] Because we often want to make inferences about the effects of organizations, I hope to see much more work on job satisfaction at higher levels of analysis.

In sum, it appears that March and Simon's (1958) propositions, organizational justice approaches (e.g., Greenberg, 1987), the job characteristic model (Hackman & Lawler, 1971), the Cornell model (Smith et al., 1969), Porter and Lawler's (1968) proposition, and Hage's (1965) theory all deserve additional research attention. Some of these earlier approaches have fallen out of style. This does not imply that these less-than-fashionable ways of thinking about the causes of job satisfaction do not remain informative. In particular, I am eager to read research reports that pursue (a) those self-discrepancy ideas of Higgins (1987) consistent with March and Simon's; (b) a clear definition of what constitutes a just organizational context; (c) the relationships between task attributes and satisfaction, controlling for salient covariants of the attributes; (d) the effects of alternative, extra-workplace frames of reference on satisfaction; (e) the moderating effects of procedural justice on contextual performance-satisfaction relationships; and (f) virtually any question entailing job satisfaction construed at a higher than individual level of analysis. These, obviously, reflect my preferences for what I want to learn. Different readers, I hope, will formulate different issues flowing from the earlier approaches reviewed that they would like to see pursued.

More Recent Theoretical Approaches to Job Satisfaction

The last 25 years have seen a number of new attempts to explain job satisfaction. Only a few of them will be reviewed here, with the ones stimulating the most recent interests being reserved for discussion in Chapter 4. I will deal later with these attention-grabbing approaches, heavily involving dispositional determinants, to spotlight them and to have the opportunity to first lay out their psychological foundations in some detail.

Now, I begin with Salancik and Pfeffer's (1978) *social information processing* approach to job attitudes, which builds on criticisms of the previously discussed job characteristics model (Hackman & Oldham, 1975). These criticisms, largely methodological in nature (e.g., research on job characteristics-job attitude relationship is plagued by priming and consistency artifacts), have been countered adequately (e.g., Stone, 1992). Nevertheless, the content of the social information processing approach is quite informative. The guts of Salancik and Pfeffer's argument are as follows. Jobs are ambiguous stimuli, subject to being interpreted in multiple ways. How a collection of tasks is interpreted greatly influences job attitudes; important determinants of these interpretations are the opinions about the work itself voiced by coworkers. Simply, social cues contribute to the production of job attitudes. This makes sense to me, and data primarily from the laboratory generally are supportive, particularly when individual differences are taken into consideration (Zalesny & Ford, 1990). In the laboratory, however, actual task attributes and social cues are treated as orthogonal factors, and participants are not viewed as potential sources of the social cues sent by their "coworkers." In other words, the real world is more complex than the laboratory. We need to start seriously considering social cues about task attributes as dependent variables. I cannot really imagine people performing a task so ambiguous as to not emit some cues whether, for example, it is more interesting than boring. Similarly, a worker who is the target of an investigation has a voice and, therefore, his or her task opinions probably are reciprocally related to those of others performing the same job.[13]

I have one final comment on Salancik and Pfeffer's (1978) ideas. Too often, they have been pitted against those of Hackman and Oldham (1975). This seems silly to me, for the approaches appear to be more complementary than competitive. We need more integrative research efforts such as those of Griffin, Bateman, Wayne, and Head (1987), who examined both objective and social factors as determinants of task perceptions and responses.

Landy (1978), adapting the ideas of Solomon and Corbit (1973), proposed an *opponent process* theory of job satisfaction. Viewed most simply, this theory implies that each worker has a typical or characteristic level of job satisfaction that could be called the person's steady state or equilibrium level (George & Jones, 1996). Changes in the person's work situation create disequilibrium, but through time, the worker's satisfaction returns to his or her steady state. For example, a pay raise may boost satisfaction, but its effects eventually wear off, with satisfaction returning to its equilibrium level. Landy explains in detail how this process unfolds by the increase or decrease in satisfaction created by the change in the work situation generating within the individual an opponent level of the attitudes. The opponent process theory, for reasons unknown to me, has not been tested. Yet research evidence shows that job satisfaction levels do remain relatively stable through time (e.g., Staw & Ross, 1985) and that at least some types of changes in the work situation produce only temporary (e.g., 6-month) changes in job satisfaction levels (e.g., Griffin, 1991). Thus, it seems that tests of this theory are well worth the effort.

Hulin, Roznowski, and Hachiya (1985) integrated ideas advanced by March and Simon (1958), Thibaut and Kelley (1959), and Smith et al. (1969) to formulate a *combined model* of work role satisfaction. They posited that satisfaction is a joint function of work role inputs and work role outcomes. Decreases in inputs relative to outcomes or increases in outcomes relative to inputs increase satisfaction. Similarly, decreases in outcomes or increases in inputs decrease satisfaction. Moreover, Hulin et al. also incorporate the use of direct and opportunity costs as well as frames of reference for evaluating outcomes into their model. Although the model in its entirety has not been tested, data supporting a number of its linkages are available (Roznowski & Hulin, 1992). Given what I have previously said about some of the sources of the model (e.g., about Smith et al.'s Cornell model), I would like to see an empirical examination that simultaneously considers all its parts (i.e., inputs, outcomes, use of costs, and frames of reference). In addition, given the role of inputs and outcomes in the model and in Adams's (e.g., 1965) theorizing, it also may be of value to conduct a conceptual analysis of how the two approaches are alike and dissimilar.

The newest and last theory to be noted here was advanced by Motowidlo (1996). This heavily cognitive approach entails a construal of the normative favorability of work environments as populations of all positive and negative events and conditions that occur in those environments through time. Experienced favorability is a product of samples from these populations stored in memory. When workers try to judge the favorability of their work environments, they retrieve a portion of this evaluative information from memory. Finally, reported job satisfaction is, in part, a product of these retrieved memories. Motowidlo provides explanations of how individual differences affect each of these components of his model; thus, he labels his approach *a theory of individual differences in job satisfaction*. I hope I have provided enough of a description of Motowidlo's theory to entice readers to study the original presentation. There, I believe, they will find an innovative and provocative framework for considering individual differences in job satisfaction that is well worth empirical scrutiny.

In regard to individual differences, some results in the literature should be recognized, although one could hardly say they are a product of any model or theory. First, for example, gender (e.g., Witt & Nye, 1992) and race (e.g., Brush, Mock, & Pooyan, 1987) seem *not* to be reliably associated with satisfaction. The interesting question is why. For example, it is well documented that women tend to earn less than men, even when such important factors as the tasks performed are held constant (e.g., England & McLaughlin, 1979), yet women do *not* report lower levels of satisfaction. Although this question has been researched (e.g., Majors, 1994), organizational scientists have not been the principal investigators pursuing answers to it and similar puzzles—although we are the workplace experts. A second example of an interesting individual difference result is the consistent age-satisfaction relationship evident in the literature (e.g., Brush et al., 1987), with older workers reporting higher levels. This difference might be attributable to older workers occupying better jobs and having more realistic expectations (i.e., lower ones) that are met. But again, we need more theoretically driven data to help explain the observed relationship.

Before summarizing this section, I will introduce one more idea. It also does not really constitute a model or theory, just an intriguing hypothesis (Doran et al., 1991). Although Ajzen and Fishbein (1980), Ajzen (1988), and others have asserted that intentions—a product of attitudes—cause behavior, Doran et al. hypothesized the converse, predicting that workers' intentions to leave at organizational entry are negatively related to subsequent job satisfaction, with the relationship stronger for workers whose financial requirements are lower. This prediction was derived from Festinger's (1957) theory of cognitive dissonance and an extension of that theory (Brehm & Cohen, 1962) specifying that dissonance arousal is a function of the degree to which persons feel that they have chosen to put themselves in a situation in which inconsistent cognitive elements (e.g., intentions and attitudes) occur.

Doran et al.'s (1991) proxy for choice was financial requirements (e.g., number of dependents), with low requirements reflecting high choice. Thus, for instance, workers who upon organizational entry do not intend to stay, subsequently will report relatively lower levels of job satisfaction, especially if they feel little financial pressure to be on the job. Doran et al. observed a strong correlation between intent to leave (measured at entry) and overall job satisfaction (measured approximately 4 weeks later; $r = -.61, p \leq .001$) among a sample of retail sales clerks with low financial requirements but detected no relationship among clerks with high requirements ($r = .00$). These findings indicate that behavioral intentions, at least under certain circumstances, cause job satisfaction. In a way, this idea is consistent with Weick's (1969, 1995) notion of *retrospective sensemaking*—what we now see is a function of what we previously have done. Other than the possible exception of Doran et al., Weick's notion has not been applied to understanding job satisfaction. It should be.

Now, to the summary: Looking back over the advances made by organizational scientists during the last 20 years or so in understanding the causes of job satisfaction, I am not particularly impressed—at least with the results of the approaches reviewed above, with the possible exception of Motowidlo's (1996) theory, which is too new to judge. During this period, the organizational sciences became energized, attracting many more scholars who, through the years, grew increasingly methodologically sophisticated and conceptually astute. Too little of this talent, however, seems to have been directed at developing a more comprehensive theory of job satisfaction. Yes, we have made advances that tell us this or that factor (e.g., social cues) are important causes of satisfaction. But no one has seriously attempted to put the pieces of the puzzle together in a way that recognizes the interplay among person attributes (including life circumstances) and attributes of the workplace (social, emotional, and physical) and that takes advantage of the tremendous gains made in the last two decades in understanding fundamental psychological and sociological processes (e.g., how evaluative judgments are formed and how social networks function).

This is a tall order indeed. I do not want or anticipate *a* grand theory of job satisfaction. Rather, what we need are a number of competing, integrated approaches considerably more holistic than what we now have but not attempts to model fully the causes of job satisfaction. Theories are simplified abstractions of reality. In the chapters ahead, additional ideas to fuel to these theoretical approaches will be introduced. The challenge of taking such ideas and creatively modifying and combining them lies ahead. If this challenge is not taken up, I fear that our understandings of the causes of job satisfaction will remain overly piecemeal. This is not to say that progress will not be made also by pursuing the approaches of Salancik and Pfeffer (1978), Landy (1978), and others reviewed above. It will. But I am confident that giant leaps forward are to be made by attempts, albeit difficult ones, to construct more unified theories. A preview of what these theories might look like is provided in Chapter 4. That preview is such a long way off because many pieces of the job satisfaction puzzle remain to be put into place. A number of these pieces pertain to the consequences of job satisfaction, which are dealt with below.

Consequences

I have the impression that researchers have attempted to establish a relationship between job satisfaction and almost every dependent variable considered in organizational behavior. Here, therefore, only major categories of consequences will be discussed. One I will *not* discuss is job-related distress. Indeed, as will be shown, it even is awkward to raise the issue of stress in this section, rather than in the preceding one on antecedents, but I do so following the leads of Locke (1976) and Cranny et al. (1992).

More often than not, job satisfaction is treated in the job stress literature as an indicator of distress (Brief & Atieh, 1987). For example, if perceptions of a supposedly stressful condition of work (e.g., role conflict) are found to be negatively associated with job satisfaction, it is concluded that the condition is a source of job-related distress (e.g., Jackson & Schuler, 1985). This reasoning is troublesome because of the construal of distress it implicitly or explicitly entails. That is, the reasoning is dependent on a belief in context-specific mental health (e.g., Warr, 1987). This belief suggests, for instance, that clinical depression, somehow stemming from one's conditions at work, is evident from 9:00 to 5:00, but not before or after. But we know better. Clinical depression exists across the contexts of a person's daily life; it is something the person carries about through the day—not something that can be left behind at work. So, to demonstrate that job satisfaction is a sign of distress, it must be shown to converge with indicators of subjective well-being in life, such as life satisfaction. Some reviews of the relationship, however, indicate job satisfaction, on average, explains less than 10% of the variance in life satisfaction (e.g., Rice, Near, & Hunt, 1980).[14]

Moreover, in interpreting observed job-life satisfaction relationships, it is important to recognize that at least at the conceptual level, they represent part-whole correlations (Quinn, Staines, & McCullough, 1974) and that measures of the constructs generally are collected at one time, often with scales using similar or identical formats (Rice et al., 1980). Both these factors likely inflate observed relationships. I am not arguing that job satisfaction per se is unimportant to workers; it clearly is (Nord, 1977). Rather, it seems that there are better indicators of distress (so-called context-free ones) than measures of job satisfaction. In addition, in arguing for this conclusion, the evidence presented in regard to observed job-life satisfaction relationships could be interpreted as supportive of subjective well-being causing job satisfaction. Although the relationship is quite modest, there does exist evidence for this alternative (e.g, Schmitt & Mellon, 1980).[15] Whatever the case, to dig deeper into the voluminous stress literature is beyond the scope of this book. (For a sampling of that diffuse body of knowledge, see Barley & Knight, 1992; Burke, Brief, & George, 1993; and Dooley & Catalano, 1980.) Now, to the major categories of the consequence of job satisfaction addressed in this chapter.

Role Withdrawal

My use of the term *role withdrawal* differs a bit from that of Hulin's (1991), primarily because I include psychological as well as behavioral forms of withdrawal as consequences of job dissatisfaction. Specifically, this section addresses turnover, absenteeism, and the like, as well as, briefly, reduced organizational commitment.

Organizational scientists have long theorized about the causes of *turnover;* in the majority of these models, job satisfaction plays a role (e.g., Farrell & Rusbult, 1981; Hulin et al., 1985; Hom & Griffeth, 1991; Lee & Mitchell, 1994; March & Simon, 1958; Mobley, 1977; Mobley, Griffeth, Hand, & Meglino, 1979; Muchinsky & Morrow, 1980; Porter & Steers, 1973; Price, 1977; Steers & Mowday, 1981). What follows is intended to provide merely a taste of how job satisfaction has been treated in these models. For a more comprehensive coverage, see, for example, Hulin (1991) and Hom and Griffeth (1995).

The interesting part of the theories incorporating a relationship between satisfaction and turnover is not that dissatisfied workers tend to voluntarily leave their employing organizations. Rather, it is the *linkages* between the two constructs that help explain why the average observed correlation between satisfaction and turnover is a quite modest -.17 (Hom & Griffeth, 1991).[16] Mobley, Honer, and Hollingsworth (1978) posit that satisfaction is linked to thinking of quitting, intention to search, and intention to quit or stay, with the latter directly affecting quitting or staying. In addition, they recognize that the probability of finding an acceptable alternative affects both intentions to search and to quit or stay. Support for the model can be found, for instance, in Miller, Katerberg, and Hulin (1979) and Micheals and Spector (1979).

Hulin et al. (1985), consistent with Fishbein and Ajzen's (1975) work on the formation of attitudes, posited that the availability of alternative job opportunities affects satisfaction, which, in turn, influences behavioral intentions to quit and, through these intentions, quitting. They also reason, however, that dissatisfaction alternatively might result in intentions to reduce job inputs or to change the work situations (e.g., unionization activity). For empirical support of the Hulin et al. model, see, for instance, Hom and Hulin (1981).

Extending the sort of thinking evident in models such as those of Mobley et al. (1978) and Hulin et al. (1985) is Lee and Mitchell's (1994) rather complex unfolding model, based on Beach's (1993) image theory. In the model, job dissatisfaction is depicted as a product of some shock to the system that results in a person traveling down one of four decision paths to quitting. One path, for example, portrays leaving as a script-driven response; in another, it is seen as a product of assessing one's alternatives as three internal images reflecting (a) the general values and standards that define the self, (b) the goals that energize and direct the person's behaviors, and (c) the behavioral tactics and strategies the person wants to rely on for attaining his or her goals. Lee, Mitchell, Wise, and Fireman (1996) provide the only test to date of the Lee and Mitchell model. These researchers interpret their finding as generally consistent with the model and as showing that different people use different paths in deciding to quit, with only some of these represented in earlier theoretical approaches.

On the basis of the research generated by the sorts of voluntary turnover models described above, it is clear that real and/or imagined job alternatives, often empirically captured by the unemployment rate (e.g., Gerhart, 1990), affect reactions to dissatisfaction in significant ways. Not at all surprising, it seems that dissatisfied workers who cannot (or believe they cannot) find an attractive alternative, stay. This raises an important research question: How do workers, who can be thought of as feeling trapped in their organizations, adapt? Although a few have theorized about such adaptation (e.g., Hulin,

1991; Rusbult, Farrell, Rodgers, & Mainous, 1988; Withey & Cooper, 1989), we have a long way to go toward understanding why a trapped worker selects a given adaptive response over another. This puzzle is complicated by the number of options workers can choose from and because many of these are not mutually exclusive.

The following are some of the options identified by Hulin et al. (1985): stealing, using work time for personal tasks, moonlighting on the job, long coffee breaks, wandering around and looking busy, talking with coworkers about trivia, tardiness, absenteeism, retirement, and unionization activity. I am sure the reader is creative enough to come up with a bunch more. But again, how do workers choose among the options to respond to their dissatisfaction? I do not see a concerted effort under way to tackle this question. Rather, organizational scientists largely continue to construe adaptive responses to dissatisfaction as uniquely determined; therefore, for any given potentially adaptive response that catches an investigator's interest (e.g., theft), we have a model (e.g., Greenberg & Scott, 1996) that does not adequately recognize that the potential response can be considered as part of a set of options. I am not arguing against the development of theories focusing on a single adaptive response. The world is complex, and, I am sure, as further demonstrated below, singular responses (e.g., absenteeism) do have unique causes worthy of attention. My concern is with these singular responses attracting so much attention that the question of how people choose among them remains in the background.

Following turnover, *absenteeism* seems to be the form of role withdrawal that has gotten the most research attention. As in the turnover literature, the action is in understanding the weak "direct effects" of job satisfaction. Several reviews of the satisfaction-absence relationship indicate an average correlation of less than -.15 across studies (Farrell & Stamm, 1988; Hackett & Guion, 1985; Scott & Taylor, 1985). Because it seems logical that if people do not like their jobs, they are less prone to show up, then why such a weak relationship? One answer is that the relationship may be a function of the sorts of absenteeism investigated (e.g., Dalton & Mesch, 1991; Kohler & Mathieu, 1993). For example, if a person trips and falls on the way to work and breaks a wrist, therefore, missing work, one would not expect satisfaction to predict the absence. Alternatively, satisfaction might predict a choice to play tennis instead of going to work. Thus, a typology of absence behaviors is needed that distinguishes between volitional and involuntary acts, articulated in such a way that makes measurement of different sorts of absenteeism feasible.

Another factor influencing the satisfaction-absenteeism relationship may be the absence policies governing workers' behaviors, as suggested, for instance, by the findings of Dalton and Mesch (1991) and Farrell and Stamm (1988). For example, one expects the satisfaction-absenteeism relationship to be weaker in an organization with a clearly communicated absence policy entailing a low tolerance for absenteeism, close monitoring of absence behaviors, and swift disciplinary actions in response to violations, than in an organization with no clearly understood absence policy, sporadic monitoring of absence behaviors, and little if any managerial reactions to employees missing work. Simply, workers subjected to restrictive absence policies may feel they have less choice about missing work and, therefore, be less likely to act on their experienced dissatisfaction. Given the way absence policies were described above, it is easy and appropriate to construe them as organizational phenomena. Thus, rather than merely studying individual perceptions of absence policies, it seems appropriate to gauge policy attributes at the organizational level of analysis and observe their effects on the satisfaction-absenteeism relationship.

An organizational or at least work group-level approach also applies to the next factor considered as potentially affecting the satisfaction-absenteeism relationship: *absence culture* (Johns & Nicholson, 1982; Martocchio, 1994; Nicholson & Johns, 1985). The relationship likely would be weaker in a culture characterized by strict *social* rules that dictate people are expected to be at work unless it is virtually impossible for them to attend than in one in which norms encourage frequent absences, no matter what the reason.[17]

The three factors discussed above, as well as others that likely affect the satisfaction-absenteeism relationship, are recognized in Steers and Rhodes (1978, 1984) process model of attendance behavior. In that model, satisfaction is posited to directly affect attendance motivation, which, in turn, directly causes attendance behavior. Moreover, motivation is depicted also to be influenced by pressures to attend (e.g., incentive systems and work group norms). In addition, the motivation-behavior relationship is posited to be moderated by ability to attend (e.g., illnesses/accidents and family responsibilities). The Steers and Rhodes model, like the turnover models previously noted, does not recognize substitutes for its focal withdrawal behavior, yet it does specify unique causes of absenteeism.

Moving beyond behaviors to reduced *organizational commitment* as a form of role withdrawal, I essentially recognize the obvious: Behavioral adaptions to dissatisfaction (for example, turnover and absenteeism as well as the likes of theft, long coffee breaks, and unionization activity) should be accompanied by supportive thoughts. Indeed, for instance, commitment and turnover are associated rather strongly (e.g., Cohen, 1993; Mathieu & Zajac, 1990).

Organizational commitment, like job satisfaction, is a fuzzy construct (Morrow, 1983). Recognizing that numerous alternatives exist, I will begin with Steer's (1977) definition of it as "the relative strength of an individual's identification with and involvement in a particular organization" (p. 46). So construed, commitment is characterized further as accepting an organization's goals, expressing a willingness to work hard to achieve those goals, and desiring to stay with the organization (e.g., Mowday, Steers, & Porter, 1979; Porter, Steers, Mowday, & Boulian, 1974). Measures of commitment and job satisfaction have been found to be related highly (e.g., Mathieu & Zajac, 1990) yet to tap distinct constructs (Tett & Meyer, 1993). Recently, three components of organizational commitment have been conceptualized (e.g., Meyer, Allen, & Smith, 1993), and their measurement has been confirmed (e.g., Dunham, Grube, & Castaneda, 1994). These components, presumably reflecting separate determinants, are a product of (a) emotional attachments (affective commitment); (b) the costs of leaving, such as losing attractive benefits or seniority (continuance commitment); and (c) the individual's personal values (normative commitment). I am a bit uncomfortable with these components because they seem to be defined conceptually by their causes, and the items used to operationalize them do not seem to mesh well with the words used to label them. Regarding the latter source of discomfort, "I really feel as if this organization's problems are my own," for example, is an item used to measure affective commitment (Meyer et al., 1993), but such an item, to me at least, does not seem to be particularly emotionally charged. (The next two chapters both touch on the measurement of affect.)

For a somewhat more comforting conceptual approach to the bases of organization commitment, see O'Reilly and Chatman's (1986) article that is firmly grounded in Kelman's (1958) work on attitude change.[18] My concern here, however, is not really with the origins of commitment or even necessarily its forms; rather, I am interested in what we know about commitment as a consequence of satisfaction. Regrettably, the answer is very, very little. As has been indicated, the association between the two variables is strong, and this relationship, logically, has been attributed to satisfaction promoting organizational identification and involvement and dissatisfaction reducing them (e.g., Bluedorn, 1982; Koch & Steers, 1978). Although some data do support this attribution (e.g., Williams & Hazer, 1986), other data indicate that commitment causes satisfaction (e.g., Bateman & Strasser, 1984). The commitment-causes-satisfaction idea is consistent with the notion that people can interpret their behavior in ways that lead to commitment to those behaviors and, in turn, positive attitudes toward them (Weick, 1977).[19]

For the converse, organizational scientists seem to have thought little about the underlying processes that might bind job satisfaction to organizational commitment or about under what conditions the two might be *dis*connected. If an employer supplies a satisfying job, does an employee, because of some reciprocity norm, evidence commitment in return? If so, are all facets of satisfaction equally important to the exchange relationship? If not, what are the more central facets, and why are they so? Perhaps these are the sorts of questions that need be pursued in attempting to understand the satisfaction-commitment relationship. But I am wed not to those particular questions, just to the need for some sort of systematic effort to be applied to unmasking the nature of the relationship.

In sum, job satisfaction does seem to be related to various forms of role withdrawal but not directly so. In addition, I am persuaded by Hulin's (e.g., 1991) arguments that various forms of withdrawal can serve as substitutes for one another. But as of now, neither the mechanisms linking dissatisfaction to some forms of withdrawal or to substitution choices are as well articulated as they should be. Of course, in studying the relationships between dissatisfaction and the domain of withdrawal, it would be foolhardy to ignore other potential causes of turnover, absenteeism, and so on. These other potential causes have not been the concern of this chapter on job satisfaction. This lack of attention merely is a pedagogical device and is not intended to be interpreted as an implicit claim that job satisfaction is where all the action should be centered. The questions posed in this section do demonstrate (I hope), however, that the role of satisfaction in withdrawal processes is intriguing and not as obvious as one might have presumed. This intrigue likely will be heightened as we learn more about the changing nature of employment relationships (e.g., Rousseau, 1995). For instance, how might an employment relationship defined by an employer as "a fair day's pay for a fair day's work" affect the association between job satisfaction and organizational commitment? Will it serve to dissolve the association, or might it take a form we have yet to discover in the organizational sciences? In Chapter 7, these sorts of questions will be addressed in more detail.

Other Organizationally
Dysfunctional Reactions

From a managerial perspective, role withdrawal commonly is not considered a functional way to adapt to being dissatisfied (although it sometimes is organizationally beneficial, e.g., Staw & Oldham, 1978). The functionality of voluntary role withdrawal for the individual is not something organizational scientists have studied intensely (although they should have), so little is known about it. But that is another matter; here, I continue to focus on presumably organizationally dysfunctional reactions to dissatisfaction, some of which were mentioned in the previous section.

The study of dysfunctional or negative job behaviors (other than the likes of turnover and absenteeism) has been, with few exceptions, remarkably sparse, at least in the organizational sciences, but there seems to be the beginnings of a trend toward paying more attention to them (e.g., Allen & Lucero, 1996; Greenberg & Scott, 1996; Murphy, 1993; O'Leary-Kelly, Griffin, & Glew, 1996). In part because of this perceived trend, I thought a separate, albeit brief, section on dysfunctional behaviors was warranted.[20]

Regarding the relationships between job dissatisfaction and dysfunctional job behaviors, Fisher and Locke (1992) provide a selective but informative review of the research (too much of which is unpublished). They cite a study by Matheny (1988) in which six categories of negative behaviors are identified: (a) physical avoidance or escape from the job as a whole (e.g., avoiding one's job by coming in late or leaving early); (b) avoidance of the work itself (e.g., doing as little work as possible); (c) psychological adjustment (e.g., using drugs or alcohol before, during, or after work because of work problems); (d) constructive protests or problem solving (e.g., seeing a lawyer regarding one's job situation); (e) defiance or resistance to authority (e.g., deliberately ignoring rules or regulations); and (f) aggression, revenge, retaliation, and getting even (e.g., using physical violence against other employees or supervisors). Several elements in each of these categories have a distinct body of literature, more often than not, outside the organizational sciences. For example, there are numerous studies of the relationship between work and problem drinking (e.g., Brief & Folger, 1992).

Fisher and Locke (1992), however, following the leads of Rosse and Miller (1984) and Henne and Locke (1985), see dysfunctional behavior as a set from which workers choose in responding to dissatisfaction.[21] They propose a choice model in which satisfaction, dissatisfaction, and change in satisfaction are both directly and indirectly linked to action. The indirect linkages entail a search for action alternatives and an evaluation of them leading to a choice/behavioral intention. Moreover, they posit that the search for and evaluation of alternatives are influenced by several common factors (e.g., role models, group norms, personal history, company policy, contract provisions, and voice mechanism). In addition, they posit that the evaluation of action alternatives also is influenced by self-efficacy, personality/self-concept, constraints, and expected positive and negative consequences. This model, which seems simultaneously complex and somewhat vague, has yet to be tested. Perhaps any model would suffer from both vagueness and complexity if its focus was the choice among an amazingly wide array of behavior (e.g., calling in sick when not really sick, letting others do one's work, covering emotion by wearing a mask of impassivity or indifference, suggesting to other employees that they all should form a union, openly refusing to do an assignment, or lying to get one's boss in trouble). Nevertheless, on the basis of an unpublished study by Davis (1988), Fisher and Locke report some favorable results regarding direct relationships between satisfaction and self-reported measures of the earlier identified categories of negative behaviors (e.g., $r = -.43$, for the job-in-general satisfaction-psychological adjustment relationship). But they also report some rather disappointing findings (e.g., $r = .11$, *n.s.*, for the job-in-general satisfaction-aggression relationship).

From the above, it should be obvious that we have a lot to learn about how satisfaction may be tied to particular dysfunctional behaviors. As indicated, some of these behaviors are being attended to increasingly in the organizational sciences. In some cases, this probably is so because the behaviors have become problematic in the larger society, receiving considerable media exposure. In the United States, for instance, violence has reached what some consider to be epidemic proportions (e.g., 24,000 murders in 1993; Federal Bureau of Investigation, 1993). It seems to me that as people in the organizational sciences jump on the bandwagon of research on violence, they ought to be careful to somehow tease apart organizational from societal effects. I am worried that without researchers being aware of it, what is happening within the community in which an organization is embedded may distort observed relationships between organizationally relevant independent variables (e.g., job satisfaction) and relatively low base rate dysfunctional behaviors. That is, some dysfunctional behaviors, such as violence in the workplace, largely may be manifestations of problems evident in society in general and driven principally by societal, rather than organizational, forces.

Task Performance

In Chapter 1, the job satisfaction-task performance relationship was mentioned. Here, I will have a little more to say about it. Recall that in the preceding
chapter, *task performance* was defined as the proficiency with which people
perform activities that are formally recognized as part of their jobs (Borman
& Motowidlo, 1993). These role-prescribed (Katz & Kahn, 1978) activities
often are those identified by the job analysis techniques of the industrial
psychologist and evaluated by the job performer's organizational superior. It
has become the accepted wisdom in the organizational sciences that job
satisfaction does *not* cause job performance (read task performance). This
accepted wisdom is a product of several reviews of the satisfaction-performance relationship, beginning with one by Brayfield and Crockett (1955), in
which it was concluded that the two variables were related minimally, at best.
In subsequent, progressively more sophisticated reviews based on an increasing number of studies, the same conclusion was reached, with satisfaction
appearing to explain, on average, about 3% of the variance in performance
(e.g., Iaffaldano & Muchinsky, 1985; Vroom, 1964). The variation in correlations producing this low central tendency, however, has been described as
"rather large" (Katzell, Thompson, & Guzzo, 1992, p. 195).

Several explanations have been offered for the meager satisfaction-performance relationship. These include, for example, (a) measurement problems
with the criterion variable (i.e., supervisory ratings of task performance are
error laden; e.g., Spector, 1996); (b) lack of "true" variability in the criterion
variable (i.e., workers are not free to vary their behaviors, for instance, because
of the restrictive nature of organization control mechanisms; e.g., George &
Jones, 1996); and (c) failure to match general measures of job satisfaction with
a correspondingly aggregated measure of a large set of behaviors, that is, if
there was correspondence between the levels of aggregation represented in the
attitude (satisfaction) and behavior (performance) measures, the correlation
between the attitude and behavior would be strong (e.g., Fishbein & Ajzen,
1974; Fisher, 1980; see also the explanations provided by Northcraft and
Neale, 1994, and Staw, 1986).

Although I am sure that supervisory ratings of performance commonly are
error laden, that worker behavior is rather severely restricted in some settings,
and that a better correspondence between the levels at which attitudes and
behavior are measured does strengthen attitude-behavior correlations, none
of these explanations are very comforting to me. In part, this is because
performance commonly has been observed to be associated with other pre-

dictors (as in the selection literature, e.g., Schneider & Schmitt, 1976), with it being measured in the same ways and under similar circumstances as in satisfaction-performance literature and because satisfaction, as previously demonstrated, frequently has been shown to be related to other criteria, although the levels at which measures were aggregated did not mesh particularly well. Perhaps stated more simply, if the explanations for a failure to detect a significant satisfaction-performance relationship were valid, they also would hold for explaining why somewhat analogous relationships also are not observed, but these analogous relationships are evident in various literatures. So maybe the rationale for expecting job satisfaction to cause task performance is at fault.

Greene (1972) has noted that although the expectation that satisfaction causes performance has theoretical roots, it also is supported by (a) the popular belief that a happy worker is a productive worker; (b) the notion that all good things come together; and (c) the pleasantness associated with increasing a worker's satisfaction, rather than the relative unpleasantness of dealing directly with performance when a problem arises. It may be that expecting job satisfaction to cause task performance is more of a sign that one is a layperson, rather than a scientist who has digested the available evidence. Nevertheless, I still suspect a consistent, significant job satisfaction-task performance relationship is out there to be found. I must confess that the logic underlying my suspicion requires viewing both job satisfaction and job performance a "little" differently than I have thus far in this section. The view required is from the organizational level of analysis. In other words, the consistent, significant relationship I expect is out there is captured in the following proposition: Organizations with more satisfied workers perform better than organizations whose workers are less satisfied. Because I have introduced the idea of aggregating satisfaction earlier in this chapter, the tricky part of the proposition is the meaning of *organizational performance*, for which there is a lack of consensus in the literature (e.g., Ford & Schellenberg, 1982; Jobson & Schneck, 1982; Katz & Kahn, 1978). Given this lack of consensus, let me tentatively define the construct as the effectiveness with which an organization acquires and efficiently uses available resources to achieve its operative goals.[22]

Theoretical justifications for expecting organizational performance to vary as a function of member satisfaction can be found in a variety of sources, many of which were reviewed by Ostroff (1992). In a nutshell, these justifications suggest that satisfied workers will be more likely to engage in collaborative efforts and accept organizational goals, whereas dissatisfied workers may fail to work collaboratively or may collaborate such that their efforts are diverted from achieving organizational goals (e.g., Likert, 1961; Roethlisberger, 1959).[23] Beyond summarizing the theoretical literature, Ostroff conducted one of the few studies that have examined the satisfaction-performance relationship at the organizational level of analysis. She found that organizations with more-satisfied workers tended to perform better than those with less-satisfied workers. It is time to aggressively pursue the job satisfaction-task performance relationship at the organizational level of analysis. In doing so, it would be interesting to assess if collaboration and organizational goal acceptance indeed mediate the relationship. At least implicitly, the satisfaction-task performance relationship will surface again in this and later chapters.

Contextual Performance

Katz (1964) described a set of spontaneous and innovative behaviors, essential for organizations to function, that are distinguishable from role-prescribed behaviors (i.e., task performance) and that can be considered as a consequence of job satisfaction. This set of so-called extrarole behaviors includes helping coworkers, protecting the organization, making constructive suggestions, developing oneself, and spreading goodwill. These five behaviors have been labeled simply as forms of *organizational spontaneity* (George & Brief, 1992). Building on Katz's thinking, Bateman and Organ (1983) coined the term *organizational citizenship behaviors* (OCBs) to describe a similar set of voluntary acts that facilitate organizational goal attainment. The set was broadened in addressing *prosocial organizational behaviors* (Brief & Motowidlo, 1986). Van Dyne, Cummings, and Parks (1995) admirably attempted to make sense out of the often subtle differences among the meanings conveyed by these various labels. Here, I try to sidestep the confusion by adopting Borman and Motowidlo's (1993) term *contextual performance,* which to me not only captures the spirit of prior efforts to define and describe extrarole behaviors but also adds some conceptual precision. I do this although most researchers have addressed the behaviors as OCBs.[24]

Contextual performance, as noted in the preceding chapter, refers to the contributions people make to a work environment supportive of task performance. Considerable empirical evidence demonstrates that a reasonably consistent, somewhat modest relationship does exist between job satisfaction and contextual performance at the individual level of analysis, when contextual performance is conceived of and measured in OCBs (Organ, 1988b; Organ & Ryan, 1995). Why an observed satisfaction-contextual performance relationship and not one for satisfaction-task performance at the individual level of analysis? The answer probably lies in that contextual performance can be thought of as relatively more volitional in nature. Borman and Motowidlo (1993) assert that variation in task performance is attributable to individual differences in knowledge, skills, and abilities. Alternatively, however, they see the major sources of variation in contextual performance as volitional variables. Volitional variables stand out because unlike task activities, contextual behaviors are likely not be role prescribed but rather more voluntary in nature. Thus, contextual performance should be more sensitive to differences in satisfaction. It is plausible, for example, that people who are more satisfied with how their employers treat them are more likely to volunteer to take on duties beyond those regularly assigned to them (e.g., Organ, 1988b).

I strongly suspect that the modesty of observed satisfaction-contextual performance relationships will disappear if and when research moves from the individual to the organizational level of analysis. In other words, the association between the two will become considerably stronger. This suspicion is rooted in the ideas reviewed by Ostroff (1992) that were presented in the previous section (e.g., satisfied workers are more likely to engage in collaborative efforts). Perhaps even more important, it seems clear to me that several of the *consequences* of contextual performance at the individual level occur at an aggregate level. These consequences are quite evident in the following contextual activities identified by Borman and Motowidlo (1993): helping and cooperating with others and endorsing, supporting, and defending organizational objectives. Simply, these show that contextual activities are targeted at others and the organization. Thus far, my admittedly fuzzy story suggests that at the individual level of analysis, satisfaction is a cause of contextual performance, and increased contextual performance contributes to organizational performance.[25] The causal chain suggested may explain Ostroff's earlier noted finding that organizations with more-satisfied workers tend to perform better than those with less-satisfied workers.

My story should not be left so fuzzy because it addresses a potential solution to the satisfaction-performance puzzle and a key to understanding a route to enhanced organizational effectiveness. In discussing the job satisfaction-task performance relationship, I cited early works by McGregor (1960), Likert (1961), and others that may need to be reconsidered in developing a much needed theory that ties together how people feel about their jobs, how they perform, *and* the effectiveness of the organizations to which they belong. Although such a theory is beyond the scope of the current effort, it now seems plausible to accumulate what we know about satisfaction-performance relationships in such a way that recognizes conceptual and empirical consistencies and contradictions and, perhaps, explains those contradictions by being sensitive to alternative forms of performance and the levels at which they are conceived and measured. Beyond this possibility, we must be creative about visualizing the processes that might link satisfaction and performance across levels of analysis. In thinking about such processes, the reader likely will find House, Rousseau, and Thomas-Hunt's (1995) general treatment of how different levels of analysis might be related, as well as the recent theorizing of Staw and Sutton (1993), to be quite helpful.

In selectively reviewing the consequences of job satisfaction (namely, various types of role withdrawal; other organizationally dysfunctional behaviors; and task, contextual, and organizational performance), my aims were to assist the reader in appreciating what we know and in framing what we might want to learn. If an aim of science is to answer the question of "Why?" (i.e., to provide explanations for underlying processes), then some of the literature reviewed on role withdrawal indicates that we are well on the road to accumulating a rather substantial body of scientific knowledge. This observation certainly is not meant to be interpreted as accepting any theory of withdrawal (e.g., Hulin et al.'s, 1985; Lee & Mitchell's, 1994; March & Simon's, 1958; or Mobley et al.'s, 1979, models of turnover) as a truism; rather, these theories, to varying degrees, do address the mechanisms that may link satisfaction to withdrawal, are built on seemingly plausible arguments, and have led to the collection of perceptive data. Looking back, I do not think we could have asked for much more. Looking ahead, I expect we will continue to slowly accumulate process knowledge about satisfaction-withdrawal relationships. A substantial body of process knowledge (i.e., that which addresses the "Why?" question) about how satisfaction might be linked to other organizationally dysfunctional behaviors does not exist; we have only begun to expend considerable resources on studying theft, aggression, and such in organizational settings. I would be surprised and disappointed if, in a decade, we do not know much, much more than we do today. The study of satisfaction-performance relationships seems to be stuck at the point of questioning their existence. But as I have suggested, there are signs that significant leaps forward in understanding *how* they *are* connected at and between various levels of analysis are on the horizon. It is going to be exciting to see what unfolds.

Concluding Remarks

Any reader even casually familiar with the literature on job satisfaction will have noted that this chapter suffers from several major omissions. Some of these were intended and, sometimes, even noted in the text; other significant omissions reflect gaps in my knowledge or errors in my judgment. For these unintended exclusions, I am sorry.

I intentionally excluded segments of the job satisfaction literature for one of two reasons. First, I think some of the recent advances in the job satisfaction literature (e.g., the dispositional approach and Weiss and Cropanzano's, 1996, affect events theory) can be appreciated better once their social psychological foundations are presented. Those presentations are included in the next chapter. Second, some issues (e.g., the relationship between job satisfaction and customer satisfaction) simply fit more appropriately in later chapters. So, the business of this chapter, job satisfaction, is incomplete; readers will see it continue to be conducted in some of the pages ahead.

Notes

1. Also see Wanous, Reichers, and Hudy (1997).

2. To learn about alternative measures of overall job satisfaction, see Cook et al. (1981) and Ironson, Smith, Brannick, Gibson, and Paul (1989).

3. For a provocative discussion of such measures, see Porac (1987).

4. For findings that contradict Maslow's critics, see, for example, Elizur (1984); Ronen (1994); and Ronen, Kraut, Lingoes, and Aranya (1979).

5. Also see Watson, Pennebaker, and Folger (1986).

6. Kanfer (1992) drew a similar conclusion in regard to need theories helping us better understand the nature of work motivation.

7. See, for example, Lawler (1968), Pritchard (1969), and Adams and Freedman (1976) for reviews of the resulting empirical evidence.

8. For the social psychological origins of procedural justice, see Thibaut and Walker (1975).

9. For more on this line of thinking, see James and James (1992).

10. For more on the relationship between actual task properties and task perceptions, see Taber and Taylor (1990).

11. For other approaches to studying job characteristics, see Gardner and Cummings (1988) and Griffen (1987).

12 Also see, for example, Rousseau (1978), Berger and Cummings (1979), and Adler and Borys (1996).

13. For more on the true complexity of the social information processing approach, see Zalesny and Ford (1990).

14. See also the position of work in Andrews and Withey's (1974) analyses of subjective well-being.

15. For example, see also Judge and Watanabe (1993) and Weaver (1978).

16. Also see Carsten and Spector (1987) and Steel and Ovalle (1984).

17. For recent insights to the nature of absence cultures, see, for example, Harrison and Schaffer (1994) and Johns (1994, in press).

18. Also see O'Reilly and Chatman (1996).

19. Also see Berger and Luckman (1967).

20. For an overview of earlier research, see, for example, Coleman's (1994) treatment of what he calls *occupational crimes*.

21. Recall the similar view advanced by Hulin et al. (1985) noted in the previous section.

22. For a consistent definition, see Etzioni (1964).

23. For compatible rationales, see, for example, Emery and Trist (1960); Gross and Etzioni (1985); Kopelman, Brief, and Guzzo (1990); Mayo (1933); and McGregor (1960).

24. Perhaps to cloud matters even more, I refer the reader to enlightening articles by Mackenzie, Podsakoff, and Fetter (1991); Morrison (1994); and Van Dyne, Graham, and Dienesch (1994), which also characterize the nature of the construct at hand but are not necessarily consistent with the posture presented here.

25. Regarding this latter linkage, see George and Bettenhausen (1990), as well as Borman and Motowidlo's (1993) discussion of the association between individual contextual performance and organizational effectiveness.

3 The Social Psychology
of Attitudes

A LITTLE OF THIS, A LITTLE OF THAT

If the study of attitudes has a disciplinary home, it is social psychology. Since the 1920s, social psychologists have been intensely interested in how attitudes are formed and changed and in their relationships to behaviors. Although organizational scientists theorize about particular attitudes (e.g., job satisfaction), much of the social psychology literature focuses on the concept of attitude per se. I intend to convince readers that any organizational scientist would benefit from at least a casual familiarity with that literature. I have watched the organizational sciences grow up and become independent from their parental social science disciplines (e.g., psychology and sociology)— perhaps too independent. It seems that we have reached the point in our development that most of what we do clearly builds on each other's theorizing and empirical research; it also seems to me, however, that our knowledge structure would be even stronger if we more frequently returned to our roots to ensure that the foundations on which we are building are constructed appropriately and incorporate the most sound materials currently available. More simply stated, we would know a heck of a lot more, for example, about job satisfaction, if we had more often returned to the social psychology literature on attitudes to test the correctness of our fundamental assumptions and to take advantage of recent advances. I am convinced that for the time being, our discipline will be healthier if we all maintain a balance by keeping one foot in our ancestral social science, whatever it may be, and the other in the future of the organizational sciences. Hence, this chapter is about the social psychology of attitudes.

The chapter is intended to inform but mostly to entice the reader to learn more and, in no way, is meant to constitute a source supplying everything the reader might need to know about the attitude concept. For an excellent textbook on the subject, I recommend Eagly and Chaiken's (1993), and, to stay abreast with advances, the *Journal of Personality and Social Psychology* cannot be beat. What follows is either pretty basic but necessary "stuff" or a highly idiosyncratic selection of ideas to whet the appetite for the social psychology of attitudes.

Before I describe how the remainder of the chapter unfolds, let me be clearer about its goals. I want to provide enough information so that the reader can begin to sense how the study of attitudes in the organizational sciences (for example, that reviewed in the previous chapter) might be a bit shaky here and there in regard to its conceptual and/or empirical underpinnings and how that study can be made more solid. Moreover, I want to introduce some ideas, not now evident in the organizational sciences, that might supply fresh and productive ways of thinking about the tired job satisfaction construct. Finally, I want to lay the necessary social psychological foundations for the chapters ahead.

The rest of chapter is composed of three primary sections. The first section addresses definitions of the attitude concept; the cognitive, affective, and behavioral nature of attitudes will be analyzed, and methods for measuring attitudes will be reviewed briefly. The second section deals with the functions of attitudes, emphasizing the relationship between attitudes and behaviors. The last primary section focuses on the subject matter that constitutes the bulk of the social psychological literature on attitudes—how they are formed and changed. The chapter will close with a few remarks about the utility of what has been said and about how much has gone unsaid in the chapter.

The Nature of Attitudes

McGuire (1984, 1985) provides an informative history of the study of attitudes in which he describes three periods during this century as particularly exciting. The 1920s and 1930s were characterized by an intense interest in scaling attitudes (e.g., Likert, 1932; Thurstone & Chave, 1929) and, correspondingly, in behaviorally validating the measures developed (e.g., LaPiere, 1934). The 1950s and 1960s focused on the dynamics of attitude change, growing from the World War II work of Hovland, Lumsdaine, and Sheffield (1949) regarding the effects of mass communications. In 1985, McGuire described the 1980s and 1990s as an emerging era noteworthy for a surge of research on the content, structure, and functions of attitudes, exemplified by research on social judgment, inference, scripts, and cognitive responses (e.g., Hastie, 1983; Wyer, Srull, & Gordon, 1984). Retrospectively, my outsider's prospective leads me to believe that McGuire's expectations for social psychological attitude research in the 1980s and early 1990s largely were on target, with the influence of Hastie, Srull, Wyer and other *cognitive* social psychologists dominating. Even before the 1980s were over, however, criticisms appeared concerned with the exclusivity of the cognitive approach and the failure to attend adequately to the role of affect (e.g., Fiske, 1981; Higgins, Kuiper, & Olson, 1981; Zajonc, 1980a). In the pages to come will be mention of the empirical responses to these criticisms (e.g., Abelson, Kinder, Peters, & Fiske, 1982) that may lead the late 1990s and the beginning of the next century to become characterized as a period in which social psychological research on attitudes more fully recognized that people feel as well as think and act.

My overview of McGuire's historical account, in part, was provided to suggest that almost 100 years of social psychological attitude research has yielded a large and diverse literature. It is unsurprising, therefore, that this literature is populated by numerous definitions of the attitude concept—literally hundreds of them (Fishbein & Ajzen, 1972). For example, Greenwald (1989) defines attitudes as "the affect associated with a mental object" (p. 432); Kruglanski (1989), as "a special type of knowledge, notably knowledge of which content is evaluative or affective" (p. 139); and Triandis (1991), as "a state of a person that predisposes a favorable or unfavorable response to an object, person, or idea" (p. 485).[1] In large part because of the depth to which it is discussed by its authors and its representativeness, Eagly and Chaiken's (1993) definition is offered here as a currently viable model for construing what constitutes an attitude. They define an attitude as "a psycho-logical tendency that is expressed by evaluating a particular entity with some degree of favor or disfavor" (p. 1). Eagly and Chaiken refer to a "psychological tendency" as a state internal to the person that is a type of bias, predisposing the individual toward positive or negative evaluative responses and to "evalu-ating" as encompassing all classes of evaluative responses—overt or covert/af-fective, cognitive, or behavioral.

Olson and Zanna (1993) assert that most attitudes theorists, such as Eagly and Chaiken (1993), agree "(a) evaluation constitutes a central, perhaps predominant, aspect of attitudes; (b) attitudes are represented in memory; and (c) affective, cognitive, and behavioral antecedent of attitudes can be distinguished, as can affective, cognitive, and behavioral consequences of attitudes" (p. 119). As I intend to demonstrate in later chapters, each of these agreed-on points have implications for the study of attitudes in and around organizations. For now, merely reflect on how job satisfaction was defined in the previous chapter and how its antecedents and consequences were dis-cussed, then consider Olson and Zanna's noted points of agreement among social psychologists. Gaps in how we have studied job satisfaction should be-gin to surface; again, some of these will be pointed out in the chapters to come.

Affective, Cognitive, and Behavioral
Classes of Evaluative Responses

According to McGuire's (1985) historical account, the idea that an attitude is composed of three components (or, in the language of Eagly and Chaiken, 1993, that evaluative responses are divisible into three classes) can be traced back to the thinking of Hellenic and early Hindu philosophers. These com-ponents (or classes of evaluative responses) are termed as affective, cognitive, and behavioral by social psychologists (e.g., Krech & Crutchfield, 1948; Rosen-berg & Hovland, 1960; Smith, 1947). The affective component is how one *feels* about an attitude object (e.g., a boss), *including the moods, emotions, and sympathetic nervous system activity experienced in relation to the object.*

For example, for those of you who are doctoral students, does your major professor make you feel annoyed, tense, and angry or happy, calm, and relaxed? The former feelings indicate a relatively negative response to him or her, whereas the latter ones indicate a more positive reaction. Thus, it can be seen that these feelings have evaluative meaning; therefore, they are indicative of your attitude toward your major professor. What you *think* about your professor also has evaluative meaning. These thoughts are the cognitive component of your attitude toward your major professor. More generally, the cognitive component is the beliefs or ideas one has about (i.e., associates with) an attitude object. To continuing with my example: Do you think your major professor is foolish, unsafe, and worthless or wise, safe, and valuable? The third component of an attitude, the behavioral or conative one, is how one *acts* and/or *intends to act* toward an attitude object. Because behavior and stated behavioral intentions often are treated as dependent effects of attitudes or their affective or cognitive components, a two-component model of attitude structure (composed of affect and cognitions) often has been advocated (e.g., Bagozzi & Burnkrant, 1979; Petty & Cacioppo, 1986b; Rosenberg, 1968a; Zajonc & Markus, 1982). Data supporting the convergent, discriminant, and predictive validity of this model are readily available (e.g., Bagozzi, 1981; Bagozzi & Burnkrant, 1985; Fishbein & Ajzen, 1974).[2] Largely for pragmatic reasons (i.e., an interest in attitude-behavior relationships), I tend to rely on the two-component model when thinking about attitude structure, although not discounting the scientific status of the tripartite alternative.

The models of the component structure (or multidimensionality) of the attitude construct are useful. Greenwald (1968) and others (e.g., Zanna & Rempel, 1988), for instance, have argued that each component may have separate antecedents. The affective component, for example, might be a product of classical conditioning (e.g., Staats & Staats, 1958). That is, the component is a product of an attitude object being paired with a stimulus that elicits an affective response. If this happens repeatedly, the attitude object itself comes to elicit the affective response, thereby, the attitude component is formed.[3] The cognitive component may be thought of as a product of a cognitive learning process during which a person acquired information about an attitude object through direct or indirect experience with it and, thereby, forms beliefs and/or ideas about the object. For instance, people form beliefs and ideas about an organization by directly experiencing it as customers, clients, or employees and/or indirectly through advertisements, press coverage, or word of mouth. Finally, Greenwald asserts that the behavioral component may be formed through instrumental learning or operant conditioning (e.g., see Doob, 1947). The lesson I take away from writings such as Greenwald's is that attitudes can be formed by affective, cognitive, and/or behavioral processes; thus, a broad view of attitude formation and change is necessary to adequately appreciate the origins of organizationally salient attitudes and how they might be modified. Simply to assert, for example, that attitudes such as job satisfaction are a product of organizational context oversimplifies what is known about attitude formation and change processes. I will have more to say on this later—for now, back to the utility of thinking about component models of attitude structure.

It has been noted that the components of an attitude may not necessarily align (e.g., a person's feelings toward an attitude object may not be indicative of what he or she thinks about the object; e.g., Rosenberg & Hovland, 1960). Data show that the different components may be differentially affected by the same change process (e.g., Edwards, 1990; Millar & Millar, 1990) *and* differently predict the same criterion variable (e.g., Abelson et al., 1982; Millar & Tesser, 1986). Thus, one could observe, for instance, an intervention to affect an attitude, or not, or an attitude to predict a behavior, or not, depending on whether the measure of the attitude used principally captured the "right" component (e.g., affective or cognitive)!

Measuring Attitudes

Having established how social psychologists approach the definition of the attitude construct and its component structure, I now move on to briefly consider their measurement techniques. In doing so, my goals merely are to further inform the reader about the nature of attitudes and perhaps to stimulate the use of more varied attitude measurement techniques in the organizational sciences. Some of the social psychological measures to be introduced probably are not well suited to the study of attitudes in and around organizations unless the research is laboratory based. Nevertheless, the descriptions of them should help clarify the component structure of attitudes and may help get one's creative juices flowing.

Social psychologists, like organizational scientists, principally operationalize the attitude construct simply by asking people their attitudes toward some object. Work on the scales composing these self-report measures first appeared in 1928 with the publication of Thurstone's article titled "Attitudes Can Be Measured." That article emphasized the method of paired comparisons. In later publications, he and/or his colleagues emphasized the method of equal-appearing intervals (Thurstone & Chave, 1929) and successive intervals (Saffir, 1937). For a description of these methods, see Himmelfarb (1993). Another major advance in attitude measurement was based on the work of Guttman (1941, 1944), which also is described by Himmelfarb. Organizational scientists, however, likely are more familiar with Likert scaling (Likert, 1932) and the semantic differential (Osgood, Suci, & Tannenbaum, 1957). Responses to the items composing a Likert measure, which are summed, are formulated such that agreement with an item indicates a favorable or unfavorable attitude toward the object. For example, see the Minnesota Satisfaction Questionnaire (Weiss et al., 1967). A semantic differential consists of a number of bipolar adjectives (e.g., *bad-good*); respondents indicate their attitudes by checking one of several categories separating the adjectives in each pair, with a score computed by summing across these ratings. Again, I assume much of this is old hat to the reader; if not, see the previously cited chapter by Himmelfarb.

Perhaps not so familiar are a number of recent and highly provocative treatments of how the context in which the measures mentioned are used can distort the responses obtained. For example, it is well documented and reasonably understood when and why respondents use preceding items in a questionnaire to interpret later-appearing questions about their attitudes (e.g., Ottati, Riggle, Wyer, Schwarz, & Kuklinski, 1989; Sarup, Suchner, & Gaylor, 1991; Schwarz & Strack, 1991; Schwarz & Sudman, 1992; Strack & Martin, 1987; Tourangeau & Rasinski, 1988). In addition, some intriguing recent research also shows that the response categories provided respondents can be used by them to interpret attitude items (Schwarz, 1990; Schwarz & Hippler, 1991). Wittenbrink and Henly (1996), for instance, showed that the following sort of response category manipulations influenced their student participants' subsequently self-reported attitudes toward Blacks. Participants were asked, "Out of 100 Black students at your university, how many gained access primarily because of affirmative action polices?" They were randomly assigned to the following categories: (a) "less than 5," "5-14," "15-24," "25-34," and "35 or more" or (b) "less than 60," "60-69," "70-79," "80-89," "90 or more." When later asked their attitudes toward Blacks, those participants provided with response categories such as (b) reported more negative attitudes than those participants previously provided with response categories such as (a).

In total, there is a growing body of literature in which social psychological theory is being applied to understand how factors such as item positioning and response category wording affect self-reports of attitudes. Positioning and wording, in this literature, often are construed as providing respondents frames of reference for interpreting attitude questions. It is time that the organizational literature clearly reflects an appreciation of these potential frame-of-reference effects. The distortion effects described can be characterized as unmotivated ones relative to those whereby the distortion is intended by the respondents (e.g., responding in such a way to not embarrass themselves). Social psychologists have addressed methods for reducing various motivated types of distortion. For example, the "bogus pipeline" procedure presumably reduces intended distortions by leading respondents to think that the researcher has a foolproof way of gauging their real attitudes (e.g., Arkin & Lake, 1983; Jones & Sigall, 1971; Quigley-Fernandez & Tedeschi, 1978). See also the literature on the *randomized response technique* (e.g., Himmelfarb & Lickteig, 1982; Shotland & Yankowski, 1982; Warner, 1965).

As I continue with the potentially unfamiliar, an article by Crites, Fabrigar, and Petty (1994) is well worth noting. It is unusual for self-report measures of attitudes to be constructed intentionally to reflect the component structure of attitudes. Crites et al. address this concern for the affective and cognitive components. For example, they provide semantic differential scales, one composed of eight affective word pairs (e.g., *delighted/sad, annoyed/calm,* and *relaxed/angry*) and the other of seven cognitive word pairs (e.g., *beneficial/harmful, perfect/imperfect,* and *wholesome/unhealthy*) to tap a person's attitude toward some object. Moreover, Crites et al. report results supportive of these scales' internal consistencies and convergent and discriminant validities. I am eager to see these scales applied to measuring attitudes in and around organizations and to learn how the affective and cognitive component scores might differentially predict the same salient criterion variables.

Social psychologists also use a variety of measurement methods that entail procedures other than directly asking people their attitudes. Several are linked to specific attitude components, whereas others are intended to tap global attitudes. The "lost letter procedure" (Milgram, Mann, & Harter, 1965) is an example of an indirect, *global* measure that might be used within organizations. In an organization's buildings and parking lots, a researcher could drop an equal number of letters addressed to "Person A" and "Person B" or to "Unit A" and "Unit B." The number of letters returned to each person or unit supplies a crude index of the relative attitudes within the organization toward the persons or units. The research of Wells and Petty (1980) provides another example of an indirect, global measure. They unobtrusively videotaped audience members listening to a speech and found that when the speaker took a position with which listeners agreed, most made vertical head movements, but disagreement evoked horizontal movements. Thus, listeners unknowingly signaled their attitudes by nodding and shaking their heads. See Webb, Campbell, Schwartz, Sechrest, and Grove (1981) as a source for other examples of such creative, indirect, global attitude measures.

Indirect, *affective* indicators often are measures of physiological responses linked to emotional processes thought to be triggered by the attitude object under investigation (Himmelfarb, 1993). Long ago, for example, Darwin (1872) posited that different facial expressions are associated with different emotions. More recently, Cacioppo and Petty (1981) used a facial electromyograph (EMG) to gauge attitudes. This device allowed the researchers to measure facial muscle activity as participants listened to an agreeable or disagreeable message. They found that an agreeable message increased activity in the cheek muscles, a response characteristic of happiness; a disagreeable message increased activity in the forehead and brow area, a response associated with sadness or distress. These subtle changes were *not* seen by observers. Might an organizational scholar in the year 2050 assess, in her EMG-equipped laboratory, employee facial muscle activity in response to alternative announcements of a potential organization restructuring?[4]

Indirect, *cognitive* indicators are built on the belief that attitudes do affect how information is processed, and, therefore, that these systematic effects can indicate a person's attitudes (Himmelfarb, 1993). Almost five decades ago, Hammond (1948) used this idea in designing a technique (i.e., the error-choice method) to tap an organizationally salient attitude. He found that when people were asked what the average worker earned per week and were provided with two erroneous answers (one overstating the amount and the other understating it), the wrong answer they chose was associated with their affiliation with labor or management. Labor affiliates tended to choose the understated amount; management affiliates, the overstated amount. Thus, the biased judgments of Hammond's respondents can be seen to be indicative of their attitudes toward labor or management. Since Hammond's findings, researchers have assessed distortions in logical reasoning (Thistlethwaite, 1950) and judgments of the plausibility of arguments (Selltiz & Cook, 1966) as indirect measures of attitudes. To once again query the future, might an organizational scholar one day gauge racial attitudes by having managers rate the effectiveness of arguments labeled as for or against organizational diversity programs?[5]

In sum, I hope the above *very* abbreviated treatment of attitude measurement in social psychology might have suggested ways of gauging attitudes other than those currently seen in the organizational literature. Moreover, the presentation was intended to further clarify the affective and cognitive content of attitudes, an appreciation not adequately evident in our literature at this time. More about the nature of attitudes will be unveiled in the sections that follow.

The Functions of Attitudes

Much of what I say here is about how attitudes can function to shape a person's behaviors, which, as reflected in the discussion of the consequences of job satisfaction in the preceding chapter, ought to be familiar territory for the organizational scientist. Not as well represented, at least explicitly, in the organizational literature, are other functions of attitudes considered by social psychologists. I begin by presenting a well-known social psychological taxonomy of the functions of attitudes.

Building on the idea that the attitudes people hold fit their needs, Katz (e.g., 1960) advanced a four-function taxonomy. In part, the taxonomy was deduced from his research on ego defense as a source of prejudice (e.g., Sarnoff & Katz, 1954). Katz's taxonomy specifies utilitarian, knowledge, ego defense, and value expression functions for attitudes. The *utilitarian function* recognizes that attitudes can be instrumental for maximizing rewards and minimizing punishments from the environment; therefore, it reflects thinking consistent with various reinforcement theorists. For example, a worker may have a favorable attitude toward his or her boss because the worker believes the boss is a source of positive outcomes. According to Katz, the *knowledge function* refers to that attitudes can "give meaning to what would otherwise be an unorganized chaotic universe" (p. 175), that is, attitudes can serve to organize and simplify a person's experiences. Eagly and Chaiken (1993) noted that Katz's thinking about the knowledge function is consistent with the notion that attitudes may be regarded as one type of schema in that they provide a frame of reference for comprehending and categorizing the elements in one's environment.[6] Reasoning from earlier psychoanalytic accounts of prejudice, Katz saw the *ego defense function* as enabling people to deal with intrapsychic conflicts and generally protect their self-images. Prejudiced people, therefore, can be seen as unconsciously protecting their own egos by holding negative attitudes that reflect their relative superiority toward, for instance, convenient racial groups different from their own (e.g., Sarnoff & Katz, 1954). Attitudes as a means of conveying personal values and other aspects of one's self-concept are captured by Katz's *value expression function.* For example, a person who draws self-esteem from being a member of management or who desires to be a manager holds attitudes consistent with a managerial ideology. Greenwald and Breckler (1985) elaborate the value expression function by associating it with maintaining three aspects of the self-concept: private self (attitudes that meet internalized standards), public self (attitudes that secure positive evaluations from significant others), and collective self (attitudes that meet the goals of important reference groups).[7]

Techniques are available to gauge which functions an attitude might serve (e.g., Herek, 1987), and messages congruent with the function an attitude serves are more likely to change that attitude (e.g., Pryor, Reeder, & McManus,

1991; Shavitt, 1990; Snyder & Miene, 1992). Simply, it appears feasible that a concern for the functions of attitudes might improve attempts at, and understandings of efforts aimed at, changing organizationally salient attitudes.

Although contemporary social psychological approaches to the functions of attitudes emphasize how attitudes provide simple strategies for problem solving, help organize memory, and contribute to the maintenance of self-worth (e.g., Pratkanis & Greenwald, 1989), additional, more specific functions have appeared in the literature that organizational scientists might find intriguing. For instance, a variety of social psychological theories indicate that a person's attitudes are systematically interconnected (for example, Heider's [e.g., 1946] balance theory). On the basis of these theories, it is apparent that a person's current attitudes function to shape the formation of newly acquired attitudes. That is, people likely form new attitudes consistent with the ones they already possess. As one explanation for this phenomenon, personal values could be considered the glue that binds an individual's values together (e.g., Deaux & Wrightsman, 1988). Thus, a person who highly values equality is expected to possess somewhat similar positive attitudes toward civil rights movements as they pertain, for example, to Blacks, Hispanics, and women. Later in this chapter, the concept of values will surface again. For now, on values and the interconnectedness of attitudes, the interested reader should see, for example, Abelson and Prentice (1989); Ball-Rokeach, Rokeach, and Grube (1984); Johnson and Eagly (1989); Ostrom and Brock (1968); and Sherif and Cantril (1947).

Another specific function of attitudes is that they influence interpersonal attraction; people are attracted to others whom they perceive as holding similar attitudes (e.g., Byrne, 1971; Huston & Geis, 1993; McCaul, Ployhart, Hinsz, & McCaul, 1995; Smeaton, Bryne, & Murnen, 1989).[8] The interpersonal attraction function of attitudes is evident, at least implicitly, in the organizational literature on relational demography (e.g., Tsui, Egan, & O'Reilly, 1992) and on Schneider's (1987) attraction-selection-attrition framework. But to my knowledge, a direct test of it, focusing on attraction or repulsion and measurement of perceived or actual attitude similarity/dissimilarity, has not yet appeared in organizational literature.

Attitudes also may influence the information people approach and attend to, with individuals seeking and focusing on information consistent with their attitudes (e.g., Festinger, 1957; Frey, 1986).[9] For example, people with negative attitudes toward President Clinton probably seek out and attend to media coverage about "Whitewater" more than do those with favorable attitudes.[10] In the organizational literature, the closest I think we have come to examining this function is Dearborn and Simon's (1958) research on the effects of functional background (e.g., marketing and finance) on executives' perceptions of the problems an organization is experiencing. Attempts to replicate such an effect have produced mixed results (Beyer et al., 1997; Kefalas & Schoderbek, 1973; Waller, Huber, & Glick, 1995; Walsh, 1988). The Dearborn and Simon study and those following it were based on the assumption that functional experience leads to the selective perception of organizational information (e.g., marketeers focus on marketing information). The mixed results for this assumption may be a product of trying to directly measure experience (e.g., functional area) rather than the residue of experience (i.e., attitudes). My bet is that how executives vary, for instance, in their attitudes toward the importance of marketing to organizational effectiveness is more consistently related to the degree to which they focus on information about marketing in diagnosing organizational problems than is their current functional assignment.

The final example of the functions of attitudes to be introduced before turning to attitude-behavior relationships is concerned with the recollection of behaviors. Specifically, people tend to believe that they have behaved in the past consistent with their current attitudes, although those current attitudes may have been revised recently (e.g, Ross, 1989). Thus, attempting to link together *self-reports* of behaviors and attitudes may be even more problematic than many organizational researchers currently think. Beyond this methodological concern, the current function of attitudes seems to speak to popular notions of sensemaking in organizations (e.g., Weick, 1995).

In sum, people's current attitudes generally can be thought of as providing simple strategies for problem solving, helping to organize memory, and contributing to self-worth and, more specifically, for example, as influencing the new attitudes they form, to whom they are attracted, the information they seek out and focus on, and the behaviors they see themselves having performed. All these functions of attitudes seem *potentially* salient for understanding various aspects of life in and around organizations. I am not arguing that we should focus research attention on any particular function; rather, I believe we would benefit from appreciating the range of functions a person's attitudes serve. Knowing that attitudes serve utilitarian, knowledge, ego defense, and value expression functions could lead to the posing of questions not now evident in our literature. This is my hope. Now, let's move on to what has been examined extensively in our literature: attitudes as predictors of behaviors.

Attitude-Behavior Relationships

Given that the ultimate usefulness of the attitude concept can be viewed as resting on the assumption that attitudes influence behaviors (Olson & Zanna, 1993), it is surprising, to me at least, that social psychologists seem to have paid attitude-behavior relationships *relatively* little attention. For instance, in their comprehensive text, Eagly and Chaiken (1993) devoted one chapter to the impact of attitudes on behaviors and nine chapters to attitude formation and change. This is not to say that the social psychological literature has little to offer on the subjects of if, when, and how attitudes influence behaviors; rather, I felt that sharing my surprise might perhaps bring readers' expectations in line with what is to come.

Early on in the study of attitude-behavior relationships, it was observed that attitudes sometimes poorly predict behaviors (e.g., Blumer, 1955; Kutner, Wilkins, & Yarrow, 1952; LaPiere, 1934). The social psychology community really did not take these findings seriously until Wicker (1969) asserted, on the basis of his review of the available empirical evidence, that people likely do *not* possess stable, underlying attitudes that influence their overt behaviors. Today, we know Wicker's assertion is unfounded (Kraus, 1995); his article, however, helped stimulate a stream of research, still flowing (e.g., Lord, Desforges, Ramsey, Trezza, & Lepper, 1991), that allows us to understand when attitudes might be observed to predict behaviors and when they may not. Below, I offer a summary of this stream of research, beginning with what I consider to be largely methodological concerns (some of which were raised in the preceding chapter).

Attitudes may not be related to behaviors in a particular context simply because the context offers few behavioral options, that is, the situation constrains the variance in the behavior of interest. This point was raised some time ago to explain why attitude-behavior relationships appear stronger in field studies than they do in laboratory studies, where behavior presumably is more constrained (e.g., Hovland, 1959; Kelman, 1974). More generally, Snyder and Ickes (1985) distinguish between strong and weak situations, with the former ones being of the sort that specify what behaviors are possible and those that are not—thus limiting or eliminating the effects of differences between people on their behaviors. As implied in the previous chapter, some organizational settings may be considered to be strong situations; the organizational literature, however, currently supplies little conceptual guidance for identifying such situations. Moreover, not explicitly considered in either the social psychological or organizational literatures is the possibility that strong situations also constrain the variability of attitudes, thereby suppressing attitude-behavior relationships in another way. Thus, attention to identifying strong organizational settings seems particularly important.

A second methodological reason for observing weak attitude-behavior relationships has to do with measuring single versus multiple acts. Single behaviors likely are influenced by a number of factors irrelevant to the attitude thought to be a predictor of the behavior; when a composite index of attitude-relevant behaviors is formed, these factors, so long as their influence is not largely consistent across the set of behaviors composing the composite, tend to cancel one another, thereby, creating a more reliable behavioral measure and, thus, a considerably stronger attitude-behavior correlation (Eagly & Chaiken, 1993). This logic is not new to the social psychological literature (e.g., Campbell, 1963) and has been articulated most fully by Fishbein and Ajzen (e.g, 1974). In support of their reasoning, Fishbein and Ajzen report a correlation of .14 between a Likert measure of religious attitudes and a single-act criterion but a correlation of .68 with a multiple-act criterion.[11]

A third methodological concern, also discussed thoroughly by Fishbein and Ajzen (e.g., Ajzen & Fishbein, 1977), is related to the single- versus multiple-act criterion issue but more generally addresses the level of specificity at which attitudes and behaviors are operationally defined. According to their *principle of correspondence* (or of compatibility; Ajzen, 1988), attitude-behavior relationships are stronger to the degree the (a) action, (b) target, (c) context, and (d) time elements of each are measured at the same level of specificity. Although the principle may hold, the application of it, as suggested by Eagly and Chaiken (1993), might serve to mask the underlying processes of interest to investigators. That is, the constructs of interest to a researcher may not correspond in Fishbein and Ajzen's view. For instance, the principle should not be used to drive a study of attitudes toward being absent, when an investigator is interested in how job satisfaction per se is linked to absenteeism. For more on this warning, see Dawes and Smith (1985). Before moving on, I take the liberty of tentatively modifying the principle of correspondence on the basis of findings presented earlier in the chapter. Attitudes predict behaviors better if there is a correspondence between the affective/cognitive class of the attitude and the affective/cognitive class of the behavior (e.g., Millar & Tesser, 1986). Thus, level of specificity probably also should refer to the affective/cognitive class of the attitudes and behaviors in question.

Beyond these methodological concerns, one additional issue regarding the magnitude of observed attitude-behavior relationships is worthy of note.

Various attitude qualities, principally strength, affect attitude-behavior relationships—the greater the strength of the attitude, the greater the magnitude of the relationship (Petty & Krosnick, 1993). Fazio (e.g., 1990; Fazio, Chen, McDonel, & Sherman, 1982; Fazio & Zanna, 1978), construing strength as the degree of association in memory between an attitude object and its evaluation, explains the effects of attitude strength by asserting that it determines accessibility of the attitude in memory, thereby, the likelihood the attitude will come to mind when the behavior in question is being contemplated. Moreover, Fazio (e.g., 1986) has asserted that the assessibility of strong attitudes occurs automatically in the presence of the attitude object, without any conscious cognitive processing (but see Bargh, Chaiken, Govender, & Pratto, 1992, for a counter position).

A number of other attitude qualities (e.g., certainty, centrality, clarity, confidence, extremity, involvement, and stability) are thought to be equivalent to or indicative of attitude strength (e.g., Raden, 1985). What, then, influences attitude strength, a seemingly critical construct for understanding the attitude-behavior relationship? Attitude strength appears to be a function of the amount of knowledge a person has about an attitude object (e.g., Davidson, Yantis, Norwood, & Montano, 1985; Kallgren & Wood, 1986) and if that knowledge is based on direct, personal experience rather than, for instance, secondhand information (Fazio & Zanna, 1981). Moreover, attitude strength has been shown to increase when an attitude (a) directly affects a person's own outcomes and self-interest; (b) is related to deeply held philosophical, political, and/or religious values; and (c) is of concern to the person's close friends, family, and/or social in-groups (Boninger, Krosnick, & Berent, 1995). In addition, Tesser (1993) offers the provocative assertion that strong attitudes are rooted in our genetic makeup. His assertion is consistent with numerous findings in psychology. For example, ample evidence demonstrates the influence of genetics on personality (e.g., Bouchard & McGue, 1990; Eaves, Eysenck, & Martin, 1989; Loehlin, 1989; Plomin & Nesselrode, 1990; Tellegen et al., 1988). Tesser not only defends his idea regarding genetics and attitude strength by employing the findings of others; he presents the results of four original studies supportive of it. Tesser's studies generally show that attitudes with greater heritability (as identified by prior investigators, e.g., Martin et al., 1986) are stronger than attitudes with less heritability and, therefore, are more accessible as indexed by response speed, more resistant to a standard attitude change induction, and more central to attitude similarity-interpersonal attraction relationships.

In sum, psychologically weak situations, multiple-act criteria, attitudes and behaviors at the same levels of specificity, and strong attitudes all should contribute to the observation of relatively strong attitude-behavior relationships. Of these factors, attitude strength seems to me the most meaty theoretically. But the story I have told about moderators of attitude-behavior relationships is not complete. For more on such potential moderators, see Eagly and Chaiken (1993). Now, on to models of the attitude-behavior relationship.

The Theory of Reasoned Action

Fishbein and Ajzen's (1975) theory of reasoned action dominates the attitude-behavior literature in social psychology; as seen in the previous chapter, it also has influenced the thinking of organizational scientists concerned with the prediction of behaviors (e.g., turnover) from attitudes. The theory is somewhat restrictive in that it addresses attitudes toward volitional behaviors (not attitudes toward targets, e.g., Blacks). In essence, the theory posits that (a) the most proximal cause of behavior is a person's intention to engage in it; (b) intention is a function of attitude toward the behavior and subjective norms; (c) attitude toward the behavior is a function of beliefs that the behavior leads to salient outcomes; and (d) subjective norms are a function of the person's perceptions of significant others' preferences about whether he or she should or should not engage in the behavior and the person's motivation to comply with these referent expectations. Numerous applications of the theory have demonstrated its predictive validity. Recently, for example, the theory has been used successfully in regard to seat belt use (Stasson & Fishbein, 1990), applying for a nursing program (Strader & Katz, 1990), and performing a testicular self-examination, (Steffen, 1990).[12]

Although the theory of reasoned action has had many supporters, it also has attracted numerous critics. Most criticisms of it are aimed at the theory's assumption that other variables affect behavior only through their impact on the theory's variables (Eagly & Chaiken, 1993). Internalized moral rules, for instance, have been found to contribute to the prediction of behaviors, in addition to the effects of attitude toward the act and subjective norms (e.g., Pomazal & Jaccard, 1976; Schwartz & Tessler, 1972; Zuckerman & Reis, 1978). Prior behavior (or habit) seems to be an especially influential variable directly affecting subsequent behavior (e.g., Bagozzi, 1981; Bauman, Fisher, & Koch, 1989; Bentler & Speckart, 1979, 1981; Grandberg & Holmberg, 1990; Sutton & Hallett, 1989). On the basis of available evidence, Eagly and Chaiken concluded that quite a number of everyday behaviors may be controlled by habit as well as by intentions.[13] For instance, in part, someone does not miss a day of work simply because he or she has never missed a day of work.

Data also show that intentions do not always mediate the effects of attitudes on behaviors (e.g., Bagozzi & Yi, 1989; Bagozzi, Yi, & Baumgartner, 1990; Bentler & Speckart, 1981). Consistent with such evidence, Eagly and Chaiken (1993) postulated that individuals sometimes may impulsively or spontaneously act on their attitudes without forming an explicit intention. In addition, it is important to note, perhaps particularly for organizational scientists, that the theory of reasoned action has been criticized for excluding a focus on behaviors requiring skills and abilities as well as opportunities and cooperation from others (Liska, 1984). As a final example of how the theory has been criticized, several investigators have observed that reciprocal causal effects may be evident among the theory's variables (e.g., Andrews & Kandel, 1979; Doran et al., 1991; Heise, 1977). For additional concerns with the theory, see, for example, Eagly and Chaiken (1993), Liska (1984), and Olson and Zanna (1993).

Alternatives to the Theory of Reasoned Action

Given the above criticisms of Fishbein and Ajzen's (1975) theory, it is not surprising that alternatives have surfaced in the social psychology literature. I begin with the theory's closest relative, Ajzen's (e.g., 1988, 1991) *theory of planned behavior.* The essential difference between the two theories is Ajzen's inclusion of *perceived behavioral control* to expand the theory to include behaviors not fully under volitional control. This new variable is defined as a person's perception of how easy or difficult it is to perform the behavior; therefore, it is similar to Bandura's (e.g., 1977) self-efficacy construct. Most tests of Ajzen's theory show that predictions are improved by the inclusion of perceived behavioral control (e.g., Beck & Ajzen, 1991; Madden, Ellen, & Ajzen, 1992; Schlegel, d'Avernas, Zanna, DeCourville, & Manske, 1992). In their evaluation of the theory of planned behavior, Eagly and Chaiken (1993) recognized the need to attend to how individuals plan the attainment of their behavioral goals and to how such planning relates to perceived behavioral control.[14]

Fazio (1990) advanced the *MODE model* of the attitude-behavior relationship, which, according to Olson and Zanna (1993), "provides a compelling analysis of how attitudes can spontaneously affect actions" (p. 133). The model, emphasizing motivation and opportunity as determinants of how attitudes affect behaviors, indicates that the theory of reasoned action will hold when people (a) are highly motivated to think deliberately about an attitude object and (b) have the opportunity to do so. But when either of these conditions are not met, highly accessible attitudes guide behaviors. In this way, Fazio supplies an explanation of when the effects of attitudes on behaviors are automatic, rather then deliberative. (See also Fazio, Powell, & Williams, 1989, and Sanbonmatsu & Fazio, 1990.) To date, the organizational literature really has not evidenced a consideration for such automatic effects, which may be quite commonplace.

As a final example of an alternative approach to the attitude-behavior relationship, I will briefly describe Eagly and Chaiken's (1993), as of yet untested, *composite model.* In the model, behavior originates in the activation of habits, attitude toward targets, and three classes of anticipated outcomes of behavior—utilitarian, normative, and self-identity. These variables, in turn, are posited to affect attitude toward the behavior that influences intentions that affects behavior directly. (This description does not capture all the relationships contained in this rather complex model.) *Utilitarian outcomes* refer to the rewards and punishments anticipated to follow from engaging in the behavior. *Normative outcomes* refer to the approval and disapproval that significant others are expected to express in reaction to engaging in the behavior as well as to the pride and guilt the person anticipates experiencing following the behavior on the basis of his or her internalized moral rules. *Self-identity outcomes* refer to affirmations and repudiations of central aspects of the person's self-concept anticipated to follow from engaging in the behavior. As I hope the reader can see from this abbreviated description, the composite model does respond to a variety of concerns that have been expressed about the theory of reasoned action. Of course, we must await tests of the model to ascertain if this responsiveness constitutes a significant advance in the attitude-behavior literature.

None of the above approaches are intended to serve as a strict guide to attitude-behavior research in the organizational sciences. Rather, each approach contains ideas not yet exploited by us that likely could open new avenues of investigation or redirect existing ones. For instance, in thinking about Eagly and Chaiken's (1993) composite model and contextual performance, I was led to question the influence of utilitarian, normative, and self-identity outcomes on workers' attitudes toward the behavior. I do not believe that any of these questions have been entertained by contextual performance investigators, but it seems to me that provocative cases readily could be constructed for studying the potential contributions of such anticipated consequences as rewards/punishments, approval/disapproval from significant others, pride/guilt, and affirmations/repudiations of the self-concept to explaining attitudes toward contextual performance and, subsequently, the behavior itself. The model and the opportunity to use it are available; the intent to do so and the act itself are up to the reader.

Attitude Formation and Change

As suggested earlier, the literature on attitude formation and change, particularly the latter, is voluminous. By necessity, therefore, this section is especially selective. Moreover, some of what I have chosen to share is rather knotty, at least for someone like myself who is a consumer of, not a contributor to, the ideas. In attempting to untangle these ideas for presentation here, I hope that I have retained their essence and not oversimplified them. As a final warning, I suspect that because of their absence in the organizational literature, portions of what follows likely will be quite foreign to the reader. For now, please trust me that these unfamiliar ideas are important to understanding the formation and change of attitudes in and around organizations.

Attitude Formation

Rather obviously, a personal encounter with an object often leads to forming an attitude toward it (McGuire, 1985). Indeed, Zajonc (1968) hypothesized that mere repeated exposure to an object increases liking for that object. On the basis of a review of the considerable research entailing tests of the hypothesis, Bornstein (1989) concluded that the relationship between exposure frequency and attitude generally is positive, and he identified several moderators of the relationship. Perhaps most intriguing among these moderators is the subliminal manner in which stimuli are presented. When the presentation is subliminal, rather than supraliminal, the effect is larger. Several theoretical accounts have been advanced for the mere exposure effect, with Moreland and Zajonc's (1977, 1979) explanation having attracted the most attention. In part, they argued that the attitudinal effects of mere exposure sometimes may occur via a "hot" affective mechanism (i.e., one not involving a prior cognitive process). For a summary of the controversy sparked by this now seemingly reasonable claim, see, for example, Eagly and Chaiken (1993). In addition to an encounter with an object leading to the formation of an attitude, simply expecting to interact with the object (e.g., Gerard & Orive, 1987), being asked one's attitude about it (e.g., Fazio, Lenn, & Effrein, 1983-

1984), and having considerable knowledge about the object (e.g., Judd & Downing, 1990) also are associated with attitude formation.

Moreover, as was noted earlier, attitude formation can be a product of classical conditioning (Staats, 1967). That is, the pairing of an object (e.g., a company) with positive or negative affect-inducing stimuli (e.g., the label "sleazy") can produce an attitude toward the object. People do not need to be consciously aware of the unconditioned stimuli for such learning to occur (e.g., Krosnick, Betz, Jussim, & Lynn, 1992). For more on the conditioning of attitudes and the boundaries of these effects, see, for example, Cacioppo, Marshall-Goodell, Tassinary, and Petty (1992); Kuykendall and Keating (1990); Lott (1955); Lott and Lott (1960); and Perdue, Dovidio, Gurtman, and Tyler (1990).

The influence of beliefs, values, and ideologies on attitude formation has been theorized about and examined empirically. Although there is support for the claim that attitudes sometimes are derived from beliefs (e.g., Fishbein & Ajzen, 1975; also see, for instance, Anderson, 1981; Fishbein, 1967; Peak, 1955), it appears that the process often involves only a few beliefs (or even only one; e.g., Eagly & Chaiken, 1993; McGuire, 1985). Regarding values, when two or more values surface in reference to an object and those values are in conflict, the resulting attitude is moderate; alternatively, without value conflict, the attitude is extreme (Tetlock, 1986).[15] Research on the effects of ideology (which can be thought of as a cluster of beliefs organized around a dominant societal theme; e.g., Converse, 1964) on attitude formation has produced a mixed but informative set of results. Some investigators claim that U.S. citizens lack political ideologies and, for instance, that their political beliefs are relatively unformed (e.g., Converse, 1975). Others assert that overarching ideologies are common (e.g., Judd, Krosnick, & Milburn, 1981) but often are organized around themes other than conservatism and liberalism, such as "pro-labor traditionalism" (e.g., Fleishman, 1986). Another camp of investigators say that U.S. citizens often are willing to identify themselves as conservative or liberal; this identification, however, does not translate into attitudes with ideological implications (e.g., Sears & Kinder, 1985). Moreover, some evidence indicates that a politicized context may cause people who identify themselves as conservatives or liberals to think more ideologically. Perhaps the most consistent position across investigators (Eagly & Chaiken, 1993) is that people with considerable expertise about political matters do possess political ideologies (e.g., Judd & Downing, 1990; Tetlock, 1989).

Finally, I want to raise again the likelihood that some attitudes are inherited. Evidence indicates, for example, the partial heritability of attitudes toward drinking alcohol (Perry, 1973), white supremacy (Eaves et al., 1989; Martin et al., 1986), the death penalty (Eaves et al.; Martin et al.), and religion (Waller, Kojetin, Bouchard, Lykken, & Tellegen, 1990). Although such evidence has been supported strongly by some social psychologists (e.g., Tesser, 1993), others have questioned it (e.g., Olson & Zanna, 1993). The likelihood that job satisfaction partially is inherited is addressed in the next chapter.

Thus far, a personal encounter with an attitude object, including mere exposure to it, as well as expecting to interact with the object, being asked one's attitude about it, and having considerable knowledge about the object, has been identified as influencing attitude formation. In addition, it was recognized that attitude formation can be conditioned and affected by one's beliefs, values, and ideologies. Finally, the possibility that attitudes can be inherited was noted. In discussing some of these factors, I recognized that conscious awareness was not a necessary condition for attitude formation to occur. I am not finished with the attitude formation literature; several of the theories to be introduced in the remainder of the chapter can be viewed as addressing both attitude formation and change. Nevertheless, if any of what has been said above about attitude formation is new to the reader, I hope that it has stimulated thought about when and how attitudes are formed in and around organizations. As can be inferred from the preceding chapter on job satisfaction, such thinking is important because relatively little of the social psychology literature on attitude formation has been applied by organizational scientists.

Attitude Change

Given the applied bent of many organizational scientists, I will approach the topic of attitude change largely by considering how social psychologists have characterized the process of persuasion by communication. I open by describing two routes to persuasion. Next, on the basis of the elements in most persuasive situations identified by the Communications Research Program at Yale in the 1940s and 1950s (i.e., source, message, context, and recipient; e.g., Hovland, Janis, & Kelley, 1953), the findings of a large number of studies will be summarized. Third, several theories of attitude change will be reviewed. Finally, I will discuss resistance to change.

Petty and Cacioppo (e.g., 1986b) formulated the *elaboration likelihood model* (ELM) of persuasion that specifies the conditions under which people critically think about the contents of a message and what they do when those conditions are not met. Persuasion mediated by critical (argument-based) thinking is labeled by Petty and Cacioppo as the *central route*. They call the alternative the *peripheral route*.

The term *elaboration* refers to the degree to which people think about issue-relevant arguments contained in persuasive messages. When situational and individual difference variables ensure high motivation and ability for issue-relevant thinking, the *elaboration likelihood* is high and, therefore, so is the probability that the central route will be followed. Petty and Cacioppo (e.g., 1986b) posited that *attitudes formed or changed via the central route are relatively persistent, predictive of behavior, and resistant to change* (until challenged by convincing counterarguments). In earlier approaches to persuasion, it often was assumed that the central route needed to be taken for change to occur. For example, Hovland and his colleagues at Yale (e.g., Hovland et al., 1953) asserted that for a message to have influence, receivers must learn its contents and be motivated to accept it. Thus, people were seen as persuaded only by arguments they attend to, comprehend, and accept. McGuire (1968), building on the work of Hovland et al., proposed that the persuasive impact of messages could be viewed as the multiplicative product of six information-processing steps: presentation, attention, comprehension, yielding, retention, and behavior. These distinctions in information-processing steps have yielded interesting empirical results. For instance, people high in intelligence are better able to comprehend (learn) a message but less likely to retain (accept) it; people lower in intelligence are more willing to accept a message but may have more trouble learning its contents; thus, intelligence does not generally influence vulnerability to persuasion (Rhodes & Wood, 1992).[16]

According to the ELM, when motivation or ability for elaboration is low, attitudes still can be formed and changed, but the peripheral route to persuasion is followed. This route encompasses a number of mechanisms that cause persuasion in the absence of argument scrutiny (e.g., Petty & Cacioppo, 1986b), for instance, attributional reasoning (e.g., Kelley, 1972), classical conditioning (e.g., Staats, 1983), and maintaining social relationships (e.g., Eagly & Chaiken, 1993; Smith, Bruner, & White, 1956). As noted by Brehm and Kassin (1996), recognition of the peripheral route to persuasion is consistent with Adolf Hitler's (1933) observation that "the receptive ability of the masses is very limited, their understanding small" (p. 77) and with his carefully planned use of lighting, background music, the timing of entrances, and so on at the meetings at which speeches were made (Qualter, 1962). Simply, Hitler saw that people sometimes responded to superficial cues, and he used such cues to spread his hate.[17]

Research generally supports the ELM prediction that the quality of persuasive arguments influences attitudes more often when people are highly motivated and/or able to engage in elaboration processing (Eagly & Chaiken, 1993). Moreover, the list of variables known to motivate and/or enable central route processing is quite extensive (e.g., Chaiken & Stangor, 1987; Petty & Cacioppo, 1986b; Tesser & Shaffer, 1990). Perhaps at the top of that list in research attention received is involvement with the contents of the message, defined as the relevancy of the message to the recipient's goals and values. This research appears to show that the likelihood of taking the central route increases with involvement (Petty & Cacioppo, 1990; but also see Johnson & Eagly, 1989). An example of a variable that has received considerably less attention is the race/ethnic origin of the sender. It seems that White Americans are more likely to follow the central route if the sender is Black or Hispanic rather than White (White & Harkins, 1994; but also see, for example, Mackie, Gastardo-Conaco, & Skelly, 1992).

Chaiken and her colleagues (e.g., Chaiken, 1980, 1987; Chaiken, Liberman, & Eagly, 1989) have advanced the *heuristic-systematic model,* similar to the ELM. In *heuristic processing,* similar to the peripheral route, people focus on the subset of available information that enables them to use relatively simple rules, schemas, or heuristics that mediate attitude judgments tasks. In *systematic processing,* similar to the central route, recipients access and scrutinize a great deal of information for its relevance to their attitude judgments tasks. The heuristic-systematic model posits that people prefer less to more effortful means of information processing; they exert whatever effort is required for them to feel sufficiently confident that their processing goals have been satisfied. The model also posits that in some situations, people use both heuristics and systematic processing. This proposition is not explicitly evident in the ELM. Finally, similar to the ELM, the heuristic-systematic model posits that *attitudes formed or changed on the basis of heuristic processing alone tend to be less stable, less resistant to counterarguments, and less predictive of behavior* than when systematic processing is used. In the discussions that follow, ideas relevant to both routes or means of processing are presented.

As noted earlier, Hovland et al. (1953) identified *source, message, context,* and *recipient* as elements evident in most persuasive situations. In discussing these elements, my aim simply is to exemplify what is known about the effects of each, sampling from both earlier and contemporary research. I begin with the *source* of persuasive messages. It is well known that particular categories of sources (e.g., parents [McGuire, 1985] and the media [Roberts & Maccoby,

1985]) can be especially influential in persuasion. Regrettably, it appears that social psychologists have lost interest in identifying these categories and in investigating when and how any given category is particularly influential. Rather, it seems that a long-term interest in the attributes of sources, such as their expertise, trustworthiness, likability, and attractiveness, has continued (Chaiken, 1986; McGuire, 1985; Petty & Cacioppo, 1981). Several of these attributes pertain to the *credibility* of the source. *Generally,* the more credible the source, the more recipients agree with the content of the message sent (e.g., Hovland & Weiss, 1951; Kelman & Hovland, 1953). Often, credibility effects are attributed to the source's expertise as evidenced by how recipients perceive his or her credentials, knowledge, and intelligence *as well as* how well-spoken he or she is seen (Hass, 1981). Regarding the speech of the source, recent research shows, for example, that rapid speech inhibits the generation of unfavorable thoughts to a counterattitudinal message and, thereby, enhances agreement, whereas it inhibits the generation of favorable thoughts to a proattitudinal message and, thereby, reduces agreement (Smith & Shaffer, 1991); women who speak tentatively are more persuasive with men than are women who speak assertively, whereas tentative speech reduces the effectiveness of women speaking to other women (Carli, 1990).

Trustworthiness also explains credibility effects. For instance, people tend to be leery of those who have something to gain from their successful persuasion (Brehm & Kassin, 1996). This explains why a person seen as arguing against his or her own interests is more persuasive (e.g., Eagly, Wood, & Chaiken, 1978; Walster, Aronson, & Abrahams, 1966) and why sources are seen as more credible if they acknowledge and refute opposing arguments rather than presenting only one side (Crowley & Hoyer, 1994). In addition, it probably also explains why the more products a celebrity endorses, the less trustworthy the celebrity is seen by consumers (Tripp, Jensen, & Carlson, 1994). The robustness of trustworthiness perhaps is most vividly established by the finding that people are more influenced when they think they accidentally overheard a persuasive communication than when they receive the same message but thought it was intended for their ears (Walster & Festinger, 1962). Although the influence of trustworthiness may seem logical, recent evidence suggests that perceptions of it may not be so rational. For instance, sources with a babyish facial appearance are perceived as more trustworthy (Brownlow & Zebrowitz, 1990; also see Burgoon, Birk, & Pfau (1990).

Like credibility, *likability* pertains to several source attributes. In particular, similarity and physical attractiveness, principal determinants of likability, have been investigated as source effects on attitude formation and change.

Similarity has been defined operationally in a number of ways in the similarity-likability and similarity-attitude change literatures, for example, in attitudes (e.g., McCaul et al., 1995), demographic characteristics (e.g., Dembroski, Lasater, & Ramerez, 1978), moods (e.g., Locke & Horowitz, 1990), and personalities (e.g., Caspi & Harbener, 1990). Research appears to indicate that similarity enhances attitude change in conjunction with strong but not weak messages (Mackie, Worth, & Asuncion, 1990) and that when the similarities seem relevant to the content of the message, similarity increases persuasion the most (Berscheid, 1966).

Although similarity in physical attractiveness has been investigated in the similarity-likability literature (e.g., Carli, Ganley, & Pierce-Otay, 1991), the physical attractiveness of the source per se has been the focus of attention in the attitude change literature. This literature demonstrates that the attractiveness of a source enhances his or her persuasiveness (e.g., Chaiken, 1979; Kahle & Homer, 1985; Pallak, 1983). Credibility and likability do not cover all the literature on source effects. Cialdini, Green, and Rusch (1992), for example, show that attitude change is enhanced when a source has yielded to a recipient's persuasive attempt on a prior topic compared with when a source had resisted the recipient's persuasive attempt. That is, a norm of reciprocity appears to have been operating. As another example, multiple sources who advocate a similar position are more persuasive than a single source (e.g., Harkins & Petty, 1987). This effect may be a function of the multiple sources increasing the "consensus" (Kelley, 1967) associated with the position (Eagly & Chaiken, 1993). Moreover, as has been indicated, there are limits to the effects of source attributes. Consistent with ELM (e.g., Petty & Cacioppo, 1986b) predictions, when personal involvement with the contents of the message is high, people follow the central route, thus reducing the effects of source attributes on attitude change (e.g., Chaiken, 1980; Petty, Cacioppo, & Goldman, 1981).

The source of a message can matter, but understanding when and how source effects occur is considerably more complex than typically is portrayed in organizational behavior textbooks. This oversimplification reflects that the contemporary organizational research literature ignores possible source effects. In providing an overview of the research on source effects, I often cited social psychological research relevant to marketing. It seems we have a lot to learn from our marketing colleagues; this opportunity extends beyond source effects to the entire communication process, as I will show.[18]

As we now begin to move through my overview of the effects of the *message* per se (i.e., what is communicated and how it is communicated) on persuasion, readers quickly will see the same sort of complexities that surrounded source effects. In discussing source effects, I used the terms *strong* and *weak* messages. What do these terms mean? In presentations of the ELM, Petty and Cacioppo (e.g., 1986b) implicitly referred, for example, to the relative plausibility or believability of a message's arguments (Eagly & Chaiken, 1993). On the basis of how the terms have been operationalized in persuasion research, Areni and Lutz (1988) observed, however, that differences between strong and weak messages are rooted in the types of evidence used to bolster the message's core arguments (e.g., statistics vs. personal opinion) and in the degree to which the attitude object is associated with *very* positive attributes as compared with *less* positive attributes.[19] The findings of investigations in which argument quality has been defined in this way indicate that strong messages do produce more attitude change consistent with the direction of the arguments presented than do weak ones (Eagly & Chaiken, 1993).

Intuitively, the perceived truth value of a message ought to influence attitude change. Merely repeating a statement causes it to be judged more truthful (Arkes, Boehm, & Xu, 1991). This may explain why, at least for a high-quality message, merely increasing exposure to it enhances persuasion (Cacioppo & Petty, 1985, 1989). The "newness" of a statement also affects its judged validity. Gruenfeld and Wyer (1992) demonstrated that recipients assume that communicators intend their statements to convey new information; therefore, if the information conveyed is redundant with a recipient's prior knowledge, then the recipient apparently wonders why the statement was made and may suspect the communicator actually possesses information disconfirming the statement, leading to the statement's being judged less than truthful.

Supportive of the ELM (e.g., Petty & Cacioppo, 1986b), considerable evidence shows that when motivation and/or ability for argument processing is low, message attributes such as length and the number of persuasive arguments presented exert a greater positive impact on attitude change (e.g., Harkins & Petty, 1987; Petty & Cacioppo, 1984; Wood, Kallgren, & Preisler, 1985). In addition, the same moderating effects for motivation and/or ability are evident regarding the effects of humorous messages (Chattopadhyay & Basu, 1990) and vivid messages (McGill & Anand, 1989; but also see, for example, Collins, Taylor, Wood, & Thompson, 1988; Fiske & Taylor, 1991). Moreover, positively framed messages (describing potential gains) are more effective than negatively framed messages (describing potential losses from not "embracing" the attitude object) when elaboration is minimal, but the reverse is true when it is extensive (Maheswaran & Meyers-Levy, 1990).

The fear appeal of a message probably has received more research attention than any other message attribute (Olson & Zanna, 1993). Perhaps the most popular theoretical approach is Roger's (e.g., 1983) *protection motivation theory* (but also see alternatives advanced by Janis, 1967, and McGuire, e.g., 1969). The theory postulates that threatening messages are effective to the degree that they convince recipients that the problem is serious (severity), the recipient is susceptible to the problem (vulnerability), and the problem can be avoided by engaging in a behavior the recipient is capable of performing (efficacy). Support for the theory has been obtained in both the laboratory (e.g., Rippetoe & Rodgers, 1987) and the field (e.g., Meyerowitz & Chaiken, 1987). Recent examples of successful applications of the theory have been concerned with earthquake preparedness (Mulilis & Lippa, 1990), condom use (Struckman-Johnson, Gilliland, Struckman-Johnson, & North, 1990), and parental discussions about child abuse (Campis, Prentice-Dunn, & Lyman, 1989).[20] Does protection motivation theory have any relevancy to attitude change in organizations? Just think about how the threat of a downsizing might be framed to produce an attitude change among organizational members that management would see as desirable.

As was the case for source attributes, I have not fully covered the territory of message attributes. Once again, my intent merely was to provide an enticing taste of the social psychological literature. But before I move on, I do want to mention one last aspect of the message: People tend to miscomprehend everyday communications (e.g., magazine articles) at rates ranging from 15% to 40% (e.g., Jacoby & Hoyer, 1982, 1987). Clearly, therefore, message comprehension ought to be at the top of one's head in considering the effects of the message on attitude change.

I have embarrassingly little to say about the effects on attitude change of the *context* in which the message is delivered. Although, as I previously noted, the Communication Research Program at Yale (e.g., Hovland et al., 1953) did identify context as an element in the process of persuasion, context seems to have disappeared, for reasons unknown to me, from the social psychology literature as a key ingredient for understanding attitude change. What presumably passes for research on the influence of context generally is concerned with the effects of distractions. Petty, Wells, and Brock (1976) posited that distraction inhibits a recipient's dominant cognitive responses to a message. More precisely, they hypothesized that for a message eliciting primarily unfavorable thoughts, distraction enhances persuasion because it reduces the ability to generate counterarguments; for a message eliciting primarily favorable thoughts, distraction inhibits persuasion because it reduces the ability to generate supportive arguments. Several experiments have yielded results consistent with these hypotheses (Petty, Ostrom, & Block, 1981). But such findings obviously supply little substance for understanding potential context effects. Organizational scientists, as experts in the workplace context, should take this near void as a challenge. We need to start thinking about how organizational settings might influence attitude change attempts. In doing so, the implications of the ELM (e.g., Petty & Cacioppo, 1986b) should not be ignored. Moreover, the extensive social psychological literature on social influence, although not as integrated into the attitude change literature as one might wish, also is a valuable source of ideas for contemplating context effects on attitude change in organizations. This literature, for example, ranges from Asch's (e.g., 1951) research on conformity to Milgram's (e.g., 1974) studies of obedience to Moscovici's (e.g., 1980) explorations of minority influence. For a recent and provocative example of how ideas evident in the social influence literature might be applied to understanding attitudes in organizations, see O'Reilly and Chatman's (1996) analysis of organizational culture as social control.

Recipient (or audience) attributes have been more extensively reported in the recent literature on attitude change. These effects address both relatively enduring and more transient characteristics of recipients. The least investigated enduring recipient attributes are demographic ones. Meyers-Levy and Sternthal (1991), however, recently have argued and demonstrated in two experiments that women, as compared with men, are more likely to follow the central route in processing message cues. As another example of such demographic research, Krosnick and Alwin (1989) showed that older persons are less susceptible to attitude change (but also see Tyler & Schuller, 1991).

Perhaps more extensively studied are the effects of the recipient's personality. A meta-analytic study by Rhodes and Woods (1992) showed, for instance, that self-esteem is related reliably to persuasion, with recipients of moderate self-esteem influenced more by attitude change attempts than those of either high or low self-esteem. Investigations into the role of another personality construct, self-monitoring (Snyder, 1974), also have yielded an intriguing set of findings. "High self-monitors" regulate their behaviors across situations with the aim of favorably impressing others; alternatively, "low self-monitors" are less interested in impressing others and are more concerned with behaving true to their own beliefs and values. Snyder and DeBono (1985), on the basis of these descriptions, hypothesized and found that high self-monitors are more responsive to social adjustive than to value expressive messages. A social adjustive message contains information, for example, about attitudes of the recipient's peer group (DeBono, 1987). Snyder and DeBono's results have been constructively replicated on a number of occasions (e.g., DeBono & Edmonds, 1989). A final example of the influence of the recipient's personality involves findings regarding "need for cognition." People high in need for cognition tend to enjoy and participate in effortful cognitive activity (Cacioppo & Petty, 1982). On the basis of a series of studies, people high in need for cognition, as expected, tend to take the central route to persuasion as contrasted with those low in need for cognition, who are more likely to follow the peripheral route (e.g., Cacioppo, Petty, & Morris, 1983).

Considerable attention has focused on how the recipient's mood affects attitude change. Available results generally indicate that people in positive moods process messages less systematically than those in neutral moods (Eagly & Chaiken, 1993; Petty, Gleicher, & Baker, 1991; Schwarz, Bless, & Bohner, 1991). Two explanations for this effect, both with empirical support, are evident in the literature. First, good moods elicit positive thoughts from memory, which take up limited cognitive capacity, thereby reducing the *ability* to elaborate (i.e., to think about the issue-relevant arguments contained in the message; e.g., Mackie, Asuncion, & Rosselli, 1992; Mackie & Worth, 1989, 1991). Second, the *motivation* of people to elaborate in a good mood is reduced because they do not want to ruin their mood by expending cognitive effort (e.g., Bless, Bohner, Schwarz, & Strack, 1990; Isen, 1984; Worth & Mackie, 1987). Petty et al. (1991) have advanced a third, more condition-laden alternative. For example, under conditions of low personal involvement with an issue, attitudes move in the direction of the mood because the mood serves as a peripheral cue, but under conditions of high involvement, the movement of attitudes in the direction of the mood can be caused by the mood-biasing systematic processing (e.g., a positive mood can cause positive information to be more accessible).[21] Moreover, I suspect that Forgas's (1995) affect infusion model, which in part deals with when affect serves as a prime and when it is used as information, will further inform the process by which a recipient's mood affects attitude change.

I assume that some to most of the territory I have covered regarding the influence of source, message, context, and recipient is familiar to the reader; it often is how portions of the organizational communications literature are framed in textbooks for undergraduate and MBA students (e.g., Robbins, 1993). As I indicated earlier, as a teacher I find these textbook presentations disappointing because they present an oversimplified picture and fail to depict adequately the influence of the elements *in organizational settings.* This latter concern probably arises because the organizational literature contains few studies in which the effects of source, message, and so forth on attitude formation or change have been investigated systematically. On the basis of intuition and descriptions of managerial work (e.g., Mintzberg, 1973), it seems to me that the study of persuasion in organizations ought to be a hot topic. Why it is not, I do not know, but given the complexities evident in the social psychological literature, such research should prove to be a challenge— one well worth taking on.[22]

So far, in discussing attitude change, I really have not detailed, except for the ELM (e.g., Petty & Cacioppo, 1986b), alternative theoretical approaches evident in the social psychological literature. Here, I remedy this deficiency by providing a sampling of these approaches, beginning with Festinger's (1957) *cognitive dissonance theory*, mentioned previously. The theory has attracted a remarkable amount of interest by both social psychologists and others. This likely is attributable to the scope of the theory, which principally posits that people's cognitive elements tend to exist in harmony with one another, and when they do not, people are motivated to make cognitive changes to restore harmony. Festinger broadly construed what constitutes a *cognitive element* to include the likes of beliefs, attitudes, commitments, decisions, and (mental representations of) behaviors. The theory's central prediction, that people seek to reduce dissonance (disharmony), was assessed empirically early on with a now classic experiment by Festinger and Carlsmith (1959). The results of the experiment demonstrated a "self-persuasion" phenomenon, which refers to the process of people changing their attitudes in response to their behaviors. Essentially, the researchers found that participants induced to engage in a counterattitudinal behavior but supplied with an insufficient rationale for doing so changed their attitudes in a direction to be more consistent with the behavior. This result produced a considerable number of reactions, both positive (e.g., Zajonc, 1960) and negative (e.g., Chapanis & Chapanis, 1964); on balance, however, the findings of numerous attempted replications supported, with significant limitations, Festinger and Carlsmith's essential claims for cognitive dissonance theory (Brehm & Cohen, 1962; Cooper & Fazio, 1984; Wicklund & Brehm, 1976).

The currently known limitations to cognitive dissonance theory indicate that the dissonance effect (i.e., self-persuasion) occurs when people *freely choose* to engage in the counterattitudinal behavior, they feel *committed* to the behavior, the behavior produces *aversive consequences*, and people feel *personally responsible* for these consequences (Eagly & Chaiken, 1993). Cognitive dissonance theory has evolved through the years and, in its current form, remains a provocative way of thinking about the effects of behaviors on attitudes and, as will be shown later, about other dimension of attitude change.

For recent empirical applications of the theory in social psychology, see, for example, Axsom (1989), Elliot and Devine (1994), Leippe and Eisenstadt (1994), and Losch and Cacioppo (1990); for recent conceptual analyses, see Berkowitz and Devine (1989), Cooper & Scher (1992), and Schlenker (1982).

Another theory concerned with the effects of behaviors on attitudes is Bem's (1965, 1972) *self-perception theory.* Self-perception theory can be thought of as more calculative or mechanical and less emotionally driven than cognitive dissonance theory. Bem argued that people often lack strong or easily interpretable internal cues about their own attitudes. When this is the case, persons may turn to their recent behavior and the situation in which it took place to infer their attitudes. If the individuals see the situation as insufficient to have caused the behavior (e.g., there were no potent rewards evident for engaging in the behavior), then their attitudes are influenced by their perceptions of recent behavior. That is, the persons assume that their attitudes are congruent with their behaviors. Given that a condition for people to infer their attitudes from their behavior is that the attitude in question must be weak or difficult to interpret, Fazio (1987) has observed that self-perception theory may be more salient to understanding attitude formation than attitude change. He also observed, however, that attitudes based on perceptions of one's own behaviors are relatively strong ones. Correspondingly, these attitudes are more accessible from memory (Fazio, Herr, & Olney, 1984) and more predictive of subsequent behaviors (Zanna, Olson, & Fazio, 1981). For recent applications of self-perception theory, see, for instance, Damrad-Frye and Laird (1989) and Olson (1990, 1992).

Aronson (1968, 1969; Thibodeau & Aronson, 1992) suggested that dissonance arousal is a product of some threat to one's self-concept. Steele (e.g., 1988) built on this suggestion in formulating his *self-affirmation theory.* The theory, as described by Eagly and Chaiken (1993), entails viewing the self as a reservoir of self-esteem that is drawn down by the experience of dissonance. Self-justifying attitude change can bring the reservoir back up to a safe level, but so can other self-affirming thoughts—even those not obviously relevant to the circumstances that produced the initial dissonance. Steele's ideas have received some empirical support (e.g., Steele & Liu, 1983; Steele, Spencer, & Lynch, 1993). This presents somewhat of a problem for understanding attitude change processes because self-affirmation theory currently does not specify when self-justifying attitude change occurs as the means for restoring self-esteem.[23]

Also complicating matters is how *impression management* theorists have interpreted dissonance theory research findings (e.g., Tedeschi, Schlenker, &

Bonoma, 1971). Their interpretation emphasizes that what matters is the desire to appear consistent, not the motivation to be consistent. That is, people publicly report a change in their attitudes to give an impression of attitude-behavior consistency (even if their private attitudes remain unchanged). Impression management theorists also argue that rather then moderating their attitudes, people sometimes may give excuses for their behaviors, thus, minimizing their responsibility for the inconsistency.[24] Although impression management has been considered by organizational scientists (e.g., Giacalone & Rosenfeld, 1989), neither it nor self-perception theory nor self-affirmation theory have been pursued systematically to better understand attitude change in or around organizations.

It should be obvious now that the theories I have chosen to present all are alike in that they deal with how an individual might cope with counterattitudinal cognitive elements, broadly defined after Festinger (1957) to include behaviors. Dissonance theory asserts that people can change their attitudes to justify attitude-discrepant behaviors; self-perception theory asserts that change is a product of inferring one's attitudes from one's behaviors; self-affirmation theory asserts that change is motivated by threats to the self-concept; and impression management theory asserts that change is rooted in concern about how the self is seen publicly. Personally, I am not concerned with the relative truth value of these alternatives; rather, I have found that each of them has heuristic value when it comes to thinking about attitude change. I hope that the reader sees the same value. Moreover, I hope that my presentation of these theories, coupled with material that proceeded it in this chapter, has supplied some feel for the variety of ways social psychologists conceptually approach the problem of attitude change. In moving on to consider how people resist attempts to change their attitudes and, therefore, to explain the persistence of attitudes, I will complete my introduction to the social psychological literature on attitude change.

Changing another person's attitudes can be a tough business. This is so for several reasons (some of which were reviewed in my earlier discussion of the functions of attitudes). First, Allport (1935) long ago observed that "attitudes determine for each individual what he will see and hear, what he will think and what he will do" (p. 806). In part, this implies that people tend to approach and attend to information consistent with their attitudes and avoid or pay little attention to inconsistent information (Eagly & Chaiken, 1993). This idea is captured in Festinger's (e.g., 1957) prediction that to reduce dissonance or ensure consonance, people seek out information supportive of their attitudes and avoid information that challenges them. Thus, from a dissonance theory perspective, attitudes persist because of *selective exposure and attention*. According to Frey's (1986) review of the literature, research generally supports this perspective.[25]

Persistence also is a product of *selective perception and judgment*. That is, information is encoded and conclusions are drawn from it in such a way to support currently held attitudes. Support for this idea can be found in a number of streams of research (e.g., Bothwell & Brigham, 1983; Krosnick, 1990; Manis, 1960; Sherif & Hovland, 1961; Vallone, Ross, & Lepper, 1985; Vidmar & Rokeach, 1974; Zanna, Klosson, & Darley, 1976). *Selective memory* also is known to contribute to persistence. Evidence shows that attitude-congruent information is more memorable (Roberts, 1985); presumably, therefore, this stored information is accessed in defense of one's attitudes. In summarizing the evidence on selective exposure, attention, perception, judgment, and memory, Eagly and Chaiken (1993) state, "Attitudes are difficult to alter to the extent they are strong and important. Strong attitudes create biases in information processing—biases that tend to maintain and even to polarize existing attitudes" (p. 621). Below, I provide further evidence in support of this conclusion as alternative theories of resistance to attitude change are considered.

Lumsdaine and Janis (1953) observed that two-sided communications are more effective than one-sided messages in inducing resistance to propaganda and suggested that this is because counterarguments "inoculate" people against later attempts to persuade them. McGuire (1964), in pursuing this explanation, formulated *inoculation theory*. Central to the theory is the assertion that exposure to weak versions of a persuasive argument increases later resistance to that argument. These weak versions, although not strong enough to change attitudes, encourage people to develop defenses against subsequent attacks on their attitudes. McGuire further asserted that attitudes infrequently attacked, therefore, are more vulnerable to persuasive attempts; thus, he saw his theory as particularly germane to what he called *cultural truisms*—widely shared, rarely questioned attitudes. Relatively often, McGuire's ideas have been applied in the design of health education programs (e.g., Chassin, Presson, & Sherman, 1990) and to understanding resistance to negative political advertisement (e.g., Pfau, Kenski, Nitz, & Sorenson, 1990). Moreover, Pratkanis and Aronson (1992) have suggested that ideas such as McGuire's can be used by parents to protect their children from television commercials. Inoculation theory has yet to appear in the organizational literature.[26]

In a sense, McGuire (1964) thought of people as motivated to protect their attitudes. Such motivational thinking also can be seen in Brehm's (e.g., 1966) theory of psychological reactance. Most simply stated, the theory assumes that people want to feel free to hold a particular attitude toward an attitude object (or not to adopt any attitude regarding the object); it posits that high-pressure tactics to get people to adopt a particular attitude may threaten attitudinal freedom. The more important this freedom is to the person and the more persuasive pressure applied, the greater the reactance experienced. *Reactance* is a motivational state to restore a threatened or lost freedom. The greater the experienced reactance, the more the person sticks to his or her initial attitude. Research involving attempts to force people to adopt a particular attitude supports this prediction (e.g., Snyder & Wicklund, 1976; Wicklund & Brehm, 1968; Worchel & Brehm, 1970); impression management researchers have argued, however, that these findings may be a product of people wanting to be seen by others as autonomous (i.e., free and independent; e.g., Heilman & Toffler, 1976).[27] On balance, it does appear that high-pressure tactics are not particularly effective, except in situations involving extreme distress (Sargant, 1957) and a powerful agent of influence (Schein, Schneier, & Barker, 1961), as prisoners of war might experience.

In sum, strong attitudes tend to persist and be resistant to change because change might create cognitive disharmony or threaten the self. Moreover, people often seem quite capable of warding off attacks on their attitudes. Key words in the previous two sentences are *tend* and *often*. As is evident in my portrayal earlier in this section of two routes to persuasion, of the elements in most persuasive situations (i.e., source, message, context, and recipient), and of several theories of attitude change, people's attitudes need not be treated as fixed. The social psychological literature, as I sincerely hope I have demonstrated, speaks loudly and reasonably clearly about the process of attitude change in ways that should provide clues to organizational scientists for better understanding how attitudes do change and can be changed in and around organizations. Our colleagues in marketing, as I have indicated, not only have listened; they have contributed to this body of literature. It is time we do the same, because I cannot imagine someone advancing a plausible argument that understanding the process of attitude change is *un*important to us—yet no body of organizational literature on attitude change exists. Yes, we have showed some concern for the phenomenon, for example, in considering the impact of organizational development efforts (e.g., Golembiewski, Billingsley, & Yeager, 1976). But this piecemeal concern has not and likely will not yield a *fundamental* understanding of attitude change processes in the settings we claim are our territory.

Concluding Remarks

My treatment of the attitude change literature in social psychology is *not* intended to encourage, for example, the testing of this or that social psychology theory in organizations. Social psychology is *not* our business; organizations *are* what we are about. What I have reviewed is intended to stimulate organizational scientists to ask questions they otherwise might not have posed and to pursue solutions to problems in ways they might not have thought of previously. Moreover, some of what I have said does constitute a foundation on which the chapters ahead will be built.

The serious student of the social psychology of attitudes likely will be taken aback by how lightly I touch on some aspects of the literature. But the chapter did open with a warning that what was to come would in no way provide complete or broad coverage. For the topics I did cover, the many references provided should help the reader obtain a more complete picture. For the topics excluded, later chapters will return to the social psychology literature and supply a brief review of a few of these (e.g., stereotypes).

For those who still doubt the utility of the material in this chapter or are really just eager to learn more, I suggest reading Cialdini's (1993) *Influence: Science and Practice* and Pratkanis and Aronson's (1992) *Age of Propaganda: The Everyday Use and Abuse of Persuasion*—and *thinking* organizations. I am sure readers will put them down convinced as well as primed to see the study of attitudes in the organizational sciences through a different lens.

Notes

1. Compilations of definitions are provided, for example by Allport (1935); Campbell (1963); Kiesler, Collins, and Miller (1969); and Smith, Bruner, and White (1956).

2. For an alternative set of results, see, for example, Breckler (1984).

3. For an example of such a classical conditioning process, see Zanna, Kiesler, and Pilkonis, 1970.

4. For more on facial electromyographic activity and attitude research, see, for example, Petty and Cacioppo (1983). In addition, see Cacioppo, Crites, Berntson, and Coles (1993) for an example of measures of electrical activity in the brain used in attitude research.

5. Given my previously stated preference for considering behaviors as criterion variables, I will not address the possible indirect behavioral indicators of attitudes. The interested reader should see Himmelfarb (1993).

6. For more on this point, see, for example, Fazio (1989), Greenwald (1989), and Shavitt (1990).

7. For an alternative to Katz's taxonomy from the same era, see Smith, Bruner, and White (1956). The reader will not find Smith et al.'s three-function taxonomy particularly incongruent with the ideas of Katz reported here.

8. A related idea is that attitude dissimilarity produces interpersonal repulsion (Rosenbaum, 1986).

9. For more on the effects of attitudes on information processing, see, for example, Eagly (1993), Hilton and von Hippel (1990), and Kunda (1990).

10. See Sweeney and Gruber (1984) for data consistent with this speculation.

11. Also see, for example, Abelson (1982) and Dawes and Smith (1985).

12. For reviews of tests of the theory, see, for example, Ajzen and Fishbein (1980) and Fishbein (1980).

13. Also see, for example, Langer (1989) and Triandis (1980).

14. For an additional revision of the theory of reasoned action focusing on goal-oriented behaviors, see Bagozzi and Warshaw (1990).

15. For an alternative view, see Katz and Hass (1988); for discussions of the issue, see, for example, Liberman and Chaiken (1991) and Tesser and Shaffer (1990).

16. For more on McGuire's ideas, see, for example, McGuire (1972) and Eagly and Chaiken (1993).

17. On the modern uses of propaganda, see Pratkanis and Aronson (1992).

18. See Jacoby, Hoyer, and Brief (1992) for a general treatment of the potential contribution of consumer psychology to the organizational sciences.

19. Also see Boller, Swasy, and Munch (1990).

20. For more on the fear appeal literature, see Boster and Mongeau (1984), Eagly and Chaiken (1993), and Gleicher and Petty (1992).

21. Also see Petty, Schumann, Richman, and Strathman (1993).

22. The literature on influence tactics in organizations might represent a minor exception to the observed lack of persuasion research in the organizational literature. See, for example, Kipnis and Schmidt (1988), Yukl and Falbe (1990), and Yukl and Tracey (1992).

23. Nevertheless, I felt it particularly important to raise the theory because, at least in academic settings, interventions consistent with self-affirmation notions have produced impressive improvements in performance (Steele & Aronson, 1995).

24. Also see, for example, Baumeister (1982), Baumeister and Tice (1984), Leary and Kowalski (1990), and Schlenker (1982).

25. For a more complete picture of the evidence, also see Cotton (1985), Freedman and Sears (1965a), and Wicklund and Brehm (1976).

26. Inoculation research might be seen as a subset of that concerned with *forewarning* effects. Forewarning can entail, for example, knowing in advance what position a communicator intends to change in audiences attitudes (Freedman & Sears, 1965b). Presumably, forewarning allows a listener the time to recall and/or come up with evidence and arguments that counter the communicator's position. See Cialdini and Petty (1981), for example, for a review of the literature.

27. Also see Baer, Hinkle, Smith, and Fenton (1980) and Wright and Brehm (1982).

4 Job Satisfaction Redux

Although I like the story that Kuhn (1962) tells about scientific revolutions, I am not sure it applies to the organizational sciences. In part, this is because I really cannot identify such a revolution in our literatures. Perhaps the organizational sciences are just too new a discipline for a paradigm shift to have occurred. Therefore, I am hesitant to predict that we are about to see a revolutionary change in the study of job satisfaction. My aim in this chapter, however, is to make the case that there are clear signs of at least a fresh approach to studying job satisfaction. Moreover, I want to convince the reader that this approach is more than promising; it is downright exciting. Not only is the approach likely to yield new ways of addressing existing questions, but also it may provide a frame of reference that stimulates the asking of research questions not now conceived.

As implied in the above paragraph, the fresh approach I will be introducing is not yet solidified. It now is represented in the organizational literature by a loosely connected set of provocative ideas and empirical findings. I will do more than present a sampling of these ideas and findings. More so than in the preceding chapters, I intend to take the liberty of adopting a speculative posture by advancing positions not wholly defensible now but indicative of what I think we will come to know.

In this chapter, first I will redefine job satisfaction and discuss implications of this alternative construal for measurement. Second, the causes of job satisfaction previously not considered or detailed in the earlier chapter on the construct are presented. Third, different ways of thinking about the consequences of job satisfaction will be explored. Fourth, a further peek at the next wave of job satisfaction research is provided.

Job Satisfaction Redefined

Job satisfaction is "a pleasurable or positive emotional state resulting from the appraisal of one's job or job experiences" (Locke, 1976, p. 1300). This was the working definition of the construct adopted in Chapter 2, in part because it appears to be widely used and consistent with other definitions evident in the organizational literature. Building on the social psychological foundations laid in the preceding chapter, I will offer a redefinition supportive of the aim of framing the fresh approach to studying job satisfaction now beginning to emerge: *Job satisfaction is an internal state that is expressed by affectively and/or cognitively evaluating an experienced job with some degree of favor or disfavor.* The internal state referred to is a tendency that predisposes positive or negative evaluative responses that can be either overt or covert. Behavioral responses are excluded from the definition because they often are considered consequences of job satisfaction. Jobs not experienced are excluded because job satisfaction conventionally is construed as a reaction to a job currently occupied. My definition is not at odds with the ideas recently advanced by Motowidlo (1996), who described the association between expressed job satisfaction (a judgment in his terms, an evaluation in mine) and information stored in memory.[1] Moreover, the definition offered is aimed at the individual level of analysis, but with slight modification, one could define a construct at a higher, collective level of analysis. The necessary modifications include replacing "an internal state" with "a shared internal state" and "an experienced job" with "shared job experiences" and adding a specified level of aggregation (e.g., the group level of analysis).

Adopting the view that job satisfaction entails what people feel *and* think about their jobs, Organ and Near (1985) posed an important methodological question. They asked, do conventional measures of job satisfaction capture both affective and cognitive evaluations? Organ and Near suspected that they did not, that the measures in use were cognitively laden. The only study addressing Organ and Near's question (Brief & Roberson, 1989) generally confirmed their suspicion. Our findings indicated that the Minnesota Satisfaction Questionnaire (Weiss et al., 1967) captured no affect, just cognitions; the Job Descriptive Index (Smith et al., 1969), some positive affect, but mostly cognitions; and the seemingly less used faces scale (e.g., Kunin, 1955), both affect (positive and negative) and cognitions about equally. (The current distinction between positive and negative affect is discussed later in the chapter.) Thus, the study of job satisfaction appears to have been dominated (*unknowingly*) by measures that fail to adequately gauge how people affectively evaluate their jobs. This conclusion is almost shocking given the conventional definition of job satisfaction as an emotional state. Moreover, its implications are particularly troublesome in light of the findings presented in the preceding chapter suggesting that (a) the affective and cognitive components of job satisfaction may be differentially determined (i.e., be a product of different causal influences); (b) the affective and cognitive components of job satisfaction may not necessarily align (e.g., persons' feelings about their jobs may not be indicative of what they think about them); and (c) the affective and cognitive components of job satisfaction may differentially predict the same criterion variable. That is, if we really have been concentrating *empirically* on the cognitive component of job satisfaction, yet *theoretically* we have been concerned with a construct defined as an emotional state, then it is quite possible that with more affectively laden measures we might discover our theories to be stronger than they now appear.

In addition, because most organizational scientists seem to have been blind to the affect-cognitive distinction, a host of potentially interesting questions about job satisfaction have not been posed. For example, are there identifiable aspects of job experiences that influence the affective component but not the cognitive component and vice versa? Or are certain organizationally salient behaviors predicted by the affective component but not the cognitive component and, again, vice versa? (I realize this all may sound a bit too abstract; as the chapter progresses, however, I trust the reader will find "more meat on the bone.")

Given the importance of distinguishing between the affective and cognitive components of job satisfaction and the findings (Brief & Roberson, 1989) indicating that organizational scientists often have been tapping the cognitive dimension while slighting or even excluding the affective one, I will explore how to go about measuring the way persons affectively express feelings about their jobs. Before beginning this exploration, I will review the alternatives raised in the last chapter for getting at the cognitive component of attitudes.

First, Crites, Fabrigar, and Petty's (1994) semantic differential scale, composed of seven word pairs, was developed, in part, to measure the cognitive component of an attitude toward some object. At least some of their word pairs (e.g., *safe/unsafe, beneficial/harmful, valuable/worthless,* and *perfect/imperfect*) might be useful for gauging how individuals cognitively evaluate their job experiences. In addition, assessments of distortions in logical reasoning and judgments of the plausibility of arguments have been used to get at the cognitive component. These measurement strategies reflect the belief that attitudes affect information processing, and, therefore, that these systematic information processing effects can indicate a person's attitudes. This belief is seen clearly in Motowidlo's (1996) theory of individual differences in job satisfaction briefly described in Chapter 2. In presenting his theory, which begins with a cognitive process through which information is sampled from a population of events and conditions in the work environment, Motowidlo recognized the implications of "biased" information processing (including the selective retrieval of information from memory) for measuring job satisfaction. It is hoped that in future works, he will spell out those implications in more detail, specifying the sort of instrumentation that would be consistent with his theoretical position.

In regard to self-reports of the affective component, I can identify two measurement approaches. The difference between the two approaches concerns the relative uniqueness of a job as an attitude object. Simply, a job, unlike many attitude objects such as a politician, is something that is experienced quite intimately. A job is not something evaluated from a distance on the basis of limited or no personal contact; rather, it is something evaluated through repeated, close associations. These characteristics of a job as an attitude object are evident in the second approach to measuring the affective component of job satisfaction I will present. The first approach entails asking persons how they feel about or toward their jobs. Here, an investigator might use the affective word pairs of Crites et al. (1994; e.g., *delightful/sad, happy/annoyed, calm/tense,* and *excited/bored*). The second approach entails asking persons how they feel while experiencing their jobs (e.g., "How have you felt at work during the past week?"). Empirically, I do not know how similar the two approaches may be; I have never seen the first approach reported in the literature. Conceptually, the two approaches are quite dissimilar because the latter can be viewed as a measure of mood at work. Mood at work and the affective component of job satisfaction may be different constructs, but until the first measurement approach has been pursued empirically, I tentatively accept measures of mood at work as at least crudely reflecting the affective component of job satisfaction.

One could argue legitimately with my position because mood is thought of as reasonably variable through time (e.g., Watson, 1988), but so might be the affective component of job satisfaction. We do not know. I was comfortable enough to actually use mood to capture the affective component in an earlier study (Brief & Roberson, 1989). My comfort stemmed from the commonplace measurement of mood in the social psychology literature (e.g., Watson, Clark, & Tellegen, 1988); as noted in the previous chapter, in that literature, measures of the feelings people are experiencing often have been used to index the affective components of attitudes. For instance, Cacioppo and Petty (1981), operating under the assumption that certain physiological responses are linked to emotional processes thought to be triggered by the attitude object under investigation, used a facial electromyograph to gauge attitudes. The Job Affect Scale (JAS; introduced by Brief, Burke, Atieh, Robinson, & Webster, 1988), was relied on in the previously mentioned study (Brief & Roberson). The JAS is composed of 10 clear markers of positive affect and 10 clear markers of negative affect identified by Watson and Tellegen (1985). (See Table 4.1 for the JAS.)[2]

Why did the JAS (Brief et al., 1988) include two sets of items, one to tap positive affect and the other negative affect? We did so because of Watson and Tellegen's (1985) review of the factor analytic research on the structure of self-reported mood in which it was concluded that positive and negative affect emerge as the first two varimax rotated dimensions in common orthogonal factor analyses of self-reported mood. Stated more simply, affective states are best described by two major and independent dimensions, positive and negative affect, rather than a single dimension ranging from negative to positive; considerable empirical evidence supports this description (e.g., Costa & McCrae, 1980; Diener & Emmons, 1984; Meyer & Shack, 1989; Watson, Clark, & Tellegen, 1984; Watson & Pennebaker, 1989; Zevon & Tellegen, 1982). High positive affect signals pleasure engagement (e.g., enthusiasm, elation, and peppiness); high negative affect signals unpleasant engagement (e.g., distress, nervousness, and scornfulness).[3]

I hope that I have shown that the affective component of a person's job satisfaction might be tapped appropriately by measuring mood at work and that such measurement should include two independent dimensions of affect, positive and negative. But how does this thinking apply to a higher level of analysis? Fortunately, we can turn to the research of George (e.g., 1996a) on

TABLE 4.1   Job Affect Scale

Instructions

Below you find a list of words which a person may use to describe one's feelings at work. Using the scale provided, indicate *how you felt at work during the past week.* Please be *open* and *honest* in your responding. Do *not* skip any item.

1	2	3	4	5	6	7
Extremely Slightly	*Fairly Slightly*	*Slightly*	*Moderately*	*Fairly Strongly*	*Strongly*	*Extremely Strongly*

_____ 1. Active
_____ 2. Calm
_____ 3. Distressed
_____ 4. Sleepy
_____ 5. Strong
_____ 6. Excited
_____ 7. Scornful
_____ 8. Hostile
_____ 9. Enthusiastic
_____ 10. Dull
_____ 11. Fearful
_____ 12. Relaxed
_____ 13. Peppy
_____ 14. At rest
_____ 15. Nervous
_____ 16. Drowsy
_____ 17. Elated
_____ 18. Placid
_____ 19. Jittery
_____ 20. Sluggish

SOURCE: Adapted from "Measuring Affect at Work: Confirmatory Analyses of Completing Mood Structures With Conceptual Linkages to Cortical Regulatory Systems," by M. J. Burke, A. P. Brief, J. M. George, L. Roberson, and J. Webster, 1989, *Journal of Personality and Social Psychology, 57,* pp. 1091-1102.

group affective tone for an answer. She defines "group affective tone" as "consistent or homogeneous affective reactions within a group" and states that it "can be described in terms of two dimensions, positive affective tone and negative affective tone" (p. 76). In discussing the measurement of the group-level variable, George emphasizes the importance of ascertaining if individual affective tone is homogeneous within a group (if it is not, of course, group affective tone for the group does not empirically exist) and suggests individual affect can be measured by Watson, Clark, and Tellegen's (1988) PANAS scale or the JAS (with short time frames, e.g., the past week, to avoid inadvertently measuring affect as a trait). (I will have more to say about the trait later.)[4] In total, it seems that if positive and negative affect are indicative of the affective component of job satisfaction, then positive group affective tone and negative group affective tone serve the same purpose for gauging the affective component of job satisfaction at the group level of analysis.

Regrettably, the above discussion of measuring the affective component of job satisfaction must be viewed as speculative. We really do have a lot to learn about the components of job satisfaction and their measurement. If I had to guess, however, I suspect that at some point in the future, mood at work will not be used to capture the affective component because of the likely distinctiveness of the constructs. Nevertheless, once again, I currently am reasonably comfortable in doing so. Part of this comfort, I must admit, is because construing the affective component as mood at work opens a world of opportunity to theorize about the antecedents and consequences of job satisfaction. Below, I sample from this world of opportunity.

Antecedents of the "New" Job Satisfaction

In *An Essay Concerning Human Understanding,* John Locke (1894/1979) refuted the doctrine of innate ideas and, in essence, argued that people know the world only by experience. This argument is related to the view that people judge how satisfied they are with their lives by using some mental calculation to sum their momentary pleasures and pains. Such a view is consistent with a *bottom-up theory* of the psychology of subjective well-being (cf. Diener, 1984). It also is consistent with how organizational scientists generally had approached the antecedents of job satisfaction (up until the mid-1980s, at least). This approach dictates that job satisfaction (either overall or with a particular facet) is a combination of the "pleasures and pains" associated with one's job experiences (either in general or a category of them). Several variants of such "it's the situation" approaches were reviewed in Chapter 2, for example, Hackman and Oldham's (1975) job characteristic model and Salancik and Pfeffer's (1978) ideas about social information processing. The basic notion is that job satisfaction is a product of the events and conditions that people experience on their jobs. For instance, if a person's work is interesting, her pay is fair, her promotional opportunities are good, her supervisor is supportive, and her coworkers are friendly, then a situational approach leads one to predict she is satisfied with her job.

Immanuel Kant (1781/1969) provides on alternative to Locke's argument that nothing is in the mind save what gets there through the senses (Bruner, 1986). In *The Critique of Pure Reason,* Kant asserted that the mind is an instrument of construction. Kant argued that people have certain knowledge, a priori, by having human minds; this knowledge precedes all reasoning. Diener (1984) noted the Kantian view corresponds to what psychologists call a *top-down theory* of subjective well-being. Such a theory holds for example, that there is a general propensity to experience things in a positive way such that "despite circumstances, some individuals seem to be happy people, some unhappy people" (Costa, McCrae, & Norris, 1981, p. 79). Barry Staw and his colleagues (e.g., Staw, Bell, & Clausen, 1986) brought attention to this approach in the organizational sciences and with it much controversy.[5] This so-called dispositional approach to job satisfaction is predicated on the notion that a person's job satisfaction is influenced by an enduring characteristic of the individual (an affective dispositional trait).

Staw and Ross (1985) observed, during 3- and 5-year intervals, significant consistency in job satisfaction when individuals changed both the employer for whom they worked and their occupation.[6] This finding led Staw et al. (1986) to examine the relationship between a measure of affective disposition constructed from participants' responses to a set of affective items completed during adolescence and measures of job satisfaction taken during adulthood. The former predicted the latter surprisingly well (e.g., affective disposition gauged when participants were 15 to 18 years of age was correlated significantly, $r = .35$, $p \le .01$) with a facet measure of satisfaction taken when the participants ranged from about 54 to 62 years of age). I said *surprisingly* because I believe that Staw et al.'s findings were unexpected by the field; as Chapter 2 demonstrated, thinking among organizational scientists was dominated by bottom-up (or situational) approaches to job satisfaction. Along with this one-sided thinking came a general disregard for the role of personality in explaining job satisfaction, a disregard I fortunately will be able to demonstrate is waning.

Staw and his colleagues' (1986) ideas and findings, as was indicated, attracted a lot of attention, much of it negative—because conventional "wisdom" was being questioned. These criticisms (e.g., Davis-Blake & Pfeffer, 1989, 1996; Gerhart, 1987), as I read them, raised three concerns about the dispositional approach to job attitudes. First, some attacks were aimed at a strict interpretation of the dispositional approach, one that advocates job satisfaction is a function *only* of disposition. The problem with this concern is that to my knowledge, no one in the organizational sciences has staked out and sought to defend such a strict interpretation; therefore, the disposition's only position is "straw man." Staw et al. early on recognized the desirability of sorting out the interaction of dispositional traits and job characteristics on job attitudes.[7]

Another criticism of the dispositional approach to job satisfaction has been concerned with ambiguities surrounding the definitions of dispositional constructs and their measurement. Often, these criticisms have been on target. For instance, readers will not find Staw et al. (1986) particularly clear about what they meant by "affective disposition" (p. 60) or about the measure of it they constructed from a subset of "83 personality descriptions" that "appeared to capture some aspect of affect" (pp. 64-65). Moreover, Judge (e.g., 1993; Judge & Bretz, 1993; Judge & Hulin, 1993; Judge & Locke, 1993) has used Weitz's (1952) gripe index or a modification of it to gauge affective disposition. The essential problem I have with the use of the albeit innovative gripe index is that reliance on it ignores the tremendous volume of psychometric and theoretical knowledge organizational scientists could draw on in the personality literature to better understand observed disposition-job attitude relationships. Simply, by relying on appropriate measures of personality with well-known psychometric properties whose nomological networks are reasonably well established, we likely would be better able to explain *why* a particular dispositional variable is found to be associated with job satisfaction. The need for explanation is the third concern that has been voiced about the dispositional approach to job attitudes. More specifically, there has been a call for developing and testing models of job attitudes that include dispositional and situational variables (e.g., House, Shane, & Herold, 1996). It is a call I wholeheartedly endorse and to which I now respond. In doing so, I also will address, by necessity, definitions of specific dispositional constructs.

Arvey, Carter, and Buerkley (1991) provide an informative conceptual analysis of dispositional and situational influences on job satisfaction. They traced the dispositional approach (or what they call *person effect models*) back beyond Staw and Ross (1985), Weitz (1952), and others to as early as 1931. In that year, Fisher and Hanna, on the basis of their study of "the dissatisfied worker," observed, "In as much as his feelings and emotions are inherent aspects of himself, he carries them with him, so to speak, into every situation he enters" (p. 27). Arvey et al.'s treatment of the situational approach covered much of the same material introduced in Chapter 2 (e.g., Hackman & Oldham's [1976] job characteristics model). Regrettably, so did their presentation of person-situation (interactional) approaches, which focused on models emphasizing the importance of person-environment fit in explaining job satisfaction, for example, the theory of work adjustment (e.g., Dawis & Lofquist, 1984). Arvey et al., however, also discussed Schneider's (1987) attraction-selection-attrition (ASA) framework, which has received little empirical attention by job satisfaction researchers. This framework, although obviously in the "fit tradition," specifies that people are attracted to and selected for job environments in which they will fit and tend to leave settings where they do not fit. In addition, Schneider claimed that job environments are a product of the people in them (i.e., "the people make the place"); thereby, he, according to Arvey et al., blurred the distinction between person and situational variables.[8] Although I do not fully accept Arvey et al.'s criticism, the ASA framework does not explicitly address dispositional affect from an interactional perspective.

Perhaps the closest to the sort of treatment I believe is required is offered by Judge, Locke, and Durham (1997). They proposed a *dispositional model of job satisfaction* based on core evaluations individuals make about themselves, the world, and other people. These core evaluations, according to Judge et al., refer to an individual's fundamental (metaphysical) value judgments. One way they see these core evaluations affecting job satisfaction is through their interaction with job characteristics; more specifically, core evaluations are posited to moderate job characteristic-job satisfaction relationships.

Although one day, research based on the Judge et al. (1997) model may prove to be informative, I am concerned, for now, with the dispositional nature of their somewhat ambiguous core evaluations construct and with its distance from a logical focus of attention, affective disposition. I am not arguing that the only dispositional models we should entertain must be affect focused, but at this stage of theoretical development, I do think it makes sense first to conceptually organize the considerable empirical evidence demonstrating an affective disposition-job satisfaction relationship before charging into uncharted waters. The considerable evidence alluded to goes beyond that typically recognized by those interested in a dispositional approach to job satisfaction (e.g., Agho, Price, & Mueller, 1993; Cropanzano, James, & Konovsky, 1993; Gutek & Winter, 1992; Judge & Hulin, 1993; Levin & Stokes, 1989; Necowitz & Roznowski, 1994; Newton & Keenan, 1991; Schaubroeck, Ganster, & Kemmerer, 1996; Watson & Slack, 1993). Several students of job-related distress also have documented affective disposition-job satisfaction relationships in their attempts to explain how disposition affects observed associations between self-reports of stress and strain. (For a review of this research, see Burke, Brief, & George, 1993.)

An Integrated Model

Given that the need remains for alternative models of job satisfaction that include both dispositional and situational variables, I now turn to outlining one such model. The model capitalizes on what already is known about affective disposition and its relationship to job satisfaction. After providing an outline of the model, I present a somewhat detailed description of its dispositional components.

The *integrated model of job satisfaction* draws heavily on the thinking and findings of my earlier work (Brief, Butcher, George, & Link, 1993). In an attempt to reconcile Lockean (bottom-up) and Kantian (top-down) views of subjective well-being, we advanced a simple framework positing that global features of personality *and* an individual's objective life circumstances influence the ways in which the person interprets the circumstances of his or her life; in turn, these interpretations directly influence subjective well-being. My colleagues and I applied our framework by operationalizing personality as negative affectivity (discussed below), objective circumstances of actual health, perceived circumstances of self-rated health, and subjective well-being, for example, of life satisfaction. Using three waves of data collected at 2-year intervals, we obtained strong support for the framework. For instance, the path analytic results indicated significant direct effects of negative affectivity and actual health (both measured in the first wave) on self-rated health (measured in the second wave) (-.37 and .30, respectively) and a significant direct effect of self-rated health on life satisfaction (measured in the third wave; .26). We also observed a significant direct effect of negative affectivity on an alternative indicator of subjective well-being (measured in the third wave), namely, the state of negative affect (.33). That is, we found personality to affect subjective well-being both directly and indirectly.

On the basis of extrapolation from the research discussed above, I posit job satisfaction to be influenced directly by how people interpret their jobs and those interpretations to be influenced by both their personalities and the objective circumstances of their jobs. Moreover, job satisfaction is posited to be influenced directly by personality. The model proposed is depicted graphically in Figure 4.1.

Rather than engaging in a philosophical discussion of what constitutes objectivity, "objective circumstances of a job" simply can be taken to mean facets of the job that exist external to the mind of the job occupant whose job satisfaction is of interest. More pragmatically stated, objective job facets are

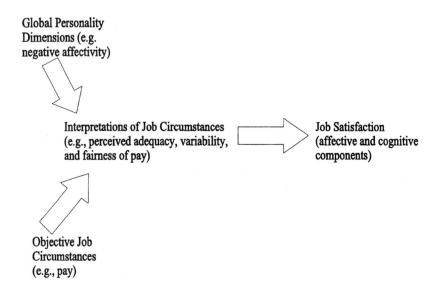

Figure 4.1. An Integrated Model of Job Satisfaction

those whose qualities are not dependent on the focal job occupant's self-reports for verification. Defined in this way, even social cues (Salancik & Pfeffer, 1978) could be taken to be objective job facets. More concretely, these facets might include compensation levels, hours worked, the repetitiveness of tasks performed, the number and quality of social interactions required and permitted, and the status attached to a job. (Recall from Chapter 2, however, that available theory does not adequately guide us to those particular job facets that should be the focus of attention in determining overall job satisfaction.)

Regarding the interpretations component of the model, concern shifts into the mind of the focal job occupant, from the objective to the subjective. That is, "interpreted circumstances of a job" refers to how a person construes or apprehends the objective circumstances of his or her job. (In this way, *interpretations* might be considered in a Kantian sense as phenomena.) In the language of Eagly and Chaiken (1993), interpretations can be thought of as that which is encoded into memory from the stimuli denoting an attitude object (e.g., the job or job facets), and the person's expressed approval or disapproval, favor or disfavor, liking or disliking, approach or avoidance, attraction or aversion, and so on constitute the attitude (job satisfaction) toward the object.[9] Thus, interpretations are descriptive, and the attitudes are affective and cognitive evaluative responses. The line between the two constructs (i.e., descriptions and evaluations) may be a thin one; one day, researchers may learn that the distinction is not warranted. For now, however, it seems reasonable to argue that how people interpret their jobs does precede their affective and cognitive evaluations of them.

The form of interaction posited (i.e., additive or main effects for both personality and the objective circumstances of the job) is only one of several meanings attached to the term *person-situation interaction* in the interactional psychology literature (e.g., Endler & Magnusson, 1976; Magnusson & Endler, 1977; Terborg, 1981). Others include, for example, the person or situation variable being construed as a moderating or mediating variable or the two being reciprocally related through time. Again, the future may hold that the currently posited model requires revision, in this case regarding the form of interaction specified. I would not be surprised, for instance, on the basis of the reasoning underlying Schneider's (1987) ASA framework, that the proposed integrated model of job satisfaction is revised to recognize the effects of personality on objective circumstances of the job. The model I advance here is merely a starting point and, admittedly, a simple and incomplete one. Indeed, I am confident that other exogenous variables could be added and moderators of the relationships depicted specified.

Addressing the concept of trait will begin to shed some light into the model's black box of personality. Trait theorists (e.g., Allport & Allport, 1921; Allport & Odbert, 1936; Cattell, 1943; Cattell & Eber, 1962; Eysenck, 1970, 1990) view traits as the fundamental building blocks of human personality; they construe these traits as broad predispositions to behave, feel, and/or think in particular ways (Pervin & John, 1997). Today, there is an emerging consensus that five robust trait superfactors provide an adequate taxonomy for personality attributes. This taxonomy is referred to as the *Big Five* (e.g., Goldberg, 1981, 1993) or the *Five-Factor Model* (FFM) of personality (e.g., Digman, 1990; McCrae & John, 1992).[10]

One of the most confusing aspects of the FFM is that different authors have attached different labels to the same personality dimensions. Rather than muddle matters here, I will rely on the labels of Costa and McCrae (e.g., 1992), influential advocates of the FFM. The Big Five and characteristics associated with high scorers on Costa and McCrae's (1985, 1992) measures of them are as follows:

1. neuroticism—worrying, nervous, emotional, insecure, inadequate, and hypo-chondriacal
2. extroversion—sociable, active, person-oriented, optimistic, fun-loving, and af-fectionate
3. openness to experience—curious, broad interests, creative, original, imagina-tive, and untraditional
4. agreeableness—soft-hearted, good-natured, trusting, helpful, forgiving, gulli-ble, and straightforward
5. conscientiousness—organized, reliable, hard-working, self-disciplined, punc-tual, scrupulous, neat, ambitious, and preserving

Evidence supportive of the FFM comes in a variety of forms. For example, the five factors show up across languages (e.g., Goldberg, 1990); there is substantial agreement of self-ratings with ratings by peers and spouses on all five factors (e.g., McCrae & Costa, 1990); and measures of the five factors exhibit logical relationships to a variety of motives (e.g., Little, Lecci, & Watkinson, 1992), emotions (e.g., Watson & Clark, 1992), and interpersonal behaviors (e.g., Shaver & Brennan, 1992).[11] Although there is solid support for the longitudinal stability of the Big Five (e.g., Costa & McCrae, 1994), the relationships between the predispositions and behaviors, feelings, and thoughts likely are somewhat less consistent; as recognized even by the pio-neers of trait theories (e.g., Allport, 1937), situations matter, too.[12]

One could perhaps construct plausible arguments for relationships be-tween each of the Big Five and job satisfaction; two of them, however, appear to fit particularly well into the proposed integrated theory of job satisfaction: neuroticism and extroversion. Regrettably, now I feel I must linguistically muddy the waters. The two personality dimensions, more often than not, appear in the literature pertaining to job satisfaction under different labels. Neuroticism is termed *negative affectivity* (NA); extroversion is termed *posi-tive affectivity* (PA). From here on, I will use these affectivity labels.

Individuals high on PA may be further characterized as tending to be engaged in the world around them, to feel good about that engagement, and to feel self-efficacious; in addition, persons with high PA tend to have a sense of overall well-being and, correspondingly, experience positive emotions and moods and perceive stimuli, think, and behave in ways to maintain these positive feelings (e.g., George, 1996b; Tellegen, 1985; Tellegen et al., 1988).

Individuals high on NA can be described as tending to have an overall negative orientation toward themselves and the world around them; they tend to think and act in ways that result in negative affect experiences and are prone to distress through time and across situations (e.g., George, 1996b; Watson & Clark, 1984; Watson & Pennebaker, 1989). Consistent with the FFM, PA and NA are independent dimensions of personality (e.g., Meyer & Shack, 1989). Thus, for example, a person could be high on PA (e.g., disposed to feel enthusiastic and active) and either high (e.g., disposed to feel distressed and hostile) or low (e.g., disposed to feel placid and relaxed) on NA. (Recall, that the *states* of positive and negative affect also were described earlier as independent dimensions.)

Given the above descriptions of PA and NA, one readily can see how these personality traits could influence the ways in which people interpret their worlds and evaluatively respond to those interpretations. In particular, for instance, it is known that individuals with high NA interpret ambiguous stimuli more negatively (e.g., Goodstein, 1954; Haney, 1973; Phares, 1961); in general, they see the world and themselves through a negative lens, thus subjectively evaluating a wide range of *potentially* negative phenomena filtered by a negative interpretive and perceptual orientation (Clark & Watson, 1991).[13] In the integrated model of job satisfaction, one would expect, therefore, that individuals with high NA are biased toward interpreting their job circumstances and evaluatively responding to those interpretations more negatively. For example, holding objective circumstances constant, a researcher could predict that as scores on a measure of NA increase, self-reports of working long hours, performing repetitive tasks, and having troublesome interactions with others (e.g., superiors, coworkers, subordinates, and customers or clients) increase and job satisfaction decreases.

Consistent with such predictions, Watson and Slack (1993), for example, observed that measures of PA and NA were related significantly with a measure of satisfaction with the work itself taken on average 2 years after the personality dimensions were gauged; these relationships held even after statistically controlling for such objective job circumstances as *Dictionary of Job Titles*-based ratings of substantive job complexity (Roos & Treiman, 1980). The researchers used the Minnesota Satisfaction Questionnaire (Weiss et al., 1967) to measure job satisfaction. Evidence previously reviewed indicates that the MSQ does not adequately tap the affective components of the attitude construct (Brief & Roberson, 1989); given the affective nature of PA and NA, I suspect that if Watson and Slack had used a measure of job satisfaction more affectively and cognitively balanced or gauged mood at work to capture the affective components, their results would have been even more impressive.

A more balanced measure of job satisfaction, a modified version of Kunin's (1955) faces scale, was used in a field experiment examining the relationship between NA and job satisfaction (Brief, Butcher, & Roberson, 1995). Employees of a hospital participating in an attitude survey were randomly assigned to either an experimental or a control condition. In the experimental condition, the employees, on arrival at the survey administration site, received cookies, soft drinks, and small, attractively gift-wrapped windup toys prior to completing a questionnaire containing a measure of NA and the faces scale. In the control condition, the survey merely was administered. Following the lead, for example, of Isen and Levin (1972), we construed the experimental manipulations as constituting a positive mood-inducing event; we predicted that this event would positively affect job satisfaction. We also predicted that NA would be negatively correlated with job satisfaction and would interact with the positive affective event. The nature of the predicted interaction was such that the effect of the positive affective event would be weaker among individuals with high NA than it would be among individuals with low NA. Results provided strong support for all three hypotheses. The observed interaction effect was attributed to (a) high NAs having a higher threshold for positive stimuli (i.e., they are less sensitive to positive events); (b) high NAs having a lower-magnitude positive mood reaction to positive events (i.e., they may react with less-positive moods); or (c) the effects of positive mood inductions wearing off more quickly among high rather than low NAs. Whatever the underlying process, the findings are consistent with the integrated model of job satisfaction advanced here.

Also supportive of an integrative model are the ideas about affective events offered by Weiss and Cropanzano (1996). These ideas constitute their *affective effects theory* (AET). Fundamental to AET is the recognition that affect levels fluctuate through time and that a person's pattern of affective experiences is influenced by both endogenous and exogenous factors. According to AET, endogenous factors include, for example, affective disposition (e.g., NA); exogenous factors include, for example, affectively relevant events that constitute shocks to existing patterns. The probability of these events (real or imagined) is portrayed in the theory as a product of work environments. Thus, Weiss and Cropanzano posited that work environment features directly influence work events; these events, along with dispositions, directly influence affective reactions. They also posited that dispositions moderate work events-affective reaction relationships. Regarding job satisfaction, Weiss and Cropanzano proposed that affective reactions, along with work environment features, directly influence work attitudes. The developers of the AET provided rather detailed rationales for each of these propositions.

The AET differs from the model shown in Figure 4.1 in at least two potentially important ways. First, AET admirably emphasizes the pattern of affective experiences, and the integrative model I have advanced here is more simplified and does not. Second, AET distinguishes between affective reactions and work attitudes, and my model does not, fully embracing the two-component (affective and cognitive) view of attitude structure. The ultimate importance of these differences for understanding job satisfaction is not now known. I would be happy if either—or better, both—theoretical approaches were to fuel empirical research in the near future. What is important is an integration of person- and situation-centered thinking that provides a distinct role for affect.

Given that mood at work is a likely indicator of the affective component of job satisfaction, my earlier theorizing (George & Brief, 1992) supplies a final example of the evidence supportive of an integrative model of job satisfaction. We addressed the antecedents of positive mood at work stemming from multiple levels of analysis. At the individual level, we specified affective disposition in the form of PA and life event history as antecedents. The treatment of life events encompassed both work-related *and* non-work-related occurrences. Thus, the perspective on events extends the territory covered thus far by recognizing that what happens to people away from work may affect their job satisfaction. We suggested, for instance, that getting married (presumably a positive non-work-related event) will positively affect positive mood at work.

Regarding work-related events and following the lead of Isen, Daubman, and Nowicki (1987), we (George & Brief, 1992) suggested that occurrences that positively reflect on a worker's competence, worth, and achievement promote positive mood at work. At the group level, we asserted that a person's mood at work is influenced by the affective tone of his or her primary work group. This implies that being a member of a group whose other members are satisfied with their jobs positively affects the individual's job satisfaction. Moreover, we argued that group affective tone is enhanced by relatively small group size, reasonably close proximity of members, the group leader's positive affect, the similarity of group members, and the dispositional composition of the group in the characteristic level of PA. Although we reviewed considerable evidence in support of these assertions, too much of it is indirect; therefore, research directly examining the antecedents of group affective tone (a component of job satisfaction at the group level of analysis) sorely is needed. We went on to assert that positive mood at work also is affected by contextual characteristics, described as relatively mundane and commonplace environmental factors. These include, for example, lighting (e.g., Oldham & Rotchford, 1983) and even the scent in the air (e.g., Baron, 1990). Finally, we argued that a variety of organizational rewards (e.g., money, recognition, and fringe benefits) affect positive mood at work. This argument is consistent with results from the social psychology literature showing that even amazingly small positive outcomes can influence mood (e.g., Isen & Levin, 1972).

The above ideas (George & Brief, 1992; Weiss & Cropanzano, 1996) as well as the empirical findings (Brief et al., 1995; Watson & Slack, 1993) all support an integrative model of job satisfaction. Once again, which particular set of ideas is pursued is considerably less important than generally heating up the pursuit of understandings of job satisfaction that entail an appreciation of the affective and cognitive components of the variable and of the influences of both person and situation factors. Will we as organizational scientists continue to define job satisfaction as an affective reaction yet mostly tap its cognitive content? Will we continue to pit situational models against dispositional approaches? I really do not think so. I truly believe we are seeing the beginning of a revolution in the study of job satisfaction, one that reflects the ideas reviewed here. Of course, where that revolution will lead us, I do not know. But I am confident, however, that both the process and outcomes of this learning will be exciting, generating answers to questions not now posed. Below, I close this section by speculating about what the future might hold for the research on the antecedents of job satisfaction.

Feeling enthusiastic, elated, and peppy at work has been argued to be indicative of being satisfied with one's job (at least in the positive affective component). This sort of job satisfaction is a product of who the person is (e.g., level of PA) and what the person experiences at work (e.g., positive mood-inducing events experienced on the job). Pragmatically, this might imply, to enhance job satisfaction, selecting workers high in PA. It also may imply managerial efforts aimed at producing positive mood-inducing events. One way to accomplish this is by injecting humor into the workplace. But few organizational scientists have taken humor seriously (e.g., Avolio, Howell, & Sosik, 1996; Baron, 1993; Duncan, 1982; Roy, 1960). I suspect that may change. What if we found that managers who keep their employees laughing keep them satisfied with their jobs? Such a result is consistent with a story told to me by a doctoral student who supplemented his meager university stipend by working as a waiter on the weekends. The manager at the restaurant where he worked always held a meeting with the wait staff prior to the dinner onslaught. The manager closed these meetings with a joke or by doing something comical. The student described the restaurant as a fun place to work. Did the manager's comic efforts really promote job satisfaction? And, as he hoped, did that job satisfaction translate into improved customer service? The latter question will be addressed in a future chapter. For now, I hope readers will take humor a bit more seriously as an antecedent of a "newly" conceived job satisfaction.

Some Consequences of the "New" Job Satisfaction

It should now be obvious that a substantial body of organizational literature does not surround how I believe job satisfaction ought to be construed and operationalized. Thus, in addressing the consequences of the new job satisfaction, little direct evidence in support of the propositions offered will be found. Moreover, in the discussion to come, the reasoning used will be laden heavily with affect, emphasizing the affective, rather than the cognitive, component of job satisfaction for two reasons. First, because of my research experience, I am more comfortable relying on affective- rather than cognitive-driven arguments. Second, and fortunately, given that often used measures of job satisfaction primarily or exclusively tap the cognitive component (Brief & Roberson, 1989), one could view the empirical literature on the consequences reviewed in Chapter 2 as cognitively laden, thus justifying the current emphasis.

I begin with the question perhaps of most interest to organizational scientists: How might the new job satisfaction be related to *task performance* at the individual level of analysis? I doubt that my answer, however, will be particularly appealing to many. I am not aware of any compelling argument for *generally* expecting job satisfaction to be predictive of task performance, defined as the proficiency with which people perform activities that are formally recognized as part of their jobs (Borman & Motowidlo, 1993). (This statement does not imply that such arguments will not one day be advanced.) One *can* speculate, however, that the strength of the job satisfaction-task performance relationship is a function of the degree to which the component of job satisfaction operationalized *matches* the types of job activities performed by the individual whose proficiency is being judged. This assertion is consistent with the flavor of some of the ideas introduced in the preceding chapter (e.g., those of Abelson et al., 1982, suggesting that the different components of an attitude differentially predict the same criterion variable); they imply, for example, that for jobs entailing activities requiring the display of positive affect, one could argue that the positive affective component of job satisfaction is predictive of task performance. Given positive mood at work as an indicator of the positive affective component, George (1991) provides support for this implication. She found that the positive moods experienced by salespeople at work were significantly and positively related to their performance of customer service behaviors.

As indicated above, a future chapter will be devoted largely to attitudes in service encounters; for now, I will not detail further the logic for expecting the positive affective component to predict task performance entailing the display of positive emotions. Rather, I return to the general case. Advances in understanding job satisfaction-task performance relationships at the individual level of analysis likely are to come from a more microapproach to the problem. Instead of thinking about the job satisfaction-task performance relationship per se, it probably will prove to be more productive to begin thinking about the job activities performed as which, if any, of them might be linked conceptually to particular components of job satisfaction. I suspect that measures of the affective (positive and negative) and cognitive components of job satisfaction likely will *not* be observed to be related consistently to task performance across jobs. Again, the magnitude of any given observed relationship is expected to be a function of the *match* between the component investigated and the job activities performed.

A lot of theoretical work lies ahead in developing the sort of micropredictions that have been offered here. For instance, there is a need to construct a framework for analyzing jobs for their potential relevancy to the different attitudinal components of job satisfaction. At least in regard to the positive affective components, reviews such as Isen and Baron's (1991) will prove valuable in tackling this assignment. Their review of positive affect as a factor in organizational behavior suggests, for example, that the positive affective component predicts task performance for individuals whose jobs entail performing activities characterized as creative (see, e.g., Isen et al., 1987).

Regarding the relationships between the components of job satisfaction and task performance, it may also be informative to examine a recent treatment (George & Brief, 1996) of the effects of feelings on work motivation. Our conclusions, based on selectively reviewing and reflecting on the literatures pertaining to moods, cognitions, and motivation, suggest a picture somewhat different from the one presented in the previous paragraph. Our conclusions, in part, suggest that favorable job attitudes in the positive affective component of job satisfaction should facilitate the initial involvement, interest, and enthusiasm for job activities, and that once workers are engaged in the process of performing those activities, these favorable attitudes also should enhance persistence. Thus, one can see the basis for an argument for a consistent relationship between the positive affective component of job satisfaction and task performance across jobs. But we appropriately observed that "the dynamic nature of performing a task, of experiencing feelings . . . make the construction of generalizable predictions remarkably complex" (p. 98). Nevertheless, the suggestions for understanding the effect of the positive affective component on task performance that follow from the study's conclusions may be on target.

Therefore, the question arises, are these effects of the components of job satisfaction constant across jobs, or are they influenced by the concept of match discussed above? My hunch is that the truth may lie somewhere in between. That is, consistent with suggestions drawn from the study, the positive affective component of job satisfaction may enhance work motivation, which, in turn, may positively influence task performance through effort. But given the complexity of their casual chain, an observed correlation between the positive affective component and task performance likely would be quite modest, at best. Moreover, consistent with the match concept, that observed correlation, however, probably would be considerably stronger among individuals whose jobs entail activities relevant to the attitude component investigated (e.g., the display of positive emotions for the positive affective component).[14]

Before leaving task performance behind, I will briefly address the effects of personality (i.e., PA and NA). There is some indication that PA is related positively to task performance and NA negatively and rather more weakly (Barrick & Mount, 1991; George, 1996b; Tett, Jackson, & Rothstein, 1991).[15] In a manner consistent with an integrated model of job satisfaction, it is quite plausible that some of these personality effects occur through the affective components of job satisfaction (positive and negative). There is a need to assess empirically this possibility because it may shed light on why and how personality affects task performance. In doing so, situational factors also ought to be taken into consideration; Murtha, Kanfer, and Ackerman's (1996) ideas about an interactionist taxonomy of personality and situations may prove to be helpful in these endeavors. These researchers, in part, were concerned with the effects of situational differences on trait self-reports and the implications of such effects for trait-behavior predictions.

Although explorations of the influence of the new job satisfaction on task performance clearly are promising, the real action likely will be in studying *contextual performance* as a consequence. As noted in Chapter 2, contextual performance, or the contributions people make to a work environment supportive of task performance (Borman & Motowidlo, 1993), is conceptually packaged under a variety of labels. For instance, I have referred to it as *organizational spontaneity* (George & Brief, 1992), shortening Katz's (1964) *spontaneous and innovative behaviors* label. Drawing considerably from the social psychology literature concerned with prosocial behavior (e.g., Carlson, Charlin, & Miller, 1988; Isen & Levin, 1972; Levin & Isen, 1975), we (George & Brief) argued that positive mood at work fosters or facilitates, for example, helping coworkers, a form of contextual performance. We went on to assert that observed job satisfaction-prosocial behavior relationships in work contexts (e.g., Motowidlo, Packard, & Manning, 1986; Puffer, 1987; Scholl, Cooper, & McKenna, 1987) are consistent with their reasoning. These findings, as well as our application of the social psychological literature, lead to the expectation that the positive affective component of job satisfaction should be particularly important for understanding the variance in contextual performance across individuals. The individual who reports feeling enthusiastic, excited, and peppy at work (i.e., one whose mood at work indicates favorable job attitudes in the positive affective component of job satisfaction) would be expected to exhibit a higher level of contextual performance than the individual reporting that he or she feels dull and sluggish at work. This expectation may be attributed, for example, to people seeking to maintain their positive affect through helping others (e.g., Carlson et al., 1988) or to the association of experienced positive affect with finding others more interpersonally attractive (e.g., Gouaux, 1971); the more attractive a potential recipient, the more one is likely to help him or her (e.g., Gross, Wallston, & Piliavin, 1975).

It should be clear that the previous discussion of boosting the positive affect com ponent of job satisfaction (e.g., by taking humor seriously) may be managerially relevant to enhancing contextual performance. Indeed, we probably now know enough to justify a field study (experimental or quasi-experimental) to assess the effects of an intervention intended to boost the affective component of job satisfaction on contextual performance. As suggested in Chapter 2 and further addressed below, such a study probably would be especially informative if conducted at a unit of analysis above the individual level.

Group affective tone (i.e., the consistent or homogeneous affective reactions within a group; George, 1990) was asserted earlier to be an indicator of the affective component of job satisfaction at the group level of analysis; it has been linked conceptually and empirically to prosocial behaviors performed by a group. As noted above, these prosocial behaviors may come in a form that contributes to contextual performance (e.g., members of a work group voluntarily helping one another). George (1996a) reasoned simply that the more favorable the affective tone of a group, the more likely the group is to engage in prosocial behaviors because the work setting will be attractive to group members and, thereby, will foster positive behaviors. Empirically, her research findings generally are supportive of this reasoning (George, 1990, 1995). Thus, it seems quite advantageous to pursue an affective component of job satisfaction-contextual performance relationship *at the group level of analysis.*

I have no problem making the same assertion for units of analysis above the group level.[16] An organization's (or subunit's) policies, practices, procedures, and so on can be thought of as generally being applied to everyone in the organization (or subunit) and, thereby, producing relatively homogeneous affective reactions, leading to relatively homogeneous contextual performance. Employees of an organization who typically report feeling enthusiastic, excited, and peppy at work would be expected to make more contributions to an environment supportive of task performance than the employees of an organization who typically report feeling dull and sluggish at work, *and* the contributions of the former organization's employees should result in its being more effective. If this scenario is in any way correct, then it becomes imperative to identify *organizational* policies, practices, procedures, and so on that positively affect the affective components of job satisfaction at the organizational level of analysis.[17]

Recently, Ryan, Schmit, and Johnson (1996) investigated attitude-effectiveness relationships at the organizational level of analysis, producing a mixed set of findings, with some attitudes, but not others, found to be related to some indicators of organizational performance. In discussing their findings, Ryan et al. admirably stated,

> The theoretical underpinnings of this study were not strong. The literature suggest there are "effects" on performance at the group or unit level that are influenced by employee attitudes. Such effects might be unit norms, organizational citizenship behaviors on the part of unit members, and perhaps the level of contextual performance evidenced. Further theoretical development is needed to understand why attitudes relate to organizational effectiveness at the unit level. (p. 877)

Some of the ideas advanced here should help fuel this needed theoretical development; in particular, it may be helpful to reconsider possible linkages between attitudes and performance at the organizational level of analysis through the lens of the new job satisfaction concept—especially its affective components and their likely correlates. Questions to pursue include these: What about a work context leads those employed in it to affectively express a favorable evaluation of the setting? What specific employee behaviors might be associated with such collective positive affect? How might these employee behaviors collectively influence particular indicators of organizational effectiveness?

More than a decade ago, Schneider (1984) observed

> that while no meaningful relationship between individual satisfaction and individual productivity may exist, the relationship between an aggregate of employees and various aggregate outcomes can be clearly demonstrated (Beer, 1980; Katz & Kahn, 1978). Unfortunately, few direct utility analyses of the importance of job satisfaction have been reported. (p. 197)

Although some of the studies that have been cited temper his observation, it still rings true to me today.[18] Schneider went on to say that "satisfaction does appear to be reflected in smoother organizational functioning and less absenteeism, turnover" (p. 198). Regarding the withdrawal behaviors he noted, it seems reasonable that the lower the rates of absenteeism and turnover an organization experiences, the more productive it should be in its ratio of product or service output to its labor costs.

Now, I turn to plausible relationships between the new job satisfaction and *withdrawal behaviors.* Continuing with the supposition that positive mood at work is an indicator of the positive affective component of job satisfaction, George's (1989) research once more comes back into the spotlight. She found positive affect at work to be associated negatively with absenteeism and explained this finding using Clark and Isen's (1982) mood maintenance hypothesis previously mentioned. This hypothesis asserts that people consciously strive to experience and maintain positive mood states. Thus, workers who experience positive moods at work should be motivated to attend to maintain their satisfaction level, but those who do not feel active, enthusiastic, elated, and so on at work should be motivated to seek satisfaction elsewhere and, therefore, be more absent from work.

This reasoning was supported by a recent study (Dietz, Brief, Hayes, Callahan, & McCline, 1997) that replicated George's results. Moreover, the study found the dispositional trait, positive affectivity, to moderate the positive mood at work-absenteeism relationship such that it was stronger (i.e., more nega-tive) among low-PA workers than among high-PA workers. Dietz et al. ex-plained this finding by reasoning that because persons with low PA are less likely to experience positive affect across settings (e.g., home and work; Watson & Slack, 1993), they are particularly dependent on those settings in which they experience positive affect to maintain a positive feeling state. Therefore, if persons with low PA experience positive affect at work, they are particularly likely to attend. This would not be so among persons with high PA because they could choose among settings to maintain their positive moods.[19]

It seems reasonable to extend George's (1989) thinking to the problem of *turnover* (see George, 1996b) and perhaps to some forms of *organizational commitment*. Perhaps the positive affective component of job satisfaction is negatively related to turnover and positively related to affective commitment. The rationale for the former relationship appears rather straightforward; the more people experience positive feelings on their jobs, the less likely they are to voluntarily leave them. The positive mood at work-affective commitment relationship is a bit more intriguing. As defined in Chapter 2, *affective com-mitment* refers to identification with, involvement in, and emotional attach-ment to an organization (e.g., Allen & Meyer, 1990; Meyer & Allen, 1991). This form of commitment, presumably entailing an emotional attachment, may be a product of the feelings (e.g., elation and enthusiasm) experienced while on the job. Empirical evidence suggests this is so (Cropanzano et al., 1993; Reilly & Orsak, 1991).

These same studies also suggest that positive mood at work may not be associated with an alternative form of commitment. That form is *continuance commitment,* which is based on an employee's cognitive assessment of the costs associated with leaving an organization (e.g., Allen & Meyer, 1990). This form of commitment might be more closely related to the cognitive compo-nent of job satisfaction because both constructs entail thoughts (evaluative on the one hand, judgmental on the other) that one might presume are subject to pressures that lead to consistency (see, e.g., Festinger, 1957).

There is some indication that the affective components of job satisfaction also influence withdrawal behaviors at aggregate levels of analysis. George (1990) found positive affective tone related negatively and negative affective tone related positively to group absence rates. In regard to high positive affective tone, she reasoned this was because people enjoy being in a group whose members are nice to each other, are likely to laugh and display other signs of positive feelings, and generally are more pleasant to be around;

conversely, high negative affective tone may lead to withdrawal because the group members, rather than interacting with pleasant others, are surrounded by people who are feeling bad and have a negative outlook (George, 1996a).

Consistent with George's (e.g., 1996a) descriptions of the consequences of groups' affectively expressing their job satisfaction are studies by Baron (e.g., 1974; Baron & Ball, 1974). The findings of this research suggest that humor and the pleasant feelings it generates are incompatible with anger and overt aggression. (Recall the earlier mention in this chapter of humor in the work-place as a means of positively influencing the affective component of job satisfaction.) Thus, shared positive feelings at work ought to be associated with a less hostile social climate in work groups and organizations. A payoff for such a climate should be "smoother organizational functioning" (Schneider, 1984, p. 198); indeed, in another series of studies, Baron and others (e.g., Baron, 1984; Baron, Fortin, Frei, Hauvner, & Shack, 1990; Carnevale & Isen, 1986) have produced results indicating this is probably so. Specifically, it appears that inducing positive affect (for example, through exposure to humorous materials) encourages the adoption of *constructive approaches to conflict resolution* (collaboration) while discouraging less desirable means of dealing with disagreements (avoidance and direct competition).[20] If one assumes that when organizational members seek to resolve disagreements through collaboration, rather than, for instance, threatening one another, the organization does function more smoothly, making the leap to the claim that positive affective tone contributes to organizational performance does not seem particularly risky. Once again, we see that construing job satisfaction as its component structure leads to viewing the satisfaction-performance relationship from a new perspective, or at least one not currently emphasized in the organizational literature.

Staw (1991) and Staw and Sutton (1993) asserted, not inconsistently with the above ideas, that the psychology of powerful organizational members plays a central role in explaining behavior at the organizational level of analysis. Support for this assertion is readily available (e.g., Kets de Vries & Miller, 1986; Miller & Dröge, 1986; Schein, 1983). Here, I argue that the psychology of powerful organizational members, in the form of their job satisfaction, is an important but largely unrecognized factor in influencing organizational (or subunit) functioning. Imagine two leaders, one satisfied with her job and the other not. The satisfied leader feels peppy, enthusiastic, and active at work; the other feels sluggish, dull, and sleepy. Further imagine how these two leaders might differentially affect their subordinates. My hunch is that the list of the consequences for subordinates is quite extensive. Therein lies a problem with the current literature. As of now, few consequences of leader affect have been investigated. We do know, however, for instance, that positive leader affect is associated positively with lower levels of subordinate turnover (George & Bettenhausen, 1990) and, in retail settings, with subordinates supplying higher levels of customer service (George, 1995).

Staw and Sutton's (1993) discussion of *macro organizational psychology* suggests another potential consequence of the new job satisfaction to be considered. More precisely, this final consequence to be considered in this section stems from the notion of person (really people in this case)-organization fit, with the people variable being affective tone, as an indicator of the positive affective component of collective job satisfaction, and the organization variable being *display rules,* the feelings the organization deems ought to be expressed by its employees (Hochschild, 1979, 1983).

Take the case of a hospital whose staff is expected to smile at and otherwise act pleasantly toward patients and their families. If that staff's collective job satisfaction is high (in positive affective tone), then one could argue there is a fit between what is expected of them, the display rules, and how they feel toward their jobs. As Staw and Sutton (1993) note, this is because "smiling at and helping others comes more naturally to people in positive moods" (p. 365).

Given such a fit, one could argue further that the display rules would be adhered to more closely than in the case of a misfit between the rules and collective job satisfaction. This misfit could take a number of forms; for instance, an organization might expect positive feeling to be displayed, but its workforce's collective job satisfaction is low in regard to the positive affective component, the negative affective component, and/or, the cognitive component. Are the consequences of the different forms of misfit the same? I suspect not; my suspicion, however, is based largely on intuition, rather than theory and research. I hope that this is only a temporary state of affairs (i.e., that relevant theory and findings will be forthcoming).

In sum, the above discussion of the potential consequences of the new job satisfaction largely stemmed from a recognition of the component structure of the attitude construct conceived of at individual and higher levels of analysis. In particular, I focused on the positive affective component, on the basis of the commonly accepted notion in social psychology that feelings experienced in reaction to an object are indicative of a person's attitude toward that object. I did not have much to say about the negative affective or cognitive components. Speculations regarding their potential effects largely have been left up to others. On the consequent or dependent variable side, I covered mostly familiar territory (e.g., various types of performance and withdrawal). As the following section suggests, however, I anticipate that once organizational scientists begin thinking about job satisfaction in the ways described here, potential consequences that have yet to enter the literature or my mind will surface and capture the attention of the field.

The Next Wave

In this concluding section of the chapter, I intend to continue to take liberties with what we know and to speculate about the directions the study of job satisfaction might take. Here, my speculations will take the form of research questions not yet raised but suggested by viewing job satisfaction as an attitude. What follows, therefore, is influenced by the social psychology literature reviewed in Chapter 2 and not yet adequately capitalized on in the preceding sections. The rationale for the questions to be posed often is thin, typically relying only on the relevant citations in social psychology. My goal is to entice, not to argue truth value. Again, I am posing questions awaiting answers.

1. When does job satisfaction come into the conscious mind of an individual or group of workers?[21] Do people, merely on encountering the attitude object (e.g., on arriving at work), think about their job satisfaction? Or does some other sort of event trigger such thoughts? If it is other-event driven, what types of "happenings" serve as the stimulus conditions? These types of questions may be particularly important given that people (perhaps groups, too) have limited cognitive resources (e.g., Kahneman, 1973; Kanfer & Ackerman, 1989); the effects of job satisfaction may vary, depending on whether it is a focus of cognitive attention or remains stored in memory.[22]

2. Can people be ambivalent in regard to their job satisfaction? If so, what is the nature of the ambivalence? *Ambivalence* here refers to a person inconsistently evaluating his or her job. On the basis of the prior descriptions of the components of job satisfaction, I suspect ambivalent job attitudes are far from rare; understanding such inconsistency may go a long way toward explaining when overall job attitudes do and do not predict organizationally relevant behaviors. For instance, increased ambivalence is associated with lower attitude stability (Vallacher, Nowak, & Kaufman, 1994), and lack of stability may

explain the failure to predict behaviors from the attitude. At the group level of analysis and above, ambivalence may be indicated by the failure to demonstrate an adequate degree of interrater agreement to justify the computation of, for example, a group affective tone score. The need to understand the conditions under which such failures occur leads to another set of research questions to be pursued.[23]

3. Although previously raised, the following is well worth restating: How might one go about measuring the affective and cognitive components of job satisfaction? The origins and consequences of these different evaluative responses likely are quite different.[24]

4. How might the values of an organization affect the job satisfaction of the individuals and groups contained in it? Although the utility of the organizational values construct has been demonstrated from the perspective of person-organization fit (e.g., O'Reilly, Chatman, & Caldwell, 1991), the direct role of the construct in shaping job attitudes remains to be explored in detail. I hope, for instance, that the members of an organization emphasizing such instrumental values (e.g., Rokeach, 1973) as sincerity, truthfulness, and working for the welfare of others would evidence higher levels of job satisfaction compared with the members of organizations whose value profile is void of these elements.[25]

5. Do persons' organizational commitments affect how they process information pertinent to their job satisfaction? Perhaps highly committed organizational members interpret pertinent information in biased ways such that their job satisfaction is enhanced. Conversely, less committed members may process the same information in ways that their job satisfaction is reduced. If this is so, does the effect hold across different dimensions of organizational commitment (e.g., affective and continuance) in combination with different components of job satisfaction (e.g., affective and cognitive)? The answers to such questions are relevant to understanding how job satisfaction levels change in organizations. Pragmatically, we might learn that organizational commitment inoculates job satisfaction against the delivery of bad news.[26]

6. Is the observed positive relationship between organizational tenure and job satisfaction (e.g., Bedeian, Ferris, & Kacmar, 1992) a product of people choosing to stay longer on jobs they like and/or of repeated exposure to the jobs (i.e., longer tenure) promoting higher levels of satisfaction? Organizational scientists have devoted an enormous amount of attention to job satisfaction's contribution to turnover but ignored the possibility of a somewhat reverse association—mere exposure to a job increases liking for it. Moreland

and Beach (1992) have demonstrated that among college students, class attendance promotes positive attitudes toward the class. Might the same hold true for the workplace?

7. Do attempts aimed at changing job satisfaction vary in their effectiveness across the culture in which organizations are embedded? Cultures can be distinguished from one another along a collectivist-individualist dimension (e.g., Erez & Earley, 1993; Markus & Kitayama, 1991; Triandis, 1994). Collectivist cultures emphasize harmony, conformity, obedience, reliability, and interdependence, whereas the normative imperative in individualistic cultures is to become independent from others, to be self-reliant, and to discover and express one's unique attributes. Hofstede (1984) argued that in collectivist cultures, job attributes associated with prestige, harmony, serving a larger collective, and allowing one to save face and avoid shame are particularly important; in individualist cultures, the salient attributes are recognition for personal accomplishments, serving the self, and avoidance of guilt. Thus, a message from management, for example, emphasizing serving a larger collective may have a more positive effect on job satisfaction in an East Asian (collectivist) culture than in a North American (individualist) one.[27]

8. How might one go about measuring the attitude strength of job satisfaction? Such attitudinal qualities as certainty, centrality, clarity, and confidence have been conceptualized as equivalent to or indicators of *attitude strength* (e.g., Raden, 1985). Gauging the attitude strength of job satisfaction is potentially important because it often has been found to moderate attitude-behavior relationships (Petty & Krosnick, 1995). Therefore, historically weak relationships (e.g., between job satisfaction and task performance) may be considerably stronger among those individuals who, for instance, are highly confident in their evaluations of their job experiences. This implies that some people may actually report they are not sure how much they like or dislike their jobs. Indeed, a response alternative of the Job Descriptive Index (Smith et al., 1969) is "?" (cannot decide). Perhaps these responses to JDI items are indicative of attitude strength (and not job satisfaction) and, thus, may moderate such relationships as the one between job satisfaction and task performance.

9. Is the relationship between job satisfaction and salient organizational behaviors weaker among those individuals relatively dependent on social cues to regulate their behaviors? The theorizing of Deci and Ryan (e.g., 1985) suggests this is so. They propose that people particularly sensitive to external cues have only a limited awareness of their needs and feelings, with the

consequence being a lack of congruence among their behaviors, thoughts, and feelings. Perhaps a somewhat related but more interesting question in light of Salancik and Pfeffer's (1978) social information processing model is the following: Is the relationship between job satisfaction and salient organizational behaviors weaker among individuals embedded in work environments in which the social cues are consistent rather than in work environments in which the cues constitute a mixed message? I could go one step further by posing another question entailing a potential interaction effect of person (sensitivity to external cues) by environment (consistency of cues) on the attitude-behavior relationship. I trust, however, the reader sees the potential line of questioning and its likely import.[28]

10. When might job satisfaction, at any given level of analysis, serve a value expressive function? Such value expressive attitudes communicate important values and/or seek social approval. Regarding the latter, for example, under what conditions might a work group's expression of positive group affective tone serve as a means for that group to acquire social approval from others in the organization in which it is embedded? Identifying these conditions is potentially important because they might affect how job attitudes are formed in the group; when the conditions are met, positive job attitudes would be promoted, assuming social approval is salient to the group. Moreover, knowing that job satisfaction serves a value expressive function should influence the choice of strategies used to change the attitude. That is, persuasive appeals congruent with an attitude's function are more effective.[29]

My attitudes toward the above questions run from "warm" to "a bit cool." That is, I do not see the above as a "top 10" list of questions about job satisfaction that ought to be pursued vigorously. Rather, they were intended merely to demonstrate the sorts of questions that might be posed if one took job satisfaction seriously as an attitude. I would, however, be pleased if one or more of the questions were pursued. But I would be happier if my questions stimulated readers to devise their own job satisfaction puzzles to be solved.

If I were to construct a top 10 list, the flavor of it would be influenced considerably by several issues: (a) the component structure of job satisfaction—measuring the components at varying levels of analysis, investigating their independent origins and consequences, and studying the effects of their being in and out of alignment with one another; (b) job satisfaction-performance relationships at aggregate levels of analysis—principally identifying potential moderators of these relationships; (c) extraorganizational influences on job satisfaction—for instance, exploring, at the individual level of analysis, the possible effects of family background and responsibilities, socioeconomic status, and other characteristics of a person's life circumstances and, at higher levels of analysis, the possible effects of geographic, occupation, and/or industry "satisfaction norms" and the mass media and other aspects of popular culture (e.g., "Dilbert"); and (d) the influences of job satisfaction at higher levels of analysis beyond the boundaries of an organization—for instance, exploring the possible effects on external labor markets (e.g., their size, composition, and draw to the organization), regulatory bodies, and, of course, the markets for the organization's goods and services. These concerns reflect my tastes and, once again, are not intended to be a guide to action.

In the 1990s, we have seen a renewed interest in job satisfaction. If that interest is going to pay off in enhanced levels of understanding, old methods coupled with old questions will not work. We need to be methodologically and conceptually daring. This chapter, combined with the two previous chapters, was aimed at encouraging such daring and fueling it with some food for thought. I could not be more optimistic about the next wave of job satisfaction research, both its breadth and depth. But optimism alone does not create a future. It is up to a sizable segment of the field to embrace job satisfaction as an exciting construct and to do so in bold, imaginative ways.

Although the focus of this book will shift away from job satisfaction in the following chapters, it will not be neglected completely. Particularly in Chapter 6, in which attitudes around organizations come into focus, job satisfaction will be seen again.

Notes

1. Also see Pratkanis and Turner (1994), whose implicit definition of job satisfaction also appears consistent with the one offered here.

2. Some of the items composing the JAS are identical to the affective words used by Crites et al. (1994), that is, *calm* and *excited*. For more on the JAS, see Burke, Brief, George, Roberson, and Webster (1989).

3. See, for example, George (1996b) for more on the distinction between positive and negative affective states; for a recent, enlightening social psychological argument in support of considering two affective components of attitudes, see Cacioppo, Gardner, and Berntson (1997).

4. For more on group affective tone, see, for example, George (1990, 1995) and George and James (1993).

5. About the same time, Schmitt and Bedeian (1982) and Schmitt and Pulakos (1985) introduced ideas similar to Staw et al. (1986), but they did not grab nearly as much attention; also see Weitz (1952), whose historical import is addressed by Judge (1992).

6. See also Schneider and Dachler (1978).

7. In the subjective well-being literature, however, strict top-down interpretations are evident (e.g., Schroeder & Costa, 1984) and have led to a debate that has been informative in unmasking the influence of dispositional variables on the self-reports of life events (e.g., Brett, Brief, Burke, George, & Webster, 1990; Maddi, Bartone, & Puccetti, 1987; Rowlison & Felner, 1988).

8. See George (1990) and Schneider, Goldstein, and Smith (1995) for more on the ASA framework.

9. For a somewhat analogous point of view, see Motowidlo (1996).

10. See John (1990) for a historical account of the emerging consensus; for a critical analysis of the FFM, see, for example, Hough and Schneider (1996) and Pervin (1994).

11. For an analysis of the relationships between the Big Five and behaviors in organizations, see, for example, Barrick and Mount (1991) and Tett, Jackson, and Rothstein (1991).

12. In the preceding chapter, I noted that some social psychological evidence, although quite limited, indicates that certain types of attitudes may be genetically influenced. Such limited evidence regarding job satisfaction also can be found in the organizational literature (e.g., Arvey, Bouchard, Segal, & Abraham, 1989; Arvey, McCall, Bouchard, Taubman, & Cavanaugh, 1994). Arvey and Bouchard (1994) provide a useful discussion of these genetic job satisfaction findings. Also noted in the preceding chapter was the considerable evidence demonstrating the influences of genetics on personality, some of which addresses the components of the FFM. Thus, genetics may influence attitudes, including job satisfaction, through effects on personality. But any serious discussion of genetic influences clearly is beyond the scope of this book. Simply, I do not have the expertise to thoughtfully analyze the issues.

13. For more on the NA construct, see, for example, Watson and Clark (1984) and Burke et al. (1993).

14. The examples used in this and the previous paragraph obviously have not pertained to the negative affective component. This is because as is noted (George & Brief, 1996), the effects of negative mood are more difficult to interpret. This in no way implies that the negative affective component is less important; rather, the literature available on which to base speculations about it contains more ambiguous findings.

15. Also see, for example, Barrick and Mount (1993); Barrick, Mount, and Strauss (1993); Ones, Mount, Barrick, and Hunter (1994); Staw and Barsade (1993); and Tett, Jackson, Rothstein, and Reddon (1994).

16. See George and Jones (1997).

17. For more on the idea of shared attitudes and the concept of organizational performance, see, for example, Kozlowski and Hattrup (1992) and Guzzo (1988), respectively; regarding the link between the two, recall Ostroff's (1993) argument, noted in the previous chapter, that positive employee attitudes in an organizational unit relate to norms of cooperation and collaboration.

18. On the link between individual performance and aggregate productivity, see Campbell and Campbell (1988).

19. See Judge (1993) for a set of findings seemingly inconsistent with Dietz et al. (1997). Judge found that the more positive the disposition of the individual, the stronger the relationship between job dissatisfaction and turnover. But as noted earlier, given his reliance on Weitz's (1952) dispositional measure, it is unclear what personality construct, if any, he gauged.

20. For more on affect and organizational conflict, see Baron (1993).

21. On the concept of "groupmind," see, for example, Klimoski and Mohammed (1994).

22. On the accessibility of attitudes, see, for example, Bargh, Chaiken, Govender, and Pratto (1992) and Fazio (1995).

23. For more on ambivalence, see, for example, Cacioppo and Berntson (1994) and Thompson, Zanna, and Griffin (1995).

24. On measuring the affective and cognitive components of attitudes, see, for example, Crites et al. (1994) and Eagly, Mladinic, and Otto (1994).

25. On values as a basis for attitudes, see, for example, Feather (1995) and Stern, Dietz, Kalof, and Guagnano (1995).

26. On the social psychology of the questions posed, see Pomerantz, Chaiken, and Tordeisillas (1995); but organizationally, also see, for example, Brockner, Tyler, and Cooper-Schneider (1992).

27. For more on matching persuasive messages to culture and the effects of doing so on attitude change, see Han and Shavitt (1994).

28. For more on the effects of self-regulation on attitude-behavior relationships, see Koestner, Bernieri, and Zuckerman (1992).

29. For more on a functional approach to attitudes, see, for example, Shavitt and Brock (1994).

5 Attitudinal Baggage

NEGATIVE RACIAL ATTITUDES
AS AN EXEMPLAR

People bring an awful lot of baggage to work with them. Some of it may contain the tools necessary for them to perform successfully the jobs they were hired to do (e.g., their job-relevant knowledge, skills, and abilities). The contents of other bags, however, make them better left unopened in the workplace. Such excess baggage is the principal focus of this chapter. Some of the questions to be addressed are these: What exactly might this baggage contain? How does it get opened at work? Once unpacked, what are the organizationally relevant consequences?

It should come as no surprise that the metaphorical baggage of interest is loaded with attitudes. Given, for instance, the previous coverage of the dispositional approach to job satisfaction, the idea that people bring attitudes to work also should not be surprising. But job satisfaction is not of concern here; rather, a host of other attitudes could be considered excess baggage in the workplace. For example, a person, on the basis of prior experiences, may enter an organization with pro-union and antimanagement attitudes. Regarding the latter, for instance, the telling of "dean jokes" among some faculty members is commonplace, and doing so might be quite reflective of the attitudes toward administrators these professors carry with them from institution to institution. One easily can identify many other attitudes that people bring to work that could come in to play on the job and be seen as problematic, depending, in part, on the organizational context experienced. This set might include negative attitudes toward various governmental agencies or public policies. An employee, for example, holds a generally negative attitude toward public policies supporting aid to the poor; when his employing organization initiates a program, in conjunction with a state agency, to train and hire welfare recipients, the employee's attitude leads him to resist the initiative. Positive attitudes can be problematic, too. Take the case of an employee who, for years before joining her current work organization, held strong, pro-environmental attitudes. At work, these attitudes have led management to view her as a real pain. She constantly complains that the organization is not environmentally responsible, even in the face of management-supplied evidence that her pro-environmental proposals are not economically sound. Brought-to-work attitudes about a company's products or services can even come to be seen as troublesome. For example, a longtime employee of a retail chain begins to act out against management when the company starts selling firearms. She had brought to work rather firm antigun attitudes.

The above paragraph demonstrates that the set of attitudes a person brings to work that somehow can be seen as problematic is potentially large and varied. Yet organizational scientists have paid little heed to them. I would like to offer some topology of these attitudes, and, even better, a theoretical framework suggesting when a given type of attitude comes into organizational play. But such conceptual devices do not now exist, and attempts to develop them remain to be undertaken. I will address, therefore, the attitudinal baggage people bring to work with an example. The example is drawn from those attitudes people hold toward groups to which they do not belong. More precisely, the attitude objects of interest can be thought of as stigmatized groups (Stone, Stone, & Dipboye, 1992) and could include, for example, older persons, women, persons who are disabled, Asians, Hispanics, and Jews. The specific target selected is Blacks. My reasons for doing so are twofold. There is a considerable body of knowledge about White attitudes toward Blacks, and there is considerable evidence showing that the treatment of Blacks in many work organizations remains a significant social problem in the United States. Both these reasons are documented in the pages to come. Although, as indicated, how negative racial attitudes affect Blacks in (or trying to get in) organizations will be discussed, what follows also is germane to the treatment of Black customers and other Black organizational stakeholders.

In this chapter, I will first lay a foundation for a discussion of racism in contemporary American business organizations. That foundation will consist of general treatments of (a) stereotypes (for example, how they are formed, how they can distort perceptions of individuals, and how they persist); (b) prejudice and the theories explaining it; and (c) racism. With this foundation in place, the organizational aspects of racism will be discussed beginning with evidence of its prevalence and concluding with potential tactics for combating it. Following this discussion, negative attitudes toward other groups (e.g., women) in organizations in both the United States and elsewhere will be raised briefly. Finally, I will return to the general notion of excess attitudinal baggage to emphasize how much has gone unsaid.

Stereotypes

In the 18th century, the word *stereotype* was coined to describe a printing process involving the use of fixed casts of the pages of type (Ashmore & Del Boca, 1981); it was not used in the context of social and political ideas until 1922, when Walter Lippman, an American journalist, evoked the word to refer to the "picture in our heads" of various social groups (Stroebe & Insko, 1989). In the first study of ethnic or national stereotypes, the term referred to incorrect generalizations that are rigid, oversimplified, and biased (Katz & Braly, 1933). In that study, stereotypes were measured by having participants identify, for 10 ethnic or national groups, the five traits most typical of each group from a list of 84 traits. On the basis of this procedure, Germans, for instance, were stereotyped by a sample of Princeton University students as scientifically minded, industrious, extremely nationalistic, stolid, and efficient.[1]

Today, social psychologists generally think of a stereotype simply as a set of beliefs about the personal attributes of a group of people (e.g., Hamilton & Sherman, 1994; Hilton & von Hippel, 1996; Stroebe & Insko, 1989). This set of beliefs is not necessarily negative in nature, but stereotypes of out-groups typically have more negative connotations than those of in-groups, even if they include seemingly positive attributes (e.g., Esses, Haddock, & Zanna, 1993.) For example, Allport (1954) noted that the "personality qualities admired in Abraham Lincoln are deplored in the Jews" (p. 189). The import of distinguishing between in-groups and out-groups should become clear as I move on to discuss the formation of stereotypes and other characteristics of them.

Stereotype Formation

Theories concerned with the origins of stereotypes tend to focus on either a sociocultural level of analysis or the individual level of analysis (Allport, 1954; Ashmore, 1970; Stroebe & Insko, 1989). The former are addressed first. Stroebe and Insko identified two metatheoretical approaches to the sociocultural causes of stereotypes. These are coercion versus integration theories of society (Dahrendorf, 1959). Coercion theories assume that societies are characterized by conflicts of interests, stemming, for example, from an economic mode of production yielding a bipolar system of social classes—one exploiting, the other exploited (e.g., Marx, 1913). The powerful (the exploiting class), according to coercion theories, ideologically justify suppression of the powerless (the exploited class), in part, by devaluing those outside their group. Such devaluations can come in the form of stereotypes. Integration theories, alternatively, assume that societies are held together by a consensus on common values (e.g., Parsons, 1951) and not by a dominant and suppressive elite. These values are transmitted to the members of a society through various socialization processes; these processes produce a social heritage that, in part, contains stereotypes.

I will hold off addressing the implications of coercion theories until the concept of prejudice is explored because these theories contribute more directly to understanding the negative stereotypes that prejudice entails. For now, consistent with integration theories, I emphasize socialization processes (involving schooling, parents, peer groups, and the mass media) as the mechanisms through which stereotypes are transmitted. Because many stereotypes stabilize by the early age of 6 or 7 (e.g., Koblinsky, Cruse, & Sugawara, 1978), parents are assumed to play a particularly important role in their transmission. Children learn not only from what their parents say but also from observing how their parents behave toward members of various groups. Moreover, children can acquire stereotypic beliefs on the basis of how their parents regulate their contacts with other children. For example, if White parents forbid their children to play with Black children, they create the impression these children are bad or nasty (Stroebe & Insko, 1989).

But where did the parents' and previous generations' stereotypic beliefs come from? Eagly (e.g., 1987, 1995) suggested that people form stereotypes on the basis of the social roles group members are observed to occupy. In some communities, for examples, Whites may observe menial jobs to be performed largely by Hispanics and virtually never by members of their own group; on the basis of these observations (which are probabilistic because no White person observes all menial laborers or all Hispanics), attributions are made about the characteristics of Hispanics as a group.[2] Closely associated with Eagly's idea is the notion that stereotypes originate from characteristics of social structures; for instance, stereotypes of racial groups may reflect the confounding of social class and race differences in society (e.g., Smedley & Bayton, 1978).

These social roles and structural characteristics need not be current to fuel the continued transmission of a stereotype. Stephan and Rosenfield (1982) argued that a stereotype of Blacks as lazy, ignorant, and dirty may be a reflection of the situation Blacks occupied during slavery. In bondage, Blacks had limited access to education, working hard was not generally a means to improve one's lot in life, and living conditions did not typically promote personal hygiene. But slavery died in America well more than a hundred years ago; how can a stereotype based on it still endure? The answer may be what already has been discussed: socialization processes, the inferior social roles Black still often are seen to occupy, and the persistent likelihood that an encountered Black is more likely to be poor than an encountered White. Moreover, if stereotypes, in part, are a product of probabilistic exposure to a group's members, then falsification of them through informal observation would be difficult (Eagly, 1987) and, even given changes in the social roles and stratification of the targeted group's members, a slow process. Later, the issue of stereotype maintenance will be addressed in somewhat more detail.

In summary, the stereotypes of at least some groups (e.g., women and Blacks) are formed on the basis of observed social roles and structures and are transmitted generationally through various socialization processes. The implication of this is that some stereotypes can be thought of as relatively enduring cultural phenomena. There are individual differences in the stereotypes people hold; these are discussed below. But within a culture, there likely is little variance in the knowledge of what constitutes the stereotypes of some groups. I would be surprised if many readers could not articulate accurately the attributes of a stereotypic man or woman. Yet it will be argued later that readers do differ in the degrees to which they believe the articulated stereotype and behave consistently with it toward members of the stereotyped group. Nevertheless, stereotypes as knowledge can and should be viewed as baggage we all carry with us.[3]

At the individual level of analysis, stereotype formation can be thought of as involving two related cognitive processes (Brehm & Kassin, 1996). The first is *social categorization* or the classification of people into groups based on perceived common attributes. Such sorting of people simply may be a natural way individuals lessen the cognitive demands placed on them. The use of social categories makes information processing easier by allowing reliance on previously stored knowledge (attributes of a social category) in place of new incoming information (e.g., Macrae, Milne, & Bodenhausen, 1994). The second cognitive process, following directly from the first, entails the tendency to assume that there is greater similarity among members of out-groups (i.e., groups with which the perceiver does not identify) than of in-groups (i.e., groups with which the perceiver does identify.) That is, there may be fine and subtle differences between "us," but "they" are all alike (Linville & Jones, 1980). For instance, I am likely to judge organizational scientists (a group with which I identify) more different from one another than I am accountants (a group with which I definitely do not identify). This out-group homogeneity effect has been attributed to limited personal contact with out-group members (e.g., Linville & Fischer, 1993).[4] The effect is salient for the formation of stereotypes because it results in people quickly generalizing from a single individual to a whole group (e.g., Quattrone & Jones, 1980). For more on the out-group homogeneity effect, see, for example, Judd, Ryan, and Park (1991); Ostrom and Sedikides (1992); and Park and Judd (1990).

Other explanations for the emergence of stereotypes can be found in the literature. For example, they arise in response to group conflicts (Robinson, Keltner, Ward, & Ross, 1995) and differences in power (Fiske, 1993), to justify the status quo (Jost & Banaji, 1994), to fulfill the perceiver's prophecies about the members of a group (Jussin, 1991), and to satisfy a need for social identity (Hogg & Abrams, 1988).[5] Some of these explanations will be pursued when the problem of prejudice is tackled; now, however, I move on to recognize explicitly an important reason to be concerned with stereotypes: They distort perceptions of individuals. For instance, given my previously alluded to but unspecified stereotype of accountants, I am likely to error in perceiving a person introduced to me as an accountant. This should come as no surprise given the previous discussion of the out-group homogeneity effect. Thus, although my stereotype provides me a quick and convenient summary of accountants, as an overgeneralized set of beliefs (Brehm & Kassin, 1996), it leads me to overlook diversity among accountants and, thereby, to form a mistaken impression of the specific accountant to whom I am introduced. But let us assume I get to know this accountant and learn that my initial stereotype-based impression of her was in error. Am I then likely to alter my beliefs about account-ants or to maintain my stereotype? This question is next on the agenda.

The Survival of Stereotypes

As already noted, stereotypes once formed tend to persist. In this section, several cognitive mechanisms are described that explain this persistence. I begin with *assimilation effects,* or the tendency to perceive individuals as more similar to their stereotypes than they really are (Hilton & von Hippel, 1996; obviously, this tendency also accounts for stereotypes distorting perceptions of individuals). For example, von Hippel, Sekaquaptewa, and Vargas (1995) have shown, consistent with a stereotype of Blacks as aggressive, that a Black panhandler is seen as more threatening than a White panhandler. Thus, if individuals are perceived more similar to their stereotype than they really are, the likelihood of encountering individuals who disconfirm a stereotype is reduced, thereby, contributing to stereotype maintenance. *Attributional pro-cesses* also can contribute to stereotype maintenance. Perceivers, when con-fronted with an individual who is incongruent with his or her stereotype, simply may make no attributions at all about the inconsistent evidence (e.g., Mass, Milesi, Zabbini, & Stahlberg, 1995; Rubini & Semin, 1994). Such infer-ential failures obviously do not lead to stereotype revisions. But even when attributions are made, they also are likely to support the status quo. People tend to infer dispositional, or stable internal, causes (a) for stereotype-congruent ver-sus stereotype-incongruent behaviors (e.g., Jackson, Sullivan, & Hodge, 1993) and (b) for negative out-group/positive in-group versus positive out-group/ negative in-group behaviors (e.g., Hewstone & Jaspars, 1984).[6]

At a more general level, assimilation effects and the described attributional processes exemplify confirmation biases (von Hippel et al., 1995). Another example of these biases is supplied by Johnston and Macrae (1994). They found that when participants were offered the opportunity to learn more about a stereotyped group, they tended to pose stereotype-consistent ques-tions about the group (i.e., to seek stereotype-consistent information).[7] Taken together, such biases lead people to recall, believe, rely on, and communicate stereotype-congruent information more than stereotype-incongruent infor-mation (Hilton & von Hippel, 1996; Semin & Fiedler, 1988; Srull & Wyer, 1989). As suggested already, although the current focus is on the contribution of these biases to the maintenance of stereotypes, their consequences for distorting how an individual member of a stereotyped group is perceived and judged cannot be ignored. But the effects of stereotype confirmation biases on how people in organizations react to one another and to outsiders have yet to appear systematically on the organizational science research agenda. This is a sad state of affairs. It would be interesting to know, for example, if members of stereotyped groups applying for jobs are asked questions by interviewers that are stereotype consistent. I suspect the answer is yes. If it is, what are the consequences of such interviewer tactics?

People tend to overestimate the joint occurrence of distinct variables. The resulting overestimation of the association between the variables has been labeled an *illusory correlation* (Chapman, 1967). These erroneous correlations, as will be shown, also contribute to the maintenance of stereotypes. Minority groups are distinctive simply by virtue of their relationships to majority groups (e.g., Sherman, Hamilton, & Roskos-Ewoldson, 1989). Thus, if members of a minority group are seen engaging in some deviant act, an illusory correlation between membership in that group and the deviant act likely will be produced (Schaller, 1991), providing "evidence" of a stereotype of the group as deviant.[8]

The final cognitive mechanism to be addressed as contributing to the survival of stereotypes is *subtyping,* the tendency to create a subsidiary classification for individuals who are members of a stereotyped group but who are seen as inconsistent with the group stereotype (Brewer, Dull, & Lui, 1981). By subtyping, stereotype-incongruent individuals are judged to be atypical. But stereotypes are revised on the basis of exposure to cases viewed as typical (e.g., Johnston & Hewstone, 1992). Thus, encountering a highly intelligent Black may not lead to a revision of a stereotype of Blacks as ignorant; the encountered stereotype-inconsistent Black could have been placed into a "Black intellectual" subcategory and judged atypical of Blacks.[9] Subtyping may not always contribute to stereotype maintenance; some even view it as a means to stereotype change (e.g., Brewer, 1988). This possibility is considered later.

Considerably more could be said about the survival of stereotypes, but I hope that the limited territory that has been covered provides an adequate lay of the land. The "take-home" message intended is that powerful sociocultural and psychological forces contribute to the survival of stereotypes. One implication of this conclusion is that organizations seeking to modify the stereotypes people bring to work with them face an uphill battle. Before moving on to explicate why stereotypes are relevant to the problem of prejudice, I present a quick review of the stereotype change and, more important, the stereotype inhibition, literatures.

Stereotype Change and Inhibition

Four models of stereotype change can be identified (Hilton & von Hippel, 1996): (a) the "bookkeeping model"—each bit of stereotype-inconsistent information processed leads to a small change in the stereotype (Rothbart, 1981); (b) the "exemplar model"—stereotypes consists of representations of specific individuals and, thus, they change (in an incremental fashion similar to that posited by the bookkeeping model) when new exemplars are added or when different ones are retrieved from memory (Smith & Zárate, 1992); (c) the "conversion model"—after some critical level of inconsistency in formation has been encountered, a dramatic change in the stereotype occurs (Rothbart, 1981); and (d) the "subtyping model"—subtypes replace superordinate categorizations and become base-level categories themselves (e.g., Brewer, 1988). In regard to the latter model, it seems that activation of one subtype even may inhibit the activation of competing subtypes (Rudman & Borgida, 1995). Moreover, subtyping may contribute to greater variability being reflected in a perceiver's responses to members of some superordinate category (Park, Ryan, & Judd, 1992).

The subtyping model of change has received the most research attention, but some evidence is available to support each of the models (Hewstone, Johnston, & Aird, 1992). In addition, it seems that the models may differentially hold, dependent on the particular function served by a stereotype in a particular context (Snyder & Miene, 1994). Beyond finding this potential complexity troublesome, I do not find the reviewed models particularly rich prescriptively. Although they may be descriptively interesting, they are not especially suggestive, to me at least, of procedures that might be used in organizations to alter people's stereotypes, but altering people's stereotypes may not be what is required.

According to Greenwald and Banaji's (1995) theorizing, stereotypes often are activated without awareness and operate at an implicit (i.e., unconscious) level. Their position is supported by an increasing body of empirical evidence (e.g., Banaji, Hardin, & Rothman, 1993; Devine, Monteith, Zuwerink, & Elliot, 1991; Perdue & Gurtman, 1990).[10] This automaticity makes the following question particularly salient: Can stereotypes be inhibited consciously? Put into an organizational context, the question becomes, "Does it make sense to train people to consciously suppress their stereotypic thinking?" Regrettably, the answer may be no. Research based on Wegner's (1994) model of thought suppression indicates that attempts to suppress (at least certain types of) stereotypes actually lead to increased activation of the stereotypes (e.g., Macrae et al., 1994).[11]

All is not lost, however. Although the activation of stereotypes may not be suppressible, people, as suggested in the earlier discussion of stereotypes as part of our social heritage, may be able to control their reactions to members of stereotyped groups. This possibility is explored in somewhat more detail next.

Stereotypes and Prejudice

The concept of stereotype has been dwelled on, in large part, because of its assumed association with prejudice. Allport (1954) defined *prejudice* as "an antipathy based on a faulty and inflexible generalization" (p. 9). Thus, he apparently saw prejudice as negative evaluations of group members growing from stereotyping (Hilton & von Hippel, 1996). His view came to be accepted widely (e.g., Ehrlich, 1973; Hamilton, 1981; Tajfel, 1982); indeed, considerable empirical evidence suggests a stereotype-prejudice link (e.g., Eagly & Mladinic, 1989; Haddock, Zanna, & Esses, 1993; Stephan, Agegev, Coates-Shrider, Stephan, & Abalakina, 1994).[12]

An alternative view can be found in the literature. Harding, Proshansky, Kutner, and Chein (1969) construed prejudice as an attitude and, adopting a three-component view of attitude, asserted that prejudice is characterized by a cognitive component (e.g., a negative stereotype of an out-group), an affective component (e.g., negative feelings toward members of the group), and a conative component (e.g., a tendency to discriminate against members of the group). As was noted in Chapter 3, the components of an attitude need not necessarily align; some evidence indicates that the cognitive component (i.e., the stereotype) is not the best predictor of one's global attitude toward an out-group (e.g., Stangor, Sullivan, & Ford, 1991).

Not necessarily inconsistent with the above view but clearly consistent with a theme previously introduced is the finding of Bettelheim and Janowitz (1964) that stereotypes about out-groups may not be related to the degree of prejudice displayed toward those groups. To understand and appreciate this finding, recall that there is strong evidence that some stereotypes are established in memory at an early age and that this is attributable to *common* socialization experiences (e.g., Katz, 1976; Porter, 1971; Proshansky, 1966). The use of the word *common* is important because it implies that the stereotypes of some groups (e.g., Blacks) are shared widely, at least in the United States. Devine (1989) argued *and* demonstrated that these cultural stereotypes are activated automatically in the presence of a member or symbolic equivalent of the target group for *both* high- and low-prejudiced individuals.[13] More precisely, people have common knowledge of these stereotypes, but knowledge does *not* equal endorsement (e.g., Ashmore & Del Boca, 1981). Knowledge of a stereotype translates into prejudice *only* when that knowledge also represents the personal beliefs of the individual.[14] Thus, given the stereotype knowledge of nonprejudiced individuals, their responses to members of a target group can be thought of as entailing the *controlled* inhibition of the automatically activated stereotype and the *conscious* activation of nonprejudiced beliefs (Devine, 1989; Devine & Monteith, 1993; Devine et al., 1991). Such thinking clearly opens the door to the idea that prejudiced responses can be regulated through conscious control (e.g., Monteith, 1993; Monteith, Devine, & Zuwerink, 1993). When the battle against racism in organizations is addressed, this idea will surface again.

In sum, it appears that a stereotype of an out-group (at least knowledge of it) does not inevitably lead to prejudice. I may have a negative picture in my head of accountants, university administrators, or some other group with which I do not identify, but knowing these stereotypes does not mean that I endorse and act on them. For prejudice, stereotypes are necessary but not sufficient. This conclusion will acquire more meaning as the concept of prejudice is explored further.

Prejudice

As evident in the previous section, the concept of prejudice has been defined in different ways. Here, I adopt a typical definition of it "as unfavorable evaluations and negative affect toward members of a group" (Olson & Zanna, 1993, p. 143). For other definitions, see, for example, Ashmore (1970).

Earlier in the chapter, explanations for prejudice were alluded to; now, some of these, as well as others, are detailed, beginning with a sociocultural approach—*realistic conflict theory* (e.g., Campbell, 1965; Sherif, 1967). This theory postulates that real, direct competition for valuable but limited resources (or the false perception of it) breeds hostility between groups (LeVine & Campbell, 1972). In-group identity and the tightness of group boundaries are increased by such conflicts. Moreover, the likelihood of group defection is decreased by increasing punishment and rejection of group defectors and deviants. Thereby, the threat associated with competition enhances *ethnocentrism,* a state characterized by heightened in-group solidarity and devaluation of out-groups (Stroebe & Insko, 1989). Such consequences of intergroup competition have been demonstrated, for example, in a classic study among boys at a summer camp (Sherif, Harvey, White, Hood, & Sherif, 1961) and in a study of corporate executives placed in competing groups as part of a training program (Blake & Mouton, 1984). In addition, it has been observed that realistic conflict theory is consistent with historical accounts of the development of prejudice toward various ethnic and national groups, both within the United States and abroad (e.g., Ashmore, 1970; Olzak & Nagel, 1986; Taylor & Moghaddam, 1994).[15]

Tajfel (e.g., 1970, 1982; Tajfel, Billig, Bundy, & Flament, 1971; Tajfel & Turner, 1979) challenged realistic conflict theory by arguing and empirically demonstrating that intergroup conflict (real or perceived) is not either a necessary or sufficient cause of ethnocentrism and antagonism between groups. He showed that membership in a *minimal group* (i.e., a group constituted by categorizing people on the basis of trivial, minimally important characteristics) whose members are not in competition for a limited resource with members of another group leads to in-group favoritism or the tendency to discriminate in favor of in-groups over out-groups.[16] Tajfel and Turner (e.g., 1985) formulated *social identity theory* as an explanation for in-group favoritism. The theory assumes that people strive to enhance their self-esteem through personal achievements and affiliations with successful groups. In-group favoritism, therefore, is the result of attempts to increase the social status of the groups to which one belongs (i.e., to increase one's social identity). Thus, threats to self-esteem should heighten the need for in-group favoritism, and the expression of in-group favoritism should heighten self-esteem. Research generally supports these predictions (Hogg & Abrams, 1990; Turner, Oakes, Haslam, & McGarty, 1994). Thus, a blow to one's self-esteem evokes prejudice; the expression of prejudice restores self-esteem (Brehm & Kassin, 1996.)[17] The relevance of social identity theory for intergroup relations has been raised in the organizational literature (e.g., Ashford & Mael, 1989; Ely, 1994), but it remains to be pursued as an explanation for prejudice in organizations.

Several psychodynamic theories have been advanced to explain prejudice, but before turning to these, I return to a finding noted earlier: Prejudiced attitudes appear to be formed at an early age (e.g., Lerner & Grant, 1990). Such a finding was presented as evidence that stereotypes and prejudice are part of our social heritage, transmitted, in part, through common socialization experiences. Although I find such an interpretation eminently plausible, it is important to note another explanation for the presence of prejudice at an early age—one that indirectly was raised in preceding chapters. Prejudiced attitudes, in part, may be inherited. For example, Eaves et al. (1989) estimated that heredity explains about 50% of the variance across individual responses to the following item: "Black people are innately inferior to White people." I am not advocating that prejudiced attitudes are inherited rather than social-ized. The message to keep in mind as I proceed to discuss psychodynamic theories is that several viable explanations exist for prejudice (including realistic conflict and social identity theories). Simply, do not expect to find *the* theory; rather, perhaps the best tactic is to select the ideas in those theories most provocative for understanding the attitudinal baggage people bring to work.

According to psychodynamic theories, prejudice is a sign of intrapersonal conflict or maladjustment (Stroebe & Insko, 1989). *Scapegoat theory,* derived from Freudian psychoanalytic theory and the frustration-aggression hypothe-sis (Dollard, Doob, Miller, Mowrer, & Sears, 1939), is a well-known psycho-dynamic (or "symptom"; Ashmore, 1970) theory of prejudice. Simply, the theory assumes that cultural restrictions in childhood and the limitations of daily life in adulthood produce frustrations that arouse hostility. This hostility (or aggression) normally is directed toward its cause, but if the cause cannot be identified or is too powerful to aggress against, then displacement occurs. Because minorities are highly visible and often relatively powerless, they are particularly likely to be the targets of displacement (i.e., to be chosen as scapegoats; Ashmore, 1970). Data support this argument. For example, White, Gentile Americans dissatisfied with their personal economic circumstances and those disturbed by the national political situation have been found to be more anti-Semitic than their less dissatisfied and disturbed counterparts (Campbell, 1947).[18]

The *authoritarian personality* explanation for prejudice also entails scape-goating (Adorno, Frenkel-Brunswik, Levinson, & Sanford, 1950). The theory posits that prejudice is part of a broader ideological framework entailing other economic, political, and social beliefs. This framework is held together by an aspect of personality that was shaped by the quality of parental control during a person's formative years (Bayton, 1946). A strict and disciplined upbringing produces a person with an authoritarian personalty who displaces the resent-ment he or she might have felt toward his or her parents on to out-groups. As described by Billig (1976), such a person is a weakling who copes with personal inadequacies, in part, by venting his or her aggressiveness on "inferior" out-groups (particularly, Blacks and Jews).[19] The early research addressing these ideas has been criticized, largely for measurement problems (e.g., Hyman & Sheatsley, 1954); more recently, however, these concerns seem to have been addressed, with research focusing on the conditions associated with the manifestation of behaviors consistent with the authoritarian personality (e.g., Altemeyer, 1988, 1994; Stone, Lederer, & Christie, 1993).

As I already have stated, no dominant theory of prejudice is evident. Rather, it is likely that prejudice is explained by some unknown combination of genetics, personality, common early socialization experiences, intergroup conflicts (real or imagined), scapegoating, attempts to enhance one's self-esteem, and other factors (e.g., religious orientation; (e.g., Batson, Flink, Schoenrade, Fulz, & Pych, 1986). In my mind, the causes of the prejudices people bring to the workplace are less important, per se, to organizational scientists than are the implications of those causes for reducing discrimination in organizations. Some of these implications are addressed later, but for now, I turn to an examination of one form of prejudice, racism, to further specify, through example, the nature of the problem.

Racism

In the preceding sections, the problem of racism was not ignored; here, however, it moves into the spotlight for a closer examination. More specifically, this section is concerned primarily with racial prejudice of White Americans directed toward Black Americans. This focus was chosen for two reasons. First, as noted earlier, a discussion of racial prejudice provides a vehicle for further unveiling the complexities of the general problem of prejudice. Second, as will be demonstrated in the next section, understanding and alleviating racism in organizations represent current and significant challenges to organizational scientists and managers alike.

It is my impression that explicit racial slurs are rarely heard in the contemporary American workplace.[20] This is consistent with the findings of survey researchers who indicate a dramatic shift in the racial attitudes *expressed* by White Americans (e.g., Schuman, Steeh, & Bobo, 1985; Smith & Sheatsley, 1984; Taylor, Sheatsley, & Greeley, 1978). In the 1930s and 1940s, public opinion polls and other sources of data indicated that the majority of White Americans endorsed stereotypes of Blacks as superstitious, ignorant, lazy, and happy-go-lucky and accepted the principle of racial segregation in virtually all aspects of people's lives (e.g., education, housing, and access to public facilities; e.g., Myrdal, 1944). Today, however, the research evidence indicates that relatively few White Americans openly endorse negative stereotypes of

Blacks or the principle of racial segregation (e.g., Sniderman & Piazza, 1993). On a more personal level, I was born in 1946 and grew up with water fountains commonly labeled as for either "Whites" or "Colored"; today, such public forms of segregation are dead.

The above indicates that "old-fashioned racism" (e.g., Sniderman & Tetlock, 1986), characterized by open bigotry and an emphasis on pre-Civil War beliefs about Blacks, is dying in the United States. This process of demise began after World War II, probably in part because the Holocaust gave racism such a horrific name, and was furthered considerably by the civil rights movement, which led to the passage of the critically important Civil Rights Act of 1964. Given that the majority of Whites now endorse the principle of integration and equal access or opportunity for persons of all races, is it safe to assume that racism no longer is a problem in America? Regrettably, the answer is *no*. Numerous studies indicate that old-fashioned racism largely has been transmuted to a subtle, indirect, and rationalizable type of racial bigotry (e.g., Crosby, Bromley, & Saxe, 1980; Dovidio & Gaertner, 1983; Frey & Gaertner, 1986; Gaertner & McLaughlin, 1983; Katz, 1981; Kinder & Sears, 1981; McConahay, 1983; Sears & Allan, 1984). As already noted, the significance of this enduring problem, particularly in organizations, will be demonstrated in the section to follow; for now, I will provide alternative descriptions of the more subtle form of racism that remains a powerful force in and around organizations.

In the face of the steady decline of Jim Crow racism (i.e., racism asserting the biological inferiority of Blacks and strict segregation), White opposition to government policies aimed at increasing opportunities for Blacks has been intense (e.g., busing for school desegregation, open housing laws, and various affirmative action efforts in education and employment; e.g., Kluegel & Smith, 1986; Schuman et al., 1985). Two principal explanations for such opposition have been studied (Kinder, 1986).

First, consistent with realistic conflict theory, White opposition to government policies aimed at increasing opportunities for Blacks is from a fear that Blacks pose a real threat (e.g., to the personal safety of Whites, to their children's education, and to their jobs). Data indicate, however, that White opposition to racial busing and antagonism toward affirmative action programs, as well as votes against Black candidates, are independent of the racial threats they see themselves facing (e.g., Kinder & Rhodebeck, 1982; Kinder & Sears, 1981; Sears, Hensler, & Speer, 1979).[21]

Second, White opposition is the result of a blending of a residue of negative racial sentiments and such treasured American values as individualism and self-reliance (Kinder, 1986). This blending of early learned racial fears and stereotypes and deep-seated feelings of social morality and propriety has been labeled *symbolic racism* (Kinder & Sears, 1981). Although the concept has been used provocatively to explore various desegregation controversies in the political arena (e.g., Sears, 1988; Sears & Allen, 1984), it has been criticized— often for its ambiguity (e.g., Bobo, 1983; Eagly & Chaiken, 1993; Sniderman, Piazza, Tetlock, & Kendrick, 1991; Weigel & Howes, 1985). Fortunately, however, similar concepts, with greater conceptual clarity, have been advanced. Some of these are described below.

Katz and Hass (1988) asserted that some White Americans harbor ambivalent beliefs and feelings about Black Americans. This ambivalence, according to them, stems from the linkage of the racial attitudes of Whites to two contrasting values: *communalism,* which expresses humanitarian and egalitarian precepts fostering concern for the well-being of others and for the community, and *individualism,* which expresses Protestant ethic precepts fostering self-denial and achieving success through hard work. The former value leads Whites to sympathize with Blacks as minority underdogs; the latter value leads Whites to criticize Blacks as socially deviant. *Ambivalent racism,* therefore, should be related to heaping great praise on successful Blacks but also denigrating Blacks not perceived to have embraced the Protestant work ethic (Hass, Katz, Rizzo, Bailey, & Eisenstadt, 1991). Generally, therefore, such racism is thought to be associated with unstable reactions to Blacks.[22]

Aversive racism represents a particular type of ambivalence entailing a conflict between a sincerely egalitarian value system and *unacknowledged* negative feelings and beliefs about Blacks (Gaertner & Dovidio, 1986).[23] The unacknowledged negative affect that aversive racists have for Blacks is not hostility or hate; rather, it involves discomfort, uneasiness, disgust, and sometimes fear, motivating not intentionally destructive behaviors but avoidance. Because aversive racists are concerned with their egalitarian self-images, however, they are motivated to avoid acting in recognizably unfavorable ways toward Blacks. Therefore, in situations in which norm-prescribing appropriate interracial behaviors are clear and unambiguous, Blacks may not be treated less favorably than Whites, because doing so would be obvious and challenge the aversive racists' nonprejudiced self-images. Even when normative guidelines are clear, aversive racists unwittingly may search for ostensibly nonracial factors to rationalize responding negatively toward Blacks. Unfavorable reactions, nevertheless, are most likely to occur in situations in which norms are weak, ambiguous, or conflicting. In these situations, the concepts of right and wrong are less applicable.[24]

Perhaps the most clearly articulated form of the new racism is that offered by McConahay (1986), *modern racism*. The principal beliefs of a modern racist are as follows:

1. Discrimination is a thing of the past because Blacks now have the freedom to compete in the marketplace and to enjoy those things they can afford.
2. Blacks are pushing too hard, too fast, and into places they are not wanted.
3. These tactics and demands are unfair.
4. Therefore, recent gains are undeserved and the prestige granting institutions of society are giving Blacks more attention and the concomitant status than they deserve. (pp. 92-93).

To these, McConahay adds two other beliefs:

5. The first four beliefs do not constitute racism because they are empirical facts.
6. *Racism is bad.*

Consequently, "those endorsing the ideology of modern racism do not define their own beliefs and attitudes as racists" (p. 93), and they act in ways to project a nonprejudicial, nondiscriminatory self-image. Thus, for modern racists to behave consistently with their negative racial attitudes requires that they be embedded in "a context in which there is a plausible, non-prejudiced explanation for what might be considered prejudiced behavior" (p. 100).[25]

To recap, modern racists *think* racism is socially undesirable yet *feel* negatively toward Blacks, particularly because they believe the gains that Blacks have made were not earned. Although their negative feelings predispose modern racists to say and do things harmful to Blacks, their desires not to be seen by themselves and others as prejudiced hold these tendencies in check. Modern racists are released to speak or act out against Blacks *only* when they have an excuse that protects them from the charge of racism. As will be shown later, the subtle yet potentially powerful force of modern racism has been examined only recently from an organizational perspective. Also to be demonstrated later, such examinations were long overdue (Brief & Hayes, 1997).

McConahay's (e.g., 1986) approach to racism has not gone uncriticized (e.g., Fazio, Jackson, Dunton, & Williams, 1995). The most enlightening alternative to McConahay's analysis that has emerged from these critical examinations is that of Devine and her colleagues, noted earlier in the chapter (Devine & Monteith, 1993; Devine et al., 1991; Monteith, 1993; Monteith et al., 1993). According to them, low-prejudice individuals (e.g., those scoring low on a measure of modern racism) have internalized standards for how they should nonprejudicially respond to out-group members (e.g., Blacks), and they experience guilt and engage in self-criticism whenever these standards are violated. Their guilt and self-criticism, in turn, motivate vigilance and consistency among personal standards, thoughts, and behaviors. High-prejudice persons, on the other hand, follow external societal standards for how they should respond to Blacks; therefore, they experience negative affect and other-directed anger and irritation only when they violate the external standards. Such other-directed feelings actually may increase prejudice because persons may blame out-group members for their anger and irritation. As I interpret Devine and her colleagues' thinking, I see no threat to McConahay's fundamental prediction that discrimination is a product of the interaction between racial attitudes (modern racism) and context (one in which a plausible, nonprejudiced explanation for what otherwise would be considered prejudiced behavior is available). Thus, in the consideration of racism in organizations below, modern racism will be used as a key explanatory construct.[26]

Racism in Organizations

Recall that modern racists believe discrimination against Blacks is a thing of the past (McConahay, 1986). What is the truth value of this belief, at least in regard to employment? To deny it, one could turn to recent claims of racial discrimination that have received considerable media exposure (for example, the claims against Texaco; e.g., Eichenwald, 1996). More striking, however, is the number of allegations of such discrimination filed with the Equal Employment Opportunity Commission (EEOC). For example, 52,000 allegations were filed during the 1992-1993 fiscal year against private sector employers. Allegations of racial discrimination in employment, of course, do not constitute proof of discrimination. Aggregate data concerning the financial and occupational position of Blacks relative to Whites, however, suggest that many EEOC complainants are not "crying wolf." According to the U.S. Census Bureau, between 1979 and 1993, the real income of White families increased by 9%, but the real income of Black families did not change. The Bureau also reported that in 1993, Blacks earned less than their White counterparts, in all jobs at all levels; moreover, such disparities persist even after controlling for differences in job qualifications (e.g., Cancio, Evans, & Maume, 1996). In addition, studies indicate that Blacks do not proportionally occupy certain types of positions, particularly those above the bottom of organizational hierarchies; indeed, although Blacks represent approximately 12% of the U.S. population, they constitute less than 5% of the management ranks and considerably less than 1% of senior executives (Morrison, 1992).

Not only are Blacks segregated vertically, but also some evidence shows rather striking forms of horizontal segregation in the workplace. In a recent study of newly hired clerical employees of a large commercial bank in the Northeast, for example, Blacks were found to be four times more likely than Whites to be assigned, after 5 months on the job, to a Black supervisor (Lefkowitz, 1994). When the researcher who discovered this pattern of segregation queried management about it, he received an enlightening response. The bank's managers reacted with surprise. Not only did they claim they were unaware of such a pattern of segregation, the managers professed no knowledge of any policy or custom of job assignments that would lead to the segregation of employees by race. It seems that the segregation that occurred was not consciously endorsed by the managers; some subtle yet powerful force was operating to match supervisors and subordinates by race.

This force not only results in segregation within an organization but apparently also may prevent Blacks from ever entering the workplace. For example, the Fair Employment Council of Greater Washington, Inc., innovatively exposed the barriers faced by Blacks seeking employment (Bendick, Jackson, & Reinoso, 1994). The council sent out teams composed of a Black and a White matched in sex, age, personal appearance, articulateness, and manner to apply for the same jobs. The pairs also were equipped with similar fictional job qualifications. Although Blacks were favored over Whites in 5% of the encounters with prospective employers, Whites were favored over Blacks in 29% of them. The Black applicants often were told the job already was filled, whereas their White counterparts were granted interviews for the "filled" position. The foregoing evidence merely is representative of a larger body of findings that Blacks *can* face discrimination in getting into, interpersonally functioning well in, and moving up in organizations (e.g., Alderfer & Thomas, 1988; Brown & Ford, 1977; Cox & Nkomo, 1986; Greenhaus, Parasuraman, & Wormley, 1990; Hayes, 1995; Kraiger & Ford, 1985; Morrison & Von Glinow, 1990; Pettigrew & Martin, 1987; Powell & Butterfield, 1997).[27]

Another body of organizational evidence indicates that Whites do react negatively to Blacks. For example, Tsui, Egan, and O'Reilly (1992), adopting a relational demography perspective, predicted and found that for Whites, being increasingly racially different from others in one's work unit is related to lower levels of organizational attachment; for nonwhites, the relationship did not hold.[28] Tsui et al.'s intriguing results, coupled with the other findings I have surveyed, lead me (and I sincerely hope the reader, too) to believe that the modern racist is wrong, that discrimination is not a thing of the past. For us, as organizational scholars, what then does this conclusion imply? Although the promotion of a just society is a responsibility of all its members (e.g., Rawls, 1971), organizational scientists have a particularly heavy obligation (Brief & Hayes, 1997). This is because of our unique ability to produce knowledge relevant to alleviating discrimination in and around organizations. Expertise in understanding the thoughts, feelings, and actions of people at work is not burden free; we have a responsibility to apply this expertise to enhance the quality of people's organizational lives (e.g., Nord, 1977). Thus, the question becomes, have we met our obligations to the victims of racial discrimination, and, thereby, to promoting a more just society through applying our expertise?

Although I have cited some exceptions and the number of them appears to be increasing, I concur with Cox and Nkomo (1990; see also Brief & Hayes, 1997) that a read of the organizational literature leads one to think that organizations largely are race neutral. In other words, our research does not adequately reflect the problem of racial discrimination.[29] Thus, we have failed to meet our *collective* obligation. Our values have been reflected in the research questions we have chosen to pursue (Kaplan, 1964); we have elected, perhaps unknowingly, to maintain the status quo (e.g., Baritz, 1960). Below, I leave behind explicit considerations of the obligations, values, and societal role of the organizational scientist and attempt to entice the reader to action by demonstrating how intellectually exciting the study of racism in organizations can be and by suggesting how such research might generally inform our understandings of attitudes in and around organizations, both within the United States and beyond.

Even among those who have studied race in organizations, the word *racism* appears to be used quite rarely.[30] It seems that use of the word, at least among organizational scientists, somehow is offensive. More rare than the use of the word *racism* in the organizational literature is direct investigation of the construct (Brief & Hayes, 1997). This is so although, as previously demonstrated, understanding new forms of negative racial attitudes among Whites toward Blacks is important for understanding discrimination. Next, I will present a case of one of those forms, modern racism, to show how its effects might be played out in organizations. First, however, recall that modern racists believe racism is bad; therefore, they act in ways to protect a nonprejudiced, nondiscriminatory self-image. Thus, for modern racists to behave consistently with their negative racial attitudes, they must have a plausible, nonprejudiced explanation for what otherwise might be considered prejudiced behavior.[31]

In late 1992, Shoney's agreed to pay $132.5 million in response to allegations that the restaurant company discriminated against its Black employees; only 1.8% of Shoney's restaurant managers were Black, and 75% of its Black restaurant employees held jobs in three low-paying, non-customer-contact positions (e.g., dishwasher). A former vice president of the company stated that the firm's discriminatory practices were the result of the CEO's unwritten policy that "Blacks should not be employed in any position where they would be seen by customers" (Watkins, 1993, p. 424). The CEO himself admitted,

> In looking for anything to identify why is this unit under-performing, in some cases, I would probably have said this is a neighborhood of predominately White neighbors, and we have a considerable amount of Black employees and this might be a problem. (p. 427)

At lower levels of the organization, such analyses by the CEO translated into some managers feeling they needed to "lighten-up" their restaurants—a company euphemism for reducing the number of Black employees—and to hire "attractive White girls" instead (p. 424).

Shoney's CEO reasoned that a restaurant's performance was affected positively if the racial makeup of the unit's customer contact personnel *matched* the customer population served. Thus, according to the reasoning of the CEO, a unit serving a White customer population should employ White customer contact personnel. I believe that the reasoning of Shoney's CEO, reflecting a bottom-line, business perspective, may be seen as plausible and may appear to many managers as nonprejudicial. Moreover, I believe that such reasonings are commonplace in business organizations *and* supply the plausible, nonprejudicial explanations necessary to release the beast of modern racism (i.e., to free modern racists to act on their negative racial attitudes).[32]

The idea of a business justification to discriminate, at first glance, may seem farfetched. It is not. Prior to the civil rights movement, these justifications were explicitly part of the content of management education. Take, for instance, the lessons taught by Chester I. Barnard (1938) in his classic *The Functions of the Executive*. He described the informal executive organization whose purpose is to communicate "intangible facts, opinions, suggestions, suspicions, that cannot pass through formal channels" (p. 225). For this informal organization to operate effectively, Barnard prescribed selecting and promoting people to executive positions who *match* those already in place. He stated,

> Perhaps often and certainly occasionally men cannot be promoted or selected, or even must be relieved, because they cannot function, because they "do not fit" where there is no question of formal competence. This question of "fitness" involves such matters as education, experience, age, sex, personal distinctions, prestige, race. (p. 224)

More than three decades after the publication of Barnard's advice to executives, a Black manager wrote, "I believe that many of the problems I encountered were of fit. . . . I was out of the 'place' normally filled by Black people in the company" (Jones, 1973, p. 114).

Today, "race matching rules" have not disappeared from the management literature. Using the same business logic as Shoney's CEO, however, these rules are advanced by those *advocating* racial integration (e.g., Cox, 1993). The president of Avon Corporation, for example, concluded that his company's inner-city markets became significantly more profitable when additional Black and Hispanic customer contact personnel were placed in them (Cox & Blake, 1991). According to the president, this was because newly placed personnel were uniquely qualified to understand certain aspects of the worldview of the minority populations in the inner city.

I contend that it is naive to believe that if an organization uses a matching rule to include Blacks, the use of the same sort of rule to exclude Blacks is precluded. Although the staffing consequences of the two forms of the rule are different, they both rest on the same business logic—racial matching enhances organizational effectiveness.

As I have shown, justifications to discriminate occur when one advocates racially matching customers and employees (as was done by Shoney's CEO) and when one advocates person-organization fit regarding race (as was done by Barnard). The latter matching rule warrants further discussion because I am particularly fearful of its prevalence in practice. This fear stems from the increasing attention person-organization fit ideas are getting in the practice literature (e.g., Bowen, Ledford, & Nathan, 1991) and from research findings indicating that organizations do select people like those already in place (e.g., Schneider, 1987). Obviously, fit is not often explicitly raised in regard to race; rather, it is addressed regarding attitudes, beliefs, personality, style, and/or values, often vaguely defined. This vagueness, however, too easily could allow the modern racist to unknowingly translate a concern for person-organization fit into a concern for race, one that constitutes a plausible, nonprejudicially motivated business justification to discriminate.

Assume, for example, that a modern racist decides to exclude from consideration a Black job candidate for a position in an all-White work group. This decision reflected a concern for potentially disrupting interpersonal relations in a group whose members work well together. The manager also did not want "to unfairly burden" the Black job candidate with the costs of adjusting in a work group whose members might provide less than a warm reception. The modern racist simply sees such a decision as an appropriate managerial response to these realistic concerns. Indeed, he or she might even see this decision not to unfairly burden the Black job candidate as an expression of nonracist attitudes.

In sum, I have argued that racial discrimination in the employment arena can be explained, in part, by a more subtle, indirect, and rationalizable form of bigotry than old-fashioned racism. This new form, modern racism, however, explains discriminatory behavior only when a plausible, nonprejudiced explanation for the behavior is available. This explanation is required because modern racists do not want to be seen by themselves or others as bigots. Indeed, their racial attitudes can be said to be unconscious (Banaji & Greenwald, 1994). The unconscious nature of modern racism, coupled with a necessary prerequisite for action (i.e., a plausible, nonprejudiced explanation for the behavior), leads me to describe it as "subtle, indirect, and rationalizable." Moreover, I asserted that the explanations necessary to release modern racists to act on their negative attitudes can be race based as well as racially free in content. Finally, I argued that in the workplace, they may be quite common and be termed "business justifications to discriminate."

Does modern racism operate in organizations in a fashion consistent with the arguments advanced? Candidly, I do not know; to my knowledge, the construct has not been measured and examined in an organizational setting. But a series of three laboratory experiments designed to simulate organizational processes do speak to the utility of the ideas presented (Brief, Reizenstein, Pugh, Vaslow, & Dietz, 1997). The experiments entailed either (a) participants led to believe they were assisting a faculty member with a consulting project or (b) participants completing an elaborate in-basket exercise.[33] In both types of experiments, participants' racial attitudes were measured well in advance of the experiments with McConahay et al.'s (1981) Modern Racism Scale; participants were assigned randomly to receive or not, from their "bosses," a business justification to discriminate in regard to screening applicants for a job. Across the experiments, two justifications were used: one based on racially matching sales personnel to customers or one based on racially matching managers to employees. The results were consistent across all three experiments, showing, as predicted, no main effects for modern racism and an interaction effect between modern racism and justifications on discriminatory behaviors. That is, scores on the measure of modern racist attitudes were predictive of discriminatory behaviors *only* when a business justification to discriminate was provided. The scores were unrelated to discriminatory behaviors when no justification was supplied *or* when a blatantly racist justification was offered.

Thus, it appears that modern racism may be a useful concept for understanding discrimination in organizations. The important next step is to take the concept into the field. More generally, the cumulative evidence is compelling that the new forms of racism described here are a subtle but powerful force in American society; therefore, it is essential to begin examination of them in organizational contexts. Although racism is offensive, the study of it cannot be avoided if organizational scientists are to fulfill their obligation to enhance the quality of people's organizational lives—no matter what their color.

To proceed, I will assume that modern racism (or something akin to it), can be part of the attitudinal baggage people bring to work. What, then, are the implications of this assumption for creating knowledge to inform the practice of managing diversity in organizations? As these implications are pursued, I will not be drawing on a scientifically rigorous, unified body of literature that speaks directly to the efficacy of interventions aimed at promoting significant racial integration in organizations. To my knowledge, such evidence does not exist; rather, the learned diversity literature that is evident does a good job of describing the naturally occurring consequences of racial heterogeneity in organizations (e.g., Tsui et al., 1992). This is surprising, given that many organizations now rely on interventions such as diversity training (e.g., Conference Board, 1994). Clearly, rigorous assessments of these interventions are needed, but because they are not now available, what follows necessarily will be speculative. Before considering the more narrow topic of the implications of modern racism for managing diversity, let me share a failed dream, one that generally informs the problem at hand.

In 1954, the U.S. Supreme Court ruled that racially separate schools were inherently unequal, in violation of the Constitution. The decision was intended to lead to school desegregation—some people believed (including myself), ultimately to reduced prejudice. My naive belief was based on the idea that forcing Blacks and Whites together would facilitate their getting to know one another as individuals and, thereby, produce an improvement in Whites' attitudes toward Blacks. Unknowingly at the time, my belief also was supported by scientific thinking (e.g., Allport, 1954). As will be shown, however, the scientific approach to the effects of interracial contact is considerably more informative than was the basis for my naive belief.

What do we know now about the effects of school desegregation on racial attitudes? According to Stephan's (1986) review of the literature, 13% of the studies conducted showed a decrease in prejudice among Whites, 34% reported no change, and 53% reported an increase! The dream of the positive consequences of contact per se failed.[34] By inference, therefore, one should *not* expect the mere integration of an organization to lead to improved race relations in the organization.

Considerable research evidence now suggests that contacts between Whites and Blacks can improve race relations if four conditions are met (Brehm & Kassin, 1996): (a) The Blacks and Whites who come into contact with one another are of *equal status* (e.g., Pettigrew, 1969); (b) the contacts involve *intimate, one-on-one interactions* (e.g., Wilder, 1986); (c) the contacts entail *cooperative activities aimed at achieving superordinate goals* (e.g., Gaertner, Mann, Dovidio, Murrell, & Pomare, 1990); and (d) the contacts are supported by *social norms* (e.g., Cohen, 1982).[35]

Given Stephan's (1986) disappointing finding regarding the effects of desegregation, it seems that the above conditions often were not met in school settings. I strongly suspect that the same holds in work organizations. For example, in classrooms, students compete for the attention and approval of their teachers, interfering with attempts to construct a cooperative climate (Aronson, 1988); in the workplace, employees likewise may compete for their supervisors' approval as well as for financial rewards, promotions, and the like. Thus, racial contact should not be expected to lead to a reduction in prejudice in many, if not the vast majority of, organizational settings. An exception might be in those settings in which "real teams" are used. The members of such teams are highly interdependent because the teams, not the individual members, are assigned tasks, evaluated, and rewarded (e.g., Guzzo & Shea, 1992). This possibility of work teams promoting racial harmony is supported by assessments of the *jigsaw classroom* (Aronson, 1990; Aronson, Blaney, Stephan, Sikes, & Snapp, 1978). The jigsaw classroom refers to a cooperative learning method in which the material to be learned is divided into subtopics, and each student is assigned a subtopic to learn and teach to the class; thus, for the class as a whole to succeed, everyone needs everyone else. Jigsaw classrooms, compared with traditional classrooms, have been shown to produce less prejudice and other positive outcomes. Therefore, it appears worthwhile to assess how teams may influence the effects of interracial contacts on prejudice in organizations. Such research should attend systematically to the levels of status equality, cooperative behaviors, personal interactions, and racial harmony-supporting norms within teams, to ascertain which, if any, of these attributes are necessary conditions for prejudice reduction in organizations. Such research not only may produce results that are academically enlightening but also may contribute to formulating solutions to one of American society's most nagging problems.

The research on the effects of school desegregation demonstrates that prejudice, indeed, is a sticky problem. In part, interventions aimed at reducing prejudice may have failed because of the nature of modern racism. Because modern racists believe that racism is bad and do not see themselves as racist, attempts to train them to understand and to see the need for respecting people of color is analogous to preaching to a choir—one composed of sinners who do not know they are such. Because diversity training in organizations typically has an aim of creating such awareness (Conference Board, 1994), it is quite doubtful that currently formulated interventions are successful with a principal target audience—modern racists (Brief & Hayes, 1997; Pettigrew & Martin, 1987). A strategy suggested by Devine and Monteith (1993) does appear promising, however.

The strategy is predicated on descriptions of modern and other new forms of racism as entailing a mix of egalitarian values and anti-Black feelings (e.g., Dovidio & Gaertner, 1986; McConahay, 1986). Given that egalitarian values are integral to a modern racist's self-conception and inconsistent with racist behaviors, they may serve as a focus for attempting to reduce discrimination in organizations. Simply, if a training program could be devised to heighten the importance of egalitarian values (those already salient to the modern racist's self-image), then those values may outweigh anti-Black feeling in responding to Blacks.[36] Rokeach and his colleagues (e.g., Rokeach & Cochrane, 1972; Rokeach & Grube, 1979) often have shown that the relative importance of a value (e.g., equality) can be manipulated quite readily. With a training focus on egalitarian values, the topic of racism or perhaps even Blacks may not even need to be raised. Clearly, such a training program ought to be designed, implemented, and evaluated rigorously.

Another promising, albeit rather obvious, intervention strategy worthy of assessment focuses on norms, or more precisely stated, rules. In discussing Black-White contacts as a means of reducing prejudice, I raised the issue of norms; now, I essentially, will expand on that potential condition for success.

Several investigators have shown, in nonwork settings, that when discriminatory behaviors can be detected, the availability of norms directly relevant to situationally appropriate behaviors, coupled with negative sanctions for violating those norms, minimizes discrimination in interracial encounters (e.g., Blanchard, Lilly, & Vaughn, 1991; Cohen, 1982; Cook, 1978; Donnerstein & Donnerstein, 1976; Pettigrew, 1985; Yarrow, Campbell, & Yarrow, 1958). When these norms emanate from authority figures (e.g., Pettigrew, 1961; Weigel & Howes, 1985), they can be thought of as rules. Thus, research is needed on the effects of the articulation of organizational rules governing the treatment of Blacks, the monitoring of how Blacks actually are treated, and the imposition of sanctions for rule violations. Not only do we need to know if rules and enforcement of them in organizations reduce discrimination, we also need to understand how variants on rules, monitoring, punishments, and so on affect salient outcomes. Would it not be wonderful to find that simple rules, *appropriately implemented,* alleviate racial discrimination in organizations?

In closing my perhaps too brief examination of reducing the effects of racism in organizations, I shift to concern with those organizational members who can be characterized as nonprejudiced (e.g., those scoring low on a measure of modern racism). In particular, I think it is important to explore how they might be enlisted in the fight against racism in organizations. Nonprejudiced Whites have been described as having established and internalized standards for nonprejudicially responding to Blacks and as capable of controlled inhibition of automatically activated stereotypes and of conscious, deliberate activation of nonprejudiced beliefs (e.g., Devine & Monteith, 1993, but see Gilbert & Hixon, 1991). Thus, nonprejudiced people know the right thing to do, want to do it, and can do so.

Let me couple this description of nonprejudiced individuals with several assumptions: Organizations are populated with significant numbers of nonprejudiced individuals; they, at least occasionally, are instructed either explicitly or implicitly by their organizational superiors to do the wrong thing and/or see others acting inappropriately toward Blacks; despite their favorable racial attitudes, they tend to comply with their bosses' wishes and, generally, to remain silent in the face of wrongdoing. The previously discussed Shoney's case (Watkins, 1993), data from the earlier described organizational simulation studies of business justifications to discriminate and modern racism (Brief, Reizenstein, et al., 1997), and more general treatments of the negative consequences of compliance pressures in organizations (e.g., Brief, Buttram, & Dukerich, 1997; Brief, Buttram, Elliott, Reizenstein, & McCline, 1995; Jackall, 1988; Kelman & Hamilton, 1989) all suggest that the assumption that nonprejudiced organizational members will comply with instructions from above to discriminate is quite plausible. In addition, given the attention organizational scholars have paid to understanding how to encourage whistle-blowing (e.g., Miceli & Near, 1992), it seems that the assumption that nonprejudiced individuals, having observed incidents of racial discrimination, tend to remain silent also is reasonable. Two questions then surface: (a) How might nonprejudiced organizational members be motivated to resist either explicit or implicit instructions from above to discriminate? and (b) how might nonprejudiced organizational members be motivated to blow the whistle on racial discrimination?

Heightening the importance of nonprejudiced organizational members' egalitarian values (as already discussed in reference to modern racists) may be an answer to both the above questions. Perhaps organizations, as has been done for customer service (e.g., Schneider & Bowen, 1995), can seek to create a *climate for equality*. Such a climate can be thought of as composed of organizational members' collective perceptions of those management-supplied goals, means, rewards, and task and social emotional support (e.g., Kopelman, Brief, & Guzzo, 1990) aimed at establishing policies, practices, and routines intended to create equality (e.g., racial). Measuring this type of organizational climate and examining its antecedents and consequences represent significant but potentially important challenges for us.

Another response to both the questions might be to encourage *principled disobedience* (Brief et al., in press). Such disobedience may entail subordinates questioning the perceived wishes of their superiors or alerting appropriate organizational officials to potential cases of racial discrimination. Knowledge about how to encourage principled disobedience is scarce. Kelman and Hamilton (1989), however, do provide a number of suggestions, all awaiting empirical scrutiny. First, disperse authority. By holding managers accountable both to their line superiors and to a human resources executive for hiring, promotion, and other personnel decisions, a window is left open to question directives from either party or to voice other concerns. Second, redefine the role of the loyal subordinate. By condemning loyalty construed as unquestioning servitude to one's superior or "the organization" and by praising the people who have the courage to question troublesome orders or practices, blind obedience may become stigmatized. Third, endorse peer discourse. By creating a norm of openness among subordinate managers, the critical discussion of instructions from above, the articulation of other misgivings, the reinforcement of doubts, and analyses of how to respond may be facilitated. I imagine that acting on these sorts of suggestions in most organizations would constitute nothing less than a revolutionary change in management style. But assessments of such revolutions may be exactly what is required to enlighten organizational practices that encourage nonprejudiced individuals to do the right thing.

I am sure that other potential strategies for holding modern racists in check and for capitalizing on the positive tendencies of nonprejudiced individuals in organizations can be articulated. (For example, on the specific issues at hand, see Brief et al., in press; on the more general problem of inhibiting wrongdoing in organizations, see Brief, Buttram, & Dukerich, 1997; Brief, Reizenstein, et al., 1997; Kelman & Hamilton, 1989; Miceli & Near, 1992.) I hope that the strategies I presented, however, demonstrated that accumulating a body of knowledge aimed at informing remedies for racism in organizations will require us to stretch the horizon of the research questions we now pose. In other words, continuing to pursue the consequences of demographic diversity is not enough; we need to start tackling research questions targeted on solving the problems already unmasked by organizational demographers and other diversity researchers. Again, questions about promoting egalitarian values and principled disobedience represent merely two of many options that can and should be pursued aggressively. Before offering these potential strategies for managing diversity, I devoted considerable attention to showing that the underlying cause of the dilemma, racism, is an enduring, complex, subtle force in American society, including in its organizations. Thus, as potential solutions to the problems associated with racially integrating organizations are formulated and examined, it is important to keep in mind that these difficulties are mere symptoms of a chronic disease, racism.

Concluding Thoughts

This chapter's story about the attitudinal baggage people bring to work in the form of negative racial attitudes is limited in several ways. For example, the discussion of new forms of racism was restricted to the American context; it was asserted that these forms entail a blend of traditional American values and anti-Black feelings. This assertion may be questionable, however, because similar, subtle forms of prejudice have been described in Britain, France, and Germany (Pettigrew & Meertens, 1995). In addition, Swim, Aikin, Hall, and Hunter (1995) asserted that the same sort of beliefs that underline modern racism also form the foundation of modern sexism (e.g., denial of continuing discrimination). Empirically, these researchers demonstrated a distinction between old-fashioned and modern beliefs about women, with the latter characterized, for instance, by antagonism toward women's demands and lack of support for policies designed to help women. These exemplary limitations of the story told should not come as a surprise because it was introduced as only an illustration of attitudinal baggage. As such, the story was intended to demonstrate that people do bring attitudes to work with them that are important for understanding their organizational behaviors. Moreover, the story was intended to be sufficiently detailed to show that the subject matter of attitudinal baggage can be intellectually provocative and that research on how organizations can modify the attitudes people bring to work is sorely needed.

In opening this chapter, I provided a few other examples of attitudinal baggage organizational scientists may want to consider. The set is large, and its boundaries are undefined. In addition to organizational members' attitudes toward Blacks, concern for attitudes toward any out-group represented in an organization's employee or customer/client population may be worthy of more direct attention. This might include attitudes toward Asian Americans, Hispanic Americans, foreigners, members of certain religious groups (e.g., Muslims and Jews), persons who are disabled (physically and mentally), gays, lesbians, and so on.[37] Moreover, the attitudes toward other potential organizational stakeholder groups that people bring to work may also warrant more research attention (e.g., attitudes toward investors, unions, and regulatory bodies). To these lists, attitudes toward certain organizational policies, practices, and procedures (e.g, empowerment) as well as toward certain products and services (e.g., tobacco and alcoholic beverages) could be added. Indeed, any strong attitude people form prior to organizational entry that is salient for understanding how they think, feel, or act in the workplace is fair game. Again, the attitudinal baggage research domain is ill defined, poorly developed, yet potentially critical to a fuller appreciation of how individuals in organizations function.

In general, within this research domain, the answers to two sorts of questions should be pursued: (a) What mechanisms might link the attitudinal baggage of concern to the organizational behavior or other outcome of interest? and (b) how might an organization intentionally or unintentionally affect the attitude of concern and/or the relationships between the attitude and outcomes of interest? The material presented on the nature of prejudice, its potential effects, and how those effects might be avoided should have demonstrated the theoretical and practical import of these questions. As I have said in closing previous chapters, my job was to entice the reader to become engaged; only time will tell if the study of attitudinal baggage takes its rightful place on the organizational science research agenda.

Notes

1. For modifications of Katz and Braly's (1933) measurement method, see Brigham (1971) and McCauley and Sitt (1978).

2. Also see Hoffman and Hurst (1990).

3. On the consensus and stability of ethnic or national stereotypes, see, for example, Gilbert (1951) and Karlins, Coffman, and Walters (1969).

4. But also see, for example, Park, Judd, and Ryan (1991) and Quattrone (1986).

5. Also see Snyder and Miene (1994).

6. For more on these attributional errors, see Pettigrew (1979) and Hewstone (1990).

7. Also see Trope and Thompson (1997).

8. For reviews of the literature pertaining to the distinctiveness rationale presented, see Hamilton and Sherman (1989) and Mullen and Johnson (1990); for alternative explanations of illusory correlations, see Hilton and von Hippel (1996).

9. See Weber and Crocker (1983).

10. But also see Gilbert and Hixon (1991).

11. For a somewhat more optimistic view on the likelihood that stereotypic thoughts can be controlled, see, for example, Brewer (1988), Fiske and Neuberg (1990), Fiske and Pavelchak (1986), and Fiske and Von Hendy (1992).

12. See also, for example, Esses et al. (1993) regarding potential mediators of the relationship.

13. Also see, for example, Dovidio and Gaertner (1991).

14. For an alternative position, see Crosby, Bromley, and Saxe (1980).

15. For a fascinating variant on realistic conflict theory, see Sidanius's (e.g., 1992) social dominance theory. This theory posits that all social systems consist of at least two castes, a hegemonic group at the top and a negative reference group on the bottom. Further, the stability of this social hierarchy is produced and maintained by (a) the differential allocation of social value by institutions, (b) the accumulated effects of discrimination by members of a hegemonic group against members of a negative reference group, and (c) behavioral asymmetries (e.g., deference to out-groups with higher status). An observed association between support for free-market capitalism and prejudice toward Blacks has been explained by the tenets of social dominance theory (Sidanius & Pratto, 1993). Also see, for example, Pratto, Sidanius, Stallworth, and Malle (1994) and Sidanius, Pratto, and Bobo (1994, 1996).

16. See also Brewer (1979); Messick & Mackie (1989); Perdue, Dovidio, Gurtman, and Tyler (1990); and Weber (1994).

17. For example, also see Brewer (1991, 1993); Crocker and Luhtanen (1990); and Noel, Wann, and Branscombe (1995).

18. Also see, for example, Allport and Kramer (1946), Epstein and Komorita (1966), and Stagner and Longdon (1955).

19. See also Rokeach (1960).

20. Nevertheless, for the likely effects of such slurs, see, for example, Greenberg, Kirkland, and Pyszczynski (1988) and Simon and Greenberg (1996).

21. But also see Citrin and Green (1990), Sears and Funk (1991), and Bobo and Kluegel (1993).

Regarding the particular problem of opposition to affirmative action in employment, see, for example, Kravitz (1995); Kravitz and Platania (1993); and Parker, Baltes, and Christiansen (1997).

22. Also see, for example, Hass, Katz, Rizzo, Bailey, and Moore (1992); Katz (1981); Katz and Glass (1979); and Katz, Wackenhut, and Hass (1986).

23. See also Kovel (1970). Recall the previously introduced idea of implicit (or unconscious) attitudes (Greenwald & Banaji, 1995).

24. Also see, for example, Dovidio and Gartner (1991); Dovidio, Mann, and Gaertner (1989); Gaertner and Dovidio (1981); and Gaertner and McLaughlin (1983).

25. See also, for example, McConahay (1983) and McConahay, Hardee, and Batts (1981).

26. I have not even come close to presenting a complete picture of the diverse and complex literature on racism. For example, the ideas of Brewer (1994) and von Hippel et al. (1995) about an information-processing component of prejudice are missing. Nevertheless, what I presented should be an ample serving for most organizational scientists, in light of the extent to which our literature is underdeveloped in regard to the treatment of racism. For those seeking more comprehensive treatment of the literature on racism and prejudice in general, see Fiske (in press).

27. The use of the word *can* is meant to imply that not all Blacks *will* be victims of discrimination in all employment settings. Some studies do report no discrimination (e.g., Sackett & Dubois, 1991). See Stone et al. (1992) for a balanced review of the literature. Although not necessarily addressing discrimination only in work organizations, the following demonstrate the often rather subtle ways Blacks can be treated disadvantageously: Biernat and Kobrynowicz (1997); Carter (1993); Davis and Watson (1982); and Yarkin, Town, and Wallston (1982).

28. See also Ibarra (1995) for more on the consequences of racial heterogeneity in organizations and Lawrence (1997) for a general discussion of organizational demography.

29. Also see Nkomo (1992).

30. See Tsui et al. (1992) and Powell and Butterfield (1997) for examples of exceptions.

31. In most research, consistent with extant theorizing, the plausible, nonprejudiced explanations used to free adherents to the new forms of racism to act on their negative attitudes have been designed to enhance the saliency and potency of nonracial factors that would justify unfavorable responding regardless of the race of the target person. See, for example, Gaertner (1976) and Gaertner and Dovidio (1981). In the story about to unfold, explanations that are explicitly racial in nature are used. Research results to be introduced later support this use.

32. See Brief et al. (in press).

33. On in-basket exercises, see Thornton (1992), for example.

34. Also see Cook (1984), Gerard (1983), and Miller and Brewer (1984).

35. Regarding the four conditions, see also, for example, Bettencourt, Brewer, Croak, and Miller (1992); Brewer and Miller (1984); Cook (1984); Fiske and Ruscher (1993); Johnson, Johnson, and Maruyama (1984); and Slavin and Madden (1979).

36. Such a relative importance notion influencing choice behavior is evident in the values literature (e.g., Brief, Dukerich, & Doran, 1991; Tetlock, 1986).

37. For a review of the limited literature on such stigmatized groups in organizations, see Stone et al. (1992).

6 Goodwill

AN ATTITUDINAL PERSPECTIVE

A dvertising, public relations, and the like are not really the subject matter of this chapter. But perhaps they should be; such devices are part of the tool kit an organization can use to mold how those beyond its boundaries evaluatively respond to it. These evaluative responses, or *attitudes of outsiders,* are what this chapter is about.

Being more businesslike, I could assert that this chapter is about such things as brand equity (e.g., Farquhar, 1989), corporate reputation (e.g., Weigelt & Camerer, 1988), firm quality (e.g., McGuire, Schneeweis, & Branch, 1990), or, my favorite, goodwill (e.g., Kieso & Weygandt, 1992). I like the accounting term, *goodwill,* because of its inclusiveness, incorporating the value of all a firm's intangible assets (including those already listed as well as others). Indeed, this chapter could be construed as providing an attitudinal perspective on the familiar business concept of goodwill. This is particularly so if goodwill is thought of as something residing in an organization's environment and varying across segments of that environment. That is, it is the attitudes of outsiders that count here; different groups of outsiders may hold quite different attitudes toward any given organization or attribute of it.

Who are these groups of outsiders? I think of them as the firm's external stakeholders. They include customers/clients, investors, the community(ies) in which the firm operates, regulatory agencies at all levels of government, and the public at large (Freeman, 1984). Although this list is daunting, it is incomplete. To it, I might add such potential constituencies as prospective employees and customers.

Why would an organization's management or we as organizational scientists care about the attitudes of these various groups? The answers are many and mostly obvious. For example, favorable organizational attitudes held by outsiders may enable a firm to charge premium prices (e.g., Klein & Leffler, 1981), to attract better-quality job applicants (e.g., Stigler, 1962), and to enhance access to capital markets (Beatty & Ritter, 1986).[1] More generally, the attitudes of outsiders matter, as suggested by Baron (1996), because of the following:

1. Negative attitudes may force organizations to take costly actions in attempting to avoid being damaged. For example, in light of the negative attitudes held by some environmental groups toward its disposable diaper product line, Proctor & Gamble produced and mailed pamphlets with such titles as "Diapers and the Environment" to 14 million households.

2. Positive attitudes may lead to organizations benefiting from sustained support. For example, satisfied customers increase purchases for those goods and services where volume discretion is possible, decrease their purchases much less sharply in the face of increasing prices, and are less attentive to competitive overtures (e.g., Andersen, Fornell, & Lehmann, 1994; Kalyanaram & Little, 1994).

3. Positive attitudes are associated with establishing implicit contracts, understandings, and expectations that can be more efficient than explicit bargaining and contracting. For example, Barney and Hansen (1994) argue that goodwill, in the form of trustworthiness, can serve as a substitute for more costly means of governing economic exchange relationships such as that between a buyer and a seller of raw materials.

Given that goodwill (i.e., the positive attitudes held by outsiders) appears to be linked to organizations avoiding costs and reaping benefits, one assumes that they engage in a host of activities aimed at promoting goodwill. This is so. In addition to specific product or service advertising, U.S. companies spend hundreds of millions of dollars each year on corporate advertising aimed at maintaining or enhancing company image (Schumann, Hathcote, & West, 1991). To this can be added what is in the public relations professional bag of tricks, for example, establishing cozy relationships with the news media, lobbying elected officials, and mobilizing grassroots political support among pensioners (Baron, 1996). But advertising and public relations are only two of several types of tactics organizations can and do employ in their attempts to influence the attitudes of outsiders. These tactics often are organized internally around the external group being targeted. In discussing corporate reputation building, Fombrun (1996) noted that companies commonly have a department for customer relations, for investor relations, for community relations, for government relations, for public relations, and so on.

In light of the considerable resources organizations seem to expend on promoting goodwill among their external constituencies, one expects that the study of the effects of these expenditures also would be considerable. This also is so, particularly among those investigators concerned with the impact of advertising and other marketing methods (cf. Jacoby, Hoyer, & Brief, 1992). The organizational community, however, at least compared with the marketing community, seems not to have taken the promotion of goodwill especially seriously (with a significant exception I will deal with later). In the organizational literature, the research closest to the general topic of goodwill addresses corporate reputation, but as recognized by Fombrun and Shanley (1990), few investigators have sought to identify factors that influence corporate reputations (e.g., Chakravarthy, 1986; Koys, 1997; McGuire et al., 1990). And it appears that most of this research is somewhat problematic because the same database is relied on—*Fortune* magazine's survey of corporate reputations. The concern is that *Fortune* surveys only executives, directors, and corporate analysts, yet the investigators using these data claim they are studying reputations per se, not corporate reputations among business elites. This may seem like a picky point; it is not. Recall that goodwill can be thought of as varying across external groups; moreover, the factors that affect it among business elites may affect, say, goodwill among customers or government officials quite differently *or* not at all.

In addition to overgeneralizing their results, corporate reputation researchers have tended to produce findings that are not particularly stimulating, at least for me. Fombrun and Shanley (1990), for example, reported that the two principal contributors to corporate reputation (as rated by *Fortune's* business elites) are recent economic performance (the more profitable, the better a firm's reputation) and riskiness (the greater the variation in profits through time, the worse a firm's reputation). Returning to my earlier point, I seriously doubt that variability in profits has the same effect it does among corporate analysts as it might, for example, among customers.

Enough negativity—on to a more detailed consideration of goodwill. Note, I said *detailed,* not fuller or more comprehensive, treatment. In the preceding chapter, racism was used to exemplify attitudinal baggage; in this chapter, the same sort of strategy is adopted. Only one facet of goodwill will be examined in attempting to entice organizational scientists to take the study of outsiders' attitudes more seriously. This facet is *customer satisfaction,* especially with service encounters. I do so because customer satisfaction is one of the few facets of goodwill that has caught the eye of organizational scholars, and coupling findings in the organizational literature with those in marketing presents a provocative picture of what can be learned by focusing on the attitudes held by outsiders toward an organization. Again, my intent is to stimulate organizational research interest in the attitudes of other external stakeholder groups, not necessarily to promote more research on customer satisfaction (but that would be all right, too).

My exploration of customer satisfaction below will begin by probing a little bit deeper into the organizational effects of customer goodwill, both short- and long-term. Next, largely to demonstrate the distinctive nature of satisfaction research in marketing, the expectancy disconfirmation model of consumer satisfaction will be described and examined briefly. As I continue with a focus on the marketing literature, I will then contrast the so-called objective of the consumer's desire, quality (Oliver, 1997), with satisfaction; as a transition to the organizational literature, emotional expression in the consumer satisfaction response will be considered. Finally, I will present and attempt to integrate two approaches to the organizational behaviors thought to directly affect customer satisfaction. One of these approaches is represented by the work of Anat Rafaeli and Bob Sutton (e.g., 1987, 1989, 1990), the other by the work of Ben Schneider and his colleagues (e.g., Schneider, 1990; Schneider & Bowen, 1985; Schneider, Parkington & Buxton, 1980). The chapter will close by returning to a more general concern with an attitudinal perspective on goodwill, to once again emphasize the need for organizational scholars to more seriously attend to how organizations influence the attitudes of their external stakeholders.

Customer Satisfaction

Fortunately, it appears that *the* book in marketing on customer satisfaction recently has been published. The book is Rich Oliver's (1997) *Satisfaction: A Behavioral Perspective on the Consumer.* I said its publication was fortunate because I clearly am no marketeer, and Oliver's book does seem to provide an excellent, although sometimes troublesome, guide for the marketing novice. The troublesome part is that the book, understandably, too lightly touches on the albeit limited organizational literature on customer satisfaction. But not to fret; this inadequacy I hope will be compensated for in the pages to come.

Now, on to a closer look at why goodwill among customers, principally in the form of customer satisfaction, can be so attractive to an organization. I begin by noting the immediate reaction to be expected from the *dis*satisfied customer. The reaction to expect, more often than not, is none. That is, the vast majority of people do not complain to the seller when dissatisfied with a good or service. For instance, data indicate that only about 20% of Americans complain in response to dissatisfying service encounters (Day, Grabicke, Schaetzle, & Staubach, 1981).[2] A reason for raising the "do nothing" response is to alert organizational researchers that complaints likely are rather poor indicators of customer goodwill, grossly underrepresenting the true levels of those who are dissatisfied. Again, the complaints being addressed are to the seller; what about complaints (or for that matter, compliments) conveyed to others (e.g., family and friends) by word of mouth? It appears that neither marketeers nor organizational scientists have taken such potential data very seriously (but see Swan & Oliver, 1989). It seems to me that word of mouth is a potentially significant means of spreading goodwill (or negative attitudes) toward an organization, and, therefore, difficult as it might be to measure, we ought to give it a go.

Again, the "do nothing" response is the likely short-term consequence of customer dissatisfaction (Oliver, 1997). As already noted, the potential array of longer-term consequences of failing to satisfy customers cannot be construed as nearly so benign. Research testing Hirschman's (1970) "exit, voice, and loyalty" framework (well known to many organizational scientists) in a marketing context indicates that dissatisfied customers tend to choose between voice (complaining) and exit (switching to another supplier); exit barriers (e.g., a monopolistic market) decrease switching and increase complaining (e.g., Andreasen, 1985; Maute & Forrester, 1993; but also see, e.g., Ping, 1993; Singh, 1991). Thus, negative customer attitudes (at least in non-monopolistic markets) can be expected to lead to the loss of business; or, more positively stated in the converse, customer satisfaction promotes loyalty. In the marketing literature, the definition of *customer loyalty* is not as straightforward as one might assume. For example, Jacoby and Chestnut (1978), followed by Dick and Basu (1994), show that it is unwise to equate loyalty solely to a pattern of repeat purchases; rather, so-called true loyalty entails both a repeat purchase pattern and favorable cognitive, affective and conative evaluations of the product or service in question. That is, purchase behaviors plus attitudes equal "true loyalty." It is easy to imagine purchases decoupled from attitudes, for instance, buying Brand X instead of the more favored Brand Y, simply because Brand Y is not available.[3]

True customer loyalty, dependent on and entailing customer satisfaction, can translate into increased profits (e.g., Andersen et al., 1994; Fornell, 1992). This is because such loyalty leads to a guaranteed customer base and, correspondingly, more accurate budgeting, more efficient strategic planning, and decreased marketing costs (Oliver, 1997). For example, Ford Motor Company has estimated that a percentage increase in owner loyalty translates into an additional $100 million in profits (Jewett, 1994).

The Expectancy Disconfirmation Model

Given that customer satisfaction can matter to organizations (especially business ones) and presumably does matter to the individuals experiencing it, I now turn to perhaps the dominant explanation in the marketing literature for customer satisfaction, the *expectancy disconfirmation model* (e.g., Oliver, 1980; Oliver & DeSarbo, 1988; Oliver & Swan, 1989; Westbrook & Oliver, 1991). In essence, the model describes consumers as forming expectations regarding the performance (quality) of a product or service (based, for example, on prior experience with the product or service and/or on communications implying its level of quality), and the state of disconfirmation of these expectations following purchase of the product or service determines the level of customer satisfaction.

Three possible states of disconfirmation are considered: *negative disconfirmation*—performance is below standard (i.e., expectations); *positive disconfirmation*—performance is above standard; and, *zero disconfirmation*—performance confirms expectations. The model posits that satisfaction occurs when performance is at least as good as expected and dissatisfaction when performance is worse than expected (but also see Oliver, 1997, pp. 112-113). Several reviews of the empirical literature generally show support for the model's predictions (e.g., Erevelles & Leavitt, 1992; Tse, Nicosia, & Wilson, 1990; Yi, 1990; but also see Churchill & Suprenant, 1982). In particular, Oliver (1977) and Iacobucci, Grayson, and Ostrom (1994) have found that the highest level of satisfaction occurs when people enter into a purchase with high expectations and experience positive disconfirmation; the lowest levels of satisfaction occur when expectations are low and negative disconfirmation is experienced.

Oliver (1997) traces the history of the expectancy disconfirmation model in consumer research to the organizational sciences, for instance, to Porter's (1961) investigation of job satisfaction involving the comparison between how much of a job facet there "should be" to how much of it "is there now." Moreover, he notes that the expectancy disconfirmation model is reflective of two somewhat competing hypotheses in social psychology. The *assimilation effect* hypothesis (Hovland, Harvey, & Sherif, 1957) suggests that consumers may assimilate performance of a product or service in such a way that satisfaction tracks those expectations (e.g., higher prior expectations and higher subsequent satisfaction), thereby creating a sort of self-fulfilling prophecy.[4] In the marketing literature, empirical support for such an assimilation effects readily can be found (e.g., Anderson, 1973; Olson & Dover, 1979; Tse & Wilson, 1988). Alternatively, the *contract effect* hypothesis (e.g., Dawes, Singer, & Lemons, 1972) suggests that consumers magnify their satisfaction reactions to performance discrepancies in the direction of the discrepancy; thus, performance above expectations is rated more highly than it really is, and performance below expectations is rated too poorly.[5]

Marketing scholars have theorized about when the assimilation effect dominates (i.e., when customer satisfaction tends to conform to prior expectations independent of performance). According to Oliver (1997), three conditions may contribute to consumers' not attending to the performance of a product or service and their reporting of satisfaction levels consistent with prior expectations. First, consumers may not be able to judge performance, for example, because it is an ambiguous concept (Hoch & Ha, 1988), as might be the case with the postpurchase evaluation of the "performance" of a piece of artwork. Second, consumers may not be interested in evaluating performance of a product or service because doing so is too inconvenient or cumbersome. Third, consumers simply may be unwilling to assess performance because the results might be disturbing, reflect poorly on their decision-making ability, and/or contradict previously drawn conclusions. Alternatively, Oliver also addressed the conditions that would make it unlikely for the assimilation effect to hold. For example, he asserted that any factor affecting the saliency of performance to the consumer should increase the extent to which disconfirmation, more so than expectation, affects satisfaction; in support of this proposition, Oliver cited the research findings of Babin, Griffin, and Babin (1994); Oliver and Bearden (1983); and others.

Clearly, research on the expectancy disconfirmation model has proven to be informative.[6] Regrettably, it seems that those few organizational scholars with a serious interest in customer attitudes are not aware of or have ignored the model.[7]

Quality

Previously, the concept of quality was evolved loosely. Now, I turn briefly to how marketeers treat *quality*, including how they relate it to customer satisfaction. Among consumer behaviorists, quality is in the eye of the beholder; it is defined as consumers' perceptions and judgments of products and services (e.g., Oliver, 1997). Subjective assessments of quality by consumers clearly can differ from assessments of quality based on objective evaluations of product or service attributes, as might be supplied by the application of industrial engineering principles (e.g., Gummesson, 1992; Ozment & Morash, 1994; Zeithaml, 1988). Correspondingly, these different assessments are influenced by different factors. Particularly interesting to me are those research findings indicating that consumers often infer quality from price (e.g., Rao & Monroe, 1989). Thus, a firm, merely by raising its prices, may enhance consumer perceptions of the quality of its products and/or services. But what impact might such a change in perceptions ultimately have on customer satisfaction?[8]

According to the expectancy disconfirmation model, if performance is salient to the consumer and if the purchased product or service does not deliver the quality expected (for example, as indicated by price), then customer dissatisfaction is predicted. This prediction highlights that quality and satisfaction can be thought of as distinct concepts (Oliver, 1993)—but maybe not. On the basis of my selective read of the salient marketing literature (e.g., Andersen et al., 1994; Bitner, 1990; Bolton & Drew, 1991; Cronin & Taylor, 1992; Gotlieb, Gerwall, & Brown, 1994), it seems to me that pre- and postconsumption judgments of quality are different beasts, with the latter, experienced quality, bearing a different relationship to satisfaction than the former. I think of preconsumption judgments as expectations and operating as posited in the expectancy disconfirmation model; postconsumption judgements, because they can be construed as cognitive evaluative reactions, arguably could be thought of as a component of customer satisfaction. Later, that argument will be made; for now, I apologize for proceeding without having clarified the quality concept further. But there is a lesson in the ambiguity. The confusion about quality *and* recognition of such in the marketing literature (e.g., Bitner & Hubert, 1994; Dabholkar, 1993; Oliver, 1994) typically are not evident among those organizational scholars with an expressed interest in customer attitudes. For instance, I do not recall seeing in the organizational literature the distinction between perceived quality as an expectation and quality as an evaluative reaction.

Service Quality: An Organizational Perspective

Customer attitudes toward products do not seem to have surfaced clearly in the organizational literature as an identifiable concern; rather, attention has focused on attitudes resulting from service encounters. Perhaps this imbalance is understandable. As will be addressed more below, service encounters have been described as a "game between people" (Bowen & Schneider, 1988, p. 45) and as "first and foremost social encounters" (McCallum & Harrison, 1985, p. 35); one might suspect that organizational scientists, as social scientists, find such social phenomena, entailing interactions between organizational insiders (employees) and outsiders (customers), as more appealing subject matter than customer attitudes toward inanimate attitude objects such as a box of cereal or a dishwasher. Yet I cannot imagine a convincing argument that customer product attitudes are irrelevant to understanding organizational functioning and effectiveness, and I readily can imagine the study of those attitudes being intriguing. For instance, some may be turned on to learn which, if any, shop floor human resource management practices are associated with product attributes that affect customer perceptions of quality and, in turn, their levels of satisfaction. Again, however, research on the production of such attitudes is difficult to locate (indeed, I failed). So, what follows is concerned exclusively with customers' reactions to service consumption. I hope that the challenge of studying customer product attitudes will be tackled and that the future will hold the opportunity to write a fuller story about how organizations and the people in them affect the attitudes of customers.

The story I will be telling about service encounters partially tracks the one told by Pugh (1997). At the core of his story is the recognition that the provision of service is *emotional labor* (e.g., Hochschild, 1983; Rafaeli & Sutton, 1987). I begin by explaining why.

Emotional Labor

Two decades ago, Shostack (1977), a marketeer, made the now abundantly clear observation that one cannot effectively think about the production and consumption of goods and services in identical ways. She stated, "A service is rendered. A service is experienced. A service cannot be stored on a shelf, touched, tasted, or tried on for size" (p. 73). Shostack saw that the key characteristic distinguishing services from goods is the former's intangibility; others have concurred (e.g., Schneider & Bowen, 1992).[9]

The intangibility of service, in part, stems from its interpersonal aspects, the interactions between service employees and customers (e.g., Gronroos, 1990; Kelley, Donnelly, & Skinner, 1990; Zeithaml, 1981), which have been suggested to be the most important contributor to customers' assessments of quality (e.g., Tansik, 1985). An element of these important employee-customer interactions is emotions, or more precisely and aptly stated by Hochschild (1983), the "emotional style of offering the service is part of the service itself" (p. 5). This component of service encounters, on the employee's side, Hochschild termed *emotional labor.* According to her, jobs that involve emotional labor are those requiring face-to-face or voice-to-voice contact with customers, thereby, affecting the emotional state of customers, and, correspondingly, necessitating the exercise of a degree of control by employers over the emotional activities of employees. Rafaeli and Sutton (1989) used the term *display rules* to describe the emotional activities required of employees as part of their jobs. From a managerial perspective, the idea is a simple one. If employees display the right emotions, the customers will have the intended emotional reaction to the service encounter (e.g., a smiling bank teller produces a smiling customer).

Employee Attitudes

The import of the feelings service workers display toward customers contributes to the need to understand what drives these behaviors. In the organizational sciences, the most prominent line of research germane to fulfilling this need addresses *climate for service,* a concept formulated by Schneider and his colleagues and subsequently aggressively pursued by them as well as others (e.g., Burke & Borucki, 1995; Schneider & Bowen, 1985; Schneider, Parkington, & Buxton, 1980; Schneider, Wheeler, & Cox, 1992). A general (but definitely *not* singular) conclusion drawn from this research is that when organizations treat their employees well, the employees treat the customer well. Schneider and Bowen (1992) found that "employee attitudes about their employing organization are significantly correlated with their customers' perceptions of the quality of service they receive" (p. 5).[10]

An adequate theory addresses not only outcomes (e.g., "A" leads to "B") but also processes (e.g., *why* "A" leads to "B"; Dubin, 1976a). Schmit and Allscheid (1995) assert (correctly I think) that the answer to the "why" question in the climate for service literature is underdeveloped. As of now, declarative statements such as the following constitute the explanations available for observed employee attitude-customer perceptions of quality relationships: "When employees encounter human resource practices that facilitate a more positive experience for them, they will create a more positive experience for customers" (Schneider, 1990, p. 398).[11] Although not providing a complete account, I, as previously indicated, will follow the lead of Pugh (1997), who, building on Rafaeli and Sutton (1989), asserted that the emotions employees express on their jobs are related to those they feel and, on the basis of the work of Hatfield, Cacioppo, and Rapson (1994), that customers "catch" these expressed feelings. Moreover, I will borrow from Pugh's rationale as to why these "caught" feelings influence customer perceptions of quality and satisfaction with service. Recall from earlier chapters that feelings experienced at work are indicative of the affective component of job satisfaction; in an extrapolation of this idea, feelings experienced by customers during a service encounter are indicative of the affective component of their satisfaction with the service received. So, the feelings to be addressed (moods and emotions) speak to the attitudes of employees and customers.

"Leaky" Attitudes

Rafaeli and Sutton (1989) asserted that internal feelings exert a major impact on the display of the emotions at work (but see Hochschild, 1983, and Stenross & Kleinman, 1989). According to them, these displayed emotions (or expressive behaviors) include facial expressions, bodily gestures, tone of voice, and language.[12] This is consistent with Hatfield, Cacioppo, and Rapson's (1992) treatment of emotions as a "package," including, for example, expressions, patterned physiological tracings, and instrumental behaviors. Support abounds for Rafaeli and Sutton's claim of an internal feeling-expressed emotion link. For example, Ekman (e.g., 1993; Ekman & Oster, 1979) repeatedly has shown that particular experienced emotions are associated with certain universal and spontaneous facial expressions. His research indicates that even when people try to conceal or fake a particular emotion with their facial expressions, true emotions "leak" through (e.g., Ekman, 1985; Ekman, Friesen, & O'Sullivan, 1988). These findings are supported by the results of Ambady and Rosenthal's (1992) meta-analytic study of the consequences (e.g., detection of deception) of thin slices of expressive behavior (e.g., those less than 30 seconds in length). Thus, it seems that although an organization's display rules may mandate service workers to express positive emotions to customers, it should be anticipated that at least sometimes, workers' true feelings will leak through and be interpreted accurately by customers. This conclusion is in line with Rafaeli and Sutton's asserted internal feeling-expressed emotion at work link and with the idea that customers are likely to read rather accurately the job satisfaction levels of the service workers with whom they come into contact.[13]

"Caught" Attitudes

What are the consequences of customers reading the job attitudes of service providers? As already noted, climate for service researchers claim that customers adopt the attitudes expressed by the service workers they encounter (e.g., Schneider & Bowen, 1992). Similar claims are evident throughout the broader literature on customer service. For instance, Romm, a restaurant executive, stated, "If you don't have happy employees, you don't have happy guests" (Stephens & Akers, 1985, p. 134); Ulrich et al. (1991), on the basis of their findings from studies of a variety of service workers and their customers across three organizations, stated, "Employees who act surly and irascible communicate such attitudes to customers and are likely to create similar attitudes among customers" (p. 92). But again, why? The concept of *emotional contagion* advanced by Hatfield et al. (1992, 1994) may supply the answer (but also see George, 1991).

"Emotional contagion" is "the tendency to automatically mimic and synchronize facial expressions, vocalizations, postures, and movements with those of another person and, consequently to converge emotionally" (Hatfield et al., 1992, pp. 153-154). The essence of emotional contagion is the notion that through interaction with another person (e.g., a service provider), one "catches" that person's feelings. Consistent with much theorizing on mood and emotion (e.g., Isen, 1984; Zajonc, 1980b, 1984), emotional contagion is thought to occur largely outside conscious awareness (Hatfield et al., 1994). The following story demonstrates this point:

> I am reminded of the feelings I sometimes have after completing a lecture to a large class, a sense that it went particularly well or particularly badly, but I cannot determine why I feel that way. I suspect that the expressions of students, which are detected during the perfunctory scanning of audience faces . . . directly engage affective responses in me. (Morris, 1989, p. 14)

Hatfield et al. (1994) offered a detailed explanation of how emotional contagion occurs. First, in a manner consistent with research demonstrating that people tend to display facial expressions like those shown in pictures they view (e.g., Dimberg, 1982; McHugo, Lanzetta, Sullivan, Masters, & Englis, 1985; Vaughan & Lanzetta, 1980), they posited that in interactions, people synchronize and mimic the other person's expressions of emotions. Second, consistent with evidence in support of the "facial feedback" hypothesis, which depicts a correspondence between facial expressions and subjective experience (e.g., Adelman & Zajonc, 1989; Zajonc, 1993), Hatfield et al. posited that moment by moment, mimicked expressions activate the experience of similar emotions. Finally, on the basis of the reasoning underlying their first two propositions, they asserted that people tend to catch the emotions of others with whom they interact. Hatfield et al. provide a thorough review of the evidence pertaining to emotional contagion, demonstrating convincing support for their ideas. It appears that service employees leak their true feelings; customers correctly interpret these expressions; *and,* indeed, they catch the feelings expressed by the employees.[14]

Before turning to the consequences of emotional contagion in service encounters for customer satisfaction, I will address a conceptual/methodological ambiguity I noted earlier. Iacobucci et al. (1994) observed that service researchers often appear not to appreciate adequately possible distinctions between customers' perceptions of the quality of service they have received and their satisfaction with that service. They went on to express concern about their observation because it seemed to them that measures of service quality and satisfaction appear to be tapping different components of the same underlying attitude, customer satisfaction, with the former being more cognitive and the latter more affective in nature.[15] For example, take the widely used measure of service quality, SERVQUAL (Parasuraman, Zeithaml, & Berry, 1985, 1988). The measure, in part, entails customers rating the levels of several dimensions of experienced service quality (e.g., tangibles, reliability, responsiveness, courtesy, and access); such ratings can be seen to capture customers' thoughts about the service experience (the attitude object) and, therefore, to gauge the cognitive component of the attitude.[16] Below, to avoid the difficulties noted by Iacobucci et al., only the term *customer satisfaction* will be used, but consistent with prior construals, the term should be taken to refer to both the affective and cognitive components of the attitude, unless otherwise indicated.[17]

As readers already have been alerted, the caught emotions of customers can be taken to be indicative of their satisfaction, at least of the affective component. Think about a restaurant customer served by a waiter or waitress who obviously appears to be feeling enthusiastic and peppy at work. The idea is that the customer catches these feelings and, thereby, experiences the service provided as satisfying (i.e., the customer's affective evaluative response to the service is positive). Given that an employee's feelings at work are indicative of the affective component of job satisfaction and that a customer's feelings during a service encounter are indicative of customer satisfaction, a link between employee and customer attitudes has been made.

Employee and customer attitudes also can be tied together by a focus on the cognitive component of the latter (Pugh, 1997). A study by Isen, Shalker, Clark, and Karp (1978) supports this assertion. They approached people in a shopping mall and asked them to respond to a survey including questions about some of their household appliances. Some participants, earlier and in a different part of the mall, had been given small gifts by the experimenters (but not those researchers subsequently administering the survey); other participants had received no gifts. Those who received a gift reported more favorable experiences with the household appliances they were questioned about than those who did not receive a gift. Isen et al. attributed their results to the receipt of the gift creating a positive affective state, which, in turn, influenced the judgments of survey respondents.

Two explanations have been advanced for such an effect, Bower's (1981) *affect priming model* and Schwartz and Clore's (1983, 1988) *affect as information model* (but also see Forgas's, 1995, *affect infusion model* and the empirical results of Martin, Abend, Sedikides, and Green, 1997). The affect priming model posits that affective states facilitate the recall of mood-congruent information from memory (e.g., a positive affective state leads to positive memories about experiences with home appliances). Alternatively, the affect as information model posits that people rely on their current moods as information in making evaluative judgments. For instance, when asked how satisfied they are with their clothes dryer, people can be thought of as asking themselves, "How do I feel about it?" (Schwartz & Clore, 1988, p. 46) and using their current, unrelated feelings as information in forming their responses. This explanation is consistent with Parasuraman et al.'s (1985) observation that "in the absence of tangible evidence to evaluate quality, consumers must depend on other cues" (p. 42). Either model leads to the same place; customer emotions caught from service employees affect their satisfaction in the direction of the caught emotion. In other words, how people cognitively evaluate a service encounter is influenced by their feelings, and those feelings are affected by the leaked attitudes of service workers.

In summary, a detailed account has been provided for observed associations between employee and customer attitudes. The story blended findings evident in the climate for service, emotional labor, marketing, and social psychology literatures. Reliance on prior findings to construct the story should not lead one to take it in its entirety as "truth." Rather, the story will have served its purpose if it provokes empirical scrutiny.

In wrapping up the topic of customer satisfaction, I return to a theme evident in prior chapters: The real action may be at higher levels of analysis (e.g., group or organization). For example, recall from Chapter 4 that the case was made for group affective tone (i.e., the homogeneous affective reactions within a group; e.g., George, 1990, 1996a) as an indicator of the affective component of job satisfaction at the group level of analysis and for this tone, through its effects on contextual performance (the contributions people make to a work environment supportive of task performance, e.g., Borman & Motowidlo, 1993), influencing group effectiveness.[18] Now, couple these recalled arguments with the idea, advanced by Cameron (1986) and Steers (1991), that the effectiveness of a unit (e.g., an organization) can (or, indeed, should) be gauged, at least in part, by stakeholder (e.g., customer) satisfaction. Thus, prior chapters already have provided a rationale for considering linkages between employee and customer satisfaction at a higher level of analysis. Support for doing so is readily available in the service literature cited in the preceding paragraphs.

In the climate for service literature, attention has been focused at the organizational level of analysis with *climate* defined as the *shared* perceptions of organizational policies, practices, and procedures (formal and informal; e.g., Reichers & Schneider, 1990). Thus, the notion that employee and customer attitudes are tied together at the organizational level is not new, but as already recognized (Schmit & Allscheid, 1995), the notion is clearly worthy of more conceptual analysis. Perhaps the suggested affective tone-contextual performance-customer satisfaction chain is not to the reader's liking; fine. Other explanations ought to be formulated and pursued empirically. The aim is to enhance our understanding of how organizations influence the attitudes of a crucial group of outsiders, their customers; the aim is not to prove that this or that particular theoretical approach is on target.

Back to the "Big Picture"

The previously introduced idea that stakeholder satisfaction is an indicator of organizational effectiveness is appealing to me. Candidly, this appeal stems from normative approaches to the claims of stakeholders that describe a person's or group's stake in an organization in moral terms (in addition to economic and legal ones; e.g., Bowie & Duska, 1990; Donaldson & Preston, 1995; Evans & Freeman, 1988; Weiss, 1994). At the beginning of this chapter, a focus on stakeholder satisfaction (i.e., a facet of goodwill) was justified because of the benefits organizations economically can accrue from it; now, in closing the chapter, I assert that stakeholder satisfaction, in and of itself, warrants attention from the organizational research community simply because it is the right thing to do.[19]

The importance of studying customer satisfaction (the now obvious thrust of this chapter) stems from its previously demonstrated association with significant economic outcomes for organizations, its probable but seemingly unexamined association with the extent to which organizations have fulfilled their legal obligations to consumers (e.g., those pertaining to product safety), and, as claimed above, its being a moral end, in and of itself. Recall, however, that customer satisfaction was chosen to exemplify the study of outsider attitudes largely because other options, providing an identifiable stream of organizational research, simply were not available. There are the earlier cited research on reputation (e.g., Fombrun, 1996) and a few other efforts that cannot yet be described as either as extensive or as systematic as the climate for service or emotional labor streams of research. For example, it has been suggested that a firm's image as a responsible corporate citizen influences its attractiveness in the labor markets (e.g., Rynes, 1991); a handful of studies indicate this may be so (e.g., Gatewood, Gowan, & Lautenschlager, 1993; Turban & Greening, 1997).

Whether the reasoning is economically, legally, or morally rooted, the same conclusion is evident: Organizational scientists need to devote considerably more energy to thinking about the attitudes of external stakeholders. In particular, we need to attend to how organizations affect their environments regarding these attitudes. Indeed, in *organization-centered* (Davis & Powell, 1992) approaches to organization-environment relations (e.g., Pfeffer & Salancik, 1978; Thompson, 1967; Williamson, 1981), the concept of attitudes plays virtually no role at all. But it takes exceedingly limited imagination to conjure up rationales for the potential import of the attitudes held by various external stakeholders (e.g., investors, suppliers, local community groups, consumer groups, and environmental groups). Take the obvious case of the attitudes of a special interest group that chooses to boycott an organization. Such boycotts are not rare, are increasing (e.g., between 1984 and 1990, boycotts against American companies increased more than threefold and in 1990 numbered around 150; Baron, 1996), and often inflict harm on their targets (Vogel, 1978). How are these negative attitudes formed? When do they lead to activism? What might organizations do to change them? All seem to be interesting questions waiting to be pursued by organizational scholars.

The picture that I have painted thus far is overly bleak. Organizational scientists have demonstrated concern for external stakeholders attitudes (e.g., Shenkar & Yuchtman-Yaar, 1997); they just have not tended to use the term *attitude* and, more important, to take full advantage of the extensive literatures on attitude formation and change. Recent and intriguing research *implicitly* concerned with external stakeholders attitudes has been conducted by Elsbach (e.g., 1994; Elsbach & Sutton, 1992). She tied her work to Pfeffer's (1981) analysis of the symbolic actions managers engage in to affect the images of their organizations. More specifically, Elsbach was interested in the organizational image of legitimacy; she approached it by blending two theoretical orientations: institutional theory (e.g., DiMaggio & Powell, 1983; Meyer & Rowan, 1977) and impression management theories (e.g., Schlenker, 1980; Tedeschi, 1981). The former orientation suggests that organizations project an image of legitimacy by developing and retaining normative and widely endorsed structures, procedures, and personnel (e.g., Brint & Karabel, 1991; Covaleski & Dirsmith, 1988; Galaskiewicz, 1991).[20] The latter orientation suggests that managers actively take on roles, display social affiliations, and provide verbal explanations of behavior to project legitimacy (Leary & Kowalski, 1990).[21] By combining institutional and impression management orientations, Elsbach demonstrated empirically that at least under limited conditions, organizations can protect their image of legitimacy by acknowledging image-threatening events and by providing evidence that their actions related to these events are in accordance with widely endorsed and normative practices.

Although the literature cited in the above paragraph is enlightening, the question at hand is, "Would explicit attention to the attitude concept contribute to current explorations regarding organizational image?" What immediately comes to my mind, given Elsbach's (1994) reliance on the impression management literature, is the idea that managers, in communicating to stakeholders, are likely to express *attitudes* they do not endorse privately. That is, in the impression management literature, people are portrayed as motivated to express themselves in ways to be seen favorably by others; such expressions need not be consistent with their private attitudes (e.g., Baer, Hinkle, Smith, & Fenton, 1980; Tedeschi, Schlenker, & Bonoma, 1971; also see Chapter 3). This perspective leads to a host of questions not now considered seriously by those organizational scholars interested in organizational reputation, image, legitimacy, and the like. For example, does striving for organizational legitimacy prompt managers to dishonestly express their attitudes to stakeholders? Assuming that managers do not honestly express their private attitudes, do stakeholders sense such deceptive actions? The latter question implies that organizations, in their quest for goodwill, might produce the converse.

Obviously, there is no strong tradition in the organizational sciences of gauging the attitudes of outsiders (except for those of customers). Although we lack experience in studying the attitudes of investors, governmental officials, social activists, and other organizational stakeholders, I see no great methodological challenge in doing so, except perhaps for gaining access. The access problem can be thought of as manifesting itself in at least two ways: noncoverage and nonresponse errors. *Noncoverage errors* refer to some members of a population not being covered by the sampling frame used and, therefore, having no chance of being selected into the sample (Dillman, 1991). For example, this might occur in seeking to construct a sample of social activists with a stake in a given organization. The *nonresponse error,* all too familiar to many organizational scientists, could occur, for example, if some sampled social activists failed to respond to the survey administered to them. Fortunately, methods for reducing both errors, the nonfamiliar and familiar one, are available (e.g., Dillman, 1991; Groves, 1990). Captive audiences (for example, employees at work and customers in a store) may be nice but are not essential to the conduct of organizational research.

The study of outsider attitudes, in a way, affords us the opportunity to learn more about the influences of organizations on society; my sense is that we are too focused on economic criteria of organizational effectiveness and how the internal functioning of organizations affects these criteria. Many groups of stakeholders are nonmarket players who have real interests in organizational outcomes. Knowing more about what these nonmarket players think and feel about organizations, particularly economic ones, is bound to be enlightening.

Notes

1. Also see, for example, Fombrun (1996), Fombrun and Shanley (1990), and Milgrom and Roberts (1986).

2. For more data, see, for example, Andreasen (1985); Best and Andreasen (1977); and Rust, Subramanian, and Wells (1992). For explanations as to why dissatisfied customers so often fail to complain, see, for example, Gronhaug and Gilly (1991), Ross and Oliver (1984), and Ursic (1985).

3. Regarding the psychology of encountering such obstacles to consumption, see, for example, Bagozzi and Warshaw (1990).

4. For a similar idea in the organizational sciences, recall from Chapter 2 Schneider, Gunnarson, and Wheeler's (1992) treatment of the role of opportunity in job satisfaction.

5. For more on the nature of the hypothesized contrast effect, see Oliver (1980).

6. In addition to the work cited above, see Spreng, Mackenzie, and Olshavsky (1996) and Zwick, Pieters, and Baumgartner (1995).

7. More generally, the model appears to be germane to the study of job attitudes yet also has not been so applied. In particular, for example, the model might shed additional light on the effectiveness of *realistic job preview* processes (e.g., Wanous, 1992), helping to explain the varying effects of preemployment expectations on job satisfaction.

8. For more on the subjective nature of quality, see, for example, Jacoby and Olson (1985); Reeves and Bednar (1994); and Zeithaml, Parasuraman, and Berry (1990).

9. For more on the uniqueness of service, see, for example, Bowen & Schneider, 1988; Kelley, 1993; Mills, Hall, Leidecker, & Marguiles, 1983; Parasuraman, Zeithaml, & Berry, 1985; Tansik, 1985; Zeithaml, 1981.

10. Also see Tornow & Wiley (1991); Ulrich, Halbrook, Mecker, Stucklik, & Thorpe (1991); and Wiley (1991).

11. See Schneider and Bowen (1985, p. 427; 1992, pp. 7, 17) for analogous kinds of explanations.

12. For more exposure to Rafaeli and Sutton's thinking, see, for example, Rafaeli (1989a, 1989b), Rafaeli and Sutton (1990, 1991), and Sutton (1991).

13. For an engaging analysis of employees violating display rules and showing customers their real feelings, see Van Maanen and Kunda (1989).

14. Pugh (1997) noted and then assumed away the possibility that the causal direction might be from customer to employee rather than as currently portrayed; here, I do likewise.

15. Recall from the previous discussion of quality that the measures Iacobucci et al. (1994) are concerned with must be postconsumption ones.

16. For more on SERVQUAL, see, for example, Cronin and Taylor (1992) and Finn and Lamb (1991).

17. On the component structure of customer satisfaction, see, for example, Mano and Oliver (1993) and Oliver (1993); recall from Chapter 3 that the different components of an attitude can have different antecedents and consequences.

18. For recent empirical support of portions of this posited causal chain, see Podsakoff, Ahearne, and Mackenzie (1997), who investigated, at the group level of analysis, the relationship between organizational citizenship behavior and performance.

19. Nord (1977) makes a similar assertion in regard to the satisfaction of a particular group of stakeholders—employees.

20. For more on institutional theory, see, for example, Powell and DiMaggio (1991) and Scott (1995).

21. For applications of impression management theory to the problems of projecting and maintaining organizational legitimacy, see, for example, Salancik and Meindl (1984); Staw, McKechnie, and Puffer (1983); and Sutton and Kramer (1990).

7 The Study of Attitudes in the Organizational Sciences as History

I had considered constructing this concluding chapter as a catalog of the numerous propositions that have been presented in previous chapters. On reflection, however, I decided that doing so was excessive. Although some of the propositions offered rest on sound conceptual foundations, others are nothing more than my speculations. Moreover, although some are supported by considerable empirical evidence, others await to be tested. So, instead of closing with a catalog, I will close with an observation—one that holds for all the propositions presented, independent of the quality of their conceptual foundations and the quantity of empirical evidence in their support.

The observation I offer (as well as the title of the chapter) is influenced heavily by Gergen (1973). Below, I will begin by briefly recounting his story of why theories of social behavior are primarily reflections of contemporary history. I intend to show how Gergen's conclusions apply to what this book is about by examining the possible effects of changes in the nature of work on the study of job attitudes. Thus, changes in the contemporary history of work (at least in the United States) will be discussed next. Then I will address the implications of these changes for some of the propositions offered in earlier chapters. Finally, and briefly, the effects of history are extended to the study of attitudes in and around organizations, in general.

Theory as History

Gergen (1973) claimed that his tale of theory as history is about social psychology, but as should become evident, it is germane to any of the social sciences, including organizational sciences. So, in summarizing his story, I will substitute social or organizational sciences for social psychology. Gergen opens with the assertion that the aim of science is to understand the factors responsible for stable relationships between events (also see Jones & Gerard, 1967), but he goes on to argue that such understandings (i.e., theories) "cannot readily be developed over time because the facts on which they are based do not generally remain stable" (p. 310). Thus, theory in the social (e.g., organizational) sciences primarily is a reflection of contemporary history.

The above line of reasoning, according to Gergen (1973), is dependent on two arguments, the first of which I reject: (a) The dissemination of social science knowledge results in changes in the patterns of behaviors on which the knowledge is based (e.g., the managerial community applies a given theory derived from observations of that community, thereby, the facts on which the theory was based are modified); and (b) as cultures change, so do the premises on which the theories were built, thereby, invalidating the theories. My rejection of the first argument largely is based on the belief that organizational science theories do not widely affect managerial behavior. Consistent with that belief is the growing body of literature indicating that the adoption of new management techniques is not necessarily dependent on organizational scholars providing guidance but more so on other "fashion setters" (e.g., the business media and management consultants) exploiting the sociopsychological vulnerabilities (e.g., the striving for novelty) of "fashion followers" (i.e., managers; e.g., Abrahamson, 1991, 1996; see also Hambrick, 1994). In addition, my rejection of Gergen's first argument is influenced by the belief that theory in the organizational sciences should not be used as a strict guide for managerial action. Very, very simply, this belief is rooted in the philosophical idea that all scientific theories are fallible (e.g., Bhaskar, 1986; Harré, 1986; Popper, 1935/1959; and, as applied to the organizational sciences, Brief & Dukerich, 1991).[1]

Gergen (1973) successfully argued his second point (that observed regularities and, therefore, the theories explaining them are wedded to cultural stability, i.e., to historical circumstance) by demonstrating, with several examples, that as a culture changes, the theoretical premises regarding social behavior in it become invalidated. For instance, he showed that the variables predicting political activism during the early stages of the Vietnam War were dissimilar from those predicting activism during later periods, and, therefore, theories of political activism built from earlier findings were invalidated by later results. Concern in the organizational sciences for the temporal instability of results as a product of cultural change is exceedingly limited. Although a few scholars have addressed "time" as a construct salient for understanding organizational behaviors (e.g., Katz, 1978; McGrath & Rotchford, 1983), only Wagner and Gooding (1987), to my knowledge, have shown how a body of organizational research (that addressing employee participation) has been affected by trends within a society. Wagner and Gooding are not the only source of proof in the organizational sciences supportive of Gergen's arguments regarding the effects of cultural change on the truth value of theory. For instance, although Gergen addressed the effects of changes in a culture through time, I see the organizational evidence demonstrating the variable results produced by tests of a theory in different cultures (e.g., Earley, 1986, 1989; Erez & Earley, 1987) as support for his position.

For now, assume along with me, that theories in the organizational sciences might be invalidated by cultural or societal trends. A general implication of this assumption is that our theories, as already noted above, may not be particularly good guides for managerial action. Gergen (1973), likewise, does not see theory as a specific guide to action but rather as a *sensitizing device* by enlightening us as to the range of factors *potentially* influencing behavior under various conditions. In the organizational sciences, others (e.g., Brief & Dukerich, 1991) have staked out a similar position. Although such general implications are not without value, concern here is specifically with how cultural or societal changes might affect what we think we now understand about attitudes in and around organizations. To draw more specific implications, one needs to address specific cultural and societal changes. This is done in the next section in which the changing nature of work is considered. Characterizations of how work has changed in the 1980s and 1990s subsequently will be used to speculate about the effects of such changes on what organizational scientists now theoretically know about attitudes, namely, employee attitudes.

The Changing Nature of Work

My colleagues and I previously have noted the importance of recognizing that what is taken to constitute work is not a historical constant (e.g., Aldag & Brief, 1979; Brief & Nord, 1990b). Doing so was an easy task because we relied on analyses of how the nature of work has changed *through the ages* (e.g., from precivilized times to the industrial revolution).[2] But attempting to characterize *contemporary* changes in the nature of work (e.g., during the last decade or so) is a much more difficult task because gauging such short-term changes essentially requires that they be measured as they occur (i.e., the target is moving). Of the numerous attempts to meet this challenge, it seems to me that Cappelli et al. (1997) have provided the clearest picture of change.[3] The following, therefore, draws heavily, but not exclusively, from Cappelli et al.'s analyses. Other evidence of change (e.g., Howard, 1995) will be brought to bear as needed.

What Was

The nature of work that was evident until the 1980s developed in corporate America after World War I (Cappelli, 1995). Its development was influenced by several forces, according to Cappelli et al. (1997), for example, the application of Frederick W. Taylor's (e.g., 1903, 1911) principles of scientific management; the availability of the military as a role model for employee selection and placement and human resources planning; and the demands of trade unions and managerial attempts to resist them.

The nature of work prevalent from around the 1930s until the 1980s rested on three principles (Cappelli et al., 1997). First, shareholders were the risk takers, and management acted to reduce their uncertainness. Second, management made all the important decisions, and nonmanagement (i.e., labor) carried out these decisions (i.e., they were not responsible for "thinking"). Third, personnel (e.g., promotion) decisions entailing the fate of nonmanagers were based on objective criteria such as seniority and not on criteria dependent on the subjective judgments of supervisors, such as performance ratings. The application of these principles played out in a variety of ways. Companies often hired inexperienced, unskilled workers and, consequently, took on the responsibility of training and developing them. Workers were promoted exclusively on the basis of seniority or seniority plus some minimum skills test. Workers were subject to temporary layoffs associated with business cycles, but union contracts protected workers from the harshness of these temporary bouts of unemployment. The wages for workers reflected their job titles and seniority (e.g., Medoff & Abraham, 1980), and the variability of a worker's paycheck was a product of the overtime he or she worked. Jobs had clearly specified job descriptions, tasks were differentiated sharply across jobs, and decision making was concentrated at the top of corporate hierarchies. I imagine to those of my generation (i.e., baby boomers), at least, the description provided is not a foreign one because it portrays a facet of the world in which we grew up. Associated with this familiarity is a certain comfort; change and the uncertainness associated with it bring discontent. What then brought the discontent I now see around me? This is the question to which I now turn.[4]

Forces for Change

The nature of work outlined above, although far from perfection, did benefit employees and employers alike. It protected workers from the turbulent environments in which their employing organizations were embedded, and it aided employers by making much more predictable the quantity and quality of labor inputs (Cappelli et al., 1997). It seems that forces beyond the control of both benefiting parties began to alter the nature of work in the United States beginning in the early 1980s. Examples of these forces, drawn from Cappelli et al., include the following:

- *Changes in public policy.* The 1975 Employee Retirement Income Security Act, for example, required that generous retirement programs for management employees be offered proportionally to all employees (Pfeffer & Barron, 1988), thereby creating an incentive to move lower-level people with now costly benefits packages off the payroll and to use contingent labor with no attached benefit costs.
- *Increased competitiveness.* The economy of Dallas, Texas, provides evidence of this. In 1970, less than 7% of all businesses in Dallas failed, but by the mid-1980s, the annual failure rate rose to about 21% (Tully, 1993). Moreover, in 1980, imports averaged less than 8% of the U.S. gross domestic products, but by 1994, they rose to 14% (*Economic Report of the President,* 1995).
- *Increased pressures for quicker responses to product markets.* For example, in the 1970s, new products accounted for 20% of corporate profits, but by the 1980s, one third of profits came from new products (Slater, 1993).
- *Increased turbulence in financial markets.* For instance, between 1980 and 1990, one third of *Fortune's* list of top manufacturing companies had been threatened with a hostile takeover, and one third ceased to exist as an independent business (Cappelli et al., 1997).

- *Increased pressures from investors.* Small investors were displaced by large, vocal investors.[5] For example, between 1985 and 1994, the percentage of shares of the 1,000 largest U.S. companies owned by individual investors dropped by about 14%, and the percentage of shares owned by institutional investors increased up to about 57% ("21st Century Capitalism," 1994).[6]

What Is

As a result of the forces noted above, how has the nature of work changed in the United States? According to numerous accounts (e.g., Applebaum & Batt, 1994; Doeringer et al., 1991; Handy, 1989; Heydebrand, 1989; Jensen, 1989; Leicht & Fennel, 1997; Osterman, 1996; Reich, 1991; Rousseau & Wade-Benzoni, 1995; Smith, 1997; Zuboff, 1988), the answer is in many ways. To greatly simplify matters, I once again largely will borrow from Cappelli et al. (1997) and list a few of the facts they reported.

Job loss and insecurity. In the 1980s and 1990s, numerous American corporations downsized. These events often received considerable media attention; as a result, job insecurity became a national problem. This reasoning appears to rest on several facts. For example, about 20% of workers saw their jobs disappear during the 1980s; toward the end of that period, job loss was higher among older and more educated workers (Farber, 1993). Consistent with this, Cappelli and O'Shaughnessy (1995) reported that the number of top executives, middle managers, and supervisors *each* fell by 6% between 1986 and 1992. As a final example, this one emphasizing the job insecurity of workers less well off, the probability of remaining on a job for less than a year among those with less than a high school education rose 6% during the last two decades (Farber, 1995).

The rise in contingent workers. Between 1980 and 1991, the number of temporary workers increased by 225% (Parker, 1994). Obviously, not all these temporary workers are so by choice. It has been estimated that the number of persons wanting to work more hours (involuntary part-timers and persons who are unemployed) rose from about 7% of the labor force in 1969 to more than 14% in 1989 (Leete & Schor, 1994; but also see Nardone, Herz, Mellor, & Hipple, 1993).

Wages, hours, and income insecurity. It seems to me that organizational scientists have demonstrated some concern for the problem of *job* insecurity (e.g.,

Ashford, Lee, & Bobko, 1989; Brockner, Grover, Reed, & DeWitt, 1992; Greenhalgh & Rosenblatt, 1984) but virtually no interest in *income* insecurity. Job insecurity essentially stems from the threat of losing one's job, whereas income insecurity also can stem from the threat of a reduction in hours, wages, and/or benefits (Brief & Atieh, 1987). Income insecurity appears to be a fact of work in the 1990s. For instance, losing one's job does not necessarily mean a loss in income because a displaced worker might obtain another job at the same or higher wage level. But as reported by Cappelli et al. (1997), less than 28% of displaced workers in 1992 did so. Between 1979 and 1989, real wages rose by less than 1%, but they *dropped* by more than 12% for those workers with only a high school education (Mishel & Bernstein, 1994). Not only have average wages fallen for many Americans, but also the variance in their incomes has increased. The variance in earnings between 1980 and 1987 was 41% higher than it was between 1970 and 1978 (Gottschalk & Moffit, 1994). Regarding hours, self-reported work rose about 6 hours a week between 1973 and 1987 (Harris & Associates, 1988; but also see Coleman & Pencavel, 1993; Robinson, 1990). More germane to the problem of insecurity, "the variance in hours worked has been rising" (Cappelli et al., 1997, p. 194).

Declining satisfaction, increasing stress. Cappelli et al. (1997) reported the results of surveys conducted by Roger Starch Worldwide showing that from 1976 to 1994, the number of people indicating they were "extremely satisfied" with their work fell from 41% to 27%. Stress-related disabilities more than doubled during the 1980s, accounting for 13% of all worker compensation claims by 1990 (Labs, 1992).

Again, the above characteristics of the nature of work today is far from a complete one, nor is the claim made that it will stand the test of time. Historians may one day look back at the 1980s and 1990s and see a period quite different from the one I have described. Nevertheless, the contemporary view is rather bleak for many workers, with the "rules of working" (or, in the words of some, the "psychological contract" between employees and employers; e.g., Rousseau, 1995) having changed for the worse. For too many Americans, working today means living in fear—fear of losing one's job, of becoming an involuntary contingent worker, of learning how to manage a family budget with a variable income.

The changing nature of work per se is fascinating, but it is not the focus of attention here. Rather, that focus remains on attitudes—as seen below, specifically on the implications of the changing nature of work for the study of job attitudes.

Change and the Study of Job Attitudes

The changing nature of work can affect the study of job attitudes in at least three ways. First, what was considered to be an antecedent or consequence of job satisfaction may change in meaning or in type. Second and likewise, the meaning or substance of the focal attitude (e.g., job satisfaction) might be altered. Third, the relationship between the job attitude and some other variable of interest may be different. Each of these possibilities is discussed in turn.[7]

In Chapter 2, the extensive literature on the job satisfaction-employee turnover relationship was recognized. I will use that relationship to begin addressing the first way how the changing nature of work might affect the study of job attitudes. Given the apparent rise in temporary employees and independent contractors, it seems legitimate to question what turnover means among these peripheral workers. Although I cannot adequately articulate why, it seems clear to me that the act of a temporary worker quitting after 4 days into a 5-day assignment is not equivalent to a worker within 5 years of tenure voluntarily leaving his or her job. The difference simply may lie in the magnitude of the acts, but I sense there is more to it that ought to be considered by those researchers interested in turnover as a consequence of job satisfaction. Another way turnover might be different today pertains to the idea that it may no longer be described adequately as a result of being *pushed* out by dissatisfaction and/or *pulled* out by an attractive alternative. For example, Hall and Mirvis (1995) wrote about the *adaptive organization* that values impermanence and the *protean career* involving work in several organizations. Their descriptions suggest that it may become commonplace for people to join an organization to fulfill a rather specific developmental need and, having had that need satisfied, to move on. Again, this sort of turnover seems different from, say, a worker in the 1960s or 1970s changing organizations largely for a sizable pay increase.

Turnover is one of several traditionally investigated consequences of job satisfaction whose meaning and/or substance likely have been affected by the changing nature of work. Other forms of role withdrawal as well as task and contextual performance may need to be reconsidered in light of the new rules of working. Likewise, the meaning and/or substance of several traditionally investigated antecedents of job satisfaction probably should be analyzed in light of the changing nature of work. For example, as noted in Chapter 2, newly hired employees who have their expectations met are more likely to be satisfied with their jobs. Might not the changing nature of work lead to certain expectations (e.g., those regarding job security) being truncated across wide segments of the population and to other expectations being more commonly salient (e.g., those regarding short-term developmental or credentialing outcomes)? If either of these are so, old approaches to construing and measuring expectations simply will not wash.

The second way the changing nature of work might affect the study of job attitudes entails rethinking the meaning and/or substance of job satisfaction (or some other focal job attitude). Recall from Chapter 2 that overall job satisfaction can be thought of as a combination of a person's satisfaction with various job facets. Given what was said above about expectations, it is not a great leap (a) to question whether the facet(s) most central to overall job satisfaction have shifted through time and (b) to examine if facets not traditionally considered have emerged as important. Regarding the former, it is known that reports of overall job satisfaction at least used to primarily reflect satisfaction with the work itself (e.g., Aldag & Brief, 1978). Is this true today? Does some other facet dominate (e.g., job security)? Or does facet contribution systematically vary across segments of the labor force (e.g., core versus peripheral employees)? Such questions *might* be thought of as pertaining to the problem of *gamma change* that organizational change researchers contend with (e.g., Golembiewski, Billingsley, & Yeager, 1976) or the problem of *functional equivalence* confronted by multinational survey researchers (e.g., Alwin, Braun, Harkness, & Scott, 1994).

Here, of course, the concern is with changes *through time* in what overall job satisfaction really means to respondents. Regarding emergent job facets, I suspect that changes in the nature of work have made salient to many workers features of jobs previously considered important to the satisfaction of only a relatively few. For instance, I imagine, as suggested above, that more people now are interested in a job principally as a stepping-stone than was the case, and, not inconsistently, that fewer people see promotional opportunities within the organization housing their current job as a significant contributor to satisfaction. These examples, of course, assume that organizational tenure is down along with upward organizational mobility. The issue is that serious students need to ponder the possibility that what was studied as a job attitude two or three decades ago now has a different meaning; in other words, it exists in the mind of the American worker as a different aim or purpose. Such an assertion is consistent with Weick's (1979) notion of retrospective sensemaking. People may retrospectively construe as important to their satisfaction that which they acted to obtain. Thus, if the changing nature of work has altered behavioral options, then what is considered satisfying in work may follow. Alternatively, what is now readily available in work could represent a need unsatisfied. Whatever the underlying process, evidence is beginning to emerge that what is in the mind of the American worker has changed. According to Cappelli et al. (1997), a recent Roper poll shows that for the first time in 15 years, newer entrants to the labor market (i.e., members of "Generation X"; Coupland, 1991) are reporting that leisure counts the most to them.

The third way that the changing nature of work might affect the study of job attitudes is closest to that articulated by Gergen (1973): The relationship between the job attitude and some other variable of interest may be affected. In prior chapters, I have argued for a positive relationship between job satisfaction and performance, at an organizational level of analysis. Maybe I was (or will be) wrong. *Implicitly,* the prior arguments for a satisfied workforce contributing to a work environment supportive of task performance and thereby, enhancing organizational effectiveness, were predicated on the assumption that a *relational* form of psychological contract exists between employees and employer. According to Rousseau (1995), this form of contract involves an open-ended, often long-term relationship with considerable economic and socioeconomic investments by both parties. These investments entail a high degree of mutual interdependence and barriers to exit and, from the employee's perspective, result in high levels of affective and continuous commitment as well as strong organizational integration/identification. Thus, one readily can see how, with a relational contract in place, a satisfied workforce translates into enhanced organizational effectiveness; simply, under a relational contract, the satisfied employee is motivated to contribute to the attainment of organizational goals, *knowing full well his or her contributions beyond the call of duty will be paid back by the employer.*

But the new rules of working dictate that the prevalence of relational contracts has declined (or will do so) and that the *transactional* form has increased (or will do so). Again, according to Rousseau, this form of psychological contract focuses on short-term, monetizable exchanges such as "a fair day's work for a fair day's pay." "Transactional contracts are limited, arm's-length agreements, low on involvement and of short duration" (Rousseau & Wade-Benzoni, 1995, pp. 294-295). From the employee's point of view, transactional contracts result in low levels of commitment and weak organizational integration/identification.[8] Thus, the worker subjected to a transactional contract (perhaps a temporary or independent contractor), although satisfied with his or her job, may be reluctant to go beyond the call of duty (for example, by engaging in so-called organizational citizenship behaviors) because the worker knows that such contributions are unlikely to be repaid in kind. So, theoretical arguments under one set of rules of working simply may not hold under a newer, different set of rules. That is, Gergen's (1973) assertion that observed regularities and, therefore, the theories explaining them are wedded to historical circumstance appears quite applicable to the study of attitudes in organizations.

Final Observations

A theme evident in prior chapters was that although job attitudes have been the mainstay of those of us interested in organizational behavior, there exists a seemingly huge and largely uncharted and untapped reservoir of attitude concepts germane to the breadth of the organizational sciences. When the notions of attitudinal baggage and goodwill among external stakeholders were explored, this theme came into focus. Both these areas of inquiry, perhaps, are even more subject to the sorts of historical forces explored above in regard to the study of job attitudes.

To examine the idea of attitudinal baggage, the racial attitudes people bring to work with them were addressed in some detail. That examination clearly documented the study of prejudice as contemporary history. First, it was shown that during the last 50 years, the self-reported attitudes of White Americans toward Blacks have improved dramatically. Second, and more interestingly, a rationale was presented as to why conscious racial attitudes such as those reflected in blatant racism are considerably less salient today for understanding unfair discrimination in the workplace than are such unconscious attitudes as modern racism (e.g., McConahay, 1983). Historical forces, likely beginning with American reactions to the Holocaust, drove racism underground and changed what was thought to be known about it in significant ways. More generally, as the legally sanctioned, morally governed, culturally supported behaviors in a society evolve, so too do the attitudes held by people in that society.[9] This generalization applies to the study of attitudes among external stakeholders as well as to the study of attitudinal baggage. Our colleagues in marketing, for example, have incorporated explicitly a concern for the effects of societal trends on consumer attitudes and behaviors (e.g., Belk, 1990; McCracken, 1986; Wallendorf, 1980). I am reasonably confident that even a cursory survey, for example, of the political science or sociology literatures would produce evidence of such explicit concern pertaining to other stakeholder groups (e.g., government officials). I am not sure, however, if that would be so if the literature within our domain were so surveyed.[10]

The message of this chapter should now be loud and clear: With the passage of time, what we know about attitudes in and around organizations likely erodes. This erosion is to be taken not as something to be avoided but rather as a natural happening that provides a stimulus for us to continuously question ourselves. Indeed, it is my aspiration that this book will be received mostly about question raising, not answer supplying. As Einstein put it, "To raise new questions, new possibilities, to regard old questions from a new angle, requires creative imagination and marks real advance in science" (Einstein & Infeld, 1938, p. 92). In the end, I can only hope that your "creative imagination" has been sparked, contributing to an organizational science not now conceived of by any of us.

Notes

1. For a more radical view of theory in the organizational sciences see, for instance, Gergen and Thatchenkery (1996).

2. Highly informative examples of analyses of changes in the nature of work through the ages include Dubin (1976b), Heneman (1973), and, especially, Tilgher (1931).

3. Other attempts I have described elsewhere (Brief, 1995).

4. For more on how work was, see, for example, Baritz (1960); Barron, Dobbins, and Jennings (1985); Ginzberg and Berman (1963); Jacoby (1985); and Nelson (1980).

5. On increased pressures from investors, an absolute must read is Useem's (1993) *Executive Defense.*

6. Cappelli et al. (1997) also asserted that management techniques were a force for change. Because I am not confident these techniques are an effect rather than a cause, they are not listed here. Indeed, I have told only a small fraction of Cappelli et al.'s story about the forces for change. Of their untold story, I urge the reader to consider their analysis of the effects of executive incentives benchmarked on shareholder value. These incentives probably enhanced greatly the "we-they" distinction between management and labor in organizations. Clearly, many executives no longer can claim "we are all in this together" (p. 218). For more on the negative consequences of recent change in how executives are compensated, see, for example, Bok (1993), Crystal (1991), and Frank and Cook (1995).

7. For a clarification of how the word *meaning* has been used in this paragraph, see Brief and Nord (1990b).

8. For more on Rousseau and her colleagues' insights on psychological contracts, see, for example, Robinson, Kraatz, & Rousseau (1994); Rousseau (1989); and Rousseau & Parks (1993).

9. The societal forces identified are in line with those considered by contemporary institutional theorists (Scott, 1995).

10. See Zald (1990), although not explicitly concerned with attitudes, for an important exception.

Postscript

A lthough the preceding section was labeled "Final Observations," I do have a few more words to share. (Sorry.) These words do not pertain to the implications of Gergen's (1973) story; rather, they are more pragmatic in nature, addressing where the study of attitudes in and around organizations should be headed *now*. I offer this direction because I suspect that some readers might expect a book such as this to close by suggesting those research questions that ought to be answered to ensure a bright future for the area of inquiry. But please recall that each of the previous chapters was loaded with questions in need of answers, and, more important, in each chapter a serious attempt was made to entice readers to create their own mysteries to be solved. So in the next (and I promise final) paragraphs, the future is addressed in broad strokes by reiterating those questions previously posed, whose answers I suspect may open many, many doors.

The study of job attitudes would be enlivened considerably by attempts to construct grounded theories explaining what constitutes a satisfying job and how the effects of these salient features of work vary across different groups of people. Also sorely needed in the study of job attitudes is research aimed at discovering the mechanism that might link an individual's job satisfaction to organizational effectiveness. Finally, in regard to the study of job attitudes, attention to shared attitudes ought to be increased considerably, with the earlier proposed integrated model of job satisfaction (combining person and situation attributes) as a prime target. For example, how do the dispositional composition of a work group and the characteristics of the environment in which that group is embedded combine to influence the level of job satisfaction?

Perhaps more intriguing than the study of job satisfaction is the wide-open area of attitudinal baggage. Because so few questions have been posed about the attitudes people bring to work, it is unrealistic to presume that any particular question now evident is likely to be the one to open up fertile theoretical territory. I am certain, however, that a tremendous effort should be expended on understanding how organizations can modify the prejudices their members carry with them.

Like the area of attitudinal baggage, the topic of goodwill among organizational stakeholders approached from an attitudinal perspective is so poorly developed as to make isolating especially promising research questions darn near impossible. Nevertheless, I will give it a shot. Most globally, research is required to facilitate articulating the ways in which organizations affect the attitudes of key external constituencies (other than customers) and how these attitudes affect organizational processes and outcomes. If such research were to be pursued, I hope that careful attention would be paid to the role of the popular press, an obviously powerful voice in society rarely focused on by organizational scientists.

I am done. I trust the above does not fall short of the expectations of those who had envisioned a close with a glimpse of a desired future. It is your move now.

References

Abelson, R. P. (1982). Three modes of attitude-behavior consistency. In M. P. Zanna, E. T. Higgins, & C. P. Herman (Eds.), *Consistency in social behavior: The Ontario Symposium* (Vol. 2, pp. 131-146). Hillsdale, NJ: Lawrence Erlbaum.

Abelson, R. P., Kinder, D. R., Peters, M. D., & Fiske, S. T. (1982). Affective and semantic components in political person perception. *Journal of Personality and Social Psychology, 42,* 619-630.

Abelson, R. P., & Prentice, D. A. (1989). Beliefs as possessions: A functional perspective. In A. R. Pratkanis, S. J. Breckler, & A. G. Greenwald (Eds.), *Attitude structure and function* (pp. 361-381). Hillsdale, NJ: Lawrence Erlbaum.

Abrahamson, E. (1991). Managerial fad and fashion: The diffusion and rejection of innovations. *Academy of Management Review, 16,* 586-612.

Abrahamson, E. (1996). Management fashion. *Academy of Management Review, 21,* 254-285.

Adams, J. S. (1963). Toward an understanding of inequity. *Journal of Abnormal Social Psychology, 67,* 422-436.

Adams, J. S. (1965). Inequity in social exchange. In L. Berkowitz (Ed.), *Advances in experimental social psychology* (Vol. 2, pp. 267-299). New York: Academic Press.

Adams, J. S., & Freedman, S. (1976). Equity theory revisited: Comments and annotated bibliography. In L. Berkowitz & E. Walster (Eds.), *Advances in experimental social psychology* (Vol. 9, pp. 43-90). New York: Academic Press.

Adelman, P. K., & Zajonc, R. B. (1989). Facial efference and the experience of emotion. *Annual Review of Psychology, 40,* 249-280.

Adler, P. S., & Borys, B. (1996). Two types of bureaucracy: Enabling and coercive. *Administrative Science Quarterly, 41,* 61-89.

Adorno, T. W., Frenkel-Brunswik, E., Levinson, D. J., & Sanford, R. N. (1950). *The authoritarian personality.* New York: Harper & Row.

185

Agho, A. G., Price, J. L., & Mueller, C. W. (1993). Discriminant validity of measures of job satisfaction, positive affectivity and negative affectivity. *Journal of Occupational and Organizational Psychology, 66*(2), 196.

Ajzen, I. (1988). *Attitudes, personality, and behavior.* Chicago: Dorsey.

Ajzen, I. (1991). The theory of planned behavior. *Organizational Behavior and Human Decision Processes, 50,* 179-211.

Ajzen, I., & Fishbein, M. (1977). Attitude-behavior relations: A theoretical analysis and review of empirical research. *Psychological Bulletin, 84,* 888-918.

Ajzen, I., & Fishbein, M. (1980). *Understanding attitudes and predicting social behavior.* Englewood Cliffs, NJ: Prentice Hall.

Aldag, R. J., Barr, S. H., & Brief, A. P. (1981). Measurement of perceived task characteristics. *Psychological Bulletin, 90,* 415-431.

Aldag, R. J., & Brief, A. P. (1978). Examinations of alternative models of job satisfaction. *Human Relations, 31,* 91-98.

Aldag, R. J., & Brief, A. P. (1979). *Task design and employee motivation.* Glenview, IL: Scott, Foresman.

Alderfer, C. P. (1969). An empirical test of a new theory of human needs. *Organizational Behavior and Human Performance, 4,* 142-175.

Alderfer, C. P. (1972). *Human needs in organizational sciences.* New York: Free Press.

Alderfer, C. P., & Thomas, D. A. (1988). The significance of race and ethnicity for understanding organizational behavior. In C. L. Cooper & I. T. Roberson (Eds.), *International Review of Industrial and Organizational Psychology* (pp. 1-41). New York: John Wiley.

Allen, N. J., & Meyer, J. P. (1990). Organizational socialization tactics: A longitudinal analysis of links to newcomers' commitment and role orientation. *Academy of Management Journal, 33*(4), 847-858.

Allen, R. E., & Lucero, M. A. (1996). Beyond resentment: Exploring organizationally targeted insider murder. *Journal of Management Inquiry, 5,* 86-103.

Allport, F. H., & Allport, G. W. (1921). Personality traits: Their classification and measurement. *Journal of Abnormal and Social Psychology, 16,* 1-40.

Allport, G. W. (1935). Attitudes. In C. Murchison (Ed.), *A handbook of social psychology* (pp. 798-844). Worcester, MA: Clark University Press.

Allport, G. W. (1937). *Personality: A psychological interpretation.* New York: Holt, Rinehart & Winston.

Allport, G. W. (1954). *The nature of prejudice.* Cambridge, MA: Addison-Wesley.

Allport, G. W., & Kramer, B. M. (1946). Some roots of prejudice. *Journal of Psychology, 22,* 9-39.

Allport, G. W., & Odbert, H. S. (1936). Trait-names: A psycho-lexical study. *Psychological Monographs, 47*(1, Whole No. 211).

Altemeyer, R. (1988). *Enemies of freedom: Understanding right-wing authoritarianism.* San Francisco: Jossey-Bass.

Altemeyer, R. (1994). Reducing prejudice in right-wing authoritarians. In M. P. Zanna & J. M. Olson (Eds.), *The psychology of prejudice: The Ontario Symposium* (Vol. 7, pp. 131-148). Hillsdale, NJ: Lawrence Erlbaum.

Alwin, D. F., Braun, M., Harkness, J., & Scott, J. (1994). Measurement in multinational surveys. In I. Borg & P. Mohler (Eds.), *Trends and perspectives in empirical social research.* New York: Walter De Gruyter.

Ambady, N., & Rosenthal, R. (1992). Thin slices of expressive behavior as predictors of interpersonal consequences: A meta-analysis. *Psychological Bulletin, 111,* 256-274.

Andersen, E. W., Fornell, C., & Lehmann, D. R. (1994). Customer satisfaction, market share, and profitability: Findings from Sweden. *Journal of Marketing, 58,* 53-66.

Anderson, N. H. (1981). Integration theory applied to cognitive responses and attitudes. In R. E. Petty, T. M. Ostrom, & T. C. Brock (Eds.), *Cognitive responses in persuasion* (pp. 361-397). Hillsdale, NJ: Lawrence Erlbaum.

Anderson, R. E. (1973). Consumer dissatisfaction: The effect of disconfirmed expectancy on perceived product performance. *Journal of Marketing Research, 10,* 38-44.

Andreasen, A. R. (1985). Consumer responses to dissatisfaction in loose monopolies. *Journal of Consumer Research, 12,* 135-141.

Andrews, F. M., & Withey, S. B. (1974). Developing measures of perceived life quality: Results from several national surveys. *Social Indicators Research, 1,* 1-26.

Andrews, K. H., & Kandel, D. B. (1979). Attitude and behavior: A specification of the contingent consistency hypothesis. *American Sociological Review, 44,* 298-310.

Applebaum, E., & Batt, R. (1994). *Transforming work systems in the United States.* Ithaca, NY: ILR.

Areni, C. S., & Lutz, R. J. (1988). The role of argument quality in the elaboration likelihood model. *Advances in Consumer Research, 15,* 197-203.

Arkes, H. R., Boehm, L. E., & Xu, G. (1991). Determinants of judged validity. *Journal of Experimental Social Psychology, 27,* 576-605.

Arkin, R. M., & Lake, E. A. (1983). Plumbing the depths of the bogus pipeline: A reprise. *Journal of Research in Personality, 17,* 81-88.

Aronson, E. (1968). Dissonance theory: Progress and problems. In R. P. Abelson, E. Aronson, W. J. McGuire, T. M. Newcomb, M. J. Rosenberg, & P. H. Tannenbaum (Eds.), *Theories of cognitive consistency: A sourcebook* (pp. 5-27). Chicago: Rand McNally.

Aronson, E. (1969). The theory of cognitive dissonance: A current perspective. In L. Berkowitz (Ed.), *Advances in experimental social psychology* (Vol. 4, pp. 1-34). San Diego, CA: Academic Press.

Aronson, E. (1988). *The social animal.* New York: Freeman.

Aronson, E. (1990). Applying social psychology to desegregation and energy conservation. *Personality and Social Psychology Bulletin, 16,* 118-132.

Aronson, E., Blaney, N., Stephan, C., Sikes, J., & Snapp, M. (1978). *The jigsaw classroom.* Beverly Hills, CA: Sage.

Arvey, R. D., & Bouchard, T. J., Jr. (1994). Genetics, twins, and organizational behavior. In B. M. Staw & L. L. Cummings (Eds.), *Research in organizational behavior* (Vol. 16, pp. 47-82). Greenwich, CT: JAI.

Arvey, R. D., Bouchard, T. J., Jr., Segal, N. L., & Abraham, L. M. (1989). Job satisfaction: Environmental and genetic components. *Journal of Applied Psychology, 74,* 187-192.

Arvey, R. D., Carter, G. W., & Buerkley, D. K. (1991). Job satisfaction: Dispositional and situational influences. In C. L. Cooper & I. T. Robertson (Eds.), *International review of industrial and organizational psychology* (Vol. 6, pp. 359-383). New York: John Wiley.

Arvey, R. D., McCall, B. P., Bouchard, T. J., Jr., Taubman, P., & Cavanaugh, M. A. (1994). Genetic influences on job satisfaction and work values. *Personality and Individual Differences, 17*(1), 21-33.

Asch, S. E. (1951). Effects of group pressure upon the modification and distortion of judgments. In H. Guetzkow (Ed.), *Groups, leadership and men* (pp. 177-190). Pittsburgh, PA: Carnegie Press.

Ashford, B. E., & Mael, F. (1989). Social identity theory and the organization. *Academy of Management Review, 14,* 20-39.

Ashford, S. J., Lee, C., & Bobko, P. (1989). Content, causes, and consequences of job insecurity: A theory-based measure and substantive test. *Academy of Management Journal, 32,* 803-829.

Ashmore, R. D. (1970). The problem of intergroup prejudices. In B. E. Collins (Ed.), *Social psychology* (pp. 246-296). Reading, MA: Addison-Wesley.

Ashmore, R. D., & Del Boca, F. K. (1981). Conceptual approaches to stereotypes and stereotyping. In D. L. Hamilton (Ed.), *Cognitive processes in stereotyping and intergroup behavior* (pp. 1-36). Hillsdale, NJ: Lawrence Erlbaum.

Assouline, M., & Meir, E. I. (1987). Meta-analysis of the relationship between congruence and well-being measures. *Journal of Vocational Behavior, 31,* 319-332.

Avolio, B. J., Howell, J. M., & Sosik, J. J. (1996, April). *A funny thing happened on the way to the bottom line.* Paper presented at the meeting of the Society for Industrial and Organizational Psychologists, San Diego, CA.

Axsom, D. (1989). Cognitive dissonance and behavior change in psychotherapy. *Journal of Experimental Social Psychology, 25,* 234-252.

Babin, B. J., Griffin, M., & Babin, L. (1994). The effect of motivation to process on consumers' satisfaction reactions. In C. T. Allen & D. R. John (Eds.), *Advances in Consumer Research* (Vol. 21, pp. 406-411). Provo, UT: Association for Consumer Research.

Baer, R., Hinkle, S., Smith, K., & Fenton, M. (1980). Reactance as a function of actual versus projected autonomy. *Journal of Personality and Social Psychology, 38,* 416-422.

Bagozzi, R. P. (1981). Attitudes, intentions, and behavior: A test of some key hypotheses. *Journal of Personality and Social Psychology, 41,* 607-627.

Bagozzi, R. P., & Burnkrant, R. E. (1979). Attitude organization and the attitude-behavior relationship. *Journal of Personality and Social Psychology, 37,* 913-929.

Bagozzi, R. P., & Burnkrant, R. E. (1985). Attitude organization and the attitude-behavior relation: A reply to Dillon and Kumar. *Journal of Personality and Social Psychology, 49,* 47-57.

Bagozzi, R. P., & Warshaw, P. R. (1990). Trying to consume. *Journal of Consumer Research, 17,* 127-140.

Bagozzi, R. P., & Yi, Y. (1989). The degree of intention formation as a moderator of the attitude-behavior relationship. *Social Psychology Quarterly, 52,* 266-279.

Bagozzi, R. P., Yi, Y., & Baumgartner, J. (1990). The level of effort required for behaviour as a moderator of the attitude-behaviour relation. *European Journal of Social Psychology, 20,* 45-59.

Ball-Rokeach, S. J., Rokeach, M., & Grube, J. W. (1984). *The great America values test: Influencing behavior and belief through television.* New York: Free Press.

Banaji, M. R., & Greenwald, A. G. (1994). Implicit stereotyping and unconscious prejudice. In M. P. Zanna & J. M. Olson (Eds.), *The psychology of prejudice: The Ontario Symposium* (Vol. 7, pp. 55-76). Hillsdale, NJ: Lawrence Erlbaum.

Banaji, M. R., Hardin, C., & Rothman, A. J. (1993). Implicit stereotyping in person judgment. *Journal of Personality and Social Psychology, 65,* 272-281.

Bandura, A. (1977). Self-efficacy: Toward a unifying theory of behavioral change. *Psychological Review, 84,* 191-215.

Bargh, J. W., Chaiken, S., Govender, R., & Pratto, F. (1992). The generality of the automatic attitude activation effect. *Journal of Personality and Social Psychology, 62,* 893-912.

Baritz, L. (1960). *The servants of power: A history of the use of social science in American industry.* Middletown, CT: Wesleyan University Press.

Barley, S. R., & Knight, D. B. (1992). Toward a cultural theory of stress complaints. In B. M. Staw & L. L. Cummings (Eds.), *Research in organizational behavior* (Vol. 14, pp. 1-48). Greenwich, CT: JAI.

Barnard, C. I. (1938). *The functions of the executive.* Cambridge, MA: Harvard University Press.

Barney, J. B., & Hansen, M. H. (1994). Trustworthiness as a source of competitive advantage. *Strategic Management Journal, 15,* 175-190.

Baron, D. P. (1996). *Business and its environment.* Upper Saddle River, NJ: Prentice Hall.

Baron, R. A. (1974). The aggression-inhibiting influence of heightened sexual arousal. *Journal of Personality and Social Psychology, 30,* 318-322.

Baron, R. A. (1984). Reducing organizational conflict: An incompatible response approach. *Journal of Applied Psychology, 69,* 272-279.

Baron, R. A. (1990). Environmentally-induced positive affect: Its impact on self-efficacy, task performance, negotiation, and conflict. *Journal of Applied Social Psychology, 20,* 368-384.

Baron, R. A. (1993). Affect and organizational behavior: When and why feeling good (or bad) matters. In J. K. Murnighan (Ed.), *Social psychology in organizations: Advances in theory and research* (pp. 63-88). Englewood Cliffs, NJ: Prentice Hall.

Baron, R. A., & Ball, R. L. (1974). The aggression-inhibiting influence on nonhostile humor. *Journal of Experimental Social Psychology, 10,* 23-33.

Baron, R. A., Fortin, S., Frei, R., Hauvner, L., & Shack, M. (1990). Reducing organizational conflict: The potential role of socially-induced positive affect. *International Journal of Conflict Management, 1,* 56-74.

Barrick, M. R., & Mount, M. K. (1991). The Big Five personality dimensions and job performance: A meta-analysis. *Personnel Psychology, 44,* 1-26.

Barrick, M. R., & Mount, M. K. (1993). Autonomy as a moderator of the relationships between the Big Five personality dimensions and job performance. *Journal of Applied Psychology, 78,* 111-118.

Barrick, M. R., Mount, M. K., & Strauss, J. P. (1993). Conscientiousness and performance of sales representatives: Test of the mediating effects of goal setting. *Journal of Applied Psychology, 78,* 715-722.

Barron, J. M., Dobbins, F. R., & Jennings, P. D. (1985). War and peace: The evolution of personnel administration in U.S. industry. *American Journal of Sociology, 92,* 350-383.

Bateman, T. S., & Organ, D. W. (1983). Job satisfaction and the good soldier: The relationship between affect and employee "citizenship." *Academy of Management Journal, 26,* 587-595.

Bateman, T. S., & Strasser, S. (1984). A longitudinal analysis of the antecedents of organizational commitment. *Academy of Management Journal, 27,* 95-112.

Batson, C. D., Flink, C. H., Schoenrade, P. A., Fulz, J., & Pych, V. (1986). Religious orientation and overt versus covert racial prejudice. *Journal of Personality and Social Psychology, 50,* 175-181.

Bauman, K. E., Fisher, L. A., & Koch, G. G. (1989). External variables, subjective expected utility, and adolescent behavior with alcohol and cigarettes. *Journal of Applied Social Psychology, 19,* 789-804.

Baumeister, R. F. (1982). A self-presentational view of social phenomena. *Psychological Bulletin, 91,* 3-26.

Baumeister, R. F., & Tice, D. M. (1984). Role of self-presentation and choice in cognitive dissonance under forced compliance: Necessary or sufficient causes? *Journal of Personality and Social Psychology, 46,* 5-13.

Bayton, J. A. (1946). Personality and prejudice. *Journal of Psychology, 22,* 59-65.

Beach, L. R. (1993). *Making the right decision.* Englewood Cliffs, NJ: Prentice Hall.

Beatty, R., & Ritter, J. (1986). Investment banking reputation and the underpricing of initial public offerings. *Journal of Financial Economics, 45,* 213-232.

Beck, L., & Ajzen, I. (1991). Predicting dishonest actions using the theory of planned behavior. *Journal of Research in Personality, 25,* 285-301.

Bedeian, A. G., Ferris, G. R., & Kacmar, K. M. (1992). Age, tenure, and job satisfaction: A tale of two perspectives. *Journal of Vocational Behavior, 40,* 33-48.

Beer, M. (1980). *Organization change and development: A systems view.* Santa Monica, CA: Goodyear.

Belk, R. W. (1990). Halloween: An evolving American consumption ritual. *Advances in Consumer Research, 17,* 508-517.

Bem, D. J. (1965). An experimental analysis of self-persuasion. *Journal of Experimental Social Psychology, 1,* 199-218.

Bem, D. J. (1972). Self-perception theory. In L. Berkowitz (Ed.), *Advances in experimental social psychology* (Vol. 6, pp. 1-62). San Diego, CA: Academic Press.

Bendick, M., Jr., Jackson, C. W., & Reinoso, V. A. (1994). Measuring employment discrimination through controlled experiments. *Review of Black Political Economy, 23,* 25-48.

Bentler, P. M., & Speckart, G. (1979). Models of attitude-behavior relations. *Psychological Review, 86,* 452-464.

Bentler, P. M., & Speckart, G. (1981). Attitudes "cause" behaviors: A structural equation analysis. *Journal of Personality and Social Psychology, 40,* 226-238.

Berger, C. J., & Cummings, L. L. (1979). Organizational structure, attitudes, and behaviors. In B. M. Staw (Ed.), *Research in organizational behavior* (Vol. 1). Greenwich, CT: JAI.

Berger, P. L., & Luckman, T. (1967). *The social construction of reality.* New York: Doubleday Anchor.

Berkowitz, L., & Devine, P. G. (1989). Research traditions, analysis, and synthesis in social psychological theories: The case of dissonance theory. *Personality and Social Psychology Bulletin, 15,* 493-507.

Berscheid, E. (1966). Opinion change and communicator-communicatee similarity and dissimilarity. *Journal of Personality and Social Psychology, 4,* 670-680.

Best, A., & Andreasen, A. R. (1977). Consumer response to unsatisfactory purchases: A survey of perceiving defects, voicing complaints, and obtaining redress. *Law & Society Review, 11,* 701-742.

Bettelheim, B., & Janowitz, M. (1964). *Dynamics of prejudice.* New York: Harper.

Bettencourt, B. A., Brewer, M. B., Croak, M. R., & Miller, N. (1992). Cooperation and the reduction of intergroup bias: The role of reward structure and social orientation. *Journal of Experimental Social Psychology, 28,* 301-319.

Beyer, J. M., Chattopadhyay, P., George, E., Glick, W. H., Ogilvie, D. T., & Pugliese, D. (1997). The selective perception of managers revisited. *Academy of Management Journal, 40,* 716-737.

Bhaskar, R. (1986). *Scientific realism and human emancipation.* Thetford, UK: Thetford Press.

Biernat, M., & Kobrynowicz, D. (1997). Gender- and race-based standards of competence: Lower minimum standards but higher ability standards for devalued groups. *Journal of Personality and Social Psychology, 72*(3), 544-557.

Bies, R. J. (1987). The predicament of injustice: The management of moral outrage. In B. M. Staw & L. L. Cummings (Eds.), *Research in organizational behavior* (Vol. 9, pp. 289-319). Greenwich, CT: JAI.

Billig, M. (1976). *Social psychology and intergroup relations.* London: Academic Press.

Bitner, M. J. (1990). Evaluating service encounters: The effects of physical surroundings and employee responses. *Journal of Marketing, 54,* 69-82.

Bitner, M. J., & Hubert, A. R. (1994). Encounter satisfaction versus overall satisfaction versus quality: The customer's voice. In R. T. Rust & R. L. Oliver (Eds.), *Service quality: New directions in theory and practice* (pp. 72-94). Thousand Oaks, CA: Sage.

Blake, R. R., & Mouton, J. S. (1984). *Solving costly organizational conflicts.* San Francisco: Jossey-Bass.

Blanchard, F. A., Lilly, T., & Vaughn, L. A. (1991). Reducing the expression of racial prejudice. *Psychological Science, 2*(2), 101-105.

Bless, H., Bohner, G., Schwarz, N., & Strack, F. (1990). Mood and persuasion: A cognitive response analysis. *Personality and Social Psychology Bulletin, 16,* 331-345.

Bluedorn, A. C. (1982). A unified model of turnover from organizations. *Human Relations, 35,* 135-153.

Blumer, H. (1955). Attitudes and the social act. *Social Problems, 3,* 59-65.

Bobo, L. (1983). Whites' opposition to busing: Symbolic racism or realistic group conflict? *Journal of Personality and Social Psychology, 45,* 1196-1210.

Bobo, L., & Kluegel, J. R. (1993). Opposition to race-targeting: Self-interest, stratification ideology, or racial attitudes? *American Sociological Review, 58,* 443-464.

Bok, D. (1993). *The cost of talent.* New York: Free Press.

Boller, G. W., Swasy, J. L., & Munch, J. M. (1990). Conceptualizing argument quality via argument structure. *Advances in Consumer Research, 17,* 321-328.

Bolton, R. N., & Drew, J. H. (1991). A multistage model of customers' assessments of service quality and value. *Journal of Consumer Research, 17,* 375-384.

Boninger, D. S., Krosnick, J. W., & Berent, M. K. (1995). Origins of attitude importance: Self-interest, social identification, and value relevance. *Journal of Personality and Social Psychology, 68,* 61-80.

Borman, W. C., & Motowidlo, S. J. (1993). Expanding the criterion domain to include elements of contextual performance. In N. Schmitt & W. C. Borman (Eds.), *Personnel selection in organizations* (pp. 71-98). San Francisco: Jossey-Bass.

Bornstein, R. F. (1989). Exposure and affect: Overview and meta-analysis of research, 1968-1987. *Psychological Bulletin, 106,* 265-289.

Boster, F. J., & Mongeau, P. (1984). Fear-arousing persuasive messages. In R. N. Bostrom (Ed.), *Communication yearbook* (Vol. 8, pp. 330-375). Beverly Hills, CA: Sage.

Bothwell, R. K., & Brigham, J. C. (1983). Selective evaluation and recall during the 1980 Reagan-Carter debate. *Journal of Applied Social Psychology, 13,* 427-442.

Bouchard, T. J., & McGue, M. (1990). Genetic and rearing environmental influences on adult personality: An analysis of adopted twins reared apart. *Journal of Personality, 58,* 263-292.

Bowen, D. E., Ledford, G. E., & Nathan, B. N. (1991). Hiring for the organization, not the job. *Academy of Management Executive, 5,* 35-51.

Bowen, D. E., & Schneider, B. (1988). Services marketing and management: Implications for organizational behavior. In B. M. Staw & L. L. Cummings (Eds.), *Research in organizational behavior* (Vol. 10, pp. 43-80). Greenwich, CT: JAI.

Bower, G. H. (1981). Mood and memory. *American Psychologist, 36,* 129-148.

Bowie, N. E., & Duska, R. (1990). *Business ethics* (2nd ed.). Englewood Cliffs, NJ: Prentice Hall.

Braithwaite, V. A., & Law, H. G. (1985). Structure of human values: Testing the adequacy of the Rokeach value survey. *Journal of Personality and Social Psychology, 49,* 250-263.

Brayfield, A. H., & Crockett, W. H. (1955). Employee attitudes and employee performance. *Psychological Bulletin, 52,* 396-424.

Breckler, S. J. (1984). Empirical validation of affect, behavior, cognition as distinct components of attitude. *Journal of Personality and Social Psychology, 47,* 1191-1205.

Brehm, J. W. (1966). *A theory of psychological reactance.* San Diego, CA: Academic Press.

Brehm, J. W., & Cohen, A. R. (1962). *Explorations in cognitive dissonance.* New York: John Wiley.

Brehm, S. S., & Kassin, S. M. (1996). *Social psychology* (3rd ed.). Boston: Houghton Mifflin.

Brett, J. F., Brief, A. P., Burke, M. J., George, J. M., & Webster, J. (1990). Negative affectivity and the reporting of stressful life events. *Health Psychology, 9,* 57-68.

Brewer, M. B. (1979). In-group bias in the minimal intergroup situation: A cognitive-motivational analysis. *Psychological Bulletin, 86,* 307-324.

Brewer, M. B. (1988). A dual process model of impression formation. In R. S. Wyer & T. K. Srull (Eds.), *Advances in social cognition* (Vol. 1, pp. 1-36). Hillsdale, NJ: Lawrence Erlbaum.

Brewer, M. B. (1991). The social self: On being the same and different at the same time. *Personality and Social Psychology Bulletin, 17,* 475-482.

Brewer, M. B. (1993). Social identity, distinctiveness, and in-group homogeneity. *Social Cognition, 11,* 15-164.

Brewer, M. B. (1994). The social psychology of prejudice: Getting it all together. In M. P. Zanna & J. M. Olson (Eds.), *Psychology of prejudice: The Ontario Symposium* (Vol. 7, pp. 315-329). Hillsdale, NJ: Lawrence Erlbaum.

Brewer, M. B., Dull, V., & Lui, L. (1981). Perceptions of the elderly: Stereotypes as prototypes. *Journal of Personality and Social Psychology, 41,* 656-670.

Brewer, M. B., & Miller, N. (1984). Beyond the contact hypothesis: Theoretical perspectives on desegregation. In N. Miller & M. B. Brewer (Eds.), *Groups in contact: The psychology of desegregation* (pp. 281-302). New York: Academic Press.

Brief, A. P. (1995). The new American workplace: Transforming work systems in the United States [Review of the book of the same title]. *Academy of Management Review, 20,* 462-478.

Brief, A. P., & Aldag, R. J. (1978). The job characteristic inventory: An examination. *Academy of Management Journal, 21,* 659-670.

Brief, A. P., & Aldag, R. J. (1989). The economic functions of work. In G. R. Ferris & K. M. Rowland (Eds.), *Research in organizational behavior* (Vol. 7, pp. 1-24). Greenwich, CT: JAI.

Brief, A. P., & Aldag, R. J. (1994). The study of work values: A call for a more balanced perspective. In I. Borg & P. P. Mohler (Eds.), *Trends and perspectives in empirical social research* (pp. 99-124). New York: Walter De Gruyter.

Brief, A. P., & Atieh, J. M. (1987). Studying job stress: Are we making mountains out of molehills? *Journal of Occupational Behavior, 8,* 115-126.

Brief, A. P., Burke, M. J., Atieh, J. M., Robinson, B., & Webster, J. (1988). Should negative affectivity remain an unmeasured variable in the study of job stress? *Journal of Applied Psychology, 73,* 199-207.

Brief, A. P., Butcher, A. H., George, J. M., & Link, K. E. (1993). Integrating bottom-up and top-down theories of subjective well-being: The case of health. *Journal of Personality and Social Psychology, 64,* 646-653.

Brief, A. P., Butcher, A. H., & Roberson, L. (1995). Cookies, disposition, and job attitudes: The effects of positive mood-inducing events and negative affectivity on job satisfaction in a field experiment. *Organizational Behavior and Human Decision Processes, 62,* 55-62.

Brief, A. P., Buttram, R. T., & Dukerich, J. M. (1997). Collective corruption in the corporate world: Towards a process model. In M. E. Turner (Ed.), *Groups at work: Advances in theory and research.* Hillsdale, NJ: Lawrence Erlbaum.

Brief, A. P., Buttram, R. T., Elliott, J. D., Reizenstein, R. M., & McCline, R. L. (1995). Releasing the beast: A study of compliance with orders to use race as a selection criterion. *Journal of Social Issues, 51,* 177-193.

Brief, A. P., Buttram, R. T., Reizenstein, R. M., Pugh, S. D., Callahan, J. D., McCline, R. L., & Vaslow, J. B. (in press). Beyond good intentions: The next steps toward racial equality in the American workplace. *Academy of Management Executive.*

Brief, A. P., & Dukerich, J. M. (1991). Theory in organizational behavior: Can it be useful? *Research in Organization Behavior, 13,* 327-352.

Brief, A. P., Dukerich, J. M., & Doran, L. I. (1991). Resolving ethical dilemmas in management: Experimental investigations of values, accountability, and choice. *Journal of Applied Social Psychology, 21*(5), 380-396.

Brief, A. P., & Folger, R. (1992). The workplace and problem drinking as seen by two novices. *Alcoholism: Clinical and Experimental Research, 16,* 190-198.

Brief, A. P., & Hayes, E. L. (1997). The continuing "American dilemma": Studying racism in organizations. In C. L. Cooper & D. M. Rousseau (Eds.), *Trends in organizational behavior* (Vol. 4, pp. 89-105). New York: John Wiley.

Brief, A. P., Konovsky, M. A., George, J. M., Goodwin, R., & Link, K. (1995). Inferring the meaning of work from the effects of unemployment. *Journal of Applied Social Psychology, 25,* 693-711.

Brief, A. P., & Motowidlo, S. J. (1986). Prosocial organizational behaviors. *Academy of Management Review, 11,* 710-725.

Brief, A. P., & Nord, W. R. (1990a). *Meanings of occupational work: A collection of essays.* Lexington, MA: Lexington Books.

Brief, A. P., & Nord, W. R. (1990b). Work and meaning: Definitions and interpretations. In A. P. Brief & W. R. Nord, *Meanings of occupational work: A collection of essays*. Lexington, MA: Lexington Books.

Brief, A. P., Reizenstein, R. M., Pugh, S. D., Vaslow, J. B., & Dietz, J. (1997). *Just doing business: Modern racism and obedience to authority as explanations for employment discrimination*. Manuscript submitted for publication.

Brief, A. P., & Roberson, L. (1989). Job attitude organization: An exploratory study. *Journal of Applied Social Psychology, 19*, 717-727.

Brigham, J. C. (1971). Ethnic stereotypes. *Psychological Bulletin, 76*, 15-33.

Brint, S., & Karabel, J. (1991). Institutional origins and transformations: The case of American community colleges. In W. W. Powell & P. J. DiMaggio (Eds.), *The new institutionalism in organizational analysis* (pp. 337-360). Chicago: University of Chicago Press.

Brockner, J., Grover, S., Reed, T. F., & DeWitt, R. L. (1992). Layoffs, job insecurity, and survivors' work effort: Evidence of an inverted-U relationship. *Academy of Management Journal, 35*, 413-425.

Brockner, J., Tyler, T. R., & Cooper-Schneider, R. (1992). The influence of prior commitment to an institution on reactions to perceived unfairness: The higher they are, the harder they fall [Special issue: Process and outcome: Perspectives on the distribution of rewards in organizations]. *Administrative Science Quarterly, 37*(2), 241-261.

Brockner, J., & Wiesenfeld, B. (1996). The interactive impact of procedural fairness and outcome favorability: The effects of what you do depend on how you do it. *Psychological Bulletin, 120*, 189-208.

Brown, H. A., & Ford, D. L. (1977). An exploratory analysis of discrimination in the employment of Black MBA graduates. *Journal of Applied Psychology, 62*, 50-56.

Brownlow, S., & Zebrowitz, L. A. (1990). Facial appearance, gender, and credibility in television commercials. *Journal of Nonverbal Behavior, 2*, 51-60.

Bruner, J. S. (1986). *Actual minds, possible worlds*. Cambridge, MA: Harvard University Press.

Brush, D. H., Mock, M. K., & Pooyan, A. (1987). Individual demographic differences and job satisfaction. *Journal of Occupational Behavior, 8*, 139-155.

Burgoon, J. K., Birk, T., & Pfau, M. (1990). Nonverbal behaviors, persuasion, and credibility. *Human Communication Research, 17*, 140-169.

Burke, M. J., & Borucki, C. C. (1995, August). *Does a climate for service matter? A test of a multiple stakeholder model of the service climate-organizational performance prediction problem*. Paper presented at the annual meeting of the Academy of Management, Vancouver, British Columbia, Canada.

Burke, M. J., Brief, A. P., & George, J. M. (1993). The role of negative affectivity in understanding relationships between self-reports of stressors and strains: A comment on the applied psychology literature. *Journal of Applied Psychology, 78*, 402-412.

Burke, M. J., Brief, A. P., George, J. M., Roberson, L., & Webster, J. (1989). Measuring affect at work: Confirmatory analyses of competing mood structures with conceptual linkage to cortical regulatory systems. *Journal of Personality and Social Psychology, 57*, 1091-1102.

Byrne, D. E. (1971). *The attraction paradigm*. San Diego, CA: Academic Press.

Cacioppo, J. T., & Berntson, G. G. (1994). Relationship between attitudes and evaluative space: A critical review, with emphasis on the separability of positive and negative substrates. *Psychological Bulletin, 115*, 401-423.

Cacioppo, J. T., Crites, S. L., Berntson, G. G., & Coles, M. G. H. (1993). If attitudes affect how stimuli are processed, should they not affect the event-related brain potential? *Psychological Science, 4*, 108-112.

Cacioppo, J. T., Gardner, W. L., & Berntson, G. G. (1997). Beyond bipolar conceptualizations and measures: The case of attitudes and evaluative space. *Personality and Social Psychology Review, 1*(1), 3-25.

Cacioppo, J. T., Marshall-Goodell, B. S., Tassinary, L. G., & Petty, R. E. (1992). Rudimentary determinants of attitudes: Classical conditioning is more effective when prior knowledge about the attitude stimulus is low than high. *Journal of Experimental Social Psychology, 28,* 207-233.

Cacioppo, J. T., & Petty, R. E. (1981). Electromyograms as measures of extent and affectivity of information processing. *American Psychologist, 36,* 441-456.

Cacioppo, J. T., & Petty, R. E. (1982). The need for cognition. *Journal of Personality and Social Psychology, 42,* 116-131.

Cacioppo, J. T., & Petty, R. E. (1985). Central and peripheral routes to persuasion: The role of message repetition. In L. F. Alwitt & A. A. Mitchell (Eds.), *Psychological processes and advertising effects* (pp. 91-111). Hillsdale, NJ: Lawrence Erlbaum.

Cacioppo, J. T., & Petty, R. E. (1989). Effects of message repetition on argument processing, recall, and persuasion. *Basic Applied Social Psychology, 10,* 3-12.

Cacioppo, J. T., Petty, R. E., & Morris, K. J. (1983). Effects of need for cognition on message evaluation, recall, and persuasion. *Journal of Personality and Social Psychology, 45,* 805-818.

Cameron, K. (1986, May). Effectiveness as paradox: Consensus and conflict in conceptions of organizational effectiveness. *Management Science, 32,* 539-553.

Campbell, A. A. (1947). Factors associated with attitudes toward Jews. In T. M. Newcomb & E. L. Hartley (Eds.), *Readings in social psychology* (pp. 518-527). New York: Holt.

Campbell, D. T. (1963). Social attitudes and other acquired behavioral dispositions. In S. Koch (Ed.), *Psychology: A study of a science* (Vol. 6, pp. 94-172). New York: McGraw-Hill.

Campbell, D. T. (1965). Ethnocentric and other altruistic motives. In D. Levine (Ed.), *Nebraska Symposium on Motivation* (pp. 283-311). Lincoln: University of Nebraska Press.

Campbell, J. P., & Campbell, R. J. (1988). *Productivity in organizations.* San Francisco: Jossey-Bass.

Campion, M. A., & Berger, C. J. (1990). Conceptual integration and empirical test of job design and compensation relationships. *Personnel Psychology, 43,* 525-553.

Campion, M. A., & McClelland, C. L. (1993). Follow-up and extension of the interdisciplinary costs and benefits of enlarged jobs. *Journal of Applied Psychology, 78,* 339-351.

Campis, L. K., Prentice-Dunn, S., & Lyman, R. D. (1989). Coping appraisal and parents' intentions to inform their children about sexual abuse: A protection motivation theory analysis. *Journal of Social and Clinical Psychology, 8*(3), 304-316.

Cancio, A. S., Evans, T. D., & Maume, D. J., Jr. (1996). Reconsidering the declining significance of race: Racial differences in early career wages. *American Sociological Review, 61,* 541-556.

Cappelli, P. (1995). Rethinking employment. *British Journal of Industrial Relations, 33,* 563-602.

Cappelli, P., Bassi, L., Katz, H., Knoke, D., Osterman, P., & Useem, M. (1997). *Change at work.* New York: Oxford University Press.

Cappelli, P., & O'Shaughnessy, K. C. (1995). *Skill and wage changes in corporate headquarters, 1986-1992.* Philadelphia: National Center on the Educational Quality of the Workforce.

Carli, L. L. (1990). Gender, language, and influence. *Journal of Personality and Social Psychology, 59,* 941-951.

Carli, L. L., Ganley, R., & Pierce-Otay, A. (1991). Similarity and satisfaction in roommate relationships. *Personality and Social Psychology Bulletin, 17,* 419-426.

Carlson, M., Charlin, V., & Miller, N. (1988). Positive mood and helping behavior: A test of six hypotheses. *Journal of Personality and Social Psychology, 55*(2), 211-229.

Carnevale, P. J. D., & Isen, A. M. (1986). The influence of positive affect and visual access on the discovery of integrative solutions in bilateral negotiation. *Organizational Behavior and Human Decision Processes, 37,* 1-13.

Carsten, J. M., & Spector, P. E. (1987). Unemployment, job satisfaction, and employee turnover: A meta-analytic test of the Muchinsky model. *Journal of Applied Psychology, 73,* 374-381.

Carter, S. L. (1993). *Reflections of an affirmative action baby.* New York: Basic Books.

Caspi, A., & Harbener, E. S. (1990). Continuity and change: Assortive marriage and the consistency of personality in adulthood. *Journal of Personality and Social Psychology, 58,* 250-258.

Cattell, R. B. (1943). The description of personality: Basic traits resolved into clusters. *Journal of Abnormal and Social Psychology, 38,* 476-506.

Cattell, R. B., & Eber, H. W. (1962). *Handbook for the Sixteen P.F. Test.* Champaign, IL: IPAT.

Chaiken, S. (1979). Communicator physical attractiveness and persuasion. *Journal of Personality and Social Psychology, 37,* 1387-1397.

Chaiken, S. (1980). Heuristic versus systematic information processing and the use of source versus message cues in persuasion. *Journal of Personality and Social Psychology, 39,* 752-766.

Chaiken, S. (1986). Physical appearance and social influence. In C. P. Herman, M. P. Zanna, & E. T. Higgins (Eds.), *Physical appearance, stigma, and social behavior: The Ontario Symposium* (Vol. 3, pp. 143-177). Hillsdale, NJ: Lawrence Erlbaum.

Chaiken, S. (1987). The heuristic model of persuasion. In M. P. Zanna, J. M. Olson, & C. P. Herman (Eds.), *Social influence: The Ontario Symposium* (Vol. 5, pp. 3-39). Hillsdale, NJ: Lawrence Erlbaum.

Chaiken, S., Liberman, A., & Eagly, A. (1989). Heuristic and systematic information processing within and beyond the persuasion context. In J. Uleman & J. W. Bargh (Eds.), *Unintended thought* (pp. 212-252). New York: Guilford.

Chaiken, S., & Stangor, C. (1987). Attitudes and attitude change. *Annual Review of Psychology, 38,* 575-630.

Chakravarthy, B. (1986). Measuring strategic performance. *Strategic Management Journal, 7,* 437-458.

Chapanis, N. P., & Chapanis, A. (1964). Cognitive dissonance: Five years later. *Psychological Bulletin, 61,* 1-22.

Chapman, L. J. (1967). Illusory correlation in observational report. *Journal of Verbal Learning and Verbal Behavior, 6,* 151-155.

Chassin, L., Presson, C. C., & Sherman, S. J. (1990). Social psychological contributions to the understanding and prevention of adolescent cigarette smoking. *Personality and Social Psychology Bulletin, 16,* 133-151.

Chatman, J. (1991). Matching people in organizations: Selection and socialization in public accounting firms. *Administrative Science Quarterly, 36,* 459-484.

Chattopadhyay, A., & Basu, K. (1990). Humor in advertising: The moderating role of prior brand evaluation. *Journal of Marketing Research, 27,* 466-476.

Churchill, G. A., Jr., & Suprenant, C. (1982). An investigation into the determinants of customer satisfaction. *Journal of Marketing Research, 19,* 491-504.

Cialdini, R. B. (1993). *Influence: Science and practice* (3rd ed.). New York: HarperCollins.

Cialdini, R. B., Green, B. L., & Rusch, A. J. (1992). When tactical pronouncements of change become real change: The case of reciprocal persuasion. *Journal of Personality and Social Psychology, 63,* 30-40.

Cialdini, R. B., & Petty, R. (1981). Anticipatory opinion effects. In R. E. Petty, T. M. Ostrom, & T. C. Brock (Eds.), *Cognitive responses in persuasion* (pp. 217-235). Hillsdale, NJ: Lawrence Erlbaum.

Citrin, J., & Green, D. P. (1990). The self-interest motive in American public opinion. *Research in Micropolitics, 3,* 1-28.

Clark, L. A., & Watson, D. (1991). General affective dispositions in physical and psychological health. In C. R. Snyder & D. R. Forsyth (Eds.), *Handbook of social and clinical psychology* (pp. 221-245). New York: Pergamon.

Clark, M. S., & Isen, A. M. (1982). Toward understanding the relationship between feeling states and social behavior. In A. H. Hastorf & A. M. Isen (Eds.), *Cognitive social psychology* (pp. 73-108). New York: Elsevier Science.

Cohen, A. (1993). Organizational commitment and turnover: A meta-analysis. *Academy of Management Journal, 36,* 1140-1147.

Cohen, E. G. (1982). Expectation states and interracial interaction in school settings. In R. H. Turner & J. F. Short (Eds.), *Annual Review of Sociology* (Vol. 8, pp. 209-235). Palo Alto, CA: Annual Reviews.

Coleman, J. W. (1994). *The criminal elite: The sociology of white collar crime* (3rd ed.). New York: St. Martin's.

Coleman, M. J., & Pencavel, J. (1993). Changes in work hours of male employees, 1940-1988. *Industrial and Labor Relations Review, 46,* 262-283.

Collins, R. L., Taylor, S. E., Wood, J. V., & Thompson, S. C. (1988). The vividness effect: Elusive or illusory? *Journal of Experimental Social Psychology, 24,* 1-18.

Conference Board. (1994). *Diversity training* (Report No. 1083-94-RR). New York: Author.

Converse, P. E. (1964). The nature of belief systems in mass publics. In D. E. Apter (Ed.), *Ideology and discontent* (pp. 206-261). New York: Free Press.

Converse, P. E. (1975). Public opinion and voting behavior. In F. Greenstein & N. W. Polsby (Eds.), *Handbook of political science* (Vol. 4, pp. 75-169). Reading, MA: Addison-Wesley.

Cook, J. D., Hepworth, S. J., Wall, T. D., & Warr, P. B. (1981). *The experience of work.* New York: Academic Press.

Cook, S. W. (1978). Interpersonal and attitudinal outcomes in cooperating interracial groups. *Journal of Research and Development in Education, 12,* 97-113.

Cook, S. W. (1984). Cooperative interaction in multiethnic contexts. In N. Miller & M. B. Brewer (Eds.), *Groups in contact: The psychology of desegregation* (pp. 155-185). Orlando, FL: Academic Press.

Cooper, J., & Fazio, R. H. (1984). A new look at dissonance theory. In L. Berkowitz (Ed.), *Advances in experimental social psychology* (Vol. 17, pp. 229-266). San Diego, CA: Academic Press.

Cooper, J., & Scher, S. J. (1992). Actions and attitudes: The role of responsibility and aversive consequences in persuasion. In T. Brock & S. Shavitt (Ed.), *The psychology of persuasion.* San Francisco: Freeman.

Costa, P. T., & McCrae, R. R. (1980). Influence of extroversion and neuroticism on subjective well-being: Happy and unhappy people. *Journal of Personality and Social Psychology, 33,* 668-678.

Costa, P. T., & McCrae, R. R. (1985). *The NEO personality inventory manual.* Odessa, FL: Psychological Assessment Resources.

Costa, P. T., & McCrae, R. R. (1992). Trait psychology comes of age. In T. B. Sonderegger (Ed.), *Nebraska Symposium on Motivation: Vol. 9. Psychology and aging* (pp. 169-204). Lincoln: University of Nebraska Press.

Costa, P. T., & McCrae, R. R. (1994). "Set like plaster?" Evidence for the stability of adult personality. In T. Heatherton & J. Weinberger (Eds.), *Can personality change?* (pp. 21-40). Washington, DC: American Psychological Association.

Costa, P. T., McCrae, R. R., & Norris, A. H. (1981). Personal adjustment to aging: Longitudinal prediction from neuroticism and extroversion. *Journal of Gerontology, 36,* 78-85.

Cotton, J. L. (1985). Cognitive dissonance in selective exposure. In D. Zillman & J. Bryant (Eds.), *Selective exposure to communication* (pp. 11-33). Hillsdale, NJ: Lawrence Erlbaum.

Coupland, D. (1991). *Generation X.* New York: St. Martin's.

Covaleski, M. A., & Dirsmith, M. W. (1988). An institutional perspective on the rise: Social transformation and fall of a university budget category. *Administrative Science Quarterly, 33,* 562-587.

Cox, T., Jr. (1993). *Cultural diversity in organizations: Theory, research, and practice.* San Francisco: Berrett-Koehler.

Cox, T., Jr., & Blake, S. (1991). Managing cultural diversity: Implications for organizational competitiveness. *The Executive, 5,* 45-56.

Cox, T., Jr., & Nkomo, S. M. (1986). Differential appraisal criteria based on race of the ratee. *Group and Organization Studies, 11,* 101-119.

Cox, T., Jr., & Nkomo, S. M. (1990). Invisible men and women: A status report on race as a variable in organization behavior research. *Journal of Organizational Behavior, 11,* 419-431.

Cranny, C. J., Smith, P. C., & Stone, E. F. (1992). *Job satisfaction: How people feel about their jobs and how it affects their performance.* New York: Lexington.

Crites, S. L., Fabrigar, L. R., & Petty, R. E. (1994). Measuring the affective and cognitive properties of attitudes: Conceptual and methodological issues. *Personality and Social Psychology Bulletin, 20,* 619-634.

Crocker, J., & Luhtanen, R. (1990). Collective self-esteem and ingroup bias. *Journal of Personality and Social Psychology, 58,* 60-67.

Cronin, J. J., Jr., & Taylor, S. A. (1992). Measuring service quality: A reexamination and extension. *Journal of Marketing, 56,* 55-68.

Cropanzano, R., & Folger, R. (1996). Procedural justice and worker motivation. In R. M. Steers, L. W. Porter, & G. A. Bigley (Eds.), *Motivation and leadership at work* (6th ed., pp. 72-83). New York: McGraw-Hill.

Cropanzano, R., James, K., & Konovsky, M. A. (1993). Dispositional affectivity as a predictor of work attitudes and job performance. *Journal of Organizational Behavior, 14,* 595-606.

Crosby, F., Bromley, S., & Saxe, L. (1980). Recent unobtrusive studies of black and white discrimination and prejudice: A literature review. *Psychological Bulletin, 87,* 546-563.

Crowley, A. E., & Hoyer, W. D. (1994). An integrative framework for understanding two-sided persuasion. *Journal of Consumer Research, 20,* 561-574.

Crystal, G. (1991). *In search of excess: The overcompensation of American executives.* New York: Norton.

Dabholkar, P. A. (1993). Customer satisfaction and service quality: Two constructs or one? In D. W. Cravens & P. R. Dickson (Eds.), *Enhancing knowledge development in marketing* (Vol. 4, pp. 10-18). Chicago: American Marketing Association.

Dahrendorf, R. (1959). *Class and class conflict in industrial society.* Stanford, CA: Stanford University Press.

Dalton, D. R., & Mesch, D. J. (1991). On the extent and reduction of avoidable absenteeism: An assessment of absence policy provisions. *Journal of Applied Psychology, 76,* 811-817.

Damrad-Frye, R., & Laird, J. D. (1989). The experience of boredom: The role of the self-perception of attention. *Journal of Personality and Social Psychology, 57,* 315-320.

Darwin, C. R. (1872). *The expression of the emotions in man and animals.* London: Murray.

Davidson, A. R., Yantis, S., Norwood, M., & Montano, D. E. (1985). Amount of information about the attitude object and attitude-behavior consistency. *Journal of Personality and Social Psychology, 49,* 1184-1198.

Davis, G., & Watson, G. (1982). *Black life in corporate America: Swimming in the mainstream.* Garden City, NY: Anchor/Doubleday.

Davis, G. F., & Powell, W. W. (1992). Organization-environment relations. In M. D. Dunnette & L. M. Hough (Eds.), *Handbook of industrial and organizational psychology* (2nd ed., Vol. 3, pp. 315-375). Palo Alto, CA: Consulting Psychologists Press.

Davis, J. A. (1982). *Cumulative general social survey 1972-1980.* Ann Arbor, MI: Inter-University Consortium for Political Research.

Davis, S. K. (1988). *Behavioral consequences of dissatisfaction: A field study.* Unpublished paper, University of Maryland, College of Business and Management, College Park.

Davis-Blake, A., & Pfeffer, J. (1989). Just a mirage: The search for dispositional effects in organizational management. *Academy of Management Review, 14,* 385-400.

Davis-Blake, A., & Pfeffer, J. (1996). Two steps forward, one step back. *Academy of Management Review, 21*(2), 340-343.

Dawes, R. M., Singer, D., & Lemons, F. (1972). An experimental analysis of the contrast effect and its implications for intergroup communication and the indirect assessment of attitude. *Journal of Personality and Social Psychology, 21,* 281-295.

Dawes, R. M., & Smith, T. L. (1985). Attitude and opinion measurement. In G. Lindzey & E. Aronson (Eds.), *Handbook of social psychology* (3rd ed., Vol. 2, pp. 509-566). New York: Random House.

Dawis, R. V. (1992). Person-environment fit and job satisfaction. In C. J. Cranny, P. C. Smith, & E. F. Stone (Eds.), *Job satisfaction: How people feel about their jobs and how it affects their performance* (Vol. 1, pp. 69-88). New York: Lexington.

Dawis, R. V., & Lofquist, L. H. (1984). *A psychological theory of work adjustment.* Minneapolis: University of Minnesota Press.

Dawis, R. V., Lofquist, L. H., & Weiss, D. J. (1968). *A theory of work adjustment* [Revision] (Minnesota Studies in Vocational Rehabilitation, No. 23). Minneapolis: University of Minnesota.

Day, R. L., Grabicke, K., Schaetzle, T., & Staubach, F. (1981). The hidden agenda of consumer complaining. *Journal of Retailing, 57,* 86-106.

Dearborn, D. C., & Simon, H. A. (1958). Selective perception: A note on the department identifications of executives. *Sociometry, 21,* 140-144.

Deaux, K., & Wrightsman, L. S. (1988). *Social psychology.* Pacific Grove, CA: Brooks/Cole.

DeBono, K. G. (1987). Investigating the social-adjustive and value-expressive functions of attitudes: Implications for persuasion processes. *Journal of Personality and Social Psychology, 52,* 279-287.

DeBono, K. G., & Edmonds, A. E. (1989). Cognitive dissonance and self-monitoring: A manner of context? *Motivation and Emotion, 13,* 259-270.

Deci, E. L., & Ryan, R. M. (1985). *Intrinsic motivation and self determination in human behavior.* New York: Plenum.

Dembroski, T. M., Lasater, T. M., & Ramerez, A. (1978). Communicator similarity, fear arousing communications, and compliance with health care regulations. *Journal of Applied Social Psychology, 8,* 254-269.

Devine, P. G. (1989). Stereotypes and prejudice: Their automatic and controlled components. *Journal of Personality and Social Psychology, 56,* 5-18.

Devine, P. G., & Monteith, M. J. (1993). The role of discrepancy-associated affect in prejudice reduction. In D. M. Mackie & D. L. Hamilton (Ed.), *Affect, cognition, and stereotyping: Interactive processes in group perception* (pp. 317-344). San Diego, CA: Academic Press.

Devine, P. G., Monteith, M. J., Zuwerink, J. R., & Elliot, A. J. (1991). Prejudice with and without compunction. *Journal of Personality and Social Psychology, 60,* 817-830.

Dick, A. S., & Basu, K. (1994). Customer loyalty: Toward an integrated conceptual framework. *Journal of the Academy of Marketing Science, 22,* 99-113.

Diener, E. (1984). Subject well-being. *Psychological Bulletin, 95,* 542-575.

Diener, E., & Emmons, R. A. (1984). The independence of positive and negative affect. *Journal of Personality and Social Psychology, 47,* 1105-1117.

Dietz, J., Brief, A. P., Hayes, E. L., Callahan, J. D., & McCline, R. L. (1997, June). *Trait affect as a moderator of the state affect-absenteeism relationship: When is attending work a means of maintaining a good mood?* Paper presented at the 2nd Industrial and Organizational Psychology Conference in Melbourne, Australia.

Digman, J. M. (1990). Personality structure: Emergence of the Five-Factor Model. *Annual Review of Psychology, 41,* 417-440.

Dillman, D. A. (1991). The design and administration of mail surveys. In W. R. Scott & J. Blake (Eds.), *Annual review of sociology* (Vol. 17, pp. 225-249). Palo Alto, CA: Annual Reviews.

DiMaggio, P. J., & Powell, W. W. (1983). The iron cage revisited: Institutional isomorphism and collective rationality in organizational fields. *American Sociological Review, 48,* 147-160.

Dimberg, U. (1982). Facial reactions to facial expressions. *Psychophysiology, 19,* 643-647.

Doeringer, P. B., Christensen, K., Flynn, P. M., Hall, D. J., Katz, H. C., Keefe, J. H., Ruhm, C. J., Sum, A. M., & Useem, M. (1991). *Turbulence in the American workplace.* New York: Oxford University Press.

Dollard, J., Doob, L. W., Miller, N. E., Mowrer, O. H., & Sears, R. R. (1939). *Frustration and aggression.* New Haven, CT: Yale University Press.

Donaldson, T., & Preston, L. E. (1995). The stakeholder theory of the corporation: Concepts, evidence, and implications. *Academy of Management Review, 20,* 65-91.

Donnerstein, M., & Donnerstein, E. (1976). Variables in interracial aggression. *Journal of Social Psychology, 27,* 143-150.

Doob, L. W. (1947). The behavior of attitudes. *Psychological Review, 54,* 135-156.

Dooley, D., & Catalano, R. (1980). Economic change as a cause of behavioral disorder. *Psychological Bulletin, 87,* 450-468.

Doran, L. I., Stone, V. K., Brief, A. P., & George, J. M. (1991). Behavioral intentions as predictors of job attitudes: The role of economic choice. *Journal of Applied Psychology, 76,* 40-45.

Dovidio, J. F., & Gaertner, S. L. (1983). Racial attitudes and the effects of a partner's race on asking for help. In B. M. DePaulo, A. Nadler, & J. Fisher (Eds.), *New directions in helping* (Vol. 2, pp. 285-303). New York: Academic Press.

Dovidio, J. F., & Gaertner, S. L. (1986). Prejudice, discrimination, and racism: Historical trends and contemporary approaches. In J. F. Dovidio & S. L. Gaertner (Eds.), *Prejudice, discrimination, and racism* (pp. 1-34). Orlando, FL: Academic Press.

Dovidio, J. F., & Gaertner, S. L. (1991). Changes in the nature and assessment of racial prejudice. In H. Knopke, J. Norrell, & R. Rogers (Eds.), *Opening doors: An appraisal of race relations in contemporary America* (pp. 201-241). Tuscaloosa: University of Alabama Press.

Dovidio, J. F., Mann, J., & Gaertner, S. L. (1989). Resistance to affirmative action: The implications of aversive racism. In F. A. Blanchard & F. J. Crosby (Eds.), *Affirmative action in perspective* (pp. 83-103). New York: Springer-Verlag.

Dubin, R. (1976a). Theory building in applied areas. In M. D. Dunnette (Ed.), *Handbook of industrial and organizational psychology* (1st ed., pp. 17-39). Chicago: Rand McNally.

Dubin, R. (1976b). Work in modern society. In R. Dubin (Ed.), *Handbook of work, organization, and society.* Chicago: Rand McNally.

Duncan, W. J. (1982). Humor in management: Prospects for administrative practice and research. *Academy of Management Review, 7*(1), 136-142.

Dunham, R. B. (1977). Relationships of perceived job design characteristics to job ability requirements and job value. *Journal of Applied Psychology, 62,* 760-763.

Dunham, R. B., Grube, J. A., & Castaneda, M. B. (1994). Organizational commitment: The utility of an integrative definition. *Journal of Applied Psychology, 79,* 370-380.

Dunham, R. B., & Herman, J. B. (1975). Development of a female faces scale for measuring job satisfaction. *Journal of Applied Psychology, 60,* 629-631.

Dunham, R. B., & Smith, F. J. (1979). *Organizational surveys: An internal assessment of organizational health.* Glenview, IL: Scott, Foresman.

Dunnette, M. D. (1966). Fads, fashions, and folderol in psychology. *American Psychologist, 21,* 343-352.

Eagly, A. H. (1987). *Sex differences in social behavior: A social role interpretation.* Hillsdale, NJ: Lawrence Erlbaum.

Eagly, A. H. (1993). Uneven progress: Social psychology and the study of attitudes. *Journal of Personality and Social Psychology, 63,* 693-710.

Eagly, A. H. (1995). The science and politics of comparing women and men. *American Psychologist, 50,* 145-158.

Eagly, A. H., & Chaiken, S. (1993). *The psychology of attitudes.* Fort Worth, TX: Harcourt Brace Jovanovich.

Eagly, A. H., & Mladinic, A. (1989). Gender stereotypes and attitudes toward women and men. *Personality and Social Psychology Bulletin, 15,* 543-558.

Eagly, A. H., Mladinic, A., & Otto, S. (1994). Cognitive and affective bases of attitudes toward social groups and social policies. *Journal of Experimental and Social Psychology, 30,* 113-137.

Eagly, A. H., Wood, W., & Chaiken, S. (1978). Causal inferences about communicators and their effect on opinion change. *Journal of Personality and Social Psychology, 36,* 424-435.

Earley, P. C. (1986). Supervisors and shop stewards as sources of contextual information in goal setting: A comparison of the United States with England. *Journal of Applied Psychology, 71,* 111-117.

Earley, P. C. (1989). Social loafing and collectivism: A comparison of the United States and the People's Republic of China. *Administrative Science Quarterly, 34,* 565-581.

Eaves, L. J., Eysenck, H. J., & Martin, N. G. (1989). *Genes, culture, and personality: An empirical approach.* London: Academic Press.

Economic report of the president. (1995). Washington, DC: Government Printing Office.

Edwards, J. R. (1991). Person-job fit: A conceptual integration, literature review, and methodological critique. *International Review of Industrial/Organizational Psychology, 6,* 283-357.

Edwards, K. (1990). The interplay of affect and cognition in attitude formation and change. *Journal of Personality and Social Psychology, 59,* 212-216.

Ehrlich, H. J. (1973). *The social psychology of prejudice.* New York: John Wiley.

Eichenwald, K. (1996, November 16). Texaco to make reward payout in bias lawsuit. *New York Times,* pp. 1, 23.

Einstein, A., & Infeld, L. (1938). *The evolution of physics.* New York: Simon & Schuster.

Ekman, P. (1985). *Telling lies.* New York: Norton.

Ekman, P. (1993). Facial expression and emotion. *American Psychologist, 48,* 384-392.

Ekman, P., Friesen, W. V., & O'Sullivan, M. (1988). Smiles when lying. *Journal of Personality and Social Psychology, 54,* 414-420.

Ekman, P., & Oster, H. (1979). Facial expressions and emotions. *Annual Review of Psychology, 30,* 527-554.

Elizur, D. (1984). Facets of work values: A structural analysis of work outcomes. *Journal of Applied Psychology, 69,* 379-389.

Elliot, A. J., & Devine, P. G. (1994). On the motivational nature of cognitive dissonance: Dissonance as psychological discomfort. *Journal of Personality and Social Psychology, 67,* 382-394.

Elsbach, K. D. (1994). Managing organizational legitimacy in the California cattle industry: The construction and effectiveness of verbal accounts. *Administrative Science Quarterly, 39,* 57-88.

Elsbach, K. D., & Sutton, R. I. (1992). Acquiring organizational legitimacy through illegitimate actions: A marriage of institutional and impression management theories. *Academy of Management Journal, 35,* 699-738.

Ely, R. J. (1994). The effects of organizational demographics and social identity on relationships among professional women. *Administrative Science Quarterly, 39,* 203-238.

Emery, R. E., & Trist, E. L. (1960). Socio-technical systems. In C. W. Churchman & M. Verhulst (Eds.), *Management science models and techniques* (Vol. 2, pp. 83-97). Elmsford, NY: Pergamon.

Endler, N. S., & Magnusson, D. (1976). Toward an interactional psychology of personality. *Psychological Bulletin, 83,* 956-974.

England, P., & McLaughlin, S. D. (1979). Sex segregation of jobs and income differentials. In R. Alvarez, K. G. Lutterman, & Associates (Eds.), *Discrimination in organizations.* San Francisco: Jossey-Bass.

Epstein, R., & Komorita, S. S. (1966). Childhood prejudice as a function of parental ethnocentrism, punitiveness, and outgroup characteristics. *Journal of Personality and Social Psychology, 3,* 259-264.

Erevelles, S., & Leavitt, C. (1992). A comparison of current models of consumer satisfaction/dissatisfaction. *Journal of Consumer Satisfaction, Dissatisfaction and Complaining Behavior, 5,* 104-114.

Erez, M., & Earley, P. C. (1987). Comparative analysis of goal-setting strategies across cultures. *Journal of Applied Psychology, 72,* 658-665.

Erez, M., & Earley, P. C. (1993). *Culture, self-identity, and work.* New York: Oxford University Press.

Esses, V. M., Haddock, G., & Zanna, M. P. (1993). Values, stereotypes, and emotions as determinants of intergroup attitudes. In D. M. Mackie & D. L. Hamilton (Eds.), *Affect, cognition, and stereotyping* (pp. 137-166). San Diego, CA: Academic Press.

Etzioni, A. (1964). *Modern organizations.* Englewood Cliffs, NJ: Prentice Hall.

Evans, W. M., & Freeman, R. E. (1988). A stakeholder theory of the modern corporation: Kantian capitalism. In T. L. Beauchamp & N. E. Bowie (Eds.), *Ethical theory and business* (3rd ed., p. 103). Englewood Cliffs, NJ: Prentice Hall.

Eysenck, H. J. (1970). *The structure of human personality.* London: Methuen.

Eysenck, H. J. (1990). Biological dimensions of personality. In L. A. Pervin (Ed.), *Handbook of personality: Theory and research* (pp. 244-276). New York: Guilford.

Farber, H. S. (1993). *The incidence and costs of job loss: 1982-1991* (Brookings Papers on Economic Activity: Microeconomics). Washington, DC: Brookings Institution.

Farber, H. S. (1995). *Are lifetime jobs disappearing? Job duration in the United States: 1973-1993* (Working Paper 341). Princeton, NJ: Princeton University, Industrial Relations Section.

Farquhar, P. (1989, September). Managing brand equity. *Marketing Research, 1,* 24-34.

Farrell, D., & Rusbult, C. E. (1981). Exchange variables as predictors of job satisfaction, job commitment, and turnover: The impact of rewards, costs, alternatives, and investments. *Organizational Behavior and Human Performance, 28,* 78-95.

Farrell, D., & Stamm, C. L. (1988). Meta-analysis of the correlates of employee absence. *Human Relations, 41,* 211-227.

Fazio, R. H. (1986). How do attitudes guide behavior? In R. M. Sorrentino & E. T. Higgins (Eds.), *Handbook of motivation and cognition: Foundations of social behavior* (pp. 204-243). New York: Guilford.

Fazio, R. H. (1987). Self-perception theory: A current perspective. In M. P. Zanna, J. M. Olson, & C. P. Herman (Eds.), *Social influence: The Ontario Symposium* (Vol. 5, pp. 129-150). Hillsdale, NJ: Lawrence Erlbaum.

Fazio, R. H. (1989). On the power and functionality of attitudes: The role of attitude accessibility. In A. R. Pratkanis, S. J. Breckler, & A. G. Greenwald (Eds.), *Attitude structure and function* (pp. 153-179). Hillsdale, NJ: Lawrence Erlbaum.

Fazio, R. H. (1990). Multiple processes by which attitudes guide behavior: The MODE model as an integrative framework. In M. P. Zanna (Ed.), *Advances in experimental social psychology* (Vol. 23, pp. 75-109). San Diego, CA: Academic Press.

Fazio, R. H. (1995). Attitudes as object-evaluation associations: Determinants, consequences, and correlates of attitude accessibility. In R. E. Petty & J. A. Krosnick (Eds.), *Attitude strength: Antecedents and consequences* (pp. 247-282). Mahwah, NJ: Lawrence Erlbaum.

Fazio, R. H., Chen, J., McDonel, E. C., & Sherman, S. J. (1982). Attitude accessibility, attitude-behavior consistency, and the strength of the object-evaluation association. *Journal of Experimental Social Psychology, 18,* 339-357.

Fazio, R. H., Herr, P. M., & Olney, T. J. (1984). Attitude accessibility following a self-perception process. *Journal of Personality and Social Psychology, 47,* 277-286.

Fazio, R. H., Jackson, J. R., Dunton, B. C., & Williams, C. J. (1995). Variability in automatic activation as an unobtrusive measure of racial attitudes: A bona fide pipeline? *Journal of Personality and Social Psychology, 69,* 1013-1027.

Fazio, R. H., Lenn, T. M., & Effrein, E. A. (1983-1984). Spontaneous attitude formation. *Social Cognition, 2,* 217-234.

Fazio, R. H., Powell, M. C., & Williams, C. J. (1989). The role of accessibility in the attitude-to-behavior process. *Journal of Consumer Research, 16,* 280-288.

Fazio, R. H., & Zanna, M. P. (1978). Attitudinal qualities relating to the strength of the attitude-behavior relationship. *Journal of Experimental Social Psychology, 14,* 398-408.

Fazio, R. H., & Zanna, M. P. (1981). Direct experience and attitude-behavior consistency. In L. Berkowitz (Ed.), *Advances in experimental social psychology* (Vol. 14, pp. 162-202). New York: Academic Press.

Feather, N. T. (1995). Values, valences, and choice: The influence of values on the perceived attractiveness and choice of alternatives. *Journal of Personality and Social Psychology, 68,* 1135-1151.

Federal Bureau of Investigation. (1993). *Uniform crime reports for the United States.* Washington, DC: Author.

Festinger, L. (1957). *A theory of cognitive dissonance.* Stanford, CA: Stanford University Press.

Festinger, L., & Carlsmith, J. M. (1959). Cognitive consequences of forced compliance. *Journal of Abnormal and Social Psychology, 58,* 203-210.

Finn, D. W., & Lamb, C. W., Jr. (1991). An evaluation of the SERVQUAL scales in a retail setting. In R. H. Holman & M. R. Soloman (Eds.), *Advances in consumer research* (Vol. 18, pp. 483-490). Provo, UT: Association for Consumer Research.

Fishbein, M. (1967). A behavior theory approach to the relations between beliefs about an object and the attitude toward the object. In M. Fishbein (Ed.), *Readings in attitude theory and measurement* (pp. 389-400). New York: John Wiley.

Fishbein, M. (1980). A theory of reasoned action: Some applications and implications. In H. E. Howe, Jr. & M. M. Page (Eds.), *Nebraska Symposium on Motivation, 1979* (Vol. 27, pp. 65-116). Lincoln: University of Nebraska Press.

Fishbein, M., & Ajzen, I. (1972). Attitudes and opinions. *Annual Review of Psychology, 23,* 487-544.

Fishbein, M., & Ajzen, I. (1974). Attitudes toward objects as predictors of a single and multiple behavioral criteria. *Psychological Review, 81,* 59-74.

Fishbein, M., & Ajzen, I. (1975). *Belief, attitude, intention, and behavior: A introduction to theory and research.* Reading, MA: Addison-Wesley.

Fisher, C. D. (1980). On the dubious wisdom of expecting job satisfaction to correlate with performance. *Academy of Management Review, 5,* 607-612.

Fisher, C. D., & Locke E. A. (1992). The new look in job satisfaction research and theory. In C. J. Cranny, P. C. Smith, & E. F. Stone (Eds.), *Job satisfaction: How people feel about their jobs and how it affects their performance* (Vol. 1, pp. 165-194). New York: Lexington.

Fisher, V. E., & Hanna, J. V. (1931). *The dissatisfied worker.* New York: Macmillan.

Fiske, S. T. (1981). Social cognition and affect. In J. Harvey (Ed.), *Cognition, social behavior, and the environment* (pp. 227-264). Hillsdale, NJ: Lawrence Erlbaum.

Fiske, S. T. (1993). Social cognition and social perception. *Annual Review of Psychology, 44,* 155-194.

Fiske, S. T. (in press). Stereotyping, prejudice, and discrimination. In D. T. Gilbert, S. T. Fiske, & G. Lindzey (Eds.), *Handbook of social psychology* (4th ed.). New York: McGraw-Hill.

Fiske, S. T., & Neuberg, S. L. (1990). A continuum of impression formation, from category-based to individuating processes: Influences of information and motivation on attention and interpretation. In M. P. Zanna (Ed.), *Advances in experimental social psychology* (Vol. 23, pp. 1-74). San Diego, CA: Academic Press.

Fiske, S. T., & Pavelchak, M. A. (1986). Category-based versus piece-meal based affective responses: Developments in schema-triggered affect. In R. M. Sorrentino & E. T. Higgins (Eds.), *Handbook of motivation and cognition: Foundations of social behaviors* (pp. 167-203). New York: Guilford.

Fiske, S. T., & Ruscher, J. B. (1993). Negative interdependence and prejudice: Whence the affect? In D. M. Mackie & D. L. Hamilton (Eds.), *Affect, cognition, and stereotyping: Interactive processes in group perception* (pp. 239-268). New York: Academic Press.

Fiske, S. T., & Taylor, S. E. (1991). *Social cognition.* New York: McGraw-Hill.

Fiske, S. T., & Von Hendy, H. M. (1992). Personality feedback and situated norms can control stereotyping processes. *Journal of Personality and Social Psychology, 62,* 577-596.

Fleishman, J. W. (1986). Types of political attitude structure: Results of a cluster analysis. *Public Opinion Quarterly, 50,* 371-386.

Folger, R. (1993). Reactions to mistreatment at work. In J. K. Murnighan (Ed.), *Social psychology in organizations* (pp. 161-183). Englewood Cliffs, NJ: Prentice Hall.

Folger, R., & Greenberg, J. (1985). Procedural justice: An interpretive analysis of personnel systems. In K. M. Rowland & G. R. Ferris (Eds.), *Research in personnel and human resource management* (Vol. 3, pp. 141-183). Greenwich, CT: JAI.

Folger, R., Konovsky, M. A., & Cropanzano, R. (1992). A due process metaphor for performance appraisal. In B. M. Staw & L. L. Cummings (Eds.), *Research in organizational behavior* (Vol. 14, pp. 129-178). Greenwich, CT: JAI.

Fombrun, C. J. (1996). *Reputation: Realizing value from the corporate image.* Boston: Harvard Business School Press.

Fombrun, C., & Shanley, M. (1990). What's in a name? Reputation building and corporate strategy. *Academy of Management Journal, 33,* 233-258.

Ford, J. D., & Schellenberg, D. A. (1982). Conceptual issues of linkage in the assessment of organizational performance. *Academy of Management Review, 7,* 49-58.

Forgas, J. P. (1995). Mood and judgment: The affect infusion model (AIM). *Psychological Bulletin, 117,* 39-66.

Fornell, C. (1992). A national customer satisfaction barometer: The Swedish experience. *Journal of Marketing, 56,* 6-21.

Frank, R. H., & Cook, P. J. (1995). *The winner-takes-all society.* New York: Free Press.

Freedman, J. L., & Sears, D. O. (1965a). Selective exposure. In L. Berkowitz (Ed.), *Advances in experimental social psychology* (Vol. 2, pp. 57-97). San Diego, CA: Academic Press.

Freedman, J. L., & Sears, D. O. (1965b). Warning, distraction and resistance to influence. *Journal of Personality and Social Psychology, 1,* 262-266.

Freeman, E. (1984). *Strategic management: A stakeholder approach.* Marshfield, MA: Pitman.

French, J. R. P., Jr., & Kahn, R. L. (1962). A programmatic approach to studying the industrial environment and mental health. *Journal of Social Issues, 18,* 1-48.

Frey, D. (1986). Recent research on selective exposure to information. In L. Berkowitz (Ed.), *Advances in experimental social psychology* (Vol. 19, pp. 41-80). San Diego, CA: Academic Press.

Frey, D. L., & Gaertner, S. L. (1986). Helping and the avoidance of inappropriate interracial behavior: A strategy that perpetuates a nonprejudiced self-image. *Journal of Personality and Social Psychology, 50,* 1083-1090.

Fried, Y., & Ferris, G. R. (1987). The validity of the job characteristics model: A review and meta-analysis. *Personnel Psychology, 40,* 287-322.

Gaertner, S. L. (1976). Nonreactive measures in racial attitude research: A focus on "liberals." In P. A. Katz (Ed.), *Towards the elimination of racism.* New York: Pergamon.

Gaertner, S. L., & Dovidio, J. F. (1981). The effects of race, status, and ability on helping behavior. *Social Psychology Quarterly, 44,* 192-203.

Gaertner, S. L., & Dovidio, J. F. (1986). The aversive form of racism. In J. F. Dovidio & S. L. Gaertner (Eds.), *Prejudice, discrimination, and racism* (pp. 61-89). Orlando, FL: Academic Press.

Gaertner, S. L., Mann, J. A., Dovidio, J. F., Murrell, A. J., & Pomare, M. (1990). How does cooperation reduce intergroup bias? *Journal of Personality and Social Psychology, 59,* 692-704.

Gaertner, S. L., & McLaughlin, J. P. (1983). Racial stereotypes: Associations and ascriptions of positive and negative characteristics. *Social Psychology Quarterly, 46,* 23-30.

Galaskiewicz, J. (1991). Making corporate actors accountable: Institution-building in Minneapolis-St. Paul. In W. W. Powell & P. J. DiMaggio (Eds.), *The new institutionalism in organizational analysis* (pp. 293-310). Chicago: University of Chicago Press.

Gardner, D. G., & Cummings, L. L. (1988). Activation theory and job design: Review and reconceptualization. In B. M. Staw & L. L. Cummings (Eds.), *Research in organizational behavior* (Vol. 10, pp. 81-122). Greenwich, CT: JAI.

Gatewood, R. D., Gowan, M. A., & Lautenschlager, G. J. (1993). Corporate image, recruitment image, and initial job choice decisions. *Academy of Management Journal, 36,* 414-427.

George, J. M. (1989). Mood and absence. *Journal of Applied Psychology, 74,* 317-324.

George, J. M. (1990). Personality, affect and behavior in groups. *Journal of Applied Psychology, 75,* 107-116.

George, J. M. (1991). State or trait: Effects of positive mood on prosocial behaviors at work. *Journal of Applied Psychology, 76,* 299-307.

George, J. M. (1995). Leader positive mood and group performance: The case of customer service. *Journal of Applied Social Psychology, 25,* 778-794.

George, J. M. (1996a). Group affective tone. In M. West (Ed.), *Handbook of work group psychology.* Sussex, UK: John Wiley.

George, J. M. (1996b). Trait and state affect. In K. R. Murphy (Ed.), *Individual differences and behavior in organizations* (pp. 145-171). San Francisco: Jossey-Bass.

George, J. M., & Bettenhausen, K. (1990). Understanding prosocial behavior, sales performance, and turnover: A group-level analysis in a service context. *Journal of Applied Psychology, 75,* 698-709.

George, J. M., & Brief, A. P. (1990). The economic instrumentality of work: An examination of the moderating effects of financial requirements and sex on the pay-life satisfaction relationship. *Journal of Vocational Behavior, 37,* 357-368.

George, J. M., & Brief, A. P. (1992). Feeling good—doing good: A conceptual analysis of the mood at work-organizational spontaneity relationship. *Psychological Bulletin, 112*(2), 310-329.

George, J. M., & Brief, A. P. (1996). Motivational agendas in the workplace: The effects of feelings on focus of attention and work motivation. In B. M. Staw & L. L. Cummings (Eds.), *Research in organizational behavior* (Vol. 18, pp. 75-109). Greenwich, CT: JAI.

George, J. M., & James, L. R. (1993). Personality, affect, and behavior in groups revisited: Comment on aggregation, levels of analysis, and a recent application of within and between analysis. *Journal of Applied Psychology, 78,* 798-804.

George, J. M., & Jones, G. R. (1996). *Understanding and managing organizational behavior.* Reading, MA: Addison-Wesley.

George, J. M., & Jones, G. R. (1997). Organizational spontaneity in context. *Human Performance, 10,* 153-170.

Gerard, H. B. (1983). School desegregation: The social science role. *American Psychologist, 38,* 869-877.

Gerard, H. B., & Orive, R. (1987). The dynamics of opinion formation. In L. Berkowitz (Ed.), *Advances in experimental social psychology* (Vol. 20, pp. 171-200). San Diego, CA: Academic Press.

Gergen, K. J. (1973). Social psychology as history. *Journal of Personality and Social Psychology, 26,* 309-320.

Gergen, K. J., & Thatchenkery, T. J. (1996). Organization science as social construction: Postmodern potentials. *Journal of Applied Behavioral Sciences, 32,* 356-377.

Gerhart, B. (1987). How important are dispositional factors as determinants of job satisfaction: Implications for job design and other personnel programs. *Journal of Applied Psychology, 72,* 366-373.

Gerhart, B. (1990, July). *The doubtful practical relevance of dispositional effects on job satisfaction* (Working Paper No. 90-06). Ithaca, NY: Cornell University, Center for Advanced Human Resource Studies.

Giacalone, R. A., & Rosenfeld, P. (1989). The effect of sex and impression management on future salary estimations. *Journal of General Psychology, 116*(2), 215-219.

Gilbert, D. T., & Hixon, J. G. (1991). The trouble of thinking: Activation and application of stereotypic beliefs. *Journal of Personality and Social Psychology, 60,* 506-517.

Gilbert, G. M. (1951). Stereotype persistence and change among college students. *Journal of Abnormal and Social Psychology, 46,* 245-252.

Ginzberg, E., & Berman, H. (1963). *The American worker in the twentieth century: A history through autobiographies.* New York: Free Press.

Glaser, B., & Strauss, A. (1967). *The discovery of grounded theory.* Chicago: Aldine.

Gleicher, F., & Petty, R. E. (1992). Expectations of reassurance influence the nature of fear-stimulated attitude change. *Journal of Experimental and Social Psychology, 28,* 86-100.

Goldberg, L. R. (1981). Language and individual differences: The search for universals in personality lexicons. In L. Wheeler (Ed.), *Review of personality and social psychology* (pp. 141-165). Beverly Hills, CA: Sage.

Goldberg, L. R. (1990). An alternative "description of personality": The Big-Five factor structure. *Journal of Personality and Social Psychology, 59,* 1216-1229.

Goldberg, L. R. (1993). The structure of phenotypic personality traits. *American Psychologist, 48,* 26-34.

Golembiewski, R. T., Billingsley, K., & Yeager, S. (1976). Measuring change and persistence in human affairs: Types of change generated by OD designs. *Journal of Applied Behavioral Science, 12,* 133-157.

Goodstein, L. D. (1954). Interrelationships among several measures of anxiety and hostility. *Journal of Consulting Psychology, 18,* 35-39.

Gotlieb, J. B., Gerwall, D., & Brown, S. W. (1994). Consumer satisfaction and perceived quality: Complimentary or divergent constructs? *Journal of Applied Psychology, 79,* 875-885.

Gottfredson, G. B., & Holland, J. L. (1990). A longitudinal test of the influence of congruence: Job satisfaction, competency utilization, and counterproductive behavior. *Journal of Counseling Psychology, 37,* 389-398.

Gottschalk, P., & Moffit, R. (1994). *The growth of earnings instability in the U.S. labor market* (Brookings Papers on Economic Activity). Washington, DC: Brookings Institution.

Gouaux, C. (1971). Induced affective states and interpersonal attraction. *Journal of Personality and Social Psychology, 20,* 37-43.

Grandberg, D., & Holmberg, S. (1990). The intention-behavior relationship among U.S. and Swedish voters. *Social Psychology Quarterly, 53,* 44-54.

Greenberg, J. (1987). A taxonomy of organizational justice theories. *Academy of Management Review, 12,* 9-22.

Greenberg, J. (1990a). Looking fair vs. being fair: Managing impressions of organizational justice. In B. M. Staw & L. L. Cummings (Eds.), *Research in organizational behavior* (Vol. 12, pp. 111-157). Greenwich, CT: JAI.

Greenberg, J. (1990b). Organizational justice: Yesterday, today, and tomorrow. *Journal of Management, 16,* 399-432.

Greenberg, J. (1993). Stealing in the name of justice: Informational and interpersonal moderators of theft reactions to underpayment inequity. *Organizational Behavior and Human Decision Processes, 54,* 81-103.

Greenberg, J., Kirkland, S. L., & Pyszczynski, T. (1988). Some theoretical notions and preliminary research concerning derogatory ethnic labels. In G. Smitherman-Donaldson & T. A. van Dijk (Eds.), *Discourse and discrimination* (pp. 74-92). Detroit, MI: Wayne State University Press.

Greenberg, J., & Scott, K. S. (1996). Why do workers bite the hands that feed them? Employee theft as a social exchange process. In B. M. Staw & L. L. Cummings (Eds.), *Research in organizational behavior* (Vol. 18, pp. 111-156). Greenwich, CT: JAI.

Greene, C. H. (1972). The satisfaction/performance controversy. *Business Horizons, 15,* 31-41.

Greenhalgh, L., & Rosenblatt, Z. (1984). Job insecurity: Toward conceptual clarity. *Academy of Management Review, 9,* 438-448.

Greenhaus, J. H., & Beutell, N. J. (1985). Sources of conflict between work and family roles. *Academy of Management Review, 10,* 76-88.

Greenhaus, J. H., Parasuraman, S., & Wormley, W. M. (1990). Effects of race on organizational experiences, job performance evaluations, and career outcomes. *Academy of Management Journal, 33,* 64-86.

Greenwald, A. G. (1968). Cognitive learning, cognitive response to persuasion, and attitude change. In A. G. Greenwald, T. C. Brook, & T. M. Ostrom (Eds.), *Psychological foundations of attitudes* (pp. 147-170). New York: Academic Press.

Greenwald, A. G. (1989). Why attitudes are important: Defining attitude and attitude theory 20 years later. In A. R. Pratkanis, S. J. Breckler, & A. G. Greenwald (Eds.), *Attitude structure and function* (pp. 429-440). Hillsdale, NJ: Lawrence Erlbaum.

Greenwald, A. G., & Banaji, M. R. (1995). Implicit social cognition: Attitudes, self-esteem, and stereotypes. *Psychological Review, 102,* 4-27.

Greenwald, A. G., & Breckler, S. J. (1985). To whom is the self presented? In B. R. Schlenker (Ed.), *The self and social life* (pp. 126-145). New York: McGraw-Hill.

Griffin, R. W. (1987). Toward an integrative theory of task design. In L. L. Cummings & B. M. Staw (Eds.), *Research in organizational behavior* (Vol. 9, pp. 79-120). Greenwich, CT: JAI.

Griffin, R. W. (1991). Effects of work redesign on employee perceptions, attitudes, and behaviors: A long-term investigation. *Academy of Management Journal, 34,* 425-435.

Griffin, R. W., Bateman, T. S., Wayne, S. J., & Head, T. C. (1987). Objective and social factors as determinants of task perceptions and responses: An integrative perspective and empirical investigation. *Academy of Management Journal, 30,* 501-523.

Gronhaug, K., & Gilly, M. C. (1991). A transaction cost approach to consumer dissatisfaction and complaint actions. *Journal of Economic Psychology, 12,* 165-184.

Gronroos, C. (1990). *Service management and marketing.* Lexington, MA: Lexington Books.

Gross, A. E., Wallston, B. S., & Piliavin, I. M. (1975). Beneficiary attractiveness and cost as determinants of responses to routine requests for help. *Sociometry, 38,* 131-140.

Gross, E., & Etzioni, A. (1985). *Organizations and society.* Englewood Cliffs, NJ: Prentice Hall.

Groves, R. M. (1990). Theories and methods of telephone surveys. In W. R. Scott & J. Blake (Eds.), *Annual review of sociology* (Vol. 16, pp. 221-240). Palo Alto, CA: Annual Reviews.

Gruenfeld, D. H., & Wyer, R. S., Jr. (1992). The semantics and pragmatics of social influence: How affirmations and denials affect beliefs in referent propositions. *Journal of Personality and Social Psychology, 62,* 38-49.

Gummesson, E. (1992). Quality dimensions: What to measure in service organizations. In T. A. Swartz, D. E. Bowen, & S. Brown (Eds.), *Advances in services marketing and management* (Vol. 1, pp. 177-205). Greenwich, CT: JAI.

Gutek, B. A., & Winter, S. J. (1992). Consistency of job satisfaction across situations: Fact or framing artifact? *Journal of Vocational Behavior, 41*(1), 61-78.

Guttman, L. (1941). The quantification of a class of attributes: A theory and method of scale construction. In P. Horst (Ed.), *The prediction of personal adjustment* (Bulletin No. 48, pp. 319-348). New York: Social Science Research Council.

Guttman, L. (1944). A basis for scaling qualitative data. *American Sociological Review, 9,* 139-150.

Guzzo, R. A. (1988). Productivity research in review. In J. P. Campbell & R. J. Campbell (Eds.), *Productivity in organizations: New perspectives from industrial and organizational psychology.* San Francisco: Jossey-Bass.

Guzzo, R. A., & Shea, G. P. (1992). Group performance and intergroup relations in organizations. In M. D. Dunnette & M. L. Hough (Eds.), *Handbook of industrial and organizational psychology* (2nd ed., Vol. 3, pp. 269-313). Palo Alto, CA: Consulting Psychologists Press.

Hackett, R. D., & Guion, R. M. (1985). A reevaluation of the absenteeism-job satisfaction relationship. *Organizational Behavior and Human Decision Processes, 35,* 340-381.

Hackman, J. R., & Lawler, E. E., III. (1971). Employee reactions to job characteristics [Monograph]. *Journal of Applied Psychology, 55,* 259-286.

Hackman, J. R., & Oldham, G. R. (1975). Development of the job diagnostic survey. *Journal of Applied Psychology, 60,* 159-170.

Hackman, J. R., & Oldham, G. R. (1976). Motivation through the design of work: Test of a theory. *Organizational Behavior and Human Performance, 16,* 250-279.

Haddock, G., Zanna, M. P., & Esses, V. M. (1993). Assessing the structure of prejudicial attitudes: The case of attitudes towards homosexuals. *Journal of Personality and Social Psychology, 65,* 1105-1118.

Hage, J. (1965). An axiomatic theory of organizations. *Administrative Science Quarterly, 10,* 289-320.

Hall, D. T., & Mirvis, P. H. (1995). The new career contract: Developing the whole person at midlife and beyond [Special issue: Careers from midlife]. *Journal of Vocational Behavior, 47,* 269-289.

Hall, D. T., & Nougaim, K. E. (1968). An examination of Maslow's need hierarchy in an organizational setting. *Organizational Behavior and Human Performance, 3,* 12-35.

Hambrick, D. C. (1994). Top management groups: A conceptual integration and reconsideration of the "team" label. In B. M. Staw & L. L. Cummings (Eds.), *Research in organizational behavior* (Vol. 16, pp. 171-213). Greenwich, CT: JAI.

Hamilton, D. L. (1981). Illusory correlations as a basis for stereotyping. In D. L. Hamilton (Ed.), *Cognitive processes in stereotyping and intergroup behavior* (pp. 115-144). Hillsdale, NJ: Lawrence Erlbaum.

Hamilton, D. L., & Sherman, J. W. (1994). Stereotypes. In R. S. Wyer & T. K. Srull (Eds.), *The handbook of social cognition* (2nd ed., Vol. 2, pp. 1-68). Hillsdale, NJ: Lawrence Erlbaum.

Hamilton, D. L., & Sherman, S. J. (1989). Illusory correlations: Implications for stereotype theory and research. In D. Bar-Tal, C. F. Graumann, A. W. Kruglanski, & W. Stroebe (Eds.), *Stereotyping and prejudice: Changing conceptions* (pp. 59-82). New York: Springer.

Hammond, K. R. (1948). Measuring attitudes by error choice: An indirect method. *Journal of Abnormal and Social Psychology, 52,* 260-268.

Han, S., & Shavitt, S. (1994). Persuasion and culture: Advertising appeals in individualistic and collectivistic societies. *Journal of Experimental Social Psychology, 30*(4), 326-350.

Handy, C. (1989). *The age of unreason.* Cambridge, MA: Harvard Business School Press.

Haney, J. N. (1973). Approach-avoidance reactions by repressors and sensitizers to ambiguity in a structured free-association task. *Psychological Reports, 33,* 97-98.

Harding, J., Proshansky, H., Kutner, B., & Chein, I. (1969). Prejudice and ethnic relations. In G. Lindzey & E. Aronson (Eds.), *The handbook of social psychology.* Reading, MA: Addison-Wesley.

Harkins, S. G., & Petty, R. E. (1987). Information utility and the multiple source effect. *Journal of Personality and Social Psychology, 52,* 260-268.

Harré, R. (1986). *Varieties of realism.* New York: Blackwell.

Harris, L., & Associates. (1988). *America and the arts V.* New York: Louis Harris Associates.

Harrison, D. A., & Schaffer, M. A. (1994). Comparative examinations on self-reports and perceived absenteeism norms: Wading through Lake Wobegon. *Journal of Applied Psychology, 79,* 240-251.

Harrison, R. V. (1978). Person-environment fit and job stress. In C. L. Cooper & R. Payne (Eds.), *Stress at work* (pp. 175-205). New York: John Wiley.

Hass, R. G. (1981). Effects of source characteristics on cognitive responses and persuasion. In R. E. Petty, T. M. Ostrom, & T. C. Brock (Eds.), *Cognitive responses in persuasion* (pp. 141-172). Hillsdale, NJ: Lawrence Erlbaum.

Hass, R. G., Katz, I., Rizzo, N., Bailey, J., & Eisenstadt, D. (1991). Cross-racial appraisal as related to attitude ambivalence and cognitive complexity. *Personality and Social Psychological Bulletin, 17,* 83-92.

Hass, R. G., Katz, I., Rizzo, N., Bailey, J., & Moore, L. (1992). When racial ambivalence evokes negative affect: Using a disguised measure of mood. *Personality and Social Psychology Bulletin, 18*(6), 786-797.

Hastie, R. (1983). Social inference. *Annual Review of Psychology, 34,* 511-542.

Hatfield, E., Cacioppo, J. T., & Rapson, R. L. (1992). Primitive emotional contagion. In M. S. Clark (Ed.), *Review of personality and social psychology: Vol. 14. Emotion and social behavior* (pp. 151-177). Newbury Park, CA: Sage.

Hatfield, E., Cacioppo, J. T., & Rapson, R. L. (1994). *Emotional contagion.* Cambridge, UK: Cambridge University Press.

Hayes, E. (1995, August). *It's not what you know, it's who you know: The effects of human and social capital on race differences in promotion and support.* Paper presented at the meeting of the Academy of Management, Vancouver, British Columbia, Canada.

Heider, F. (1946). Attitudes and cognitive organization. *Journal of Psychology, 21,* 107-112.

Heilman, M. D., & Toffler, B. L. (1976). Reacting to reactance: An interpersonal interpretation of the need for freedom. *Journal of Experimental Social Psychology, 12,* 519-529.

Heise, D. R. (1977). Group dynamics and attitude-behavior relations. *Sociological Methods and Research, 5,* 259-288.

Heneman, H. G., Jr. (1973). *Work and nonwork: Historical perspectives.* In M. D. Dunnette (Ed.), *Work and nonwork in the year 2001.* Monterey, CA: Brooks/Cole.

Heneman, H. G. (1985). Pay satisfaction. In K. M. Rowland & G. R. Ferris (Eds.), *Research in personnel and human resources management* (Vol. 3). Greenwich, CT: JAI Inc.

Heneman, H. G., & Schwab, D. P. (1985). Pay satisfaction: Its multidimensional nature and measurement. *International Journal of Psychology, 20,* 129-141.

Henne, D. L., & Locke, E. A. (1985). Job dissatisfaction: What are the consequences? *International Journal of Psychology, 20,* 221-240.

Herek, G. M. (1987). Can functions be measured? A new perspective on the functional approach to attitudes. *Social Psychology Quarterly, 50,* 285-303.

Hersey, R. B. (1932). *Workers' emotions in shop and home: A study of individual workers from the psychological and physiological standpoint.* Philadelphia: University of Pennsylvania Press.

Herzberg, F. (1968, January). One more time: How do you motivate employees. *Harvard Business Review, 46,* 53-62.

Herzberg, F., Mausner, B., & Snyderman, H. (1959). *The motivation to work.* New York: John Wiley.

Hewstone, M. (1990). The "ultimate attribution error"? A review of the literature on intergroup causal attribution. *European Journal of Social Psychology, 20,* 311-335.

Hewstone, M., & Jaspers, J. M. F. (1984). Social dimensions of attribution. In H. Tajfel (Ed.), *The social dimension: European developments in social psychology* (Vol. 2, pp. 379-404). New York: Cambridge University Press.

Hewstone, M., Johnston, L., & Aird, P. (1992). Cognitive models of stereotype change: II. Perceptions of homogeneous and heterogeneous groups. *European Journal of Social Psychology, 22,* 235-249.

Heydebrand, W. V. (1989). New organizational forms. *Work-and-Occupations, 16,* 323-357.

Higgins, E. T. (1987). Self-discrepancy: A theory relating self and affect. *Psychological Review, 94,* 319-340.

Higgins, E. T., Bond, R. W., Klien, R., & Strauman, T. (1986). Self-discrepancies and emotional vulnerability: How magnitude, accessibility, and type of discrepancy influence affect. *Journal of Personality and Social Psychology, 51,* 5-15.

Higgins, E. T., Kuiper, N. A., & Olson, J. M. (1981). Social cognition: A need to get personal. In E. T. Higgins, C. P. Herman, & M. P. Zanna (Eds.), *Social cognition: The Ontario Symposium* (Vol. 1, pp. 395-420). Hillsdale, NJ: Lawrence Erlbaum.

Higgins, E. T., Simon, M., & Wells, R. S. (1988). A model of evaluative processes and "job satisfaction": When differences in standards make a difference. In R. L. Cardy, S. M. Puffer, & J. M. Newman (Eds.), *Advances in information processing in organizations* (Vol. 3, pp. 81-105). Greenwich, CT: JAI.

Hilton, J. L., & von Hippel, W. (1990). The role of consistency in the judgement of stereotype-relevant behaviors. *Personality and Social Psychology Bulletin, 16,* 430-448.

Hilton, J. L., & von Hippel, W. (1996). Stereotypes. *Annual Review of Psychology, 47,* 237-271.

Himmelfarb, S. (1993). The measurement of attitudes. In A. H. Eagly & S. Chaiken (Eds.), *The psychology of attitudes.* Fort Worth, TX: Harcourt Brace Jovanovich.

Himmelfarb, S., & Lickteig, C. (1982). Social desirability and the randomized response technique. *Journal of Personality and Social Psychology, 43,* 710-717.

Hirschman, A. O. (1970). *Exit, voice, and loyalty: Responses to decline in firms, organizations, and states.* Cambridge, MA: Harvard University Press.

Hitler, A. (1933). *Mein Kampf* [My struggle] (E. T. S. Dugdale, Trans.). Cambridge, MA: Riverside.

Hoch, S. J., & Ha, Y. W. (1988). Consumer learning: Advertising and the ambiguity of product experience. *Journal of Consumer Research, 13,* 221-233.

Hochschild, A. R. (1979). Emotion work, feeling rules, and social structure. *American Journal of Sociology, 85,* 551-575.

Hochschild, A. R. (1983). *The managed heart.* Berkeley: University of California Press.

Hoffman, C., & Hurst, N. (1990). Gender stereotypes: Perception or rationalization? *Journal of Personality and Social Psychology, 58,* 197-208.

Hofstede, G. (1984). The cultural relativity of the quality of life concept. *Academy of Management Review, 9,* 389-398.

Hogg, M. A., & Abrams, D. (1988). *Social identification: A social psychology of intergroup relations and group processes.* New York: Routledge.

Hogg, M. A., & Abrams, D. (1990). Social motivation, self-esteem, and social identity. In D. Abrams & M. Hogg (Eds.), *Social identity theory: Constructive and critical advances* (pp. 28-47). New York: Springer.

Holland, J. L. (1985). *Making vocational choices: A theory of careers* (2nd ed.). Englewood Cliffs, NJ: Prentice Hall.

Hom, P. W., & Griffeth, R. W. (1991). Structural equations modeling test of a turnover theory: Cross-sectional and longitudinal analyses. *Journal of Applied Psychology, 76,* 350-366.

Hom, P. W., & Griffeth, R. W. (1995). *Employee turnover.* Cincinnati, OH: South-Western College Publishing.

Hom, P. W., & Hulin, C. L. (1981). A competitive test of predictions of reenlistment by several models. *Journal of Applied Psychology, 66,* 23-39.

Homans, G. C. (1961). *Social behavior: Its elementary forms.* New York: Harcourt, Brace, & World.

Hoppock, R. (1935). *Job satisfaction.* New York: Harper.

Hough, L. M., & Schneider, R. J. (1996). Personality traits, taxonomies, and applications in organizations. In K. R. Murphy (Ed.), *Individual differences and behavior in organizations* (pp. 31-88). San Francisco: Jossey-Bass.

House, R. J., Rousseau, D. M., & Thomas-Hunt, M. (1995). The meso paradigm: A framework for the integration of micro and macro organizational behavior. In L. L. Cummings & B. M. Staw (Eds.), *Research in organizational behavior* (Vol. 17, pp. 71-114). Greenwich, CT: JAI.

House, R. J., Shane, S. A., & Herold, D. M. (1996). Rumors of the death of dispositional research are vastly exaggerated. *Academy of Management Review, 21,* 203-224.

House, R. J., & Wigdor, L. A. (1967). Herzberg's dual-factor theory of job satisfaction: A review of the evidence and a criticism. *Personnel Psychology, 20,* 369-389.

Hovland, C. I. (1959). Reconciling conflicting results derived from experimental and survey studies of attitude change. *American Psychologist, 14,* 8-17.

Hovland, C. I., Harvey, O. J., & Sherif, M. (1957). Assimilation and contrast effects in reactions to communication and attitude change. *Journal of Abnormal and Social Psychology, 55,* 244-252.

Hovland, C. I., Janis, I., & Kelley, H. H. (1953). *Communication and persuasion.* New Haven, CT: Yale University Press.

Hovland, C. I., Lumsdaine, A. A., & Sheffield, F. D. (1949). *Experiments on mass communication.* Princeton, NJ: Princeton University Press.

Hovland, C. I., & Weiss, W. (1951). The influence of source credibility on communication effectiveness. *Public Opinion Quarterly, 15,* 635-650.

Howard, A. (Ed.). (1995). *The changing nature of work.* San Francisco: Jossey-Bass.

Hulin, C. L. (1966). Job satisfaction and turnover in a female clerical population. *Journal of Applied Psychology, 50,* 280-285.

Hulin, C. L. (1991). Adaptation, persistence, and commitment in organizations. In M. D. Dunnette & L. M. Hough (Eds.), *Handbook of industrial and organizational psychology* (Vol. 2, pp. 445-505). Palo Alto, CA: Consulting Psychologists Press.

Hulin, C. L., Roznowski, M., & Hachiya, D. (1985). Alternative opportunities and withdrawal decisions: Empirical and theoretical discrepancies and an integration. *Psychological Bulletin, 97,* 233-250.

Huston, T. L., & Geis, G. (1993). In what ways do gender-related attributes and beliefs affect marriage? *Journal of Social Issues, 49,* 87-106.

Hyman, H. H., & Sheatsley, P. B. (1954). The authoritarian personality: A methodological critique. In R. Christie & M. Jahoda (Eds.), *Studies in the scope and method of the authoritarian personality* (pp. 50-122). Glencoe, IL: Free Press.

Iacobucci, D., Grayson, K. A., & Ostrom, A. L. (1994). The calculus of service quality and customer satisfaction: Theoretical and empirical differentiation. In T. A. Swartz, D. E. Bowen, & S. Brown (Eds.), *Advances in services, marketing and management* (Vol. 3, pp. 1-67). Greenwich, CT: JAI.

Iaffaldano, M. T., & Muchinsky, P. M. (1985). Job satisfaction and job performance: A meta-analysis. *Psychological Bulletin, 97,* 251-273.

Ibarra, H. (1995). Race, opportunity, and diversity of social circles in managerial networks. *Academy of Management Journal, 38,* 673-703.

Ironson, G. H., Smith, P. C., Brannick, M. T., Gibson, W. M., & Paul, K. B. (1989). Construction of a job in general scale: A comparison of global, composite, and specific measures. *Journal of Applied Psychology, 74,* 193-200.

Isen, A. M. (1984). Toward understanding the role of affect in cognition. In R. S. Wyer, Jr. & T. K. Srull (Eds.), *Handbook of social cognition* (Vol. 3, pp. 179-236). Hillsdale, NJ: Lawrence Erlbaum.

Isen, A. M., & Baron, R. A. (1991). Positive affect as a factor in organizational behavior. In B. M. Staw & L. L. Cummings (Eds.), *Research in organizational behavior* (Vol. 13, pp. 1-53). Greenwich, CT: JAI.

Isen, A. M., Daubman, K. A., & Nowicki, G. P. (1987). Positive affect facilitates creative problem solving: When we are glad, we feel as if the light has increased. *Journal of Personality and Social Psychology, 51,* 1122-1131.

Isen, A. M., & Levin, A. F. (1972). Effects of feeling good on helping: Cookies and kindness. *Journal of Personality and Social Psychology, 21,* 384-388.

Isen, A. M., Shalker, T., Clark, M., & Karp, L. (1978). Affect, accessibility of material in memory and behavior: A cognitive loop? *Journal of Personality and Social Psychology, 36,* 1-12.

Jackall, R. (1988). *Moral mazes: The world of corporate managers.* New York: Oxford University Press.

Jackson, L. A., Sullivan, L. A., & Hodge, C. (1993). Stereotype effects on attributions, predictions, and evaluations: No two social judgments are quite alike. *Journal of Personality and Social Psychology, 65,* 69-84.

Jackson, S. E., & Schuler, R. S. (1985). A meta-analysis and conceptual critique of research on role ambiguity and role conflict in work settings. *Organizational Behavior and Human Decision Processes, 36,* 16-78.

Jacoby, J., & Chestnut, R. W. (1978). *Brand loyalty: Measurement and management.* New York: John Wiley.

Jacoby, J., & Hoyer, W. (1982). Viewer miscomprehension of televised communication: Selected findings. *Journal of Marketing, 46*(4), 12-26.

Jacoby, J., & Hoyer, W. (1987). *The comprehension and miscomprehension of print communication: An investigation of mass media magazines.* Hillsdale, NJ: Lawrence Erlbaum.

Jacoby, J., Hoyer, W., & Brief, A. (1992). Consumer psychology. In M. D. Dunnette & L. M. Hough (Eds.), *Handbook of industrial and organizational psychology* (2nd ed., Vol. 3, pp. 377-441). Palo Alto, CA: Consulting Psychologists Press.

Jacoby, J., & Olson, J. C. (Eds.). (1985). *Perceived quality: How consumers view stores and merchandise.* Lexington, MA: Lexington Books.

Jacoby, S. M. (1985). *Employing bureaucracy managers, unions, and the transformation of work in American industry, 1900-1945.* New York: Columbia University Press.

Jacques, E. (1956). *Measurement of responsibility.* London: Tavistock.

James, L. R., & James, L. A. (1992). Psychological climate and affect: Test of a hierarchical dynamic model. In C. J. Cranny, P. C. Smith, & E. F. Stone (Eds.), *Job satisfaction: How people feel about their jobs and how it affects their performance* (Vol. 1, pp. 89-117). New York: Lexington.

James, L. R., & Jones, A. P. (1980). Perceived job characteristics and job satisfaction: An examination of reciprocal causation. *Personnel Psychology, 33,* 97-135.

James, L. R., & Tetrick, L. E. (1986). Confirmatory analytic test of three causal models relating job perceptions to job satisfaction. *Journal of Applied Psychology, 71,* 77-82.

Janis, I. L. (1967). Effects of fear arousal on attitude change: Recent developments in theory and experimental research. In L. Berkowitz (Ed.), *Advances in experimental social psychology* (Vol. 3, pp. 166-224). San Diego, CA: Academic Press.

Jensen, M. C. (1989). Eclipse of the public corporation. *Harvard Business Review, 67*(5), 61-74.

Jewett, D. (1994, July 25). Ford's service quest: Raise owner loyalty. *Automotive News,* p. 3.

Jobson, J. D., & Schneck, R. (1982). Constituent views of organizational effectiveness: Evidence from police organizations. *Academy of Management Journal, 25,* 25-46.

John, O. P. (1990). The "Big Five" factor taxonomy: Dimensions of personality in the natural language and in questionnaires. In L. A. Pervin (Ed.), *Handbook of personality: Theory and research* (pp. 66-100). New York: Guilford.

Johns, G. (1994). Absenteeism estimates by employees and managers: Divergent perspectives and self-serving perceptions. *Journal of Applied Psychology, 79,* 229-239.

Johns, G. (in press). Contemporary research on absence from work: Correlates, causes, and consequences. *International Review of Industrial and Organizational Psychology.*

Johns, G., & Nicholson, N. (1982). The meaning of absence: New strategies for theory and research. In B. M. Staw & L. L. Cummings (Eds.), *Research in organizational behavior* (Vol. 4, pp. 127-172). Greenwich, CT: JAI.

Johnson, B. T., & Eagly, A. H. (1989). The effects of involvement on persuasion: A meta-analysis. *Psychological Bulletin, 106,* 290-314.

Johnson, D. W., Johnson, R. T., & Maruyama, G. (1984). Goal interdependence and interpersonal attraction in heterogeneous classrooms: A meta-analysis. In N. Miller & M. B. Brewer (Eds.), *Groups in contact: The psychology of desegregation* (pp. 187-212). Orlando, FL: Academic Press.

Johnston, L. C., & Hewstone, M. (1992). Cognitive models of stereotype change: III. Subtyping and the perceived typicality of disconfirming group members. *Journal of Experimental Social Psychology, 28,* 360-386.

Johnston, L. C., & Macrae, C. N. (1994). Changing social stereotypes: The case of the information seeker. *European Journal of Social Psychology, 24,* 581-592.

Jones, E. E., & Gerard, H. B. (1967). *Foundations of social psychology.* New York: John Wiley.

Jones, E. E., & Sigall, H. (1971). The bogus pipeline: A new paradigm for measuring affect and attitude. *Psychological Bulletin, 76,* 349-364.

Jones, E. W. (1973, July). What it's like to be a Black manager. *Harvard Business Review, 51,* 114.

Jost, J. T., & Banaji, M. R. (1994). The role of stereotyping in system-justification and the production of false consciousness. *British Journal of Social Psychology, 33,* 1-27.

Judd, C. M., & Downing, J. W. (1990). Political expertise and the development of attitude consistency. *Social Cognition, 8,* 104-124.

Judd, C. M., Krosnick, J. W., & Milburn, M. A. (1981). Political involvement and attitude structure in the general public. *American Sociological Review, 46,* 660-669.

Judd, C. M., Ryan, C. S., & Park, B. (1991). Accuracy in the judgment of in-group and out-group variability. *Journal of Personality and Social Psychology, 61,* 366-379.

Judge, T. A. (1992). The dispositional perspective in human resource research. In G. Ferris & K. Rowland (Eds.), *Research in personnel and human resource management* (pp. 31-72). Greenwich, CT: JAI.

Judge, T. A. (1993). Does affective disposition moderate the relationship between job satisfaction and voluntary turnover? *Journal of Applied Psychology, 78,* 395-401.

Judge, T. A., & Bretz, R. D., Jr. (1993). Report on an alternate measure of disposition. *Educational and Psychological Measurement, 53,* 1095-1104.

Judge, T. A., & Hulin, C. L. (1993). Job satisfaction as a reflection of disposition: A multiple source causal analysis. *Organizational Behavior and Human Decision Processes, 56,* 388-421.

Judge, T. A., & Locke, E. A. (1993). Effect of dysfunctional thought processes on subjective well-being and job satisfaction. *Journal of Applied Psychology, 78,* 475-490.

Judge, T. A., Locke, E. A., & Durham, C. C. (1997). The dispositional causes of job satisfaction: A core-evaluations approach. In L. L. Cummings & B. M. Staw (Eds.), *Research in organizational behavior.* Greenwich, CT: JAI.

Judge, T. A., & Watanabe, S. (1993). Another look at the job satisfaction-life satisfaction relationship. *Journal of Applied Psychology, 78,* 939-948.

Jussin, L. (1991). Social perception and social reality: A reflection-construction model. *Psychological Review, 98,* 54-73.

Kahle, L. R., & Homer, P. M. (1985). Physical attractiveness of the celebrity endorser: A social adaptation perspective. *Journal of Consumer Research, 11,* 954-961.

Kahneman, D. (1973). *Attention and effort.* Englewood Cliffs, NJ: Prentice Hall.

Kallgren, C. A., & Wood, W. (1986). Access to attitude-relevant information in memory as a determinant of attitude-behavior consistency. *Journal of Experimental Social Psychology, 22,* 328-338.

Kalyanaram, G., & Little, J. D. C. (1994). An empirical analysis of latitude of price acceptance in consumer package goods. *Journal of Consumer Research, 21,* 408-418.

Kanfer, R. (1992). Motivation theory and industrial and organizational psychology. In M. D. Dunnette & L. M. Hough (Eds.), *Handbook of industrial and organizational psychology* (2nd ed., Vol. 1, pp. 75-170). Palo Alto, CA: Consulting Psychologists Press.

Kanfer, R., & Ackerman, P. L. (1989). Motivation and cognitive abilities: An integrative/aptitude-treatment interaction approach to skill acquisition [Monograph]. *Journal of Applied Psychology, 74,* 657-690.

Kant, I. (1969). *The critique of pure reason* (N. K. Smith, Ed.). New York: St. Martin's. (Original work published 1781)

Kaplan, A. (1964). *The conduct of inquiry: Methodology for the behavioral sciences.* Scranton, PA: Chandler.

Karlins, M., Coffman, T. L., & Walters, G. (1969). On the fading of social stereotypes: Studies in three generations of college students. *Journal of Personality and Social Psychology, 13,* 1-16.

Katz, D. (1960). The functional approach to the study of attitudes. *Public Opinion Quarterly, 24,* 163-204.

Katz, D. (1964). The motivational basis of organizational behavior. *Behavioral Science, 9,* 131-146.

Katz, D., & Braly, K. N. (1933). Verbal stereotypes and racial prejudice. *Journal of Abnormal and Social Psychology, 133,* 280-290.

Katz, D., & Kahn, R. L. (1978). *The social psychology of organizations* (2nd ed.). New York: John Wiley.

Katz, I. (1981). *Stigma: A social psychological analysis.* Hillsdale, NJ: Lawrence Erlbaum.

Katz, I, & Glass, D. C. (1979). An ambivalence-amplification theory of behavior toward the stigmatized. In W. G. Austin & S. Worchel (Eds.), *The social psychology of intergroup relations* (pp. 55-70). Monterey, CA: Brooks/Cole.

Katz, I., & Hass, R. G. (1988). Racial ambivalence and American value conflict: Correlational and priming studies of dual cognitive structures. *Journal of Personality and Social Psychology, 55,* 893-905.

Katz, I., Wackenhut, J., & Hass, R. G. (1986). Racial ambivalence, value duality, and behavior. In J. F. Dovidio & S. L. Gaertner (Eds.), *Prejudice, discrimination, and racism* (pp. 35-59). Orlando, FL: Academic Press.

Katz, P. A. (1976). Racism and social science: Towards a new commitment. In P. A. Katz (Ed.), *Towards the elimination of racism.* New York: Pergamon.

Katz, R. (1978). Job longevity as a situational factor in job satisfaction. *Administrative Science Quarterly, 23,* 204-223.

Katzell, R. A. (1964). Personal values, job satisfaction, and job behavior. In H. Borow (Ed.), *Man in a world at work* (pp. 341-361). Boston: Houghton Mifflin.

Katzell, R. A., Thompson, D. E., & Guzzo, R. A. (1992). How job satisfaction and job performance are and are not linked. In C. J. Cranny, P. C. Smith, & E. F. Stone (Eds.), *Job satisfaction: How people feel about their jobs and how it affects their performance* (Vol. 1, pp. 195-217). New York: Lexington.

Kefalas, A., & Schoderbek, P. P. (1973). Scanning the business environment: Some empirical results. *Decision Sciences, 4,* 63-74.

Kelley, H. H. (1967). Attribution theory in social psychology. In D. Levine (Ed.), *Nebraska Symposium on Motivation* (Vol. 15, pp. 192-238). Lincoln: University of Nebraska Press.

Kelley, H. H. (1972). Causal schemata and the attribution process. In E. E. Jones, D. E. Kanouse, H. H. Kelley, R. E. Nisbett, S. Valins, & B. Weiner (Eds.), *Attribution: Perceiving the causes of behavior* (pp. 151-174). Morristown, NJ: General Learning Press.

Kelley, S. W. (1993). Discretion and the service employee. *Journal of Retailing, 69,* 104-126.

Kelley, S. W., Donnelly, J. H., & Skinner, S. J. (1990). Customer participation in service production and delivery. *Journal of Retailing, 66,* 315-333.

Kelman, H. C. (1958). *A time to speak: On human values and social research.* San Francisco: Jossey-Bass.

Kelman, H. C. (1974). Attitudes are alive and well and gainfully employed in the sphere of action. *American Psychologist, 29,* 310-324.

Kelman, H. C., & Hamilton, V. L. (1989). *Crimes of obedience: Toward a social psychology of authority and responsibility.* New Haven, CT: Yale University Press.

Kelman, H. C., & Hovland, C. I. (1953). "Reinstatement" of the communicator in delayed measurement of opinion change. *Journal of Abnormal and Social Psychology, 48,* 327-335.

Kets de Vries, M. F. R., & Miller, D. (1986). Personality, culture, and organization. *Academy of Management Review, 11,* 266-279.

Kiesler, C. A., Collins, B. E., & Miller, N. (1969). *Attitude change: A critical analysis of theoretical approaches.* New York: John Wiley.

Kieso, D., & Weygandt, J. (1992). *Intermediate accounting.* New York: John Wiley.

Kinder, D. R. (1986). The continuing American dilemma: White resistance to racial change 40 years after Myrdal. *Journal of Social Issues, 42,* 151-171.

Kinder, D. R., & Rhodebeck, L. A. (1982). Continuities in support for racial equality, 1972 to 1976. *Public Opinion Quarterly, 46,* 195-215.

Kinder, D. R., & Sears, D. O. (1981). Prejudice and politics: Symbolic racism versus racial threats to the good life. *Journal of Personality and Social Psychology, 40,* 414-431.

King, W. (1970). Clarification and evaluation of the two-factor theory of job satisfaction. *Psychological Bulletin, 74,* 18-31.

Kipnis, D., & Schmidt, S. M. (1988). Upward influence styles: Relationship with performance evaluations, salary, and stress. *Administrative Science Quarterly, 33*(4), 528-542.

Klein, B., & Leffler, K. (1981). The role of market forces in assuring contractual performance. *Journal of Political Economy, 89,* 615-641.

Klimoski, R., & Mohammed, S. (1994). Team mental model: Construct or metaphor? *Journal of Management, 20,* 403-437.

Kluegel, J. R, & Smith, E. R. (1986). *Beliefs about inequality: Americans' views about what is and what ought to be.* New York: Walter De Gruyter.

Koblinsky, S. G., Cruse, D. F., & Sugawara, A. I. (1978). Sex role stereotypes and children's memory of story content. *Child Development, 49,* 452-458.

Koch, J. L., & Steers, R. M. (1978). Job attachment, satisfaction, and turnover among public employees. *Journal of Vocational Behavior, 12,* 119-128.

Koestner, R., Bernieri, F., & Zuckerman, M. (1992). Self-regulation and consistency between attitudes, traits, and behaviors. *Personality and Social Psychology Bulletin, 18,* 52-59.

Kohler, S. S., & Mathieu, J. E. (1993). Individual characteristics, work perceptions, and affective reactions influences on differentiated absence criteria. *Journal of Organizational Behavior, 14,* 515-530.

Kopelman, R. E., Brief, A. P., & Guzzo, R. A. (1990). The role of climate and culture in productivity. In B. Schneider (Ed.), *Organizational climate and culture* (pp. 282-318). San Francisco: Jossey-Bass.

Korman, A. K. (1971). *Industrial and organizational psychology.* Englewood Cliffs, NJ: Prentice Hall.

Kovel, J. (1970). *White racism: A psychological history.* New York: Pantheon.

Koys, D. J. (1997). Human resource management and *Fortune*'s corporate reputation survey. *Employee Responsibilities and Rights Journal, 10,* 93-101.

Kozlowski, S. W. J., & Hattrup, K. (1992). A disagreement about within-group agreement: Disentangling issues of consistency versus consensus. *Journal of Applied Psychology, 77,* 161-167.

Kraiger, K., & Ford, J. K. (1985). A meta-analysis of ratee race effects in performance ratings. *Journal of Applied Psychology, 70,* 56-65.

Kraus, S. J. (1995). Attitudes and the prediction of behavior: A meta-analysis of the empirical literature. *Personality and Social Psychology Bulletin, 21,* 58-75.

Kravitz, D. A. (1995). Attitudes toward affirmative action plans directed at Blacks: Effects of plan and individual differences. *Journal of Applied Social Psychology, 25,* 2192-2220.

Kravitz, D. A., & Platania, J. (1993). Attitudes and beliefs about affirmative action: Effects of target sex and ethnicity. *Journal of Applied Psychology, 78,* 928-938.

Krech, D., & Crutchfield, R. S. (1948). *Theory and problems of social psychology.* New York: McGraw-Hill.

Kristof, A. L. (1996). Person-organization fit: An integrative review of its conceptualizations, measurement, and implications. *Personnel Psychology, 49,* 1-49.

Krosnick, J. W. (1990). Americans' perceptions of presidential candidates: A test of the projection hypothesis. *Journal of Social Issues, 46*(2), 159-182.

Krosnick, J. W., & Alwin, D. F. (1989). Aging and susceptibility to attitude change. *Journal of Personality and Social Psychology, 57,* 416-425.

Krosnick, J. W., Betz, A. L., Jussim, L. J., & Lynn, A. R. (1992). Subliminal conditioning of attitudes. *Personality and Social Psychology Bulletin, 18,* 152-162.

Kruglanski, A. W. (1989). *Lay epistemics and human knowledge: Cognitive and motivational bases.* New York: Plenum.

Kuhn, T. S. (1962). *The structure of scientific revolutions.* Chicago: University of Chicago Press.

Kulik, C. T., & Ambrose, M. L. (1992). Personal and situational determinants of referent choice. *Academy of Management Review, 17,* 212-237.

Kunda, Z. (1990). The case of motivated reasoning. *Psychological Bulletin, 108,* 480-498.

Kunin, T. (1955). The construction of a new type of attitude measure. *Personnel Psychology, 8,* 65-78.

Kutner, B., Wilkins, C., & Yarrow, P. R. (1952). Verbal attitudes and overt behavior involving racial prejudice. *Journal of Abnormal and Social Psychology, 47,* 649-652.

Kuykendall, D., & Keating, J. P. (1990). Altering thoughts and judgments through repeated association. *British Journal of Social Psychology, 29,* 79-86.

Labs, J. J. (1992). Perspectives: Job stress. *Personnel Journal, 78,* 43.

Landy, F. J. (1978). An opponent process theory of job satisfaction. *Journal of Applied Psychology, 63,* 533-547.

Langer, E. J. (1989). *Mindfulness.* Reading, MA: Addison-Wesley.

LaPiere, R. T. (1934). Attitudes vs. actions. *Social Forces, 13,* 230-237.

Lawler, E. E. (1968). Equity theory as a predictor of productivity and work quality. *Psychological Bulletin, 70,* 596-610.

Lawler, E. E., Hackman, J. R., & Kaufman, S. (1973). Effects of job redesign: A field experiment. *Journal of Applied Social Psychology, 3,* 49-62.

Lawrence, B. S. (1997). The black box of organizational demography. *Organization Science, 8*(1), 1-22.

Leary, M. R., & Kowalski, R. M. (1990). Impression management: A literature review and two-component model. *Psychological Bulletin, 107,* 34-47.

Lee, T. W., & Mitchell, T. R. (1994). An alternative approach: The unfolding model of voluntary employee turnover. *Academy of Management Review, 19,* 51-89.

Lee, T. W., Mitchell, T. R., Wise, L., & Fireman, S. (1996). An unfolding model of voluntary employee turnover. *Academy of Management Journal, 39,* 5-36.

Leete, L., & Schor, J. B. (1994). Assessing the time-squeeze hypothesis: Hours worked in the United States, 1969-1989. *Industrial Relations, 33,* 25-43.

Lefkowitz, J. (1994). Race as a factor in job placement: Serendipitous findings of "ethnic drift." *Personnel Psychology, 47,* 497-513.

Leicht, K. T., & Fennel, M. L. (1997). The changing organizational context of professional work. In J. Hagan & K. S. Cook (Eds.), *Annual review of sociology* (Vol. 23, pp. 215-339). Palo Alto, CA: Annual Reviews.

Leippe, M. R., & Eisenstadt, D. (1994). Generalization of dissonance reduction: Decreasing prejudice through induced compliance. *Journal of Personality and Social Psychology, 67,* 395-413.

Lerner, M. J., & Grant, P. R. (1990). The influences of commitment to justice and ethnocentrism on children's allocations of pay. *Social Psychology Quarterly, 53,* 229-238.

Levin, I., & Stokes, J. P. (1989). Disposition approach to job satisfaction: Role of negative affectivity. *Journal of Applied Psychology, 74,* 752-758.

Levin, P. F., & Isen, A. M. (1975). Something you can still get for a dime: Further studies on the effect on feeling good and helping. *Sociometry, 38,* 141-147.

LeVine, R. A., & Campbell, D. T. (1972). *Ethnocentrism: Theories of conflict, ethnic attitudes, and group behavior.* New York: John Wiley.

Liberman, A., & Chaiken, S. (1991). Value conflict and thought-induced attitude change. *Journal of Experimental Social Psychology, 27,* 203-216.

Likert, R. (1932). A technique for the measurement of attitudes. *Archives of Psychology, 140,* 5-53.

Likert, R. (1961). *New patterns of management.* New York: McGraw-Hill.

Linville, P. W., & Fischer, G. W. (1993). Exemplar and abstraction models of perceived group variability and stereotypicality. *Social Cognition, 11,* 92-125.

Linville, P. W., & Jones, E. E. (1980). Polarized appraisals of out-group members. *Journal of Personality and Social Psychology, 38,* 689-703.

Liska, A. E. (1984). A critical examination of the causal structure of the Fishbein/Ajzen attitude-behavior model. *Social Psychology Quarterly, 47,* 61-74.

Little, B. R., Lecci, L., & Watkinson, B. (1992). Personality and personal projects: Linking Big Five and PAC units of analysis. *Journal of Personality, 60,* 501-525.

Locke, E. A. (1976). The nature and causes of job satisfaction. In M. D. Dunnette (Ed.), *Handbook of industrial and organizational psychology* (pp. 1297-1349). Chicago: Rand McNally.

Locke, E. A., Sirota, D., & Wolfson, A. D. (1976). An experimental case study of the successes and failures of job enrichment in a government agency. *Journal of Applied Psychology, 61,* 701-711.

Locke, J. (1979). *An essay concerning human understanding* (P. H. Nidditch, Ed.). (Clarendon Edition of the Works of John Locke Series). New York: Oxford University Press. (Original work published 1894)

Locke, K. D., & Horowitz, L. M. (1990). Satisfaction in interpersonal interactions as a function of similarity in level of dysphoria. *Journal of Personality and Social Psychology, 58,* 823-831.

Loehlin, J. C. (1989). Partitioning environmental and genetic contributions to behavioral development. *American Psychologist, 44,* 1285-1292.

Lofquist, L. H., & Dawis, R. V. (1969). *Adjustment to work.* New York: Appleton-Century-Crofts.

Loher, B. T., Noe, R. A., Moeller, N. L., & Fitzgerald, M. P. (1985). A meta-analysis of the relationship of job characteristics to job satisfaction. *Journal of Applied Psychology, 70,* 280-289.

Lord, C. G., Desforges, D. M., Ramsey, S. L., Trezza, G. R., & Lepper, M. R. (1991). Typicality effects in attitude-behavior consistency: Effects of category discrimination and category knowledge. *Journal of Experimental and Social Psychology, 27,* 550-575.

Losch, M. E., & Cacioppo, J. T. (1990). Cognitive dissonance may enhance sympathetic tones, but attitudes are changed to reduce negative affect rather than arousal. *Journal of Experimental Social Psychology, 26,* 289-304.

Lott (Eisman), B. E. (1955). Attitude formation: The development of a color preference response through mediated generalization. *Journal of Abnormal and Social Psychology, 50,* 321-326.

Lott, B. E., & Lott, A. J. (1960). The formation of positive attitudes toward group members. *Journal of Abnormal and Social Psychology, 61,* 297-300.

Lumsdaine, A. A., & Janis, I. L. (1953). Resistance to "counter-propaganda" produced by one-sided and two-sided "propaganda" presentations. *Public Opinion Quarterly, 17,* 311-318.

Mackenzie, S. B., Podsakoff, P. M., & Fetter, R. (1991). Organizational citizenship behavior and objective productivity and determinants of managerial evaluations of salespersons' performance. *Organizational Behavior and Human Decision Processes, 50,* 123-150.

Mackie, D. M., Asuncion, A. G., & Rosselli, F. (1992). Impact of positive affect on persuasion processes. *Review of Personality and Social Psychology, 14,* 247-270.

Mackie, D. M., Gastardo-Conaco, C. M., & Skelly, J. J. (1992). Knowledge of the advocated position and the processing of in-group and out-group persuasive messages. *Personality and Social Psychology Bulletin, 18,* 145-151.

Mackie, D. M., & Worth, L. T. (1989). Processing deficits and the mediation of positive affect in persuasion. *Journal of Personality and Social Psychology, 57,* 27-40.

Mackie, D. M., & Worth, L. T. (1991). Feeling good, but not thinking straight: The impact of positive mood on persuasion. In J. P. Forgas (Ed.), *Emotion and social judgments: International series in experimental social psychology* (pp. 201-219). Oxford, UK: Pergamon.

Mackie, D. M., Worth, L. T., & Asuncion, A. G. (1990). Processing of persuasive in-group messages. *Journal of Personality and Social Psychology, 58,* 812-822.

Macrae, C. N., Milne, A. B., & Bodenhausen, G. V. (1994). Stereotypes as energy-saving devices: A peek inside the cognitive toolbox. *Journal of Personality and Social Psychology, 66,* 37-47.

Madden, T. J., Ellen, P. S., & Ajzen, I. (1992). A comparison of the theory of planned behavior and the theory of reasoned action. *Personality and Social Psychology Bulletin, 18,* 3-9.

Maddi, S. R., Bartone, P. T., & Puccetti, M. C. (1987). Stressful events are indeed a factor in physical illness: Reply to Schroeder and Costa (1989). *Journal of Personality and Social Psychology, 52,* 833-843.

Magnusson, D., & Endler, N. S. (1977). *Personality at the crossroads: Current issues in inter-actionalist psychology.* New York: John Wiley.

Maheswaran, D., & Meyers-Levy, J. (1990). The influence of message framing and issue involvement. *Journal of Marketing Research, 27,* 361-367.

Majors, R. (1994). *The American Black male: His current status and his future.* Chicago: Nelson-Hall.

Manis, M. (1960). The interpretation of opinion statements as a function of recipient attitude. *Journal of Abnormal and Social Psychology, 60,* 340-344.

Mano, H., & Oliver, R. L. (1993). Assessing the dimensionality and structure of the consumption experience: Evaluation, feelings, and satisfaction. *Journal of Consumer Research, 20,* 451-466.

March, J., & Simon, H. A. (1958). *Organizations.* New York: John Wiley.

Markus, H. R., & Kitayama, S. (1991). Culture and the self: Implications for cognitions, emotion, and motivation. *Psychological Review, 98,* 224-253.

Martin, L. L., Abend, T., Sedikides, C., & Green, J. D. (1997). How would I feel if . . . ? Mood as input to a role fulfillment evaluation process. *Journal of Personality and Social Psychology, 73,* 242-253.

Martin, N. G., Eaves, L. J., Heath, A. R., Jardine, R., Feingold, L. M., & Eysenck, H. J. (1986). Transmission of social attitudes. *Proceedings of the National Academy of Science, 83,* 4364-4368.

Martocchio, J. J. (1994). The effects of absence culture on individual absence. *Human Relations, 47,* 243-262.

Marx, K. (1913). *A contribution to the critique of political economy.* Chicago: Kerr.

Maslow, A. H. (1943). A theory of human motivation. *Psychological Review, 50,* 370-396.

Maslow, A. H. (1968). *Toward a psychology of being* (2nd ed.). New York: Van Nostrand.

Mass, A., Milesi, A., Zabbini, S., & Stahlberg, D. (1995). Linguistic intergroup bias: Differential expectancies or in-group protection? *Journal of Personality and Social Psychology, 68,* 116-126.

Matheny, C. T. (1988). *Job dissatisfaction and behaviors in the work environment.* Unpublished paper, University of Maryland, College of Business and Management, College Park.

Mathieu, J. E., Hofmann, D. A., & Farr, J. L. (1993). Job perception-job satisfaction relations: An empirical comparison of three competing theories. *Organizational Behavior and Human Decision Processes, 56,* 370-387.

Mathieu, J. E., & Zajac, D. M. (1990). A review and meta-analysis of the antecedents, correlates, and consequences of organizational commitment. *Psychological Bulletin, 108,* 171-194.

Maute, M. E., & Forrester, W. R., Jr. (1993). The structure and determinants of consumer complaint intentions and behavior. *Journal of Economic Psychology, 14,* 219-247.

Mayo, E. (1933). *The human problems of industrial civilization.* New York: Macmillan.

McCallum, J. R., & Harrison, W. (1985). Interdependence in the service encounter. In J. A. Czepiel, M. R. Solomon, & C. F. Surprenant (Eds.), *The service encounter* (pp. 35-48). Lexington, MA: Lexington Books.

McCaul, K. D., Ployhart, R. E., Hinsz, V. B., & McCaul, H. S. (1995). Appraisals of a consistent versus a similar politician: Voter preferences and intuitive judgements. *Journal of Personality and Social Psychology, 68,* 292-299.

McCauley, C., & Sitt, C. L. (1978). An individual and quantitative measure of stereotypes. *Journal of Personality and Social Psychology, 39,* 929-940.

McConahay, J. B. (1983). Modern racism and modern discrimination: The effects of race, racial attitudes, and context on simulated hiring decisions. *Personality and Social Psychology Bulletin, 9,* 551-558.

McConahay, J. B. (1986). Modern racism, ambivalence, and the Modern Racism Scale. In J. F. Dovidio & S. L. Gaertner (Eds.), *Prejudice, discrimination, and racism* (pp. 91-125). Orlando, FL: Academic Press.

McConahay, J. B., Hardee, B. B., & Batts, V. (1981). Has racism declined in America? It depends on who is asking and what is asked. *Journal of Conflict Resolution, 25,* 563-579.

McCracken, G. (1986). Culture and consumption: A theoretical account of the structure and movement of the cultural meaning of consumer goods. *Journal of Consumer Research, 13,* 71-84.

McCrae, R. R., & Costa, P. T. (1990). *Personality in adulthood.* New York: Guilford.

McCrae, R. R., & John, O. P. (1992). An introduction to the first five-factor model and its applications. *Journal of Personality, 60,* 175-215.

McGill, A. L., & Anand, P. (1989). The effect of vivid attributes on the evaluation of alternatives: The role of differential attention and cognitive elaboration. *Journal of Consumer Research, 16,* 188-196.

McGrath, J. E., & Rotchford, N. L. (1983). Time and behavior in organizations. *Research in Organizational Behavior, 5,* 57-101.

McGregor, D. (1960). *The human side of enterprise.* New York: McGraw-Hill.

McGuire, J. B., Schneeweis, T., & Branch, B. (1990). Perceptions of firm quality: A cause or result of firm performance. *Journal of Management, 16,* 167-180.

McGuire, W. J. (1964). Inducing resistance to persuasion: Some contemporary approaches. In L. Berkowitz (Ed.), *Advances in experimental social psychology* (Vol. 1, pp. 191-229). San Diego, CA: Academic Press.

McGuire, W. J. (1968). Personality and attitude change: An information-processing theory. In A. G. Greenwald, T. C. Brock, & T. M. Ostrom (Eds.), *Psychological foundations of attitudes* (pp. 171-196). San Diego, CA: Academic Press.

McGuire, W. J. (1969). The nature of attitudes and attitude change. In G. Lindzey & E. Aronson (Eds.), *Handbook of social psychology* (2nd ed., Vol. 3, pp. 136-314). Reading, MA: Addison-Wesley.

McGuire, W. J. (1972). Attitude change: The information-processing paradigm. In C. G. McClintock (Ed.), *Experimental social psychology* (pp. 108-141). New York: Holt, Rinehart & Winston.

McGuire, W. J. (1984). Perspectivism: A look back at the future. *Contemporary Social Psychology, 10,* 19-39.

McGuire, W. J. (1985). Attitudes and attitude change. In G. Lindzey & E. Aronson (Eds.), *Handbook of social psychology* (3rd ed., Vol. 2, pp. 233-346). New York: Random House.

McHugo, G. J., Lanzetta, J. T., Sullivan, D. G., Masters, R. D., & Englis, B. G. (1985). Emotional reactions to a political leader's expressive displays. *Journal of Personality and Social Psychology, 49,* 1513-1529.

Medoff, J. E., & Abraham, K. G. (1980). Experience, performance, and earnings. *Quarterly Journal of Economics, 90,* 703-736.

Messick, D. M., & Mackie, D. M. (1989). Intergroup relations. *Annual Review of Psychology, 40,* 45-81.

Meyer, G. J., & Shack, J. R. (1989). Structural convergence of mood and personality: Evidence for old and new directions. *Journal of Personality and Social Psychology, 57,* 691-706.

Meyer, J. P., & Allen, N. J. (1991). A three-component conceptualization of organizational commitment. *Human Resource Management Review, 1,* 61-89.

Meyer, J. P., Allen, N. J., & Smith, C. A. (1993). Commitment to organizations and occupations: Extension and test of a three-component conceptualization. *Journal of Applied Psychology, 78,* 538-551.

Meyer, J. W., & Rowan, B. (1977). Institutionalized organizations: Formal structure as myth and ceremony. *American Journal of Sociology, 83,* 340-363.

Meyerowitz, B. E., & Chaiken, S. (1987). The effect of message framing on breast self-examination attitudes, intentions, and behavior. *Journal of Personality and Social Psychology, 52,* 500-510.

Meyers-Levy, J., & Sternthal, B. (1991). Gender differences in the use of message cues and judgments. *Journal of Marketing Research, 28,* 84-96.

Miceli, M., & Lane, M. C. (1991). Antecedents of pay satisfaction: A review and extension. In K. M. Rowland & G. R. Ferris (Eds.), *Research in personnel and human resources management* (Vol. 9). Greenwich, CT: JAI.

Miceli, M., & Near, J. P. (1992). *Blowing the whistle: The organizational and legal implications for companies and employees.* New York: Lexington Books.

Micheals, C. E., & Spector, P. E. (1979). Causes of employee turnover: A test of the Mobley, Griffeth, Hand, and Meglino model. *Journal of Applied Psychology, 64,* 53-59.

Milgram, S. (1974). *Obedience to authority: An experimental view.* New York: Harper & Row.

Milgram, S., Mann, L., & Harter, S. (1965). The lost-letter technique of social research. *Public Opinion Quarterly, 29,* 437-438.

Milgrom, P., & Roberts, J. (1986). Price and advertising signals of product quality. *Journal of Political Economy, 94,* 796-821.

Millar, M. G., & Millar, K. U. (1990). Attitude change as a function of attitude type and argument type. *Journal of Personality and Social Psychology, 59,* 217-228.

Millar, M. G., & Tesser, A. (1986). Effects of affective and cognitive focus on the attitude-behavior relation. *Journal of Personality and Social Psychology, 51,* 270-276.

Miller, D., & Dröge, C. (1986). Psychological and traditional determinants of structure. *Administrative Science Quarterly, 31,* 539-560.

Miller, H. E., Katerberg, R., Jr., & Hulin, C. L. (1979). Evaluation of the Mobley, Honer, and Hollingsworth model of employee turnover. *Journal of Applied Psychology, 64,* 509-517.

Miller, K. I., & Monge, P. R. (1986). Participation, satisfaction and productivity: A meta-analytic review. *Academy of Management Review, 29,* 727-753.

Miller, N., & Brewer, M. B. (1984). The psychology of desegregation: An introduction. In N. Miller & M. B. Brewer (Eds.), *Groups in contact: The psychology of desegregation* (pp. 1-8). Orlando, FL: Academic Press.

Mills, P. K., Hall, J. L., Leidecker, J. K., & Marguiles, N. (1983). Flexiform: A model for professional service organizations. *Academy of Management Review, 8,* 118-131.

Mintzberg, H. (1973). *The nature of managerial work.* New York: Harper & Row.

Mishel, L., & Bernstein, J. (1994). *The state of working Americans, 1994-1995.* Washington, DC: Economics Policy Institute.

Mobley, W. H. (1977). Intermediate linkages in the relationship between job satisfaction and employee turnover. *Journal of Applied Psychology, 62,* 237-240.

Mobley, W. H., Griffeth, R. W., Hand, H. H., & Meglino, B. M. (1979). Review and conceptual analysis of the employee turnover process. *Psychological Bulletin, 86,* 493-522.

Mobley, W. H., Honer, S., & Hollingsworth, A. (1978). An evaluation of the precursors of hospital employee turnover. *Journal of Applied Psychology, 63,* 408-414.

Monteith, M. J. (1993). Self-regulation of prejudiced responses: Implications for progress in prejudice reduction efforts. *Journal of Personality and Social Psychology, 65,* 469-485.

Monteith, M. J., Devine, P. G., & Zuwerink, J. R. (1993). Self-directed vs. other-directed affect as a consequence of prejudice-related discrepancies. *Journal of Personality and Social Psychology 64,* 198-210.

Moreland, R. L., & Beach, S. R. (1992). Exposure effects in the classroom: The development of affinity among students. *Journal of Experimental Psychology, 28,* 255-276.

Moreland, R. L., & Zajonc, R. B. (1977). Is stimulus recognition a necessary condition for the occurrence of exposure effects? *Journal of Personality and Social Psychology, 35,* 191-199.

Moreland, R. L., & Zajonc, R. B. (1979). Exposure effects may not depend on stimulus recognition. *Journal of Personality and Social Psychology, 37,* 1085-1089.

Morris, W. N. (1989). *Mood: The frame of mind.* New York: Springer-Verlag.

Morrison, A. M. (1992). *The new leaders.* San Francisco: Jossey-Bass.

Morrison, A. M., & Von Glinow, M. A. (1990). Women and minorities in management. *American Psychologist, 45,* 200-208.

Morrison, E. W. (1994). Role definitions and organizational citizenship behavior: The importance of the employee's perspective. *Academy of Management Journal, 37,* 1543-1567.

Morrow, P. C. (1983). Concept redundancy in organizational research: The case work of commitment. *Academy of Management Review, 8,* 486-500.

Moscovici, S. (1980). Toward a theory of conversion behavior. In L. Berkowitz (Ed.), *Advances in experimental social psychology* (Vol. 13, pp. 209-239). San Diego, CA: Academic Press.

Motowidlo, S. J. (1996). Orientation toward the job and organization. In K. R. Murphy (Ed.), *Individual differences and behavior in organizations* (pp. 175-208). San Francisco: Jossey-Bass.

Motowidlo, S. J., Packard, J. S., & Manning, M. R. (1986). Occupational stress: Its causes and consequences for job performance. *Journal of Applied Psychology, 71,* 618-629.

Motowidlo, S. J., & Van Scotter, J. R. (1994). Evidence that task performance should be distinguished from contextual performance. *Journal of Applied Psychology, 79,* 475-480.

Mount, M. K., & Muchinsky, P. M. (1978). Person-environment congruence and employee job satisfaction: A test of Holland's theory. *Journal of Vocational Behavior, 13,* 84-100.

Mowday, R. T. (1996). Equity theory predictions of behavior in organizations. In R. M. Steers, L. W. Porter, & G. A. Bigley (Eds.), *Motivation and leadership at work* (6th ed., pp. 53-71). New York: McGraw-Hill.

Mowday, R. T., Steers, R. M., & Porter, L. W. (1979). The measurement of organizational commitment. *Journal of Vocational Behavior, 14,* 224-247.

Muchinsky, P. M., & Morrow. P. C. (1980). A multidisciplinary model of voluntary employee turnover. *Journal of Vocational Behavior, 17,* 263-290.

Mulilis, J., & Lippa, R. (1990). Behavioral change in earthquake preparedness due to negative threat appeals: A test of protection motivation theory. *Journal of Applied Social Psychology, 20,* 619-638.

Mullen, B., & Johnson, C. (1990). Distinctiveness-based illusory correlations and stereotyping: A meta-analytic integration. *British Journal of Social Psychology, 28,* 123-133.

Murphy, K. R. (1993). *Honesty in the workplace.* Belmont, CA: Brooks/Cole.

Murray, H. A. (1938). *Explorations in personality.* Boston: Houghton Mifflin.

Murtha, T. C., Kanfer, R., & Ackerman, P. L. (1996). Toward an interactionist taxonomy of personality and situations: An integrative situational-dispositional representation of personality traits. *Journal of Personality and Social Psychology, 71,* 193-207.

Myrdal, G. (1944). *An American dilemma.* New York: Harper.

Nardone, T., Herz, D., Mellor, E., & Hipple, S. (1993). 1992: Job market in the doldrums. *Monthly Labor Review, 116*(2), 3-14.

Necowitz, L. B., & Roznowski, M. (1994). Negative affectivity and job satisfaction: Cognitive processes underlying the relationship and effects on employee behaviors. *Journal of Vocational Behavior, 45,* 270-294.

Nelson, D. (1980). *Frederick W. Taylor and the rise of scientific management.* Madison: University of Wisconsin Press.

Newton, T., & Keenan, T. (1991). Further analysis of the dispositional argument in organizational behavior. *Journal of Applied Psychology, 76,* 781-787.

Nicholson, N., & Johns, G. (1985). The absence culture and the psychological contract: Who is in control of absence? *Academy of Management Review, 10,* 397-407.

Nkomo, S. M. (1992). The emperor has no clothes: Rewriting race in organizations. *Academy of Management Review, 17,* 487-513.

Noel, J. G., Wann, D. L., & Branscombe, N. R. (1995). Peripheral ingroup membership status and public negativity toward outgroups. *Journal of Personality and Social Psychology, 68,* 127-137.

Nord, W. R. (1977). Job satisfaction reconsidered. *American Psychologist, 32,* 1026-1035.

Northcraft, G. B., & Neale, M. A. (1994). *Organizational behavior: A management challenge* (2nd ed.). Fort Worth, TX: Dryden.

Oldham, G. R., & Rotchford, N. L. (1983). Relations between office characteristics and employee reactions: A study of the physical environment. *Administrative Science Quarterly, 28,* 542-556.

O'Leary-Kelly, A. M., Griffin, R. W., & Glew, D. J. (1996). Organization-motivated aggression: A research framework. *Academy of Management Review, 21,* 225-253.

Oliver, R. L. (1977). Effect of expectation and disconfirmation on post exposure product evaluations: An alternative interpretation. *Journal of Applied Psychology, 62,* 480-486.

Oliver, R. L. (1980). A cognitive model of the antecedents and consequences of satisfaction decisions. *Journal of Marketing Research, 18,* 460-469.

Oliver, R. L. (1993). Cognitive, affective, and attribute bases of the satisfaction response. *Journal of Consumer Research, 20,* 418-430.

Oliver, R. L. (1994). Conceptual issues in the structural analysis of consumption emotion, satisfaction, and quality: Evidence in a service setting. In C. T. Allen & D. R. John (Eds.), *Advances in consumer research* (Vol. 21, pp. 16-22). Provo, UT: Association for Consumer Research.

Oliver, R. L. (1997). *Satisfaction: A behavioral perspective on the consumer.* New York: McGraw-Hill.

Oliver, R. L., & Bearden, W. O. (1983). The role of involvement in satisfaction processes. In R. P. Bagozzi & A. M. Tybout (Eds.), *Advances in consumer research* (Vol. 10, pp. 250-255). Ann Arbor, MI: Association for Consumer Research.

Oliver, R. L., & DeSarbo, W. S. (1988). Response determinants in satisfaction judgments. *Journal of Consumer Research, 14,* 495-507.

Oliver, R. L., & Swan, J. E. (1989). Consumer perceptions of interpersonal equity and satisfaction in transactions: A field survey approach. *Journal of Marketing, 53,* 21-35.

Olson, J. C., & Dover, P. (1979). Disconfirmation of consumer expectations through product trial. *Journal of Applied Psychology, 64,* 179-189.

Olson, J. M. (1990). *Self-inference processes: The Ontario Symposium* (Vol. 6). Hillsdale, NJ: Lawrence Erlbaum.

Olson, J. M. (1992). Self-perception of humor: Evidence for discounting and augmentation effects. *Journal of Personality and Social Psychology, 62,* 369-377.

Olson, J. M., & Zanna, M. P. (1993). Attitude and attitude change. *Annual Review of Psychology, 44,* 117-154.

Olzak, S., & Nagel, J. (1986). *Competitive ethnic relations.* New York: Academic Press.

Ones, D. S., Mount, M. K., Barrick, M. R., & Hunter, J. E. (1994). Personality and job performance: A critique of Tett, Jackson, & Rothstein (1991) meta-analysis. *Personnel Psychology, 47,* 147-171.

O'Reilly, C., III, & Chatman, J. (1986). Organizational commitment and psychological attachment: The effects of compliance, identification, and internalization on prosocial behavior. *Journal of Applied Psychology, 71,* 492-499.

O'Reilly, C., III, & Chatman, J. (1996). Culture as social control: Corporations, cults, and commitment. In B. M. Staw & L. L. Cummings (Eds.), *Research in organizational behavior* (Vol. 18, pp. 157-200). Greenwich, CT: JAI.

O'Reilly, C., III, Chatman, J., & Caldwell, D. F. (1991). People in organizational culture: A profile comparison approach to assessing person-organization fit. *Academy of Management Journal, 34,* 487-516.

Organ, D. W. (1988a). *Organizational citizenship behavior.* Lexington, MA: Lexington Books.

Organ, D. W. (1988b). A restatement of the satisfaction-performance relationship. *Journal of Management, 14,* 547-557.

Organ, D. W. (1990). The motivational basis of organizational citizenship behavior. In B. M. Staw & L. L. Cummings (Eds.), *Research in organizational behavior* (Vol. 12, pp. 43-72). Greenwich, CT: JAI.

Organ, D. W., & Near, J. P. (1985). Cognitive vs. affect measures of job satisfaction. *International Journal of Psychology, 20,* 241-254.

Organ, D. W., & Ryan, K. (1995). A meta-analytic review of attitudinal and dispositional predictors of organizational citizenship behavior. *Personnel Psychology, 48,* 775-802.

Orr, J. M., Sackett, P. R., & Mercer, M. (1989). The role of prescribed and non-prescribed behaviors in estimating the dollar value of performance. *Journal of Applied Psychology, 74,* 34-40.

Osgood, C. E., Suci, G. J., & Tannenbaum, P. H. (1957). *The measurement of meaning.* Urbana: University of Illinois Press.

Ospina, S. (1996). *Illusions of opportunity.* Ithaca, NY: Cornell University Press.

Osterman, P. (Ed.). (1996). *Broken ladders: Managerial careers in the new economy.* New York: Oxford University Press.

Ostroff, C. (1992). The relationship between satisfaction, attitudes, and performance: An organizational level analysis. *Journal of Applied Psychology, 77,* 963-974.

Ostroff, C. (1993). The effects of climate and personal influences on individual behavior and attitudes in organizations. *Organizational Behavior and Human Decision Processes, 56,* 56-90.

Ostrom, T. M., & Brock, T. C. (1968). A cognitive model of attitudinal involvement. In R. P. Abelson, E. Aronson, W. J. McGuire, T. M. Newcomb, M. J. Rosenberg, & P. H. Tannenbaum (Eds.), *Theories of cognitive consistency: A sourcebook* (pp. 373-383). Chicago: Rand McNally.

Ostrom, T. M., & Sedikides, C. (1992). Out-group homogeneity effects in natural and minimal groups. *Psychological Bulletin, 112,* 536-552.

Ottati, V. C., Riggle, E. J., Wyer, R. S., Schwarz, N., & Kuklinski, J. (1989). Cognitive and affective bases of opinion survey responses. *Journal of Personality and Social Psychology, 57,* 404-415.

Ozment, J., & Morash, E. A. (1994). The augmented service offering for perceived and actual service quality. *Journal of the Academy of Marketing Science, 22,* 352-363.

Pallak, S. R. (1983). Salience of a communicator's physical attractiveness and persuasion: A heuristic versus systematic processing interpretation. *Social Cognition, 2,* 158-170.

Parasuraman, A., Zeithaml, V. A., & Berry, L. L. (1985). A conceptual model of service quality and its implications for future research. *Journal of Marketing, 49,* 41-50.

Parasuraman, A., Zeithaml, V. A., & Berry, L. L. (1988). SERVQUAL: A multiple-item scale for measuring consumer perceptions of service quality. *Journal of Retailing, 64,* 12-40.

Park, B., & Judd, C. M. (1990). Measures and models of perceived group variability. *Journal of Personality and Social Psychology, 59,* 173-191.

Park, B., Judd, C. M., & Ryan, C. S. (1991). Social categorization and the representation of variability information. In W. Stroebe & M. Hewstone (Eds.), *European review of social psychology* (Vol. 2, pp. 211-245). Chichester, UK: Wiley.

Park, B., Ryan, C. S., & Judd, C. M. (1992). Role of meaningful subgroups in explaining differences in perceived variability for in-groups and out-groups. *Journal of Personality and Social Psychology, 63,* 553-567.

Parker, C. P., Baltes, B. B., & Christiansen, N. D. (1997). Support for affirmative action, justice perceptions, and work attitudes: A study of gender and racial-ethnic group differences. *Journal of Applied Psychology, 82,* 376-389.

Parker, R. E. (1994). *Flesh peddlers and warm bodies: The temporary help industry and its workers.* New Brunswick, NJ: Rutgers University Press.

Parsons, T. (1951). *The social system.* Glencoe, IL: Free Press.

Patchen, M. (1961). *The choice of wage comparisons.* Englewood Cliffs, NJ: Prentice Hall.

Peak, H. (1955). Attitude and motivation. In M. R. Jones (Ed.), *Nebraska Symposium on Motivation* (Vol. 3, pp. 149-188). Lincoln: University of Nebraska Press.

Perdue, C. W., & Gurtman, M. B. (1990). Evidence for the automaticity of ageism. *Journal of Experimental Social Psychology, 27,* 26-47.

Perdue, C. W., Dovidio, J. F., Gurtman, M. B., & Tyler, R. B. (1990). Us and them: Social categorization and the process of intergroup bias. *Journal of Personality and Social Psychology, 59,* 475-486.

Perry, A. (1973). Heredity, personality traits, product attitude, and product consumption: An exploratory study. *Journal of Marketing Research, 10*(4), 376-379.

Pervin, J. P., & John, O. P. (1997). *Personality: Theory and research.* New York: John Wiley.

Pervin, L. A. (1994). A critical analysis of current trait theory. *Psychological Inquiry, 5,* 103-113.

Pettigrew, T. F. (1961). Social psychology and desegregation research. *American Psychologist, 16,* 105-112.

Pettigrew, T. F. (1969). Racially separate or together? *Journal of Social Issues, 25,* 43-69.

Pettigrew, T. F. (1979). Racial change and social policy. *Annals of the Academy of Political and Social Science, 441,* 114-131.

Pettigrew, T. F. (1985). New Black-White patterns: How best to conceptualize them? In R. H. Turner & J. F. Short (Eds.), *Annual review of sociology* (Vol. 11, pp. 329-346). Palo Alto, CA: Annual Reviews.

Pettigrew, T. F., & Martin, J. (1987). Shaping the organizational context of Black American inclusion. *Journal of Social Issues, 43*(1), 41-78.

Pettigrew, T. F., & Meertens, R. W. (1995). Subtle and blatant prejudice in western Europe. *European Journal of Social Psychology, 25,* 57-75.

Petty, R. E., & Cacioppo, J. T. (1981). *Attitudes and persuasion: Classic and contemporary approaches.* Dubuque, IA: William C. Brown.

Petty, R. E., & Cacioppo, J. T. (1983). The role of bodily responses in attitude measurement and change. In J. Cacioppo & R. Petty (Eds.), *Social psychophysiology: A sourcebook* (pp. 51-101). New York: Guilford.

Petty, R. E., & Cacioppo, J. T. (1984). The effects of involvement on responses to argument quantity and quality: Central and peripheral routes to persuasion. *Journal of Personality and Social Psychology, 46,* 69-81.

Petty, R. E., & Cacioppo, J. T. (1986a). *Communication and persuasion: Central and peripheral routes to persuasion.* New York: Springer-Verlag.

Petty, R. E., & Cacioppo, J. T. (1986b). The elaboration likelihood model of persuasion. In L. Berkowitz (Ed.), *Advances in experimental social psychology* (Vol. 19, pp. 123-205). San Diego, CA: Academic Press.

Petty, R. E., & Cacioppo, J. T. (1990). Involvement and persuasion: Tradition versus integration. *Psychological Bulletin, 107,* 367-374.

Petty, R. E., Cacioppo, J. T., & Goldman, R. (1981). Personal involvement as a determinant of argument-based persuasion. *Journal of Personality and Social Psychology, 41,* 847-855.

Petty, R. E., Gleicher, F., & Baker, S. M. (1991). Multiple roles for affect in persuasion. In J. Forgas (Ed.), *Emotion and social judgments* (pp. 181-200). Oxford, UK: Pergamon.

Petty, R. E., & Krosnick, J. A. (Eds.). (1993). *Attitude strength: Antecedents and consequences.* Hillsdale, NJ: Lawrence Erlbaum.

Petty, R. E., & Krosnick, J. A. (Eds.). (1995). *Attitude strength: Antecedents and consequences.* Mahwah, NJ: Lawrence Erlbaum.

Petty, R. E., Ostrom, T. M., & Brock, T. C. (1981). Historical foundations of the cognitive response approach to attitudes and persuasion. In R. E. Petty, T. M. Ostrom, & T. C. Brock (Eds.), *Cognitive responses in persuasion* (pp. 5-29). Hillsdale, NJ: Lawrence Erlbaum.

Petty, R. E., Schumann, D. W., Richman, S. A., & Strathman, A. J. (1993). Positive mood and persuasion: Different roles for affect under high and low elaboration conditions. *Journal of Personality and Social Psychology, 64,* 5-20.

Petty, R. E., Wells, G. L., & Brock, T. C. (1976). Distraction can enhance or reduce yielding to propaganda: Thought disruption versus effort justification. *Journal of Personality and Social Psychology, 34,* 874-884.

Pfau, M., Kenski, H. C., Nitz, M., & Sorenson, J. (1990). Efficacy of inoculation strategies in promoting resistance to political attack messages: Application to direct mail. *Communication-Monographs, 57*(1), 25-43.

Pfeffer, J. (1981). Management as symbolic action: The creation and maintenance of organizational paradigms. *Research in Organizational Behavior, 3,* 1-52.

Pfeffer, J., & Barron, J. M. (1988). Taking the workers back out: Recent trends in the structuring of employment. In B. M. Staw & L. L. Cummings (Eds.), *Research in organizational behavior* (Vol. 10, pp. 257-303). Greenwich, CT: JAI.

Pfeffer, J., & Salancik, G. (1978). *The external control of organizations.* New York: Harper & Row.

Phares, E. J. (1961). TAT performance as a function of anxiety and coping-avoiding behavior. *Journal of Consulting Psychology, 25,* 257-259.

Pinder, C. C. (1984). *Work motivation.* Glenview, IL: Scott, Foresman.

Ping, R. A., Jr. (1993). The effects of satisfaction and structural constraints on retailer exiting, voice, loyalty, opportunism, and neglect. *Journal of Retailing, 69,* 320-352.

Plomin, R., & Nesselrode, J. R. (1990). Behavioral genetics and personality change. *Journal of Personality, 58,* 191-220.

Podsakoff, P. M., Ahearne, M., & Mackenzie, S. B. (1997). Organizational citizenship behavior and the quantity and quality of work group performance. *Journal of Applied Psychology, 82,* 262-270.

Pomazal, R. J., & Jaccard, J. J. (1976). An informational approach to altruistic behavior. *Journal of Personality and Social Psychology, 33,* 317-326.

Pomerantz, E. M., Chaiken, S., & Tordeisillas, R. S. (1995). Attitude strength and resistance processes. *Journal of Personality and Social Psychology, 69,* 408-419.

Popper, K. R. (1959). *The logic of scientific discovery.* New York: Basic Books. (Original work published 1935 as *Die logik de Forschung)*

Porac, J. F. (1987). The job satisfaction questionnaire as a cognitive event: First- and second-order processes in affective commentary. In K. M. Rowland & G. R. Ferris (Eds.), *Research in personnel and human resources management* (Vol. 5, pp. 51-102). Greenwich, CT: JAI.

Porter, J. D. R. (1971). *Black child, White child: The development of racial attitudes.* Cambridge, MA: Harvard University Press.

Porter, L. W. (1961). A study of perceived need satisfactions in bottom and middle management jobs. *Journal of Applied Psychology, 45,* 1-10.

Porter, L. W., & Lawler, E. E. (1968). *Managerial attitudes and performance.* Homewood, IL: Dorsey.

Porter, L. W., Lawler, E. E., & Hackman, J. R. (1975). *Behavior in organizations.* New York: McGraw-Hill.

Porter, L. W., & Steers, R. M. (1973). Organizational, work, and personal factors in employee turnover and absenteeism. *Psychological Bulletin, 80,* 151-176.

Porter, L. W., Steers, R. M., Mowday, R. T., & Boulian, P. V. (1974). Organizational commitment, job satisfaction and turnover among psychiatric technicians. *Journal of Applied Psychology, 59,* 603-609.

Powell, G. N., & Butterfield, D. A. (1997). Effect of race on promotions to top management in a federal department. *Academy of Management Journal, 40*(1), 112-128.

Powell, W. W., & DiMaggio, P. J. (1991). *The new institutionalism in organizational analysis.* Chicago: University of Chicago Press.

Pratkanis, A., & Aronson, E. (1992). *Age of propaganda: The everyday use and abuse of persuasion.* San Francisco: Freeman.

Pratkanis, A. R., & Greenwald, A. G. (1989). A sociocognitive model of attitude structure and function. In L. Berkowitz (Ed.), *Advances in experimental social psychology* (Vol. 22, pp. 245-285). New York: Academic Press.

Pratkanis, A. R., & Turner, M. E. (1994). Of what value is a job attitude? A socio-cognitive analysis. *Human Relations, 47,* 1545-1576.

Pratto, F., Sidanius, J., Stallworth, L. M., & Malle, B. F. (1994). Social dominance orientation: A personality variable predicting social and political attitudes. *Journal of Personality and Social Psychology, 67,* 741-763.

Price, J. (1977). *The study of turnover.* Ames: Iowa State University Press.

Pritchard, R. D. (1969). Equity theory: A review and critique. *Organizational Behavior and Human Performance, 4,* 176-211.

Proshansky, H. M. (1966). The development of intergroup attitudes. In L. W. Hoffman & M. L. Hoffman (Eds.), *Review of child development research* (Vol. 2, pp. 311-371). New York: Russell Sage.

Pryor, J. B., Reeder, G. D., & McManus, J. W. (1991). Fear and loathing in the workplace: Reactions to AIDS-infected co-workers. *Personality and Social Psychology Bulletin, 17,* 133-139.

Puffer, S. M. (1987). Prosocial behavior, noncompliant behavior, and work performance among commission salespeople. *Journal of Applied Psychology, 72,* 615-621.

Pugh, S. D. (1997). *Service with a smile: The contagious effects of employee affect on customer attitudes.* Unpublished doctoral dissertation, Tulane University, A. B. Freeman School of Business, New Orleans, LA.

Qualter, T. H. (1962). *Propaganda and psychological warfare.* New York: Random House.

Quattrone, G. A. (1986). On the perception of a group's variability. In S. Worchel & W. G. Austin (Eds.), *Psychology of intergroup relations* (2nd ed.). Chicago: Nelson-Hall.

Quattrone, G. A., & Jones, E. F. (1980). The perception of variability within ingroups and outgroups: Implications for the law of small numbers. *Journal of Personality and Social Psychology, 38,* 141-152.

Quigley-Fernandez, B., & Tedeschi, J. T. (1978). The bogus pipeline as a lie detector: Two validity studies. *Journal of Personality and Social Psychology, 36,* 247-256.

Quinn, R. P., Staines, G. L., & McCullough, M. R. (1974). *Job satisfaction: Is there a trend?* Washington, DC: U.S. Department of Labor.

Raden, D. (1985). Strength-related attitude dimensions. *Social Psychology Quarterly, 48,* 312-330.

Rafaeli, A. (1989a). When cashiers meet customers: An analysis of the role of supermarket cashiers. *Academy of Management Journal, 32,* 245-273.

Rafaeli, A. (1989b). When clerks meet customers: A test of variables related to emotional expressions on the job. *Journal of Applied Psychology, 74,* 185-193.

Rafaeli, A., & Sutton, R. I. (1987). Expression of emotion as part of the work role. *Academy of Management Review, 12,* 23-37.

Rafaeli, A., & Sutton, R. I. (1989). The expression of emotion in organizational life. In L. L. Cummings & B. M. Staw (Eds.), *Research in organizational behavior* (Vol. 11, pp. 1-42). Greenwich, CT: JAI.

Rafaeli, A., & Sutton, R. I. (1990). Busy stores and demanding customers: How do they affect the display of positive emotion? *Academy of Management Journal, 33,* 623-637.

Rafaeli, A., & Sutton, R. I. (1991). Emotional contrast strategies as means of social influence: Lessons from criminal interrogators and bill collectors. *Academy of Management Journal, 34,* 749-775.

Rand, A. (1964). The objectivist ethics. In A. Rand (Ed.), *The virtue of selfishness* (pp. 13-35). New York: Signet.

Rao, A. K., & Monroe, K. B. (1989). The effect of price, brand name, and store name on buyers' perceptions of product quality: An integrative review. *Journal of Marketing Research, 28,* 307-319.

Rauschenberger, J., Schmitt, N., & Hunter, J. E. (1980). A test of the need hierarchy concept by a Markov model of change in need strength. *Administrative Science Quarterly, 25,* 654-670.

Rawls, J. (1971). *A theory of justice.* Cambridge, MA: Harvard University Press.

Reeves, C. A., & Bednar, D. A. (1994). Defining quality: Alternatives and implications. *Academy of Management Review, 19,* 419-445.

Reich, R. B. (1991). *The work of nations: Preparing ourselves for 21st century capitalism.* New York: Knopf.

Reichers, A. E., & Schneider, B. (1990). Climate and culture: An evolution of constructs. In B. Schneider (Ed.), *Organizational climate and culture.* San Francisco: Jossey-Bass.

Reilly, N. P., & Orsak, C. L. (1991). Organizational commitment and psychological attachment: The effects of compliance, identification, and internalization on prosocial behavior. *Journal of Applied Psychology, 76,* 492-499.

Rhodes, N., & Wood, W. (1992). Self-esteem and intelligence affect influenceability: The mediating role of message reception. *Psychological Bulletin, 111,* 156-171.

Rice, R. W., Near, J. P., & Hunt, R. G. (1980). The job-satisfaction/life-satisfaction relationship: A review of empirical research. *Basic and Applied Social Psychology, 1,* 37-64.

Rippetoe, P. A., & Rogers, R. W. (1987). Effects of components of protection-motivation theory on adaptive and maladaptive coping with a health threat. *Journal of Personality and Social Psychology, 52,* 596-604.

Robbins, S. P. (1993). *Organizational behavior: Concepts, controversies, and applications.* Englewood Cliffs, NJ: Prentice Hall.

Roberts, D. F., & Maccoby, N. (1985). Effects of mass communication. In G. Lindzey & E. Aronson (Eds.), *Handbook of social psychology* (Vol. 2, 3rd ed., pp. 539-598). New York: Random House.

Roberts, J. V. (1985). The attitude-memory relationship after 40 years: A meta-analysis of the literature. *Basic and Applied Social Psychology, 6,* 221-241.

Roberts, K. H., & Glick, W. (1981). The job characteristics approach to job design: A critical review. *Journal of Applied Psychology, 66,* 193-217.

Robinson, J. (1990). The time squeeze. *American Demographics, 12,* 30-33.

Robinson, R. J., Keltner, D., Ward, A., & Ross, L. (1995). Actual versus assumed differences in construal: Realism in intergroup perception and conflict. *Journal of Personality and Social Psychology, 68,* 404-417.

Robinson, S. L., Kraatz, M. S., & Rousseau, D. M. (1994). Changing obligations and the psychological contract: A longitudinal study. *Academy of Management Journal, 37,* 137-152.

Roethlisberger, F. J. (1959). *Management and morale.* Cambridge, MA: Harvard University Press.

Rogers, R. W. (1983). Cognitive and physiological processes in fear appeals and attitude change: A revised theory of protection motivation. In J. T. Cacioppo & R. E. Petty (Eds.), *Social psychophysiology: A sourcebook* (pp. 153-176). New York: Guilford.

Rokeach, M. (1960). *The open and closed mind.* New York: Basic Books.

Rokeach, M. (1968). *Beliefs, attitudes and values.* San Francisco: Jossey-Bass.

Rokeach, M. (1973). *The nature of human values.* New York: Free Press.

Rokeach, M. (1979). *Understanding human values: Individual and societal.* New York: Free Press.

Rokeach, M., & Cochrane, R. (1972). Self-confrontation and confrontation with another as determinants of long-term value change. *Journal of Applied Social Psychology, 2,* 283-292.

Rokeach, M., & Grube, J. W. (1979). Can values be manipulated arbitrarily? In M. Rokeach (Ed.), *Understanding human values: Individual and societal.* New York: Free Press.

Ronen, S. (1994). An underlying structure of motivational need taxonomies: A cross-cultural confirmation. In H. C. Triandis, M. D. Dunnette, & L. M. Hough (Eds.), *Handbook of industrial and organizational psychology* (2nd ed., Vol. 4, pp. 241-269). Palo Alto, CA: Consulting Psychologists Press.

Ronen, S., Kraut, A. I., Lingoes, J. C., & Aranya, N. (1979). A nonmetric scaling approach to taxonomies of employee work motivation. *Multivariate Behavior Research, 14,* 387-401.

Roos, P. A., & Treiman, D. J. (1980). DOT scales for the 1970 consensus classification. In A. R. Miller, D. J. Treiman, P. S. Cain, & P.A. Roos (Eds.), *Work, jobs, and occupations: A critical review of the Dictionary of Job Titles* (pp. 336-389). Washington, DC: National Academy Press.

Rosenbaum, M. E. (1986). The repulsion hypothesis: On the nondevelopment of relationships. *Journal of Personality and Social Psychology, 51,* 1156-1166.

Rosenberg, M. J. (1968a). Discussion: On reducing the inconsistency between consistency theories. In R. P. Abelson, E. Aronson, W. J. McGuire, T. M. Newcomb, M. J. Rosenberg, & P. H. Tannenbaum (Eds.), *Theories of cognitive consistency: A sourcebook* (pp. 827-833). Chicago: Rand McNally.

Rosenberg, M. J. (1968b). Hedonism, inauthenticity, and other goals toward expansion of a consistency theory. In R. P. Abelson, E. Aronson, W. J. McGuire, T. M. Newcomb, M. J. Rosenberg, & P. H. Tannenbaum (Eds.), *Theories of cognitive consistency: A sourcebook* (pp. 73-111). Chicago: Rand McNally.

Rosenberg, M. J., & Hovland, C. I. (1960). Cognitive, affective, and behavioral components of attitudes. In C. I. Hovland & M. J. Rosenberg (Eds.), *Attitude organization and change: An analysis of consistency among attitude components* (pp. 1-14). New Haven, CT: Yale University Press.

Ross, I., & Oliver, R. L. (1984). The accuracy of unsolicited consumer communications as indicators of "true" consumer satisfaction/dissatisfaction. In T. C. Kinnear (Ed.), *Advances in consumer research* (Vol. 11, pp. 504-508). Provo, UT: Association for Consumer Research.

Ross, M. (1989). Relation of implicit theories to the construction of personal histories. *Psychological Review, 96,* 341-357.

Rosse, J. G., & Miller, H. E. (1984). Relationship between absenteeism and other employee behaviors. In P. S. Goodman & R. S. Atkin (Eds.), *Absenteeism: New approaches to understanding, measuring, and managing employee absence* (pp. 194-228). San Francisco: Jossey-Bass.

Rothbart, M. (1981). Memory processes and social beliefs. In D. L. Hamilton (Ed.), *Cognitive processes in stereotyping and intergroup behavior* (pp. 145-181). Hillsdale, NJ: Lawrence Erlbaum.

Rousseau, D. M. (1978). Characteristics of departments, positions, and individuals: Contexts for attitudes and behavior. *Administrative Science Quarterly, 23,* 521-540.

Rousseau, D. M. (1989). Psychological and implied contracts in organizations. *Employee Responsibilities and Rights Journal, 2,* 121-139.

Rousseau, D. M. (1995). *Psychological contracts in organizations: Understanding written and unwritten agreements.* Thousand Oaks, CA: Sage.

Rousseau, D. M., & Parks, J. M. (1993). The contracts of individuals and organizations. In B. M. Staw & L. L. Cummings (Eds.), *Research in organizational behavior* (Vol. 15). Greenwich, CT: JAI.

Rousseau, D. M., & Wade-Benzoni, K. A. (1995). Changing individual-organization attachments: A two-way street. In A. Howard (Ed.), *The changing nature of work* (pp. 290-322). San Francisco: Jossey-Bass.

Rowlison, R., & Felner, R. (1988). Major life events, hassles and adaptation in adolescence: Confounding in the conceptualization and measurement of life stress and adjustment revisited. *Journal of Personality and Social Psychology, 55,* 432-444.

Roy, D. F. (1960). Banana time: Job satisfaction and informal interaction. *Human Organization, 18,* 158-168.

Roznowski, M., & Hulin, C. L. (1992). The scientific merit of valid measures of general constructs with special reference to job satisfaction and job withdrawal. In C. J. Cranny, P. C. Smith, & E. F. Stone (Eds.), *Job satisfaction: How people feel about their jobs and how it affects their performance* (pp. 123-163). New York: Lexington.

Rubini, M., & Semin, G. R. (1994). Language use in the context of congruent and incongruent in-group behaviors. *British Journal of Social Psychology, 33,* 355-362.

Rudman, L. A., & Borgida, E. (1995). The afterglow of construct accessibility: The behavioral consequences of priming men to view women as sexual objects. *Journal of Experimental Social Psychology, 31,* 493-507.

Rusbult, C. E., Farrell, D., Rogers, G., & Mainous, A. G., III. (1988). Impact of exchange variables on exit, voice, loyalty, and neglect: An integrated model of responses to declining job satisfaction. *Academy of Management Journal, 31,* 599-627.

Rust, R. T., Subramanian, B., & Wells, M. (1992). Making complaints a management tool. *Marketing Management, 1,* 41-45.

Ryan, A. M., Schmit, M. J., & Johnson, R. (1996). Attitudes and effectiveness: Examining relations at an organizational level. *Personnel Psychology, 49,* 853-882.

Rynes, S. L. (1991). Recruitment, job choice, and post-hire consequences: A call for new research directions. In M. D. Dunnette & L. M. Hough (Eds.), *Handbook of industrial and organizational psychology* (2nd ed., Vol. 2, pp. 399-444). Palo Alto, CA: Consulting Psychologists Press.

Sackett, P. R., & Dubois, C. L. Z. (1991). Rater-ratee race effects on performance evaluation: Challenging meta-analytic conclusions. *Journal of Applied Psychology, 76,* 873-877.

Saffir, M. A. (1937). A comparative study of scales constructed by three psychophysical methods. *Psychometrika, 2,* 179-198.

Salancik, G. R., & Meindl, J. (1984). Corporate attributions as strategic illusions of management control. *Administrative Science Quarterly, 29,* 238-254.

Salancik, G. R., & Pfeffer, J. (1977). An examination of need-satisfaction models of job attitudes. *Administrative Science Quarterly, 22,* 427-456.

Salancik, G. R., & Pfeffer, J. (1978). A social information processing approach to job attitudes and task design. *Administrative Science Quarterly, 23,* 224-253.

Sanbonmatsu, D. M., & Fazio, R. H. (1990). The role of attitudes in memory-based decision making. *Journal of Personality and Social Psychology, 59,* 614-622.

Sargant, W. (1957). *Battle for the mind: A physiology of conversion and brain-washing.* Garden City, NY: Doubleday.

Sarnoff, I., & Katz, D. (1954). The motivational basis of attitude change. *Journal of Abnormal and Social Psychology, 49,* 115-124.

Sarup, G., Suchner, R. W., & Gaylor, G. (1991). Contrast effects and attitude change: A test of the two-stage hypothesis of social judgement theory. *Social Psychology Quarterly, 54,* 364-373.

Scarpello, V., & Campbell, J. P. (1983). Job satisfaction: Are all the parts there? *Personnel Psychology, 36,* 577-600.

Schaffer, R. H. (1953). Job satisfaction as related to need satisfaction in work. *Psychological Monographs, 67*(14, Whole No. 364).

Schaller, M. (1991). Social categorization and the formation of group stereotypes: Further evidence for biased information processing in the perception of group-behavior correlations. *European Journal of Social Psychology, 21,* 25-35.

Schaubroeck, J., Ganster, D. C., & Kemmerer, B. (1996). Does trait affect promote job attitude stability? *Journal of Organizational Behavior, 17,* 191-196.

Schein, E. H. (1983, Summer). The role of the founder in creating organizational culture. *Organizational Dynamics,* 13-28.

Schein, E. H., Schneier, I., & Barker, C. H. (1961). *Coercive persuasion: A socio-psychological analysis of the "brain-washing" of American civilian prisoners by the Chinese communists.* New York: Norton.

Schlegel, R. P., d'Avernas, J. R., Zanna, M. P., DeCourville, N. H., & Manske, S. R. (1992). Problem drinking: A problem for the theory of reasoned action. *Journal of Applied Social Psychology, 22,* 358-385.

Schlenker, B. R. (1980). *Impression management: The self concept, social identity, and interpersonal relations.* Monterey, CA: Brooks/Cole.

Schlenker, B. R. (1982). Translating actions into attitudes: An identity-analytic approach to the explanation of social conduct. In L. Berkowitz (Ed.), *Advances in experimental social psychology* (Vol. 15, pp. 193-247). San Diego, CA: Academic Press.

Schmit, M. J., & Allscheid, S. P. (1995). Employee attitudes and customer satisfaction: Making theoretical and empirical connections. *Personnel Psychology, 48,* 521-536.

Schmitt, N., & Bedeian, A. G. (1982). A comparison of LISREL and two-stage least squares analysis of a hypothesized life-job satisfaction reciprocal relationship. *Journal of Applied Psychology, 67,* 806-817.

Schmitt, N., & Mellon, P. M. (1980). Life and job satisfaction: Is the job central? *Journal of Vocational Behavior, 16,* 51-58.

Schmitt, N., & Pulakos, E. D. (1985). Predicting job satisfaction from life satisfaction: Is there a general satisfaction factor? *International Journal of Psychology, 20,* 155-168.

Schneider, B. (1984). Industrial and organizational psychology perspective. In A. P. Brief (Ed.), *Productivity research in the behavioral and social sciences.* New York: Praeger.

Schneider, B. (1987). The people make the place. *Personnel Psychology, 40,* 437-453.

Schneider, B. (1990). The climate for service: An application of the climate construct. In B. Schneider (Ed.), *Organizational climate and culture* (pp. 383-413). San Francisco: Jossey-Bass.

Schneider, B., & Bowen, D. E. (1985). Employee and customer perceptions of service in banks: Replication and extension. *Journal of Applied Psychology, 70,* 423-433.

Schneider, B., & Bowen, D. E. (1992). Personnel/human resources management in the service sector. In G. R. Ferris & K. M. Rowland (Eds.), *Research in personnel and human resources management* (Vol. 10, pp. 1-30). Greenwich, CT: JAI.

Schneider, B., & Bowen, D. E. (1995). *Winning the service game.* Boston: Harvard Business School Press.

Schneider, B., & Dachler, H. P. (1978). A note on the stability of the Job Descriptive Index. *Journal of Applied Psychology, 63,* 650-653.

Schneider, B., Goldstein, H. B., & Smith, D. B. (1995). The ASA framework: An update. *Personnel Psychology, 48,* 747-773.

Schneider, B., Gunnarson, S. K., & Wheeler, J. K. (1992). The role of opportunity in the conceptualization and measurement of job satisfaction. In C. J. Cranny, P. C. Smith, & E. F. Stone (Eds.), *Job satisfaction: How people feel about their jobs and how it affects their performance* (Vol. 1, pp. 53-68). New York: Lexington Books.

Schneider, B., Parkington, J. J., & Buxton, V. M. (1980). Employee and customer perceptions of service in banks. *Administrative Science Quarterly, 25,* 252-267.

Schneider, B., & Schmitt, N. (1976). *Staffing organizations* (2nd ed.). Glenview, IL: Scott, Foresman.

Schneider, B., Wheeler, J. K., & Cox, J. F. (1992). A passion for service: Using content analysis to explicate service themes. *Journal of Applied Psychology, 77*, 705-716.

Scholl, R. W., Cooper, E. A., & McKenna, J. F. (1987). Referent selection in determining equity perceptions: Differential effects on behavioral and attitudinal outcomes. *Personnel Psychology, 40*, 113-124.

Schroeder, D. H., & Costa, P. T., Jr. (1984). Influence of life events on stress on physical illness: Substantive effects or methodological flaws? *Journal of Personality and Social Psychology, 46*, 853-863.

Schuman, H., Steeh, C., & Bobo, L. (1985). *Racial attitudes in America: Trends and interpretations.* Cambridge, MA: Harvard University Press.

Schumann, D. W., Hathcote, J. M., & West, S. (1991). Corporate advertising in America: A review of published studies on use, measurement, and effectiveness. *Journal of Advertising, 20*, 35-56.

Schwartz, H. S. (1990). Toward a theory of the universal content and structure of values: Extensions and cross-cultural replications. *Journal of Personality and Social Psychology, 58*, 878-891.

Schwartz, N., & Clore, G. L. (1983). Mood, misattribution, and judgments of well-being: Informative and directive functions of affective states. *Journal of Personality and Social Psychology, 45*, 513-523.

Schwartz, N., & Clore, G. L. (1988). How do I feel about it? The informative function of affective states. In K. Fiedler & J. Forgas (Eds.), *Affect, cognition, and social behavior* (pp. 44-62). Toronto, Ontario, Canada: C. J. Hogrefe.

Schwartz, S. H., & Tessler, R. C. (1972). A test of a model for reducing measured attitude-behavior discrepancies. *Journal of Personality and Social Psychology, 24*, 225-236.

Schwarz, N. (1990). Feelings as information: Informational and motivational functions of affective states. In E. T. Higgins & R. M. Sorrentino (Eds.), *Handbook of motivation and cognition: Foundations of social behavior* (Vol. 2, pp. 527-561). New York: Guilford.

Schwarz, N., Bless, H., & Bohner, G. (1991). Mood and persuasion: Affective states influence the processing of persuasive communications. In M. P. Zanna (Ed.), *Advances in experimental social psychology* (Vol. 24, pp. 161-199). New York: Academic Press.

Schwarz, N., & Hippler, H. J. (1991). Response alternatives: The impact of their choice and presentation order. In P. Biemer, R. Groves, L. Lyberg, N. Mathiowetz, & S. Sudman (Eds.), *Measurement error in surveys* (pp. 41-56). New York: John Wiley.

Schwarz, N., & Strack, F. (1991). Context effects in attitude surveys: Applying cognitive theory to social research. In W. Stroebe & M. Hewstone (Eds.), *European review of social psychology* (Vol. 2, pp. 31-50). Chichester, UK: Wiley.

Schwarz, N., & Sudman, S. (Eds.). (1992). *Context effects in social and psychological research.* New York: Springer-Verlag.

Scott, K. D., & Taylor, G. S. (1985). An examination of conflicting findings on the relationship between job satisfaction and absenteeism: A meta-analysis. *Academy of Management Journal, 28*, 599-612.

Scott, L., & O'Hara, M. W. (1993). Self-discrepancies in clinically anxious and depressed university students. *Journal of Abnormal Psychology, 102*, 282-287.

Scott, W. R. (1995). *Institutions and organizations.* Thousand Oaks, CA: Sage.

Sears, D. O. (1988). Symbolic racism. In P. A. Katz & D. A. Taylor (Eds.), *Eliminating racism: Profiles in controversy* (pp. 53-84). New York: Plenum.

Sears, D. O., & Allen, H. M., Jr. (1984). The trajectory of local desegregation controversies and whites' opposition to busing. In N. Miller & M. B. Brewer (Eds.), *Groups in contact: The psychology of desegregation* (pp. 23-157). Orlando, FL: Academic Press.

Sears, D. O., & Funk, C. L. (1991). The role of self-interest in social and political attitudes. In M. Zanna (Ed.), *Advances in experimental social psychology* (Vol. 24, pp. 1-91). Orlando, FL: Academic Press.

Sears, D. O., Hensler, C. P., & Speer, L. K. (1979). Whites' opposition to "busing": Self-interest or symbolic politics? *American Political Science Review, 73,* 369-384.

Sears, D. O., & Kinder, D. R. (1985). Whites' opposition to busing: On conceptualizing group conflict. *Journal of Personality and Social Psychology, 48,* 1141-1147.

Selltiz, C., & Cook, S. W. (1966). Racial attitude as a determinant of judgements of plausibility. *Journal of Social Psychology, 70,* 139-147.

Semin, G. R., & Fiedler, K. (1988). The cognitive functions of linguistic categories in describing persons: Social cognition and language. *Journal of Personality and Social Psychology, 54,* 558-568.

Shaver, P. R., & Brennan, K. A. (1992). Attachment styles and the "Big Five" personality traits: Their connections with each other and with romantic relationships. *Personality and Social Psychology Bulletin, 18,* 536-545.

Shavitt, S. (1990). The role of attitude objects in attitude functions. *Journal of Experimental Social Psychology, 26,* 124-148.

Shavitt, S., & Brock, T. C. (1994). *Persuasion: Psychological insights and perspectives.* Needham Heights, MA: Allyn-Bacon.

Shenkar, O., & Yuchtman-Yaar, E. (1997). Reputation, image, prestige, and goodwill: An interdisciplinary approach to organizational standing. *Human Relations, 50,* 1361-1381.

Sherif, M. (1967). *Group conflict and cooperation.* London: Routledge & Kegan Paul.

Sherif, M., & Cantril, H. (1947). *The psychology of ego-involvements: Social attitudes and identifications.* New York: John Wiley.

Sherif, M., Harvey, O. J., White, B. J., Hood, W. R., & Sherif, C. W. (1961). *The robber's cave experiment: Intergroup conflict and cooperation.* Middletown, CT: Wesleyan University Press.

Sherif, M., & Hovland, C. I. (1961). *Social judgment: Assimilation and contrast effects in communication and attitude change.* New Haven, CT: Yale University Press.

Sherman, S. J., Hamilton, D. L., & Roskos-Ewoldson, D. R. (1989). Attenuation of illusory correlation. *Personality and Social Psychology Bulletin, 15,* 559-571.

Shostack, G. L. (1977, April). Breaking free from product marketing. *Journal of Marketing, 41,* 73-80.

Shotland, R. L., & Yankowski, L. D. (1982). The random response method: A valid and ethical indicator of the "truth" in reactive situations. *Personality and Social Psychology Bulletin, 8,* 174-179.

Sidanius, J. (1992). A comparison of symbolic racism theory and social dominance theory as explanations for racial policy attitudes. *Journal of Social Psychology, 132,* 377-396.

Sidanius, J., & Pratto, F. (1993). Racism and support of free-market capitalism: A cross-cultural analysis. *Political Psychology, 14,* 381-401.

Sidanius, J., Pratto, F., & Bobo, L. (1994). Social dominance orientation and the political psychology of gender: A case of invariance? *Journal of Personality and Social Psychology, 67,* 998-1011.

Sidanius, J., Pratto, F., & Bobo, L. (1996). Racism, conservatism, affirmative action, and intellectual sophistication: A matter of principled conservatism or group dominance. *Journal of Personality and Social Psychology, 70,* 476-490.

Simon, L., & Greenberg, J. (1996). Further progress in understanding the effects of derogatory ethnic labels: The role of pre-existing attitudes toward the targeted group. *Personality and Social Psychology Bulletin, 22,* 1195-1204.

Simond, R. H., & Orife, J. W. (1975). Work behaviors vs. enrichment theory. *Administrative Science Quarterly, 20,* 606-612.

Singh, J. (1991). Industry characteristics and consumer dissatisfaction. *Journal of Consumer Affairs, 25,* 19-56.

Slater, S. F. (1993). Competing in high velocity markets. *Industrial Marketing Management, 22,* 255-263.

Slavin, R. E., & Madden, N. A. (1979). School practices that improve social relations. *American Educational Research Journal, 16,* 169-180.

Smeaton, G., Byrne, D., & Murnen, S. K. (1989). The repulsion hypothesis revisited: Similarity irrelevance or dissimilarity bias? *Journal of Personality and Social Psychology, 56,* 54-59.

Smedley, J. W., & Bayton, J. A. (1978). Evaluation of race-class stereotypes by race and perceived class of subjects. *Journal of Personality and Social Psychology, 36,* 530-535.

Smith, C. A., Organ, D. W., & Near, J. P. (1983). Organizational citizenship behavior: Its nature and antecedents. *Journal of Applied Psychology, 68,* 453-463.

Smith, E. R., & Zárate, M. A. (1992). Exemplar-based model of social judgment. *Psychological Review, 99,* 3-21.

Smith, M. B. (1947). The personal setting of public opinions: A study of attitudes toward Russia. *Public Opinion Quarterly, 11,* 507-523.

Smith, M. B., Bruner, J. S., & White, R. W. (1956). *Opinions and personality.* New York: John Wiley.

Smith, P. C., Kendall, L. M., & Hulin, C. L. (1969). *The measurement of satisfaction in work and retirement: A strategy for the study of attitudes.* Chicago: Rand McNally.

Smith, S. M., & Shaffer, D. R. (1991). Celebrity and cajolery: Rapid speech may promote or inhibit persuasion through its impact on message elaboration. *Personality and Social Psychology Bulletin, 17,* 663-669.

Smith, T. W., & Sheatsley, P. B. (1984). American attitudes towards race relations. *Public Opinion, 14/15,* 50-53.

Smith, V. (1997). New forms of work organization. In J. Hagan & K. S. Cook (Eds.), *Annual review of sociology* (Vol. 23, pp. 315-409). Palo Alto, CA: Annual Reviews.

Sniderman, P. M., & Piazza, T. (1993). *The scar of race.* Cambridge, MA: Belknap.

Sniderman, P. M., Piazza, T., Tetlock, P. E., & Kendrick, A. (1991). The new racism. *American Journal of Political Science, 35,* 423-447.

Sniderman, P. M., & Tetlock, P. E. (1986). Symbolic racism: Problems of motive attribution in political analysis. *Journal of Social Issues, 42,* 129-150.

Snyder, M. (1974). Self-monitoring of expressive behavior. *Journal of Personality and Social Psychology, 30,* 526-537.

Snyder, M., & DeBono, K. G. (1985). Appeals to images and claims about quality: Understanding the psychology of advertising. *Journal of Personality and Social Psychology, 49,* 586-597.

Snyder, M., & Ickes, W. (1985). Personality and social behavior. In G. Lindzey & E. Aronson (Eds.), *Handbook of social psychology* (3rd ed., Vol. 2, pp. 883-947). New York: Random House.

Snyder, M., & Miene, P. (1992). On the functions of stereotypes and prejudice. In M. P. Zanna & J. M. Olson (Eds.), *The psychology of prejudice: The Ontario Symposium* (Vol. 7). Hillsdale, NJ: Lawrence Erlbaum.

Snyder, M., & Miene, P. (1994). Stereotyping of the elderly: A functional approach. *British Journal of Social Psychology, 33,* 63-82.

Snyder, M., & Wicklund, R. A. (1976). Prior exercise of freedom and reactance. *Journal of Experimental Social Psychology, 12,* 120-130.

Solomon, R. L., & Corbit, J. D. (1973). An opponent process theory of motivation: II. Cigarette addiction. *Journal of Abnormal Psychology, 81,* 158-171.

Spector, P. (1996). *Industrial and organizational psychology: Research and practice.* New York: John Wiley.

Spreng, R. A., Mackenzie, S. B., & Olshavsky, R. W. (1996). A reexamination of the determinants of consumer satisfaction. *Journal of Marketing, 60,* 15-32.

Srull, T. K., & Wyer, R. S., Jr. (1989). Person memory and judgment. *Psychological Review, 96,* 58-83.

Staats, A. W. (1967). An outline of an integrated learning theory of attitude formation and function. In M. Fishbein (Ed.), *Readings in attitude theory and measurement.* New York: John Wiley.

Staats, A. W. (1983). Paradigmatic behaviorism: Unified theory for social-personality psychology. In L. Berkowitz (Ed.), *Advances in experimental social psychology* (Vol. 16, pp. 125-179). San Diego, CA: Academic Press.

Staats, A. W., & Staats, C. K. (1958). Attitudes established by classical conditioning. *Journal of Abnormal and Social Psychology, 57,* 37-40.

Stagner, R., & Longdon, C. S. (1955). Another failure to demonstrate displacement of aggression. *Journal of Abnormal and Social Psychology, 51,* 695-696.

Stangor, C., Sullivan, L. A., & Ford, T. E. (1991). Affective and cognitive determinants of prejudice. *Social Cognition, 9,* 359-368.

Stasson, M., & Fishbein, M. (1990). The relation between perceived and preventive action: A within-subject analysis of perceived driving risk and intentions to wear seatbelts. *Journal of Applied Social Psychology, 20,* 1541-1547.

Staw, B. M. (1986). Organizational psychology and the pursuit of the happy/productive worker. *California Management Review, 28,* 40-53.

Staw, B. M. (1991). Dressing up like an organization: When psychological theories can explain organizational action. *Journal of Management, 17,* 805-819.

Staw, B. M., & Barsade, S. G. (1993). Affect and managerial performance: A test of the sadder-but-wiser vs. happier-and-smarter hypotheses. *Administrative Science Quarterly, 38,* 304-331.

Staw, B. M., Bell, N. E., & Clausen, J. A. (1986). The dispositional approach to job attitudes: A lifetime longitudinal test. *Administrative Science Quarterly, 31,* 56-77.

Staw, B. M., McKechnie, P., & Puffer, S. (1983). Justification of organizational performance. *Administrative Science Quarterly, 28,* 582-600.

Staw, B. M., & Oldham, G. R. (1978). Reconsidering our dependent variables: A critique and empirical study. *Academy of Management Journal, 21,* 539-559.

Staw, B. M., & Ross, J. (1985). Stability in the midst of change: A dispositional approach to job attitudes. *Journal of Applied Psychology, 70,* 469-480.

Staw, B. M., & Sutton, R. I. (1993). Macro organizational psychology. In J. K. Murnighan (Ed.), *Social psychology in organizations* (pp. 350-384). Englewood Cliffs, NJ: Prentice Hall.

Steel, R. P., & Ovalle, N. K. (1984). A review and meta-analysis of research on the relationship between behavioral intentions and employee turnover. *Journal of Applied Psychology, 69,* 673-686.

Steele, C. M. (1988). The psychology of self-affirmation: Sustaining the integrity of the self. In L. Berkowitz (Ed.), *Advances in experimental social psychology* (Vol. 21, pp. 261-302). San Diego, CA: Academic Press.

Steele, C. M., & Aronson, J. (1995). Stereotype threat and the intellectual test performance of African Americans. *Journal of Personality and Social Psychology, 69,* 797-811.

Steele, C. M., & Liu, T. J. (1983). Dissonance processes as self-affirmation. *Journal of Personality and Social Psychology, 45,* 5-19.

Steele, C. M., Spencer, S. J., & Lynch, M. (1993). Self-image resilience and dissonance: The role of affirmational resources. *Journal of Personality and Social Psychology, 64,* 885-896.

Steers, R. M. (1977). *Organizational effectiveness: A behavioral view.* Santa Monica, CA: Goodyear.

Steers, R. M. (1991). *Introduction to organizational behavior* (4th ed.). New York: HarperCollins.

Steers, R. M., & Mowday, R. T. (1981). Employee turnover and post decision accommodation processes. In L. L. Cummings & B. M. Staw (Eds.), *Research in organizational behavior* (Vol. 3, pp. 235-281). Greenwich, CT: JAI.

Steers, R. M., & Rhodes, S. R. (1978). Major influences on employee attendance: A process model. *Journal of Applied Psychology, 63,* 391-407.

Steers, R. M., & Rhodes, S. R. (1984). Knowledge and speculation about absenteeism. In P. S. Goodman & R. S. Atkin (Eds.), *Absenteeism* (pp. 229-275). San Francisco: Jossey Bass.

Steffen, V. J. (1990). Men's motivation to perform the testicle self-exam: Effects of prior knowledge and an educational brochure. *Journal of Applied Social Psychology, 20,* 681-702.

Stenross, B., & Kleinman, S. (1989). The highs and lows of emotional labor. *Journal of Contemporary Ethnography, 17,* 435-452.

Stephan, W. G. (1986). The effects of school desegregation: An evaluation 30 years after Brown. In M. J. Sakes & L. Saxe (Eds.), *Advances in applied social psychology* (Vol. 3, pp. 181-206). Hillsdale, NJ: Lawrence Erlbaum.

Stephan, W. G., Agegev, V., Coates-Shrider, L., Stephan, C. W., & Abalakina, M. (1994). On the relationship between stereotypes and prejudice: An international study. *Personality and Social Psychology Bulletin, 20,* 277-284.

Stephan, W. G., & Rosenfield, D. (1982). Racial and ethnic attitudes. In A. G. Miller (Ed.), *In the eye of the beholder: Contemporary issues in stereotyping* (pp. 92-136). New York: Praeger.

Stephens, N., & Akers, M. A. (1985). Implementing service excellence: How a small company can do it right. In T. A. Swartz, D. E. Bowen, & S. Brown (Eds.), *Advances in services marketing and management* (Vol. 3, pp. 127-148). Greenwich, CT: JAI.

Stern, P. C., Dietz, T., Kalof, L., & Guagnano, G. A. (1995). Values, beliefs, and preenvironmental action: Attitude formation toward emergent attitude objects. *Journal of Applied Social Psychology, 25,* 1611-1636.

Stigler, G. (1962). Information in the labor market. *Journal of Political Economy, 70,* 49-73.

Stone, E. F. (1992). A critical analysis of social information processing: Models of job perceptions and job attitudes. In C. J. Cranny, P. C. Smith, & E. F. Stone (Eds.), *Job satisfaction: How people feel about their jobs and how it affects their performance* (Vol. 1, pp. 21-52). New York: Lexington.

Stone, E. F., Stone, D. L., & Dipboye, R. L. (1992). Stigmas in organizations: Race, handicaps, and physical unattractiveness. In K. Kelly (Ed.), *Issues, theory, and research in industrial/organizational psychology.* Amsterdam: Elsevier.

Stone, W. F., Lederer, G., & Christie, R. (1993). *Strength and weakness: The authoritarian personality today.* New York: Springer.

Strack, F., & Martin, L. L. (1987). Thinking, judging, and communicating: A process account of context effects in attitude surveys. In H.-J. Hippler, N. Schwarz, & S. Sudman (Eds.), *Social information processing and survey methodology* (pp. 123-148). New York: Springer-Verlag.

Strader, M. K., & Katz, B. M. (1990). Effects of a persuasive communication on beliefs, attitudes, and career choice. *Journal of Social Psychology, 130,* 141-150.

Strauman, T. J. (1992). Self-guides, autobiographical memory, and anxiety and dysphoria: Toward a cognitive model of vulnerability to emotional distress. *Journal of Abnormal Psychology, 101,* 87-95.

Strauss, A., & Corbin, J. (1990). *Basics of qualitative research.* Newbury Park, CA: Sage.

Stroebe, W., & Insko, C. A. (1989). Stereotype, prejudice, and discrimination: Changing conceptions in theory and research. In D. Bar-Tal, C. F. Graumann, A. W. Kruglanski, & W. Stroebe (Eds.), *Stereotyping and prejudice: Changing conceptions* (pp. 3-34). New York: Springer.

Struckman-Johnson, C. J., Gilliland, R. C., Struckman-Johnson, D. L., & North, T. C. (1990). The effects of fear of AIDS and gender on responses to fear-arousing condom advertisements. *Journal of Applied Social Psychology, 20,* 1396-1410.

Sutton, R. I. (1991). Maintaining norms about expressed emotions: The case of bill collectors. *Administrative Science Quarterly, 36,* 245-268.

Sutton, R. I., & Kramer, R. M. (1990). Transforming failure into success: Impression management, the Reagan administration, and the Iceland arms control talks. In R. L. Kahn & M. W. Zald (Eds.), *International cooperation and conflict: Perspectives from organizational theory* (pp. 221-245). San Francisco: Jossey-Bass.

Sutton, S. R., & Hallett, R. (1989). Understanding seat-belt intentions and behavior: A decision-making approach. *Journal of Applied Social Psychology, 19,* 1310-1325.

Swan, J. E., & Oliver, R. L. (1989). Postpurchase communications by consumers. *Journal of Retailing, 65,* 516-533.

Sweeney, P. D., & Gruber, K. L. (1984). Selective exposure: Voter information preferences and the Watergate affair. *Journal of Personality and Social Psychology, 46,* 1208-1221.

Swim, J. K., Aikin, K. J., Hall, W. S., & Hunter, B. A. (1995). Sexism and racism: Old-fashioned and modern prejudices. *Journal of Personality and Social Psychology, 68*(2), 199-214.

Taber, T. D. (1991). Triangulating job attitudes with interpretive and positivist measurement methods. *Personnel Psychology, 44,* 577-600.

Taber, T. D., & Taylor, E. (1990). A review and evaluation of the psychometric properties of the job diagnostic survey. *Personnel Psychology, 43,* 467-500.

Tajfel, H. (1970). Experiments in intergroup discrimination. *Scientific American, 223,* 96-102.

Tajfel, H. (1982). Social psychology of intergroup relations. *Annual Review of Psychology, 20,* 1-39.

Tajfel, H., Billig, M. G., Bundy, R. P., & Flament, C. (1971). Social categorization and intergroup behavior. *European Journal of Social Psychology, 1,* 149-178.

Tajfel, H., & Turner, J. (1979). An integrative theory of intergroup conflict. In W. G. Austin & S. Worchel (Eds.), *The social psychology of intergroup relations* (pp. 33-47). Belmont, CA: Wadsworth.

Tajfel, H., & Turner, J. (1985). The social identity theory of intergroup behavior. In S. Worchel & W. G. Austin (Eds.), *Psychology of intergroup relations* (pp. 7-24). Chicago, IL: Nelson-Hall.

Tansik, D. A. (1985). Nonverbal communication and high contact employees. In J. A. Czepiel, M. R. Solomon, & C. F. Surprenant (Eds.), *The service encounter* (pp. 149-161). Lexington, MA: Lexington Books.

Taylor, D. G., Sheatsley, P. B., & Greeley, A. M. (1978). Attitudes towards racial integration. *Scientific American, 238,* 42-49.

Taylor, D. M., & Moghaddam, F. M. (1994). *Theories of intergroup relations* (2nd ed.). Westport, CT: Praeger.

Taylor, F. W. (1903). *Shop management.* New York: Harper.

Taylor, F. W. (1911). *The principles of scientific management.* New York: Harper.

Tedeschi, J. T. (Ed.). (1981). *Impression management theory and social psychological research.* New York: Academic Press.

Tedeschi, J. T., Schlenker, B. R., & Bonoma, T. V. (1971). Cognitive dissonance: Private ratiocination or public spectacle? *American Psychologist, 26,* 685-695.

Tellegen, A. (1985). Structures of mood and personality and their relevance to assessing anxiety, with an emphasis on self-report. In A. H. Tuma & J. D. Maser (Eds.), *Anxiety and the anxiety disorders* (pp. 681-706). Hillsdale, NJ: Lawrence Erlbaum.

Tellegen, A., Lykken, D. T., Bouchard, T. J., Jr., Wilcox, K. J., Segal, N. L., & Rich, S. (1988). Personality similarity in twins reared apart and together. *Journal of Personality and Social Psychology, 54,* 1031-1039.

Terborg, J. (1981). Interactional psychology and research on human behavior in organizations. *Academy of Management Review, 6,* 569-576.

Tesser, A. (1993). The importance of heritability in psychological research: The case of attitudes. *Psychological Review, 100,* 129-142.

Tesser, A., & Shaffer, D. R. (1990). Attitudes and attitude change. *Annual Review of Psychology, 41,* 497-523.

Tetlock, P. E. (1986). A value pluralism model of ideological reasoning. *Journal of Personality and Social Psychology, 50,* 819-827.

Tetlock, P. E. (1989). Structure and function in political belief systems. In A. R. Pratkanis, S. J. Breckler, & A. G. Greenwald (Eds.), *Attitude structure and function* (pp. 129-151). Hillsdale, NJ: Lawrence Erlbaum.

Tett, R. P., Jackson, D. N., & Rothstein, M. (1991). Personality measures as predictors of job performance: A meta-analytic review. *Personnel Psychology, 44,* 703-742.

Tett, R. P., Jackson, D. N., Rothstein, M., & Reddon, J. R. (1994). Meta-analysis of personality-job performance relations: A reply to Ones, Mount, Barrick, and Hunter (1994). *Personnel Psychology, 47,* 157-172.

Tett, R. P., & Meyer, J. P. (1993). Job satisfaction, organizational commitment, turnover intention, and turnover: Path analyses based on meta-analytical findings. *Personnel Psychology, 46,* 259-293.

Thibaut, J. W., & Kelley, H. H. (1959). *The social psychology of groups.* New York: John Wiley.

Thibaut, J. W., & Walker, L. (1975). *Procedural justice: A psychological perspective.* Hillsdale, NJ: Lawrence Erlbaum.

Thibodeau, R., & Aronson, E. (1992). Taking a closer look: Reasserting the role of the self-concept in dissonance theory. *Personality and Social Psychology Bulletin, 18,* 591-602.

Thistlethwaite, D. L. (1950). Attitude and structure as factors in the distortion of reasoning. *Journal of Abnormal and Social Psychology, 45,* 442-458.

Thompson, J. D. (1967). *Organizations in action.* New York: McGraw-Hill.

Thompson, M. M., Zanna, M. P., & Griffin, D. W. (1995). Let's not be indifferent about (attitudinal) ambivalence. In R. E. Petty & J. A. Krosnick (Eds.), *Attitude strength: Antecedents and consequences.* Mahwah, NJ: Lawrence Erlbaum.

Thornton, G. C. (1992). *Assessment centers in human resource management.* Reading, MA: Addison-Wesley.

Thurstone, L. L. (1928). Attitudes can be measured. *American Journal of Sociology, 33,* 529-554.

Thurstone, L. L. (1931). The measurement of attitudes. *Journal of Abnormal and Social Psychology, 26,* 249-269.

Thurstone, L. L., & Chave, E. J. (1929). *The measurement of attitude.* Chicago: University of Chicago Press.

Tilgher, A. (1931). *Work: What it has meant to man through the ages.* London: Harrop.

Tornow, W. W., & Wiley, J. W. (1991). Service quality and management practices: A look at employee attitudes, customer satisfaction, and bottom-line consequences. *Human Resources Planning, 14,* 105-115.

Tourangeau, R., & Rasinski, K. A. (1988). Cognitive processes underlying context effects in attitude measurement. *Psychological Bulletin, 103,* 299-314.

Triandis, H. C. (1980). Values, attitudes, and interpersonal behavior. In H. E. Howe, Jr. & M. M. Page (Eds.), *Nebraska Symposium on Motivation, 1979* (Vol. 27, pp. 195-259). Lincoln: University of Nebraska Press.

Triandis, H. C. (1991). Attitude and attitude change. In *Encyclopedia of human biology* (Vol. 1, pp. 485-496). San Diego, CA: Academic Press.

Triandis, H. C. (1994). Cross-cultural industrial and organizational psychology. In H. C. Triandis, M. D. Dunnette, & L. M. Hough (Eds.), *Handbook of industrial and organizational psychology* (2nd ed., Vol. 4, pp. 103-172). Palo Alto, CA: Consulting Psychologists Press.

Tripp, C., Jensen, T. D., & Carlson, L. (1994). The effects of multiple product endorsements by celebrities on consumers' attitudes and intentions. *Journal of Consumer Research, 20,* 535-547.

Trope, Y., & Thompson, E. P. (1997). Looking for the truth in all the wrong places? Asymmetric search of individuality information about stereotyped group members. *Journal of personality and Social Psychology, 73,* 229-241.

Tse, D. K., Nicosia, F. M., & Wilson, P. C. (1990). Consumer satisfaction as a process. *Psychology & Marketing, 7*, 177-193.

Tse, D. K., & Wilson, P. C. (1988). Models of consumer satisfaction formation: An extension. *Journal of Marketing Research, 25*, 204-212.

Tsui, A. S., Egan, T. D., & O'Reilly, C. A., III. (1992). Being different: Relational demography and organizational attachment. *Administrative Science Quarterly, 37*, 549-579.

Tully, S. (1993, September 20). The real key to creating wealth. *Fortune*, 38-50.

Turban, D. B., & Greening, D. W. (1997). Corporate social performance and organizational attractiveness to prospective employees. *Academy of Management Journal, 40*, 658-672.

Turner, A. N., & Lawrence, P. R. (1965). *Industrial jobs and the worker.* Boston: Harvard University Graduate School of Business Administration.

Turner, J. C., Oakes, P. J., Haslam, S. A., & McGarty, C. (1994). Self and collective: Cognition and social context. *Personality and Social Psychology Bulletin, 20*, 454-463.

21st century capitalism [Special issue]. (1994, May 18). *Business Week.*

Tyler, T. R., & Schuller, R. A. (1991). Aging and attitude change. *Journal of Personality and Social Psychology, 61*, 689-697.

Ulrich, D., Halbrook, R., Mecker, D., Stucklik, M., & Thorpe, S. (1991). Employee and customer attachment: Synergies for competitive advantage. *Human Resources Planning, 14*, 89-103.

Ursic, M. L. (1985). A model of the consumer decision to seek legal redress. *Journal of Consumer Affairs, 19*, 20-36.

Useem, M. (1993). *Executive defense.* Cambridge, MA: Harvard University Press.

Vallacher, R. R., Nowak, A., & Kaufman, J. (1994). Intrinsic dynamics of social judgement. *Journal of Personality and Social Psychology, 67*, 20-34.

Vallone, R. P., Ross, L., & Lepper, M. R. (1985). The hostile media phenomenon: Biased perception and perceptions of media bias in coverage of the Beirut massacre. *Journal of Personality and Social Psychology, 49*, 577-585.

Van Dyne, L., Cummings, L. L., & Parks, J. M. (1995). Extra-role behaviors: In pursuit of construct and definitional clarity (a bridge over muddied waters). In L. L. Cummings & B. M. Staw (Eds.), *Research in organizational behavior* (Vol. 17, pp. 215-285). Greenwich, CT: JAI.

Van Dyne, L., Graham, J. W., & Dienesch, R. M. (1994). Organizational citizenship behavior: Construct redefinition, measurement, and validation. *Academy of Management Journal, 37*, 765-802.

Van Maanen, J., & Kunda, G. (1989). Real feelings: Emotional expression and organizational culture. In L. L. Cummings & B. M. Staw (Eds.), *Research in organizational behavior* (Vol. 11, pp. 43-103). Greenwich, CT: JAI.

Vaughan, K. B., & Lanzetta, J. T. (1980). Vicarious instigation and conditioning of facial expressive and autonomic responses to a model's expressive display of pain. *Journal of Personality and Social Psychology, 38*, 909-923.

Vidmar, N., & Rokeach, M. (1974). Archie Bunker's bigotry: A study in selective perception and exposure. *Journal of Communication, 24*, 36-47.

Vogel, D. (1978). *Lobbying the corporation: Citizen challenges to business authority.* New York: Basic Books.

von Hippel, W., Sekaquaptewa, D., & Vargas, P. (1995). On the role of encoding processes in stereotype maintenance. In M. P. Zanna (Ed.), *Advances in experimental social psychology* (Vol. 27, pp. 177-254.) New York: Academic Press.

Vroom, V. H. (1964). *Work and motivation.* New York: John Wiley.

Wagner, J. A., III, & Gooding, R. Z. (1987). Effects of societal trends on participation research. *Administrative Science Quarterly, 32*, 241-262.

Wahba, M. A., & Bridwell, L. G. (1976). Maslow reconsidered: A review of research on the need hierarchy theory. *Organizational Behavior and Human Performance, 15*, 212-240.

Wallendorf, M. (1980). The formation of aesthetic criteria through social structures and social institutions. In J. C. Olson (Ed.), *Advances in consumer research* (Vol. 7, pp. 3-6). Ann Arbor, MI: Association for Consumer Research.

Waller, M. J., Huber, G. P., & Glick, W. H. (1995). Functional background as a determinant of executives' selective perception. *Academy of Management Journal, 38,* 943-974.

Waller, N. G., Kojetin, B. A., Bouchard, T. J., Jr., Lykken, D. T., & Tellegen, A. (1990). Genetic and environmental influences on religious interests, attitudes and values: A study of twins reared apart and together. *Psychological Science, 1,* 138-142.

Walsh, J. P. (1988). Selectivity and selective perception: An investigation of managers' belief structures and information processing. *Academy of Management Journal, 31,* 873-896.

Walster, E., Aronson, E., & Abrahams, D. (1966). On increasing the persuasiveness of a low prestige communicator. *Journal of Experimental Social Psychology, 2,* 325-342.

Walster, E., & Festinger, L. (1962). The effectiveness of "overheard" persuasive communications. *Journal of Abnormal and Social Psychology, 65,* 395-402.

Wanous, J. P. (1974). A causal correlational analysis of the job satisfaction and performance relationship. *Journal of Applied Psychology, 59,* 139-144.

Wanous, J. P. (1992). *Organizational entry: Recruitment, selection, orientation, and socialization of newcomers.* Reading, MA: Addison-Wesley.

Wanous, J. P., Poland, T. D., Premack, S. L., & Davis, K. S. (1992). The effects of met expectations and newcomer attitudes and behaviors: A review and meta-analysis. *Journal of Applied Psychology, 77,* 288-297.

Wanous, J. P., Reichers, A. E., & Hudy, M. J. (1997). Overall job satisfaction: How good are single-item measures? *Journal of Applied Psychology, 82,* 247-252.

Warner, S. L. (1965). Randomized response: A survey technique for eliminating evasive answer bias. *Journal of the American Statistical Association, 60,* 63-69.

Warr, P. (1987). *Work unemployment and mental health.* Oxford, UK: Clarendon.

Watkins, S. (1993, October 18). Racism du jour at Shoney's. *The Nation,* pp. 424-428.

Watson, D. (1988). The vicissitudes of mood measurement: Effects of varying descriptors, time frames, and response formats on measures of positive and negative affect. *Journal of Personality and Social Psychology, 55,* 128-141.

Watson, D., & Clark, L. A. (1984). Negative affectivity: The disposition to experience aversive psychological states. *Psychological Bulletin, 96,* 465-490.

Watson, D., Clark, L. A., & Tellegen, A. (1984). Cross-cultural convergence in the structure of mood: A Japanese replication and a comparison with U.S. findings. *Journal of Personality and Social Psychology, 47,* 127-144.

Watson, D., Clark, L. A., & Tellegen, A. (1988). Development and validation of brief measures of positive and negative affect: The Panas scales. *Journal of Personality and Social Psychology, 54,* 1063-1070.

Watson, D., & Clark, M. S. (1992). On traits and temperament: General and specific factors of emotional experience and their relation to the five-factor model. *Journal of Personality, 60,* 441-476.

Watson, D., & Pennebaker, J. W. (1989). Health complaints, stress and distress: Exploring the central role of negative affectivity. *Psychological Review, 96,* 234-254.

Watson, D., Pennebaker, J. W., & Folger, R. (1986). Beyond negative affectivity: Measuring stress and satisfaction in the workplace. *Journal of Organizational Behavior Management, 8,* 141-157.

Watson, D., & Slack, A. K. (1993). General factors of affective temperament and their relation to job satisfaction over time. *Organizational Behavior and Human Decision Processes, 54,* 181-202.

Watson, D., & Tellegen, A. (1985). Toward a consensual structure of mood. *Psychological Bulletin, 98,* 219-225.

Weaver, C. N. (1978). Job satisfaction as a component of happiness among males and females. *Personnel Psychology, 31,* 831-840.

Webb, E. J., Campbell, D. T., Schwartz, R. D., Sechrest, L., & Grove, J. B. (1981). *Nonreactive measures in the social sciences* (2nd ed.). Boston: Houghton Mifflin.

Weber, J. G. (1994). The nature of ethnocentric attribution bias: Ingroup protection or enhancement? *Journal of Experimental Social Psychology, 30,* 482-504.

Weber, R., & Crocker, J. (1983). Cognitive processes in the revision of stereotypic beliefs. *Journal of Personality and Social Psychology, 45,* 961-977.

Wegner, D. M. (1994). Ironic processes of mental control. *Psychological Review, 101,* 34-52.

Weick, K. E. (1969). *The social psychology of organizing.* Reading, MA: Addison-Wesley.

Weick, K. E. (1977). Enactment processes in organizations. In B. M. Staw & G. Salancik (Ed.), *New directions in organizational behavior* (pp. 267-300). Chicago: St. Clair.

Weick, K. E. (1979). Organization design: Organizations as self-designing systems. *Organizational Dynamics, 6,* 30-46.

Weick, K. E. (1995). *Sensemaking in organizations.* Thousand Oaks, CA: Sage.

Weigel, R. H., & Howes, P. W. (1985). Conceptions of racial prejudice: Symbolic racism reconsidered. *Journal of Social Issues, 4*(3), 117-138.

Weigelt, K., & Camerer, C. (1988). Reputation and corporate strategy: A review of recent theory and applications. *Strategic Management Journal, 9,* 443-454.

Weiss, D. J., Dawis, R. V., England, G. W., & Lofquist, L. H. (1967). *Manual for the Minnesota Satisfaction Questionnaire.* Minneapolis: University of Minnesota Press.

Weiss, D. J., Dawis, R. V., Lofquist, L. H., & England, G. W. (1966). *Instrumentation for the theory of work adjustment.* Minneapolis: University of Minnesota, Minnesota Studies in Vocational Rehabilitation.

Weiss, H. M., & Cropanzano, R. (1996). Affective events theory: A theoretical discussion of the structure, causes and consequences of affective experiences at work. In B. M. Staw & L. L. Cummings (Eds.), *Research in organizational behavior* (Vol. 18, pp. 1-74). Greenwich, CT: JAI.

Weiss, J. W. (1994). *Business ethics: A managerial, stakeholder approach.* Belmont, CA: Wadsworth.

Weitz, J. (1952). A neglected concept in the study of job satisfaction. *Personnel Psychology, 5,* 201-205.

Wells, G. L., & Petty, R. E. (1980). The effects of overt head-movements on persuasion: Compatibility and incompatibility of responses. *Basic and Applied Social Psychology, 1,* 219-230.

Westbrook, R. A., & Oliver, R. L. (1991). The dimensionality of consumption emotion patterns and consumer satisfaction. *Journal of Consumer Research, 18,* 84-91.

White, P. H., & Harkins, S. G. (1994). Race of source effects in the elaboration likelihood model. *Journal of Personality and Social Psychology, 67,* 790-807.

Whitsett, D. A., & Winslow, E. K. (1967). An analysis of studies critical of the motivator-hygiene-theory. *Personnel Psychology, 20,* 391-415.

Wicker, A. W. (1969). Attitudes versus actions: The relationship of verbal and overt behavioral responses to attitude objects. *Journal of Social Issues, 25,* 41-78.

Wicklund, R. A., & Brehm, J. W. (1968). Attitude change as a function of felt competence and threat to attitudinal freedom. *Journal of Experimental Social Psychology, 4,* 64-75.

Wicklund, R. A., & Brehm, J. W. (1976). *Perspectives on cognitive dissonance.* Hillsdale, NJ: Lawrence Erlbaum.

Wilder, D. A. (1986). Cognitive factors affecting the success of intergroup contact. In S. Worchel & W. G. Austin (Eds.), *Psychology of intergroup relations* (2nd ed., pp. 288-304). Chicago: Nelson-Hall.

Wiley, J. W. (1991). Customer satisfaction: A supportive work environment and its financial cost. *Human Resources Planning, 14,* 117-126.

Williams, L. J., & Hazer, J. T. (1986). Antecedents and consequences of satisfaction and commitment in turnover models: A reanalysis using latent variable structural equation methods. *Journal of Applied Psychology, 71,* 219-231.

Williamson, O. E. (1981). The economics of organization: The transaction cost approach. *American Journal of Sociology, 87,* 548-577.

Withey, M. J., & Cooper, W. H. (1989). Predicting exit, voice, loyalty, and neglect. *Administrative Science Quarterly, 34,* 521-539.

Witt, L. A., & Nye, L. G. (1992). Gender and the relationship between perceived fairness of pay or promotion and job satisfaction. *Journal of Applied Psychology, 77,* 910-917.

Wittenbrink, B., & Henly, J. R. (1996). Creating social reality: Informational social influence and the content of stereotypic beliefs. *Personality and Social Psychology Bulletin, 22,* 598-610.

Wood, W., Kallgren, C. A., & Preisler, R. M. (1985). Access to attitude-relevant information in memory as a determinant of persuasion: The role of message attributes. *Journal of Experimental Social Psychology, 21,* 73-85.

Worchel, S., & Brehm, J. W. (1970). Effect of threats to attitudinal freedom as a function of agreement with the communicator. *Journal of Personality and Social Psychology, 14,* 18-22.

Worth, L. T., & Mackie, D. M. (1987). Cognitive mediation of positive affect in persuasion. *Social Cognition, 5,* 76-94.

Wright, R. A., & Brehm, S. S. (1982). Reactance as impression management: A critical review. *Journal of Personality and Social Psychology, 42,* 608-618.

Wyer, R. S., Srull, T. K., & Gordon, S. (1984). The effects of predicting a person's behavior on subsequent trait judgements. *Journal of Experimental Social Psychology, 20,* 29-46.

Yarkin, K. L., Town, J. P., & Wallston, B. S. (1982). Blacks and women must try harder: Stimulus persons' race and sex attributions of causality. *Personality and Social Psychology Bulletin, 8,* 21-24.

Yarrow, M. R., Campbell, J. D., & Yarrow, L. J. (1958). Acquisition of new norms: A study of racial desegregation. *Journal of Social Issues, 14*(1), 8-28.

Yi, Y. (1990). A critical review of consumer satisfaction. In V. A. Zeithaml (Ed.), *Review of marketing 1990* (pp. 68-123). Chicago: American Marketing Association.

Yukl, G., & Falbe, C. M. (1990). Influence tactics and objectives in upward, downward, and lateral influence attempts. *Journal of Applied Psychology, 75,* 132-140.

Yukl, G., & Tracey, J. B. (1992). Consequences of influence tactics used with subordinates, peers, and the boss. *Journal of Applied Psychology, 77,* 525-535.

Zajonc, R. B. (1960). The concepts of balance, congruity, and dissonance. *Public Opinion Quarterly, 24,* 280-296.

Zajonc, R. B. (1968). Attitudinal effects of mere exposure. *Journal of Personality and Social Psychology, 9*(No. 2, Pt. 2).

Zajonc, R. B. (1980a). Cognition and social cognition: A historical perspective. In L. Festinger (Ed.), *Retrospections on social psychology* (pp. 180-204). New York: Oxford University Press.

Zajonc, R. B. (1980b). Feeling and thinking: Preferences need no inferences. *American Psychologist, 35,* 151-175.

Zajonc, R. B. (1984). On the primacy of affect. *American Psychologist, 39,* 117-123.

Zajonc, R. B. (1993). The confluence model: Differential or difference equation. *European Journal of Social Psychology, 23,* 211-215.

Zajonc, R. B., & Markus, H. (1982). Affective and cognitive factors in preferences. *Journal of Consumer Research, 9,* 123-131.

Zald, M. N. (1990). History, sociology, and theories of organization. In J. E. Jackson (Ed.), *American political and economic institutions* (pp. 81-88). Ann Arbor: University of Michigan Press.

Zalesny, M. D., & Ford, J. K. (1990). Extending the social information processing perspective: New links to attitudes, behaviors, and perceptions. *Organizational Behavior and Human Decision Processes, 47,* 205-246.

Zanna, M. P., Kiesler, C. A., & Pilkonis, P. A. (1970). Positive and negative attitudinal affect established by classical conditioning. *Journal of Personality and Social Psychology, 14,* 321-328.

Zanna, M. P., Klosson, E. C., & Darley, J. M. (1976). How television news viewers deal with facts that contradict their beliefs: A consistency and attribution analysis. *Journal of Applied Social Psychology, 6,* 159-176.

Zanna, M. P., Olson, J. M., & Fazio, R. H. (1981). Self-perception and attitude-behavior consistency. *Personality and Social Psychology Bulletin, 7,* 252-256.

Zanna, M. P., & Rempel, J. K. (1988). Attitudes: A new look at an old concept. In D. Bar-Tal & A. W. Kruglanski (Eds.), *The social psychology of knowledge* (pp. 315-334). Cambridge, UK: Cambridge University Press.

Zeithaml, V. A. (1981). How consumer evaluation processes differ between goods and services. In J. Donnelly & W. George (Eds.), *Marketing of services* (pp. 186-190). Chicago: American Marketing Association.

Zeithaml, V. A. (1988). Consumer perceptions of price, quality, and value: A means-ends model and synthesis of evidence. *Journal of Marketing, 52,* 2-22.

Zeithaml, V. A., Parasuraman, A., & Berry, L. L. (1990). *Delivering quality service: Balancing customer perceptions and expectations.* New York: Free Press.

Zevon, M. A., & Tellegen, A. (1982). The structure of mood change: An idiographic/nomothetic analysis. *Journal of Personality and Social Psychology, 43,* 111-122.

Zuboff, S. (1988). *In the age of the smart machine: The future of work and power.* New York: Basic Books.

Zuckerman, M., & Reis, H. (1978). Comparison of three models for predicting altruistic behavior. *Journal of Personality and Social Psychology, 36,* 498-510.

Zwick, R., Pieters, R., & Baumgartner, H. (1995). On the practical significance of hindsight bias: The case of the expectancy-disconfirmation model of consumer satisfaction. *Organizational Behavior and Human Decision Processes, 64,* 103-117.

Author Index

Jackson, J. R., 135
Jackson, L. A., 125
Jackson, S. E., 33
Jacoby, J., 75, 84, 153, 155, 169
Jacoby, S. M., 182
Jacques, E., 23
James, K., 94, 109
James, L. A., 47
James, L. R., 26, 47, 116
Janis, I., 69, 70, 71, 75, 81
Janowitz, M., 128
Jardine, R., 63, 68
Jaspers, J. M. F., 125
Jennings, P. D., 182
Jensen, M. C., 176
Jensen, T. D., 72
Jewett, D., 156
Jobson, J. D., 43
John, O. P., 97, 117
Johns, G., 37, 48
Johnson, B. T., 59, 71
Johnson, C., 149
Johnson, D. W., 150
Johnson, R., 107
Johnson, R. T., 150
Johnston, L., 125, 126, 127
Jones, A. P., 26
Jones, E. E., 56, 124, 172
Jones, E. F., 124
Jones, E. W., 140
Jones, G. R., 30, 42, 117
Jost, J. T., 124
Judd, C. M., 68, 124, 127, 149
Judge, T. A., 48, 93, 94, 116, 117
Jussim, L. J., 68
Jussin, L., 124

Kacmar, K. M., 113
Kahle, L. R., 73
Kahn, R. L., 3, 18, 42, 108
Kahneman, D., 112
Kallgren, C. A., 63, 74
Kalof, L., 118
Kalyanaram, G., 152
Kandel, D.B., 65
Kanfer, R., 47, 105, 112
Kant, I., 92
Kaplan, A., 14, 138
Karabel, J., 167
Karlins, M., 149
Karp, L., 164

Kassin, S. M., 70, 72, 124, 130, 143
Katerberg, R., Jr., 35
Katz, B. M., 64
Katz, D., 3, 42, 44, 58, 106, 108, 121, 149
Katz, H., 174, 175, 176, 177, 180, 182
Katz, I., 84, 133, 134, 150
Katz, P. A., 128
Katz, R., 173
Katzell, R. A., 18, 42
Kaufman, J., 112
Kaufman, S., 26
Keating, J, P., 68
Keefe, J. H., 176
Keenan, T., 94
Kefalas, A., 60
Kelley, H. H., 30, 69, 70, 71, 73, 75
Kelley, S. W., 160, 169
Kelman, H. C., 61, 72, 145, 146, 147
Keltner, D., 124
Kendall, L. M., 4, 12, 13, 26, 27, 28, 30, 87, 114
Kendrick, A., 134
Kenski, H. C., 81
Kets de Vries, M. F. R., 110
Kiesler, C. A., 83
Kieso, D., 151
Kinder, D. R., 51, 54, 68, 104, 133, 134
King, W., 21
Kipnes, D., 84
Kirkland, S. L., 149
Kitayama, S., 114
Klein, B., 152
Kleinman, S., 161
Klien, R., 23
Klimoski, R., 117
Klosson, E. C., 81
Kluegel, J. R., 133, 149
Knight, D. B., 34
Knoke, D., 174, 175, 176, 177, 180, 182
Koblinsky, S. G., 122
Kobrynowicz, D., 150
Koch, G. G., 64
Koch, J. L., 38
Koestner, R., 118
Kohler, S. S., 36
Kojetin, B. A., 69
Komorita, S. S., 149
Konovsky, M. A., 12, 24, 94, 109
Kopelman, R. E., 48, 146
Korman, A. K., 21
Kovel, J., 150
Kowalski, R. M., 84, 167

Subject Index

About the Author

Arthur P. Brief received his Ph.D. from the University of Wisconsin–Madison in 1974 and is currently the Lawrence Martin Chair of Business at Tulane's A. B. Freeman School of Business and, by courtesy, Professor of Psychology. He also is Director of the William B. and Evelyn Burkenroad Institute for the Study of Ethics and Leadership in Management. Prior to his move to Tulane in 1989, he was on the faculties of several other schools, including, most recently, New York University's Stern School of Business. In addition to lecturing throughout the United States, he has taught organizational behavior in Chile, Finland, France, Mexico, People's Republic of China, Taiwan, and elsewhere internationally. During the fall of 1995, he was in Lisbon as the Fulbright/FLAD Chair of Organizational Behavior.

Professor Brief is a recipient of the Freeman School's most prized award for teaching, the Howard Wissner Award. His scholarship, which focuses on two areas—job-related distress and ethical decision making in organizations—also has been award winning. His prior books, among others, include *Task Design and Employee Motivation, Managing Job Stress, Productivity Research in the Behavioral and Social Sciences,* and *Meanings of Occupational Work: A Collection of Essays.*

He has served on the editorial boards of the *Academy of Management Review,* the *Journal of Applied Psychology,* and other learned journals and currently is on the board of the *Academy of Management Journal.* He is a Fellow of the American Psychological Association and of the American Psychological Society as well as a member of the Society of Organizational Behavior and MESO. He has served as President of the Midwest Academy of Management and as Chair of the Academy of Management's Organizational Behavior Division.

DATE DUE

DEC 1 8 1999

MAY 0 6 1999

SEP 0 6 1999   JUN 0 6 2002

DEC 0 0 2003

JAN 3 0 2003

AUG 1 3 2001

OCT 2 4 2001

JUL 1 2 2002

AUG 2 1 2003

MAY 1 2 2001

JUL 1 1 2007